# CRIME AT THE TOP

# CRIME
# AT
# THE
# TOP:

## Deviance In Business and the Professions

Edited by
**JOHN M. JOHNSON**
*Arizona State University*
*and*
**JACK D. DOUGLAS**
*University of California at San Diego*

**J.B. Lippincott Company**
*Philadelphia   New York   San Jose   Toronto*

ISBN 0-397-47383-4

Library of Congress Catalog Card Number    78-4095

Printed in the United States of America

2   4   6   8   9   7   5   3   1


**Library of Congress Cataloging in Publication Data**

Crime at the top.

　　Includes bibliographies.
　　1. White collar crimes—United States—Addresses,
essays, lectures. I. Johnson, John M. II. Douglas,
Jack D.

HV6769.C74　　　　　　364.1'6

ISBN 0-397-47383-4

# *Contents*

# Introduction

Business and professional deviance are by far the most pervasive and massive forms of financial deviance in our society. The usual official estimates of financial loss from street crimes put that figure at approximately 1 billion dollars each year. Official estimates of insurance frauds involving arson exceed this figure by two or three times. Employee theft is estimated at 15 billion a year. No one has any clear idea how much money is lost through the various forms of business and professional deviance each year, but any realistic estimate would have to place it at 10 billion or more. All the forms of street crime, burglaries, robberies, vandalism, and so on amount to no more than a fraction of such losses.

Yet, as we all know, business and professional deviance have received little attention from social scientists when compared with the mass of studies of other forms of deviance. A look at the studies of juvenile delinquency alone shows the discrepancy to be remarkable. Beginning with the numerous studies of delinquency by the Chicago school sociologists in the 1920s and 1930s (especially the famous ones by Thrasher and Shaw and McKay), sociologists and criminologists alone have done thousands over a 50-year period. A high percentage of the basic, general theories of deviance developed in the 1920s through the 1960s were founded largely on these studies. A list of authors of those theories reads almost like a who's who of deviance theorists in that era—Thrasher, Shaw and McKay, Sellin, Merton, Kobrin, Cohen, Miller, Cloward and Ohlin, Wolfgang, Yablonsky, and many others. Compared to those thousands of works on delinquency, studies of upper-world deviance are almost nonexistent. Sutherland's well-known essay on white-collar crime, Clinard's generally overlooked study of black markets in the Second World War, Cressey's generally known study of embezzlement and, very importantly, Dalton's all too often overlooked study of executive "theft" are among the few noteworthy exceptions. Why was there such a vast discrepancy between what was obviously going on in the social world and what social scientists were studying?

Over the years one possible rational explanation of this discrepancy has been put forward many times. It is argued that the crimes of the lower

1

part of our social-economic spectrum, especially street crimes, involve far more actual or potential violence than do the forms of deviance common to the upper parts of that spectrum. We all know that there are robberies and muggings that involve murder, sometimes brutal murder. We have read of those murders in the newspapers, often in gruesome detail. Surely, it is argued, those should concern us far more than anti-trust violations, faulty auto repair jobs, arson, and so on. There is, after all, no doubt that people are far more anxious to avoid being shot to death than they are to avoid paying higher prices for electricity because manufacturers of electric circuit breakers conspire to fix prices a billion or 2 billion dollars higher than they would be under competitive pricing conditions.

Few of us studying deviance in depth would now accept this argument. We do not question that people are more fearful of violence than of fraud or theft without violence. But our studies of many different aspects of life, together with new ways of analyzing social actions and their consequences, have convinced us that it is simply not true that upperworld forms of deviance do not have grave consequences for our personal safety. For example, some of our own work on drugs has convinced us that this is an area in which the discrepancy is very high. Heroin dealers, so-called drug pushers, have long been considered by the general public to be murderers, as Harry Anslinger (long-time head of the Federal Bureau of Narcotics) called them in a famous book he wrote. The claim is that they sell (push) dangerous drugs that sometimes kill the users. Almost all serious students of heroin use would now agree that heroin itself is a nondangerous drug—far less dangerous than cigarettes or alcohol—when used in limited doses; that street deaths from heroin are caused overwhelmingly by accidental overdoses or sometimes from impurities as a result of sources being driven into illegal markets by legislation and police powers; that heroin dealers do not create drug fiends by pushing people into drug use; and that heroin dealers are almost always trying to make money or support their own habit, not to murder their customers. Many of us have become convinced that drug deaths from street drugs could be almost entirely eliminated by decriminalized use of such drugs and, more importantly, that there are more drug-related deaths from legally prescribed drugs than from street drugs. Some students of drugs even argue that doctors do far more "pushing" of drugs through prescriptions than do heroin dealers, because they sometimes own pharmacies or stock in drug companies. In a similar vein, the American College of Surgeons and other groups that have studied surgery have repeatedly concluded that thousands of people die each year from surgery that should not have been performed. Other sources of death and injury from upper-world activities are increasingly examined—police shootings of innocent people or those guilty of only minor infractions; police-induced deaths from high-speed chases; occupational hazards that could be corrected by appropriate action; production of automobiles *known* to be "unsafe at any speed"; and, of course, government waging of war. Some theorists have even begun to examine whether the psychic injuries resulting from such practices as racial repression might be far more damaging to lives than are all the injuries from robberies or muggings.

Most of these questions remain open and all of the answers are in the formative stages. But we have come to the general conclusion that all of the earlier studies and theories of deviance took for granted certain things about the social world which were simply not true. Most importantly, they assumed that the lower classes were in general more deviant than the middle to upper classes. (That, after all, was the central idea of Merton's famous theory of deviance.) The social scientists seem to have believed this primarily because their own backgrounds, predominantly middle class, socialized them to believe such things and, probably even more importantly, because they used official information about deviance which was generated by laws and policing procedures that *assumed* the lower-class forms of deviance were the only ones that mattered much. Because this was assumed, their efforts were directed toward discovering, counting, and eliminating deviance at the socioeconomic bottom of society—and thus to ignoring it at the top. Even on those rare occasions when deviance at the top was revealed, as in cases of consumer fraud, laws were written and adjudicated so as to make it almost impossible to prove fraud had actually occurred. The net result was that the official statistics used by almost all the early sociologists to develop their theories of deviance showed the lower part of society to be highly deviant and the upper part to be inhabited largely by the pure in heart.

Probably the most important revolution in social research in general, and especially on deviance, has been the discovery that much of official statistics on social class and deviance are invalid and unreliable. This revolution has been accomplished by first carrying out a great number of carefully detailed studies of the official statistics and the ways in which they are constructed and then devising more valid and reliable field-research methods of directly observing deviance in natural social settings. As these methods of direct observation have been used ever more extensively, our basic ideas about deviance have changed radically. We now know that our earlier picture of deviance, especially our picture of the socioeconomic top of society as virtuous and the lower part wicked, was a gross distortion. Anyone who is seriously concerned with financial deviance must obviously look to the upper reaches of the socioeconomic scale.

However, our studies of deviance at the top of society are far from complete. We are finding it extremely difficult to penetrate the highest reaches of corporate society to make direct observations. The reason is simple enough: people at the top systematically exclude outsiders who might observe them and carefully manage their public presentations (their "p-r work") so as to appear highly virtuous. We are all aware now of how systematically this was done by the Watergate conspirators at the very top. (Deviance of this kind is examined in our companion volume, *Official Deviance*, J. B. Lippincott Co., 1977.) But we learned of the "Watergate horrors" through means other than direct observation, primarily secret recordings and court testimony. Court records, sometimes supplemented by investigative reporting and even secret recordings, remain the primary sources of our knowledge of deviance at the top of the business and professional world. Because of this, the material in this volume draws heavily on direct field-research observations for understanding deviance at the middle level of society, but at higher levels we are usually dependent on more indirect observations obtained from court records and investigative reporting.

Our discussion to this point seems to assume that business and professional deviance are obvious events. We have simplified only as a means of introducing the subject. Some of the major sections of this volume (especially Chapter 5 on employee theft) will make it abundantly clear that the social and legal definitions of business and professional deviance are very complex and often problematic and conflicting. This is not surprising. After all, if investors involved with Equity Funding (Chapter 8) could see that they were being swindled, they obviously would avoid being swindled. Hiding, deceit, trickery, half-truths, lies, and all the complex modes of dishonest self-presentations are basic to most forms of business and professional deviance. This alone makes them very difficult to study. But there are even more problematic aspects: many of the activities, such as "employee theft," are given different meanings by the people involved. What a judge might label as "theft," employees might label as "employee benefits" or "perks," and the employers as "theft" or "benefits" in different situations. This makes it much harder to study business and professional deviance—but it also provides a much richer source of social data for understanding human society in general.

We begin this volume with three chapters that show how pervasive is deviance at the top in our world, how much the deviant shades into the nondeviant, and how "smart operators" can manipulate these complex meanings to their advantage. Many of these forms of rule violations are so pervasive in some segments of life that they come to be taken for granted and pass unnoticed. The four chapters in Part III are original articles, all but Chapter 7 being based on in-depth, direct observations of typical forms of middle-class deviance. Chapter 4, which is concerned with sales work in a burglar alarm company, is presented first because it deals with the gray region of behavior—the tactics used are rarely *clearly* definable by any of the participants as immoral or illegal. The next three chapters deal with forms of behavior which are progressively more clearly defined by the participants as illegal.

As the authors of Chapter 5 note, their study of "employee theft" is concerned, at the most general level, with deviance by "respectable" people, that is, people who are generally ranked high in status or prestige in our society and whose public identity is certainly believed to be moral, upright, honest—nondeviant. (The social meanings of "respectability" is what Sutherland had in mind when he spoke of white-collar crime. We have dropped the phrase "white collar" because "respectables" of the upper part of society often wear sport shirts today.) The basic thrust of the paper shows that extremely high percentages of these "respectable" people, the people from the middle to the top in social prestige, income and property, are very commonly involved in behavior that they themselves would regard as disreputable when committed by others and which certainly can be prosecuted as misdemeanors or felonious theft when observed by the police. The very people who would be shocked at the fantastic schemes of the frauds at Equity Funding (Chapter 8) actually often show the same kind of creativity in developing their own forms of corrupt inventory information, hiding assets, and other deceits. But they do not show shock or outrage over *their* behavior. Why? This very significant essay shows how those involved really think and feel about such acts and, especially, why they do them. It has vital theoretical importance for the rest of the book. It does not provide a complete answer to the vastly complex questions about the forms of deviance we are concerned with here, but it suggests some of the most important elements on which such a theory might be constructed.

Part IV deals with business deviance at very high levels, including the huge multinational corporations. Robert Snow's original article (Chapter 7) offers an introduction and theory that links the lower level forms of business deviance dealt with earlier with these highest levels. The same motives and forms of deviance found in his analysis of land development frauds are found expanded into far bigger schemes at the highest levels. Some of these schemes have been huge indeed, involving dozens of people in criminal conspiracies to set prices (violating anti-trust laws) or deceive investors and drain funds out of huge corporations like OIS and Equity Funding. There are actually a good number of fine accounts of such high-level schemes, almost all of them by economic journalists. We have tried to choose only the most reliable and interesting of these.

Part V is concerned with professional deviance, which has even more rarely been considered in sociological studies of deviance at the top of society. Professional deviance overlaps with business deviance. This is seen, for example, in the major questions concerning possible involvement of professional accountants in allowing frauds such as Equity Funding to continue and in various academic consulting and grantsmanship forms of fraud. But professional deviance often has far more serious consequences for the "clients" than financial deviance by businessmen. Medical malpractice can have deadly consequences and legal malpractice can result in years in prison for the client. Any particular case of professional deviance tends to be less significant than cases of business deviance, but the percentage of professionals involved may be larger.

Part VI, the conclusion, is concerned primarily with the major solutions to those problems that have been proposed in recent years. It is likely that no solutions will be found to such problems until we are able to determine and explain much better what is going on. It will be apparent throughout this volume that we believe social scientists and journalists have only begun the difficult processes of determining the facts and developing valid explanations. We have tried to avoid any hasty construction of theories that might mislead more than inform. We feel strongly that future work, especially more in-depth studies, will reveal whole new dimensions and thus inspire new theories both of the specific forms of deviance and probably of deviance more generally. After all, one of the most important general facts we learn from studying official business and professional deviance is that while the forms of deviance may vary considerably from one segment of society to another, rule evasions and violations are found at all levels of society. This has basic implications for our understanding of society generally and certainly for our understanding of deviance.

Since we must remain open and tentative in our explanations of deviance at the top, we have no novel solutions to propose. Most current proposals, which we have tried to gather together, begin by considering how complex and problematic these forms of deviance and crime are and end by asserting that no solutions will end the problem. None take simple, moralistic positions, such as attempting to banish evil by brandishing nasty labels. Clearly the complex nature of the problem demands complex approaches, and we will have to be content with imperfect measures.

Some victims of business and professional deviance suffer greatly from their misuse. Some perpetrators, though probably not a very high percentage, suffer for their victimizing. In the pages that follow, the very human drama of these episodes is fully presented. We, as sociologists, find the study of business and professional deviance to be an extremely interesting, even intriguing endeavor. We believe the study of these schemes, especially those at the very top of our society, reveal much that is basic in our society and in human beings generally. Therefore, they are fascinating to us, and we suspect that most students of society will find them equally fascinating.

John M. Johnson
Jack D. Douglas

# II

# The Nature of Business and Professional Deviance

## INTRODUCTION

The three readings in Part II begin with an examination of the nature and extent of business and professional deviance in American society. In "What's an Operator?" (Chapter 1) Frank Gibney discusses the Operator as a generic social type, which includes important features of the American national character noted on many previous occasions by foreign travelers, foreign observers, and other commentators of the American scene. An Operator is the pragmatic man-of-action, one who utilizes moral and legal sleights-of-hand to get things done, to pursue what he or she defines as the goals of the organization or business enterprise. Gibney notes an increasing number of different types of Operators in contemporary society, including sharpers, takers, boiler-room operators, fixers, pitchmen, corporate operators, crooked labor bosses, professional operators, and dodgers.

The daily routines of Operators typically include many actions which could be defined as violations of laws and other legal statutes. But of course such cases rarely find their way into the courts. A major reason for this is that such underhanded business dealings are difficult to prosecute, since most cases of business or corporate fraud hinge on proving the actor's subjective intent to defraud others. And even in those instances where a successful prosecution of business fraud has been accomplished, the convictions typically result in short sentences and light fines for those convicted. Our legislative elites and their business supporters have consciously maintained our legal statutes in their present state of ambiguity which allow these many forms of underhanded business dealings to becomes routine features of American life.

It is a mistake, however, to think that American businessmen prey on unsuspecting victims with no complicity on the part of those victimized. Gibney argues that many unscrupulous business practices owe their success in part to the desires of many consumers to "get something for

7

nothing," to the American glorification of the successful sharper, stress on material acquisition, and the belief that "you can't cheat an honest man." This fact is nicely illustrated in "Caveat Emptor" (Chapter 2) by U.S. Senator Warren G. Magnuson and Jean Carper, which describes the routine business practices known as bait and switch selling, lo-balling, chain referral selling, free gimmick advertising, special pricing, and fear selling, some of which have been known to exist for hundreds of years. Magnuson and Carper also take note of charity swindles, business opportunity rackets, unsolicited merchandise schemes, phony correspondence and vocational schools, land fraud swindles, and phony home improvement scams. All of these schemes and swindles depend in part on the consumer for their success, on the consumer's desire to "get a good deal," "get something for nothing," or "make out like a bandit." The consumer's complicity in the successful swindle is one of the factors which makes solving these problems so difficult.

Finally, in Chapter 3 by Herbert Edelhertz, the former Chief of the Fraud Section of the U.S. Criminal Division, we present a detailed consideration of many of the problematic features of business and professional deviance, from the problems of defining the phenomena to the complicated dilemmas of legislative reform, prosecution, sentencing, and other proposed solutions. Edelhertz correctly observes that our society has undergone fundamental and significant changes in recent decades, and many of the major trends continue unabated, including the increasing complexity of virtually everything, increasing reliance on computers and other technological innovations, which themselves have given rise to new forms of business deviance, and, correspondingly, the increasing problems for citizens to understand how all this operates.

One very important point is implied throughout the Edelhertz article but remains unanalyzed by the author, namely, the increasing attempts by federal, state, and local officials to "control" all kinds of business practices by using the instruments of state power. These attempts represent but one more of the various struggles for achieving a symbolic as well as legitimized dominance in our society, and will no doubt continue for many years to come. For those of us not directly involved as partisans in these struggles, either as businessmen or state officials, these trends will mean the increasing development of various kinds of *symbiotic* relations between the controllers and the controlled, a kind of antagonistic but nevertheless mutually cooperative underground, such as we now see between police officials and narcotics dealers, prostitutes, gamblers, and others who provide valued services in society.

# 1

# What's an Operator?

Frank Gibney

> . . . and there came on that foul image of fraud, came on and
> landed his head and chest, but did not draw his tail on to the bank.
> His face was the face of a just man, so gracious was its outward aspect,
> and all the rest was a serpent's trunk; he had two paws, hairy to the
> armpits, and the back and breast and both the flanks were painted with
> knots and circlets—Tartars or Turks never made stuffs with more colours
> in ground and embroidery . . .
>
> The Inferno, Canto XVII[1]

The morning of another good business day dawned bright and clear.
The reputable executive had two Alka-Seltzer tablets and a cheerful breakfast and sent his children off to school with fatherly counsel. His wife
was slightly troubled about the maid's Social Security payments, which
were long past due; he suggested that she forget about them, since the
maid was leaving soon anyway. Then he climbed into his Thunderbird
and drove downtown.

Traffic was heavy and he was forced to leave the car in a No Parking
zone across from the office. He locked it carefully and on his way down
the street ran into the veteran cop on the beat, who thanked him for a
recent Christmas gift, the usual four bottles of good blended whiskey.
Once in the office, he took care of the mail and some routine desk chores
and settled at least one small but irritating personnel problem: when one
of his middle-rank salesmen asked for a raise, he turned him down but
suggested with the broadest of winks that the man had carte blanche to go
heavy on his expense account until the matter of raises came up formally
late in the fall. Then he took an hour out with his personal income-tax
consultant, who had just found a happy devise for altering repair and
depreciation costs on some rental property, for a handsome tax "profit."
Before their conference was quite over, he handled an urgent long-distance
call from his lawyer and unofficial investment counselor, who had found

a good insolvent manufacturing company which was ripe for a nice tax-loss merger.

A few minutes before one, the reputable businessman walked over to his club, where he habitually lunched and played squash on the company expense account. There he entertained two visiting college classmates at a lavish meal; he insisted on signing the check. Back in the office, he had time to detail one of his assistants to "take care of" the building inspector with jurisdiction over their new plant site, thus getting as much red tape as possible out of the way. In the meantime his secretary had drafted several routine letters for him to sign. Among them was a note to an executive of a smaller firm with whom he had just signed a contract, thanking him for the gift of a new-model TV set.

At a brief conference later in the afternoon he congratulated his firm's controller on a bookkeeping devise that was handily padding a few of the firm's more controversial accounts. Then he went into a half-hour huddle with the account executive from the ad agency about some trouble they had lately run into with the Federal Trade Commission on the subject of misleading commercials. (He advised the advertising man to keep up the same pitch until after the fall sales drive, FTC or no FTC.) In a crucial twenty-minute session, he won the consent of the firm's board chairman to the week's Big Deal, a sleight-of-hand exchange of shares with another company which ultimately promised a really large tax saving and some big stock profits, after several platoons of lawyers had worked out the corporate footwork. This done, he felt free to leave for home. Before he turned out the light in his office, he had his secretary wrap up one of the new company desk sets, which seemed just the thing for his study.

The reputable executive, as anyone could gather from this selective but by no means improbable account of his daily rounds, is what most of his society—viewing his actions dispassionately—would call an "Operator." He is also, by legal definition, a criminal. His business day, if he were successfully prosecuted, could conceivably result in a total of $31,500 in fines and no less than 33 years' imprisonment. Specific offenses would include:

Penalty for willful nonpayment of employer's Social Security contributions: $10,000 fine and/or five years in jail.

Penalty for attempting to influence a police officer with a gift: $5,000 fine and/or 10 years in jail.

Penalty for filing a fraudulent income-tax return: $10,000 fine and/or five years in jail.

Penalty for misusing an expense account, under Section 665 of the N. Y. State Penal Law: $500 fine and/or one year in jail.

Penalty for bribing a public officer: $5,000 fine and/or 10 years in jail.

Penalty for secretly accepting a gift in return for corporate loans: $500 fine and/or one year in jail.

Penalty for appropriating company property to one's personal use: $500 fine and/or one year in jail.[2]

Yet no one would be more surprised than the businessman to be told this. About the criminal shading of some of his activities he would be blissfully ignorant. But even where his chicanery was done knowingly, his first reaction—if he were a typical Operator—would be one of surprised indignation that he, of all people, should be singled out for "persecution." After all, the reputable-looking Operator would protest, "Isn't everybody doing it?"

This [article] is about how everybody *is* doing it, a brief and necessarily undetailed survey of the vast and burgeoning volume of dishonest dealing in the United States today. The subject matter is not restricted to what criminologists, after the late Professor Ernest Sutherland, now call "white-collar crime," i.e., "a crime committed by a person of respectability and high social status in the course of his occupation." It includes the current activities, often awesomely mechanized, of the swindlers, con men, grafters and embezzlers—the compulsive type of professional thief of whom O. Henry once wrote, in *The Gentle Grafter:* "Whenever he saw someone else with a dollar in his hand, he took it as a personal grudge, if he couldn't take it." But the obviously criminal act, the acknowledged illegality, is only a small part of the Operators' total activities. We must include also the wide area of legal but immoral sharp practices in business, labor and politics, often severely damaging to society but generally subtle enough to keep just beyond effective range of society's formidable but fixed legal gun positions.

The very definition of "operator" must be made arbitrary and harshly comprehensive. For the Operator thrives on moral, not to say legal sleight-of-hand—it is no accident that modern slang use of the word derives originally from the eighteenth-century English slang for skilled pickpocket. Often the Operator is considered a pillar of the community. He may be, and in recent criminal cases has turned out to be, a Chicago architect, a prosperous automobile dealer in Denver, a member of Congress from Massachusetts, a physician in Omaha, a respected lawyer in Philadelphia or a veteran Internal Revenue Service agent in New York.

The Operator may be a bigtime juggler of corporations or a smalltime accountant skillfully barbering a friend's income tax. He may be a salesman padding his expense account to meet the payments on his car. He may take bribes or give them, whether the bribing involves a political scandal or a simple shift of business from one wholesaler to another. He may be a partner in a crooked accident-insurance racket or a prosperous store owner with a weakness for faked markdowns. Or, all too likely, he may be just a decent, God-fearing American who had to put his finger in the till one day and never found the strength to pull it out.

Many of these people become Operators without realizing it. The boundaries are slippery between what is obviously right and obviously wrong and we are rich in our mirages of private morality and pressing self-justification. But no one can *remain* an Operator for long without resorting to some form of knowing, culpable deceit.

The Operator has always been present on the American scene. Inevitably, successful fraud increased and multiplied along with the expansion of the national economy. But in the early days of the Republic it was necessarily a penny-ante operation. The Operator was likely to be a gambler, a fast-talking peddler or a sharp wit attracted by the opportunities for crookedness in the field of trading and finance. "Is there no way," the New York *Sun* apostrophized in January 1837, "to reach the knaves who have flooded this city with checks made out in the form of bills on banks in which they have not a dollar deposited?" Later nineteenth-century economic progress brought the Operator into the big time. By the 1890s, the old-time "Robber Barons" had become Operators in the grand manner. During a meeting of 17 railroad presidents at J. P. Morgan's house in New York City, one of their number, A. B. Stickney, delivered himself of the memorable observation: "I have the utmost respect for you gentlemen individually, but as railroad presidents I wouldn't trust you with my watch out of my sight."

But it was left to our own era to take the ancient art of the Operator and turn it into a broad-gauge way of life in which all Americans—regardless of race, color, creed or economic status—could participate. Never in our history has the practice of fraud been so dignified by constant use and acceptance.

Here are a few indications of the Operators' recent activities, measured in terms of cold cash. Last year, by conservative estimate, some five billion dollars, roughly one percent of the total U. S. national product, changed hands under innumerable desks, counters, or expensive restaurant tables in kickbacks, payoffs or bribes. The country's employers lost more than half a billion to embezzling employees, from pilfering shop workers to absconding assistant secretary-treasurers. More of the public's money evaporated through retail chiseling. A half billion went down the drain in home-repair frauds alone. Officials of the Securities and Exchange Commission [SEC] do not even attempt to measure the high cost of stocks worth slightly more than the paper they are printed on, aside from putting it in the "hundreds of millions." In a six-month period of 1957, six fly-by-night security outfits could make themselves an illicit profit of $4.5 millions. A big-timer like Alexander Guterma, on the other hand, was convicted of fraud by the U. S. Government in 1960, after methodically bilking several companies and their stockholders in nine busy years of entrenched business swindling.

Officers of the Bureau of Internal Revenue could display a record harvest of $1,684,465,000 in additional taxes, penalties and interest on the 1958 returns of U. S. taxpayers and squeeze out an extra $1,012,000,000 from delinquent accounts. In the course of its enforcement activity the Bureau conducted more than 25,000 separate investigations, the majority of them for tax fraud.

The aggregate of rubber checks bounced a third higher than last year and almost 100 percent higher than in 1952. The yearly loss to banks and individuals is now figured at well over a half billion. The Post Office Department, with a record number of arrests in 1958, reported an increase of 29 percent in mail-order and other fraud within its province between 1950 and 1958—$2\frac{1}{2}$ times the population increase, incidentally. Their cost was pegged at a "conservative" $100,000,000.

The aberrations of "regular" businesses are no more comforting. Although the 63 new antitrust actions brought by the Department of Justice —a 17-year high—in 1959 were sometimes as much a matter of legal interpretation as criminal corporate behavior, there was no mistaking the out-and-out crime of Operators who diverted to their own use money collected in employee's withholding and Social Security taxes: the delinquent accounts now amount to over $300 million. The Federal Trade Commission [FTC] records an alarming rise in the total of consent orders and civil and criminal actions against companies in every industry for various misrepresentations of their products. The number of actions for deceptive practices in 1959 stood at 267—twice the number instituted in 1956. And the FTC, with a staff of only 738 investigators and jurisdiction only in clearly interstate cases, is quick to admit that its cases are but a tiny percentage of the total. For 1960, the FTC has before it the additional and Herculean chore of combing the fraud out of the matted locks of the television and radio industry.

The foregoing drainage from the national pocketbook is in the record. Conspicuously not recorded are the amounts lost to stockholders and investors through issues juggled and corporations either grossly swollen or grotesquely contracted for the benefit of their exploiters. There is no count, either, of the money lost to the U. S. government in the acquisitions of insolvent companies by going concerns, as a device to obviate the paying of taxes. Of at least equal enormity is the robber baron's tax levied on the entire economy by the crookedness of bad union leadership.

Such records of the Operator's take are formidable; but they are only secondary to the real problem he poses to this country today. A habit of fraud is growing upon us. For the Operator can thrive only where he is tolerated, not to say invited. (It is the oldest maxim of the con man that "you can't cheat an honest man.") The disturbing thing about so much of the fraud in the United States is the eagerness of the suckers who succumb to it, their urge to make the fast buck faster, their alacrity at condoning sharp practices which earlier generations of Americans would at least have recognized as morally wrong—even if they helped clip the coupons.

Americans have always held a sneaking sympathy for the sharper, the gay rogue, the lad who cheats in examinations and never gets caught, the seasoned traveler who makes a work of art out of each customs declaration, the car owner—it would have to be a very skillful car owner these days—who manages to slip something over on a dealer in a trade-in. When the yegg in loud pin-stripes changes to a gray flannel suit, his transition is hailed as the American dream in action. The well-publicized entrepreneur Frank Costello was a case in point. There was never any doubt about the illicit nature of his activities. Yet he gained free access to the offices—and the parties—of some of the more respected citizens of New York, Los Angeles, and other key business centers. Long after his activities had been exposed, he remained an object of public curiosity rather than public revulsion—a legitimate target for aspiring autograph hounds.

District Attorney Frank Hogan of New York County hammers away at such public indifference to criminals wearing cuff links. "We appear," he said,

> to have developed a public morality which condemns—rather than praises—any private citizen who seeks to enforce the laws that we—as members of a free society—have called into being. . . . We make a sort of game of it, between law-enforcement officials and criminals, and sit complacently by, quite ready to applaud a brilliant stroke on either side.

This tendency to glorify the sharper has always been present in American literature and, as romance grows thinner and plots for our other native art form, the Western, exhaust themselves, it has become stronger. In some recent fictional works, notably Ayn Rand's *Atlas Shrugged*, the Operator in business comes through as a well-pressed Tamerlane, with a corps of busy appraisers, bookkeepers, and assistant vice-presidents. As sophisticated a writer as John Marquand, who began his dissections of the national character with George Apley's stiff-necked bird-watchers, switched with the years to plot mergers with ruthless old diamonds in the rough like Willis Wayde, a fit contender in any business-fiction league.

Other nations have their own images of this sort: the ruthless intellectual tearing up his library card to sway the masses to his will, the literary giant who proves that society is as corrupt as he is, the mustachioed general storming the palace, the man from the county family sewing up elections as effortlessly as he knots his old school tie. And if the American zeal to perform prodigies with money and property is less soaring than the urge to master men's souls or lead their bodies on the battlefield, it is not so dangerous.

Yet the urge to gain business success, and to cut corners in so doing, can in time produce a most unmoral tolerance for fraud. As early as 1832, Mrs. Trollope, that notoriously sharp-tongued English critic of American mores, could write (after failing in business in Cincinnati) her inflamed description of the dollar: "This sordid object forever before their eyes, must inevitably produce a sordid tone of mind and worse still, it produces a seared and blunted conscience on all questions of probity."

Almost 140 years and countless dollars later we find that the age of unparalleled abundance, of leisure, high investment profit, and vast material expectations is leaving us with a sadly blunted conscience indeed.

It is no small part of the trouble that we have become, as a society, scandalously overprotected. A web of rules, regulations, safeguards, administrations, and group thought winds its strands ever more tightly through a nation which still asserts itself to be just a bunch of good, individualistic, rugged free-enterprisers. This overprotection not only lets our guard down against chiseling, but it also encourages its own kind of revolt. The man who chuckles over a friend's tax dodge is displaying the same envy of direct action that leads him to sit night after night in a half-dark room watching TV private eyes gun down the opposition.

Then there is the urge to abundance. Each year more than $11 billion are spent in the United States on various forms of advertising. A tremendous amount of educated talent is devoted to convincing Americans that life cannot be bearable without the higher-quality dog food, the more "influential" magazine, the extra car—even more recently, the extra house. (We shall get into the question of the fraudulent or nearly fraudulent advertising claim in later chapters.) Stress on sheer acquisition naturally makes people greedy, and greed is the beginning of a cheat.

The Genial American Society of 1960 has come a long way from its watchful beginnings in the midst of what the Puritans (before they started to make money) liked to call "this evil, sinful world." The Genial Society takes abundance for granted. Its members are paradoxically careless of the possessions they seek so avidly, once they get them—they are so used to planned obsolescence. Yet while lacking the vigilance of the miser, they retain all of the miser's acquisitiveness.

The Genial Society frowns on indignation, except as directed against convicted murderers, native Communists or idealized instances of "graft and corruption"—and even in these rare cases where group anger is permitted, the members of the group seldom do much about the objects themselves. Toleration is its highest social good. Harsh words are anathema. In 1959 the U.S. Weather Bureau had to change the name of its new Discomfort Index of heat and humidity, due to public protest. And by "toleration" I mean a social philosophy that bears little relation to charity or respect for one's fellow man. We dislike surprises. We are pathetically afraid of "looking bad."

We are gullible and have a near-fatal fascination for showmanship and show. We may or may not be dedicated to a search for visible symbols of power and prestige, but we look that way. It is a tribute to our aptitude for self-deception that the modern American, one of the most face-conscious national figures in history—at least as far as his private life is concerned—can still pretend to smile patronizingly at what he regards as the Oriental "sensitivity to face."

In a memorable questionnaire of representative car owners in the 1950s about their preferences in a new model, almost all the people questioned listed as their prime criteria items like "fuel economy," "safety" or "engine performance." Since these qualities were somewhat at variance with the splayed fins and pointed windshields which everyone was then demanding in his car, a shrewd poll-taker asked another question: "What would your next-door neighbor prize in a car?" The answers came back quickly and almost uniformly: "style," "power and pickup," "chrome," etc.—all the qualities that people were actually buying. The "next-door neighbor's" criteria were obviously what each person wanted for himself. It would not have been good form to say so.

As a keynote example of the Genial Society's vulnerability, we might take the brief financial orbiting of Mr. Earl Belle of Pittsburgh. Mr. Belle is at the moment a resident of Rio de Janeiro, capital of one of the few countries which do not have an extradition treaty with the United States. For a few exciting years, he was regarded back home as a boy wonder in the finest tradition.

Belle graduated from the University of Pittsburgh in 1956 and burst upon the world with his degree, a small family benefice and a few contacts among Pittsburgh people with heavy cash balances remaining from their World War II profits. In two years he had control of the First National Bank of nearby Saltsburg and a good reputation in the town for bringing new industry into it. Working with one Edward Talenfeld and his sons Murray and Barton, he used the bank's assets to buy up the happily named firm of Cornucopia Gold Mines. This he converted into a holding company with interests—mostly on option—in several reasonably functioning concerns.

Belle exuded coolness and confidence. At the very moment the SEC was oiling up its machinery to investigate his unorthodox stock buying and selling procedures, he had set about raising money for his ventures from several widely separated but equally unsuspecting banks. He borrowed $150,000 from the Manufacturers Bank in Edgewater, N.J.: $200,000 from the McKeesport, Pa., People Union Bank; and a total of $475,000 from the Security National Bank of Huntington, N.Y. These and other activities were subsequently part of a monumental thirty-eight-count indictment.

With a flair for the *beau geste,* Belle affected a valet-companion, raccoon coats, gaily colored vests, a $5,000 Mercedes, and a superbly convincing line of chatter. He got a fine press. Barely six months before his final exposure, he was interviewed by Mike Wallace, the New York TV interlocutor, in his column in the New York *Post.* Wallace cited him as an outstanding American, "a vigorous, tough-minded 26-year-old," who had "pyramided his profits into a $10-million industrial empire." Answered Belle, in a rare burst of frankness: "A dollar is round and you figure it rolled to you so easy, it can roll away. But if you claw your way up, nobody can take anything from you, because they didn't give you anything." (He was finally given his fraud and conspiracy indictment by a federal grand jury in Pittsburgh in 1960.)

An embarrassing number of publicists and financial authorities were charmed by the boyish ruthlessness of such statements and hooked accordingly. Yet through the period of his greatest fame, he was already listed on the bulletins of the Better Business Bureau as suspect, since the SEC had early in the game undertaken action against his holding company. Any thorough reportorial investigation would have confirmed the existence of gaping loopholes in his financial log pile. But none thought of doing such a thing. He *looked* so successful.

The Operator by definition lives in a floating world[3] of big deals and ready pleasures, and he is constantly enlarging its boundaries. The fix, the bribe, the organized cheat are common in sections of American life which were once thought almost sacrosanct, like sports, art or religious activity. The more improbable his zone of operations, in fact, the better chance has the Operator to take the suckers completely unaware. He shifts his style with the ease of a stage manager adjusting the scenery—from the real-estate fraud or the crooked TV repair shop to the stock swindle to the accident insurance racket, or vice versa. But he is at least subject to a few reasonably definite categories which follow.

*The sharpers.* The most readily distinguishable group of Operators, the promoters-gone-wrong who swindle the buying or investing public by taking over once-legitimate businesses and exploiting them. A sharper generally starts out in life as a reputable businessman.

*The takers.* Their world is the exchange of bribes and kickbacks. They proliferate in wholesale businesses that require a great deal of personal contacts between buyers and suppliers. They also populate the lower fringes of politics, where the crooked building inspector or the venal police officer is an all too common fact of life.

*The boiler-room operators.* Stock swindling has become such a major criminal or (as prosecutors often find out to their sorrow) semicriminal occupation that its practitioners deserve a category all their own.

*The fixers.* The free spenders (and freeloaders) who make their way in business by greasing palms for percentages. Seldom can a criminal charge be made to stick against them. They peddle influence, jobs, and money, and they deftly drag reputable businessmen into their peculiar social and moral whirlpool.

*The pitchmen.* The custodians of false claims and fraudulent pretensions. Although related to the sharpers, they deserve a separate category— if for no other reason than that their activities, although equally debatable morally, seldom land them in jail. Most of them begin as relatively honest workers in advertising, journalism, business, or the law.

*The corporate operators.* The aristocracy of the whole movement: the king-size sharpers. They represent the class least eager to see its name linked with the other types. Their lives are often symbols of respectability; but they prey on both American business and the public through their addiction to such personally profitable devices as convenient mergers, juggled assets, and various forms of trade and competition. They use their employees and their stockholders like helpless pawns, but they rarely break the law clearly enough to warrant the court action they deserve.

*The crooked labor bosses.* Robber Barons with contempt for union democracy. Their baronies have proved extraordinarily resistant to both legal action and spurts of public indignation. (Although not specifically discussed . . . [here], . . . they are allies and supporters of most of the other categories cited, in one way or another.)

*The professionals.* Although the most established of American operators, these out-and-out criminals are probably the least important. They include swindlers and embezzlers, forgers and passers of bad checks. They extract yearly uncountable millions (90 percent of their victims never tell) from the people who P. T. Barnum said were born at the rate of 60 an hour. Many of them shift into the more modern categories of sharpers or even fixers.

*The dodgers.* Pure amateurs at first. This category, its numbers swelling hourly, comprises all those who try and succeed in evading public or business responsibility by fraudulent means. Almost everyone in it regards himself as an honest man. The more able of this sort find it easy to become dedicated full-time operators.

Whatever the type of Operator, however thin his protective coloration, we can safely assume that the Genial Society will have a hard time catching him. Where legal catching is out of the question, it may be difficult even to identify an Operator as such. For there are three heavy road blocks which can hinder pursuit. They are: (1) the federal system of government; (2) the due process of law; and (3) the Genial Society's unthinking assumption of its own honesty.

To begin with, every effective Operator is a strong states' rights man. His activities follow the flag, wherever it may wave—an epidemic of crooked car salesmen not long ago invaded U. S. Army posts in Germany; and scant days after Congress passed the Alaska Statehood bill, the New York State Attorney General's office issued a special warning to investors against the rising number of phony Alaska mining stocks. The Operator is generally careful to run back and forth among as many different state jurisdictions as possible. Nowhere else in the world can he take such advantage of rival local authorities and play out his game with so many differing sets of ground rules. A consumer fraud regarded as criminal in Connecticut might not even be mentioned on the statute books of Minnesota. The peculiarities of state laws on banking, investment, taxes, and trade are enough to delight any keen and fraudulent mind.

A murderer or a bank robber gets short shrift under any state law. And, barring the rare exception, the extradition processes are swift and sure when one state's police catch another state's violent criminal. But crimes of fraud are not so clearly defined. Most of them are too intricate and indirect in their illegality to upset a governor's or a state legislature's blood pressure. The slicker types make a specialty of American legal geography, hopping with some care from one area to another as occasion demands. Federal agencies like the SEC and the FTC grow gray trying to bring these offenders to book. Often they must resort to heavy persuasion before some state legal mechanisms can even be alerted to the danger.

There are, however, certain discernible patterns of crime, cut to areas where local conditions or sheer geography favor them. Denver, for instance, has always been known as a handy stopping place for forgers and check kiters. The reason for this is simple. Although big enough to give some protective cover, it is rather isolated, as American big cities go—a condition made to order for this sort of work. Los Angeles, it goes without saying, has been a center for numerous varieties of real-estate fraud. The general area of southern California, with its high percentage of retired people, has had more than its share of phony investment swindles, as well as a collection of heterodox swamis and nonordained soul-savers, who specialize in contributions.

Detroit's police department has not been overly troubled with fraud schemes—acute problems of race and industrial relations have been known to give the local cops enough work opportunities. Cincinnati, at the moment, is possessed of an efficient police force, and the garden variety of fraud operator, at least, has made himself scarce. Chicago, on the other hand, remains an aviary of splendidly tufted fraudsters. Their depredations are distinguished not so much by skill or suavity as [by] comprehensiveness. There is barely a corner of Chicago's civic life which has not been plucked clean by some variety of gangster or grafter, and the state of the city's law-enforcement facilities has been a national disgrace.[4]

For all the evils of Chicago, for all the temporary prominence of vest-pocket iniquity centers like Phenix City, Alabama, or Jersey City, New Jersey, or the profitable eccentricities of the corporation laws of Delaware, it is New York where the best Operators always congregate. It is no accident that a great proportion of the criminal examples noted in this book have some connection with this city. For New York fills roughly the same function in the world of white-collar crime that it fills in the legitimate theater. A crooked practice may originate in Austin, Texas, or Tacoma, Washington, but if successful it will sooner or later find its way east for the criminal equivalent of the Broadway opening. If the Manhattan "opening" proves a success, there are plenty of road-show opportunities afterward.

The one exception is political fraud, where the supreme goal, of course, lies 300 miles to the south. But cases where an entire small-town grafting operation can be transferred to Washington are fortunately few. For all the chiseling done by individuals in the Eisenhower and Truman administrations, the country will probably not tolerate again the spectacle which Warren Harding left us of Ohio's back-street politics installed in the White House. It was too embarrassing.

In dealing with white-collar criminals, crooked politicians included, the law often less than fulfills its purpose. It may be not so much a threat as a handy port in a storm. The nub of the legal problem in fraud cases was stated as well as anyone could state it in a 1917 decision by Judge Hough of the U. S. Circuit Court of Appeals: "Just when the sanguine man becomes reckless and the reckless one criminal cannot be laid down as a matter of law." The question of fraud is largely a matter of proving intent. There is nothing to stop the proprietor of, say, Sub-Arctic Tundra, Ltd., from saying in court that he honestly believed there was gold, uranium, platinum, and buried treasure in those desolate flatlands. There is no stolen car or corpus delicti to prove him wrong. For the modern operator lives in a world of paper and promises, a world which Mr. Blackstone and the constructors of the Common Law could hardly have anticipated.

Every district attorney dreads a fraud case, except the reckless legal knight in armor (and these are in short supply). It is hard to prove and, to state his problem in [nonlegal] but human terms, likely to damage his record with an acquittal. The obvious reason for this is the attitude of juries. A juror can get indignant about a murder victim, but he may feel nothing but contempt for the victim of a swindle—unless the prosecutor can produce the classic example of the woman in widow's weeds or the orphans' trust fund. Such clear-cut cases are few and far between. In most fraud actions, jurors have the attitude of spectators at a court-tennis game, trying to determine whether the effort of figuring out the complex rules is worth it.

A deeper handicap is the state of the laws. It would be a farfetched Utopia indeed which had its laws keep up step by step with the march of crime. The best we can hope for is that they will follow close enough upon cases of novel wrongdoing to restrict their spread. In the area of fraud and corporate or personal deception, this has not happened. In New York State, to give a flagrant example, it was not until 1953 that a law finally declared that it is illegal for a union leader to accept a bribe. Even now, in a world where advertising claims can be made by subliminal suggestion, only a minority of the states have thought of revising the old basis of their consumer-protection laws: Let the buyer beware.

"You have to have an evil and it has to be pretty bad," said Warren Olney, until 1958 the head of the Department of Justice's Criminal Division, "before you get enough public pressure behind it to get legislation." The trouble with laws governing the Operators' activities is the Genial Society's lack of public indignation. Ample laws exist on the statute books, both state and federal, to insure against the reincarnation of Jim Fisk, Jay Gould, or, in his more unsavory aspects, P. T. Barnum. But the *new* kind of Operator has revised his methods. Netting him can be as frustrating as trying to capture a mosquito with a lacrosse stick.

So far, so bad. But the hopeful prosecutor has to contend with yet another obstacle, the attitude of the judiciary. To say that most judges do not get indignant over the nonviolent criminal is an understatement—at least according to most prosecutors. The Operator invariably makes a better appearance in court than his violently criminal brethren do. In any case, the sentences given for fraud, swindling, or business deception are proportionately far lighter than those handed down for crimes of violence, although by volume it is the crimes of fraud which are economically and morally more expensive to society.

In January 1958 the leader of a fake insurance-claims ring in New York City was convicted on three counts of first-degree grand larceny, one count of second-degree grand larceny and three counts of conspiracy. He was convicted of swindling $11,000 from three insurance companies, the specific offense for which he was tried. The judge gave him a *suspended* sentence and ordered him to make restitution—of $3,000.

Angered by such dispositions, District Attorney Hogan was moved to comment: "It's becoming common in General Sessions for a thief after conviction to make a fractional restitution and walk out without any penalty. It's practically like paying for a license to swindle after you're caught."

If a prosecutor gets his conviction through the judge and jury, he then has to reckon with the mechanism of appeal. The process of appeal to a higher court was developed to insure an accused against any possibility of judicial or factual error in his trial. The wide channels of appeal, teeming with so many varieties of legal technicalities, permit convicted criminals to argue their cases for years before final disposition. If they are patient and wealthy, the chances are that some legal technicality may ultimately intervene in their favor. Really successful Operators have ample resources for this sort of happy procrastination. Fraud cases, often involving very complicated questions of law, generally invite appeal.

The final factor in the Operator's success is the moral problem, to which we have alluded. Fraud has become noisome, destructive and difficult to punish in America precisely because of our commitment to the copybook maxim that "Honesty is the Best Policy." Generations of Americans—sales managers, union presidents and secretaries of state—have subscribed to this principle and believed in it. Lawyers and social commentators have written volumes on that tabernacular linchpin of business society, the Honest Contract. At its best this commitment to rigid communal honesty holds our democracy together. It still enforces far more voluntary obedience than is observable in many other societies.

The trouble is that our own overprotected society takes the group commitment for granted. We believe in honesty too much and too little, for we leave the premises of honesty unexamined and forgotten. We rely on the law and our system of public order to define honesty for us, instead of going back to our own consciences, where our own honesty is in question, or critically poking beneath the fancy label or the television commercial, when it is a matter of someone else's honesty. The law cannot always tell us when a person is crooked. . . .

# NOTES

1. Translation by John D. Sinclair.

2. All these penalties noted are for violations of either federal or state laws. Only one state, New York, has been used for the sake of uniformity.

3. The term "floating world" is the direct translation of *Ukiyo*, the Japanese term for the demimonde of actors, geisha, prostitutes, pleasure-seeking gentry, crooks and bankrupts which flourished in Tokyo and other large Japanese cities of the late seventeenth century. The *Ukiyo* gave the world a brilliant genre of pictures and sketchbooks for which it is now best known. But the depredations of its crooked citizenry almost swamped the Japanese national character.

4. In January, 1960, a series of scandals—involving bail-bond deals, egregious ticket-fixing, and fine-stealing in the courts—was climaxed by the confession of a burglar that he had committed his larcenies under the direction of local police officers. Only a few days after his confession, more than a score of public officials had already been implicated.

# 2

# Caveat Emptor

*Warren G. Magnuson and Jean Carper*

One evening two men in a Cadillac paid a call on an elderly couple in a small town in Arkansas. One of the men, a Mr. G., president of the Superior Improvement Company in Little Rock, presented himself to the couple as an important executive affiliated with Alcoa Aluminum Company. He told the couple that after a careful examination of their house he had chosen it to be a model home as part of a new advertising campaign to sell aluminum siding. Photographs, he said, would be taken of the house "before" and "after" the siding was applied and would be featured in beautiful brochures. Salesmen would bring prospective customers to view the house, and for every sale made as a result, Mr. G. promised to give the couple a commission of $100. When urged to sign an agreement, the couple protested that their house was old and they were thinking of using their savings to rebuild. But the promises of Mr. G. were irresistible. He asserted he was giving them the siding at $1,000 below cost, cheaper than they could get it anywhere, and that with the commissions their house would be transformed into a showplace of beauty for virtually nothing. "Well, then, he said one thing that kind of struck me," the homeowner later recalled. "He said to say a little prayer and pray to the Lord and let Him guide us as to whether to sign the contract." Touched by this display of humility, the man and woman signed a contract for $1,480 and gave Mr. G. a down-payment check for $200.

By the next morning, the couple was no longer so spellbound by Mr. G.'s promises. Skeptical, they checked around and discovered they could buy aluminum siding for much less than Mr. G.'s "bargain factory prices." The homeowner, realizing he had been fleeced, tried to stop payment on the check, but was told that one of Mr. G.'s representatives had been there that morning as the bank opened and cashed the check. Repeated attempts to reach Mr. G. by phone at his Little Rock office were futile. He was always "out," and, said the homeowner, "His secretary kind of laughed like it was a big joke." Finally, in desperation and worry over

From Senator Warren G. Magnuson and Jean Carper. *The Dark Side of the Marketplace.* Englewood Cliffs, N.J.: Prentice-Hall, 1968, pp. 3–31. Reprinted by permission.

his wife's ill health, which had been aggravated by the transaction, the man borrowed money from a bank and paid off the bill in full. He was informed by a lawyer that if he refused to make payments, the finance company Mr. G. had sold the contract to could sue him—and collect. The workmen had already tacked up the siding, such as it was. And the contract he had signed was legally binding, regardless of the verbal misrepresentations.

Hundreds of persons in rural Arkansas, Tennessee, and Kentucky, since 1960, have been seduced by Mr. G.'s prayers and phony promises into paying exorbitant prices for shoddy workmanship and poor quality materials. Mr. G. claimed his aluminum was manufactured by Alcoa, Kaiser, or Reynolds Aluminum Co.; it was in truth an off-brand, most of it shipped from Illinois. He told customers that it would "never chip, crack, fade or soak up water, would never need paint and had a lifetime guarantee." To many a homeowner's dismay, the siding was not applied by "factory-trained personnel" as promised, but sometimes by local teenagers. It fell off; the caulking was not done properly; the upper layer of finish could be rubbed off with the sweep of a hand. Some homes were left unfinished, aluminum and trash piled high in the yard. One man's house was such a shambles within a year, pockmarked by the fallen siding, that he needed a completely new siding job. The only thing he had bought from Mr. G. was a $2,400 debt.

Mr. G. and his salesmen preyed shamelessly on the illiterate, the poor, the old, and the guileless. One man said Mr. G.'s salesmen kept him up most of the night begging him to sign a note; weary and fatigued, he finally did. An elderly Negro was coerced into putting his X mark on a contract. Many were induced to part with their pensions and Social Security checks. Others said they were tricked into signing mortgages on their homes, and one couple swore their names were forged to a promissory note. In this brutal marketplace, there was no compunction about tacking aluminum siding on a shack in the fork of a dust-covered road and proclaiming it a "showplace."

Many people understood that because of the $100 bonus, they would have to pay little or nothing for the siding. Instead, once their names were on the contract, few homeowners ever saw Mr. G. or any of his salesmen again. No one brought prospective customers to view the renovated house as the salesmen had promised. Some people waited and waited, actually stayed home for days on end, fearing to leave the house, waiting for the customers that never came, until their hope turned to anguish.

Many were left with disastrous debts. A young schoolteacher signed a contract with a total price of $3,650. By the time monthly payments were figured out—84 of them at $73.45 each—he discovered he had agreed to pay $6,132 over a period of seven years. Horrified, he borrowed money from his credit union and managed to persuade the finance company to let him pay off the debt; the company insisted, however, that he pay them more than $1,000 interest for use of the money for "less than a month."

Another couple signed a contract with Mr. G. for what they thought was about $2,000 and a mortgage on their house. Said a government lawyer: "When they sat down that night and in their sober judgment figured out what that was going to cost them over a period of 84 months —84 payments—they were not going to pay $2,000; it would be some $4,000 to $4,400. That fellow attempted to commit suicide." Another pensioned purchaser came home and found his elderly wife unconscious on the bed. She recovered but confessed she had been so worried over the transaction with Mr. G. and the prospect of losing their home that she drank Lysol.

Early in 1964, the Federal Trade Commission issued a complaint against Mr. G. and his company, charging him with a dozen "unfair and deceptive practices." After hearings, he was ordered by the FTC to stop using such sales practices in interstate commerce. Mr. G. chose to take his case through the courts, and finally in early 1967, when the Supreme Court refused to hear his case, he was forced to comply with the FTC ruling. (It is interesting to note that the primary basis for Mr. G.'s defense was not innocence of deceptive selling, for he admitted that he had promised bonuses to prospective buyers. His main contention was that he was not engaging in interstate commerce and that, therefore, the FTC had no jurisdiction over his actions. The FTC can intervene only when it can be proved that a misdoer is operating across state lines.)

It might appear that Mr. G. will be forced by the FTC to stop using his lucrative, deceptive sales pitches (his annual volume of business was estimated at $400,000). On the contrary, Mr. G. shows every intention of carrying on. He has mapped out for the FTC his blueprint for future business: he will not advertise in interstate newspapers or other media, will not use the mails to send out brochures and will not make sales to residents in other states. In other words, he pledges not to work his deceptive arts on anyone, except, of course, the unlucky prospects he may find within the borders of Arkansas.

At this writing, Mr. G. is still in business, his Superior Improvement Company still in existence. If complaints received by the Better Business Bureau of Little Rock are accurate, his salesmen are still active in Arkansas, using misrepresentations and "questionable advertising and selling practices" to unload shoddy jobs and merchandise at unconscionable prices. Who is to stop him?

Although the Federal Trade Commission may be reluctant to admit it for fear of seeming to condone deceptive practices, the sorry truth in this matter is that as long as Mr. G.'s corporation scrupulously avoids interstate commerce, it can operate with impunity, free from FTC jurisdiction or intervention, no matter how blatantly dishonest the sales practices or how appalling to human sensibilities the amount of human misery left in their wake.

It is certain that the authorities of Arkansas, when informed of this company's intention to hide behind state lines out of the reach of the FTC, will *want* to take measures to protect the residents of Arkansas. But the question is: will they be able to? Do they have the authority under existing state law? Although it is impossible to predict the outcome of any legal action—and some states have achieved surprising victories with the imaginative use of seemingly inapplicable laws—legal authorities advise me that Arkansas probably does not have the legal machinery necessary to fight companies like Mr. G.'s. Arkansas does not have a comprehensive law covering deceptive selling. It has only a variety of laws forbidding the use of certain deceptive practices to sell specific products, but aluminum siding is not among them. It is true that Arkansas, like other states, has criminal fraud and false pretenses statutes, resulting in fines or imprisonment for those adjudged guilty. But these statutes are a poor vehicle for preventing deceptive selling. Indictments under the statutes are exceedingly rare and convictions even rarer. As far as we know, neither federal, nor state, nor any other known authority can under present law take action to protect the citizens of Arkansas against the gouging of companies like Mr. G.'s.

Although the case of Mr. G. is one of the most dramatic on record of how deceptive sellers can operate outside the reach of the law, it would be a mistake to believe that Arkansas is like the old Oklahoma Strip of the 1880s: the only place where robbers could operate without interference from the law. On the contrary, although Arkansas is uncommonly hampered by weak consumer protection laws, it is hardly unique. Consumer deception flourishes nearly everywhere in the country, quite often unimpeded—and sometimes even abetted—by the law. As Helen Nelson, former consumer counsel for the governor of California, has said: "More money is being taken from Americans at penpoint than by gunpoint and the pen often makes it legal."

Deceptive selling by the unscrupulous few in the business underworld is, in fact, our most serious form of theft. It cheats Americans of several billion dollars yearly, more than is lost through robbery, burglary, larceny, auto theft, embezzlement and forgery combined. Unlike the con men of yesterday who were often so heavy-handed that they offended the law, today's modern bandits of the marketplace are the masters of the light touch. With their insidious misrepresentations, silver-tongued lies, half-truths, and exaggerated promises, these men can reach even deeper into our pockets without producing a rustle to disturb the law or often the victim himself. From coast to coast we are exposed to their Pandora's box of selling tricks—some old, but handily adapted to modern circumstances, and some new, carefully devised to outwit the law.

Although these schemes are staggering in scope and diverse in their nature (the Better Business Bureau has identified eight hundred different varieties), they invariably have several things in common: they are lucrative, they are subtle and their purveyors rarely come in conflict with the law. According to a nationwide survey for the President's Commission on Law Enforcement and Administration of Justice in 1966, nine out of every ten victims of consumer fraud do not even bother to report it to the police. Fifty percent of the victimized felt they had no right or duty to complain; forty percent believed the authorities could not be effective or would not want to be bothered; ten percent were confused about where to report.

It is startling to consider that the vast majority of Americans victimized by consumer fraud feel that the law can or will do nothing to help them; but it is even more startling to realize that in many instances those victims are absolutely correct. Our legal remedies against consumer deception and fraud, some of which were adequate fifty, even twenty, years ago, are now so outdated as to leave the consumer nearly helpless. Under our present laws, with rare exceptions, we neither give relief to the victimized consumer nor effectively halt the swindlers.

The scheme so successfully used by Mr. G. is but one of five major schemes on which today's pyramid of deceptive selling rests. Although Mr. G. combined several techniques, his primary deception consisted of convincing homeowners that by making their home a "model," he was giving them "a special low price." (The phony "special price" is also used to sell a variety of items, including encyclopedias, automobiles, carpeting, roofing and jewelry.) According to the Federal Trade Commission, the four other schemes that are currently most responsible for fleecing American consumers are *bait and switch advertising,* including "lo-balling," *chain-referral selling,* the *free gimmick* and the *fear-sell.*

Of these, the most troublesome to detect and curtail is bait and switch advertising, in which the merchant advertises goods *which he has no intention of selling* in order to switch the prospective buyer to another item, invariably higher priced and with a greater margin of profit. Not only is bait advertising perfectly legal in most states, but it is so subtle that most victims are never aware that they have been deceived. We all see bait advertising continually, but probably few of us are aware of its insidious calculated nature.

Typically, this is the way the scheme works. A housewife in Alexandria, Virginia, recently noticed this advertisement in the classified section of a newspaper:

SEW MACH.—1965 Singer
Touch and Sew ***
Reposs. Balance. $86.40
New Mach. Guar. Dealer,
Credit Dept. ***

When the salesman arrived at her home, following her telephone call to the company, she was appalled by the machine he carried. He set it down on the table and said: "Well, this is the machine." It was not the new one described in the ad. Rather, as the woman put it, it was "an old beaten-up Singer about 25 or 30 years old. . . . I'd seen machines in better shape at rummage sales." It was battered, scratched, and was a straight-stitch machine with no attachment. "I wouldn't have given more than $5 or $6 for it," she said. Noting her disappointment and admitting his "mistake," the salesman saved the day. He rushed to his car and brought in two sparkling, new, off-brand sewing machines priced at $289 and $365. The housewife chose the one for $289 and was given a discount because it was the "salesman's first day."

There were several glaring misrepresentations, designed to lure prospective customers, in this advertisement. The words "Reposs." (ostensibly standing for repossession) and "Balance" led the readers to believe the machines had been partially paid for by a previous purchaser and thus were being offered for a song. The signature "Credit Dept." created the same impression. In truth, the use of the Singer name was only a lure to support a full-time business of selling off-brand machines. This was proved by the fact that the dealer sold only two or three Singers a month, but spent $400 per month advertising them. Almost the total volume of his business was in the less well-known brand, the more expensive model to which customers were "switched."

Sometimes the salesman actually produced the advertised recent-model Singer, but then actively disparaged the "bait" by finding fault with it: "This machine is delicate and not functioning as it should." "We get a lot of complaints on these Singers." In most other instances, as in the case of the Alexandria housewife, the bait was so offensive that it had "built-in dissuaders," and prospects rejected it on sight. The way was then cleared for the salesman's pitch on the more profitable merchandise. In describing the subtlety of the approach, an FTC lawyer noted: "The prospective purchaser is led on without suspecting the insincerity of the salesman's presentation, and the switch is made to the higher-priced machine of a different make as though the transition were the suggestion of the prospect and not the salesman."

This unfair and deceptive advertising of a product without intent to sell goes on incessantly, with all kinds of merchandise: vacuum cleaners, television sets, carpeting, automobiles, radios, washing machines, furniture. Nor is it confined to door-to-door selling. For some stores, "bait and switch" advertising is the mainstay of their business. An appliance store advertises, for example, a 17-inch-screen TV for $99, but woe to the salesman who actually sells it. Said one store manager, referring to an advertised GE portable, "Any guy who lets that set go out the door goes with it." This merchandise is, in sales lingo, "nailed to the floor," and it is the salesman's job to knock it, to disparage it in any way and to switch the customer to a more expensive model.

In an exclusive series of articles for *Home Furnishings Daily,* an anonymous salesman confessed that his store in New York City periodically featured phony special items in the newspaper, "to pull the shoppers in." He described the sales items:

> First special in the ad is a 21-inch console television for $66. This always is a floor sample of ancient vintage and requires an aerial antenna of greater power than we have in the store to bring in a picture. Second special in the ad is a 10-cubic-foot refrigerator for $199. It is a make produced by a manufacturer swallowed up several mergers back. The color of the box might be described as an off-white with a slight tendency toward yellow. The guarantee on the unit is for six months. Third bargain special is a famous-make 9-pound washer for $99. We have a beautiful wringer-type washer to show those attracted by this item, but strangely enough most of those attracted somehow assumed we were referring to a fully automatic washer in the ad. Completing our quartet is a 36-inch range for $65. There is really nothing striking about this stove unless it be the fact that it is two-tone in color with the sides being black. It has no oven heat control and a speck of rust has begun to appear in the chips in the enamel on top. After a customer has viewed any of the above mentioned specials, it is quite natural that he will ask to see something a bit better. With the step-up, comes my chance to make a sale at a good price.

A variation of bait advertising is lo-balling, and it is so new that the FTC used the term for the first time in 1967 in a case involving automobile transmissions. In lo-balling, the company advertises or promises a service at an outrageously low price and actually performs the work at the advertised price, but only as an enticement to get possession of the automobile (lo-balling to date has been almost exclusively associated with automobiles) so the company can gouge the owner for additional unneeded repairs.

The lucrative routine goes this way, as illustrated by the experience of a man in Washington, D. C. He responded to an advertisement promising to reseal his car's transmission for labor charges of $22 plus an extra charge for needed parts. He was promised one-day service. When he left the car, it was functioning properly except for an oil leakage, which was to be corrected by resealing the transmission.

"About 4:15 the same day, I went back and they had a transmission lying on a work bench, and they said: 'This is your transmission and here are some parts of metal that were found in it and the pump is completely shot and needs replacing.' So I talked to the manager and said, 'What will that cost?' He said, 'Well, it would cost about another $42,' which raised the cost of the job to about $76.

"So I told him to go ahead with it, take the things that were torn down if they needed a new pump, to put it in. He said it would be ready the next afternoon.

"Well, I called the next morning to find out if the car would be ready and he examined it further and said: 'All the bushings are shot and need replacing.' I said, "What is that going to cost?' He said, 'Well, the total job is now $107. "

Through this technique, lo-ballers have been known to run the price on transmission repairs up to $400 and $500.

Some of the three hundred franchises of the Aamco Transmission Company, which sponsors television commercials starring actress Zsa Zsa Gabor and does a 25-million-dollar business in forty states, have been accused of lo-balling.

In Columbia, South Carolina, for example, three officers and employees of the local Aamco franchise were charged with conspiring to obtain money under false pretenses after a carefully marked 1959 automobile was left with them by state investigators for repairs. The transmission had previously been rebuilt, the parts marked by a competent mechanic, and was in good working order. Only the governor was defective. Aamco employees, however, tore down the transmission, declared it "burned up" and rebuilt it at a charge of $189.17. Subsequent examination of the transmission by a mechanic hired by the state revealed that some of the "new" parts listed on the bill were in fact the old parts which had been marked. Only two of the old marked parts reportedly had been replaced: the defective governor and a front seal valued at $2.25.

The attorney general of Minnesota, in October 1967, obtained an injunction prohibiting Aamco dealers in the state from continuing to use lo-balling and other misleading practices which deceive customers.

There are fads in frauds, as in other areas of life. One of the most vicious and fastest-growing is chain-referral selling. Less than ten years ago, it was of minor concern, but as United States postal officials observe, it has "snowballed overnight." It now constitutes a major problem, so much so that the U. S. Postal Inspection Service has established a special project to help combat it and has initiated 234 investigations, resulting in 34 convictions as of June 1967.

The gist of the swindle is that customers are led to believe that by referring the names of acquaintances as prospective customers they will have to pay nothing for a piece of merchandise, and very often will make money. For each friend who is sold, or who agrees to participate in the "advertising campaign," as it is invariably called, the victim is promised a commission. Salesmen frequently erase customers' doubts by telling them that 80 percent of those referred actually "participate" as proved by past experience. In truth, postal inspectors, by painstakingly searching through company records, have discovered that only about 5 percent of the referred actually sign up. And of course once they have sold the original customer, some companies don't bother to follow up the leads supplied or to remit the commission if a referred friend does buy. This deceit is all the more cruel for it is being practiced on elderly people who find the lure of making a few pennies to augment their meager income irresistible.

One could produce hundreds of cases of companies perpetrating this fraud, but an especially reprehensible example was recently seen in Oklahoma City. Of this firm's activities, an investigating postal inspector, usually unemotionally objective in his reports, was moved to remark: "The viciousness of referral selling has probably never been more dramatically portrayed." He went on to write in a final report:

> The operators through their well-schooled, high-pressure salesmen imported from faraway points, induced more than 1,000 financially distressed persons in Oklahoma to sign purchase contracts and promissory notes for the purchase of major household appliances, including food freezers, refrigerators, kitchen cooking ranges, stereos, television receivers and washing machines. Each item was sold at the grossly inflated price of $660.96 on a three-year payment contract, despite the fact that identical items could at that time have been bought in numerous retail stores in Oklahoma for less than $300 each, and some for less than $250.

Particularly saddening was the experience of one man who had recently lost his left hand in an accident and could no longer work at the trade he had practiced for years. "He was burdened by medical bills, and had just taken a job at Goodwill Industries for $1 an hour," wrote the inspector,

> when he received a neatly printed note in facsimile script signed by an acquaintance. It said:
>
>> Hi,
>> In a few days, at our request,
>> a friend of ours will call you for
>> an appointment to explain the details
>> of a *fabulous profit sharing program.*
>> You will be paid $500 for the few minutes

you devote to looking into this plan.
Since you are not obligated, hear this
out and make your own decision.
Sincerely,

After receiving the note, he got a telephone call from the company setting up an appointment for the "friend" to call on him and his wife.
With a printed chart, the salesman showed how he could make as much
as $900 in three months' time, by referring names of his acquaintances
to the company and signing little introductory notes the company would
obligingly mail to persons whose names he furnished.

The victim explained his dire financial circumstances, that he
couldn't afford to pay for anything. The salesman assured him it was an
"advertising program" and was a means to pay all his medical bills. He
was then shown the company's "Advertising Commission Warranty."
The victim said he had no need for the appliances "advertised" by the
company, but the salesman said he had to sign up for one appliance in
order to enter the program. The salesman was so convincing that the man
believed the program would relieve his financial distress and he signed
the papers to enter the program. The next day a stereophonic record player
was delivered to his home and about a week later he received notice
from a finance company that they had purchased his installment contract and that his monthly payments should be made promptly each
month to them for the next three years.

This poor man sent twenty-six names to the company, but never received a single dollar in return. He is now burdened with an unwanted
stereo and finance payments that put him more deeply and hopelessly
in debt.

The company, operated by four persons, three from one family, cost
the public an estimated $500,000 loss although it operated less than one
year. Toward the end of the company's short life, its two sales offices in
Oklahoma City and Tulsa were stuffed with thousands of unopened referral forms mailed in by numerous victims.

An interesting postscript to the case is that the officers of the company
were arrested for mail fraud, but only the sales manager was found guilty.
The other three, including the president and the vice-president, were declared innocent in a retrial in April 1967. This points up how difficult it
is to get a criminal conviction for consumer fraud and thus how inappropriate our traditional criminal remedies are in stopping consumer
deception. For it must be proved under the criminal fraud statutes that
the scheme not only deceived consumers but that the seller also consciously
and deliberately set out to deceive. No matter how distasteful the scheme
or how many hundreds of consumers were cheated, if the jury doubts that
the perpetrators sincerely *intended* to defraud, then they must find the
defendants not guilty. The defendants in this case claimed that, although

they may have been misguided, they actually believed that the scheme would work and carried it out in all good faith.

In granting a new trial on appeal (the verdict was guilty in the first trial), the appellate judge outlined the criteria by which the jury must come to a verdict by quoting a previous decision from the 10th circuit:

> It matters not how visionary you may find the enterprise to be, or how unreasonable the prospects of success . . . if the defendants actually believed in them. Promises made in good faith, whether they be glittering or attractive or not, are not criminal. If you believe . . . that the representations made by the defendants . . . although glittering, attractive, persuasive and alluring, were made in good faith and not as a part of a deliberate plan to scheme or defraud or to obtain money by false pretenses, then it is your duty to find the defendants not guilty. . . .

Being convicted of a criminal act is surely a grave matter, and I certainly would not suggest that we change the criteria for determining such convictions. No man should be branded a criminal and fined or imprisoned who has not been proved guilty of bad faith or intent to commit a wrongdoing. But the real question in protecting consumers is not whether a person who carried on such a scheme *intended* to defraud and therefore is a criminal. The pertinent question is: should the law allow a vast number of the public to be seduced into misery—have their money stolen and their lives demeaned—by the actions of *any* soul—guided or misguided, bad-intentioned or good-intentioned? Whether such a person *intended* to deceive is quite irrelevant, if in fact he *did* deceive and is allowed to continue to deceive. In some instances of consumer fraud, criminal prosecutions are warranted. But by depending excessively on laws that punish the seller rather than stop the practice, we have yet to catch up with the realities of consumer protection.

Another pernicious type of selling which is sweeping the country is the "free gimmick," invariably accompanied by innumerable misrepresentations. It is doubtful that any American of any economic class is untouched by this scheme. A lawyer in New York whose wife was tricked into subscribing to three children's magazines under the impression that it was a "service" from the Board of Education recently wrote:

> If wives of persons who are supposedly above average in education, sophistication, etc., and especially the wife of an attorney, can be so easily taken in, you can imagine what this person (a door-to-door saleswoman) must be able to do with less sophisticated persons.

The sales pitches are familiar: "This lovely $x$-cubic-foot freezer is yours absolutely free if you subscribe to our food-freezer plan." The food is usually low quality, overpriced, and the freezer is hardly free. The cost of the food more than covers the retail price of the freezer.

"Congratulations! You have just won second prize in our drawing for a vacuum cleaner, which entitles you to $150 off the purchase price." It turns out that after the $150 is subtracted from the phony $289 "regular" price, the cost is $139 which is still overpriced. The same giveaway principle is widely used in peddling sewing machines: "You have *won* a free sewing machine; the only charge to you is the price of the cabinet." The $59 "cabinet price," in truth, covers the cost of the machine and gives the seller his usual profit.

The variety is endless: "Your telephone number has been chosen for this free gift. . . ." "We want to give you five dancing lessons absolutely free if you can answer this question: Adam and Eve had two sons. One was Cain and the other was ——?" (One perverse man answered Aaron, but after the telephone solicitor recovered, she allowed that his answer was close enough—they both started with A.)

Unfortunately, another area in which the giveaway is becoming increasingly prevalent is in "educational materials," encyclopedias, magazines, and other books. In 1966, magazine subscription rose to the top of the Better Business Bureau's complaints list. That year the BBB processed 162,537 "instances of services" concerning magazines.

A magazine salesman of fifteen years' experience, who finally quit the business, came to my office last spring, anxious to make known the deplorable tactics being used in some magazine selling. He told how the sympathy "college kid gag" had given way to the something-for-nothing pitch. "Pretending you're a college kid trying to win points for a scholarship is still used in some places," he said,

> but the biggest thing these days is the free-postage pitch. We tell people they get the magazine free if they will only pay the 42 cents a week postage. And they really believe it! I know some salesmen making $20,000 a year this way. Using this pitch myself I have sold $99 worth of magazines to people who are blind, who don't have shoes for their kids or a stitch of carpet on the floor. It's a rotten business, and I'm sorry I stayed in it as long as I did.

Certainly not all magazines are sold this way, and it is unfortunate that a handful of offenders are marring the reputation of the ethical dealers and publishers. The same can be said for encyclopedias, although it can also be said that many famous-name encyclopedias from supposedly reputable companies are sold by deceptive salesmanship. Consistently, the FTC has warned and brought complaints against companies that misrepresent their sets of encyclopedias as being free, an advertising promotion gift, if the customer will only pay to keep it up to date. In July 1967, my staff and I asked William Hesse, a graduate student at the University of Washington, and one of the congressional interns in my office, to discover whether a newly established encyclopedia sales office in Washington, D. C., was engaging in deceptive selling by pretending to give away free sets. Hesse answered an ad promising $550 per month guaranteed salary for doing "advertising and promotion," and was put into training. The sales pitch turned out to be laden with falsifications. Hesse was repeatedly warned never to admit he was a salesman, but to say he was "with the Promotional Division of E. E. (Educational Enterprises, Inc.) and only seeking "testimonial advertising" for the "first Major International Reference Library," whose first major sales campaign was to get under way in 1968.

Door opener (to wife only): "Hi there, I have to see your *husband*" (say it like you know him).

Door opener (to husband only): "Hi there, I have to see you for a minute!" (say it like you made a special trip just to see him; give him your name and shake his hand).

"The reason we call in the evening like this is because we have to talk to the man of the house and the wife together. OK?" (*Smile*) "I'm not a salesman so please don't be alarmed. I've been asked to interview some of the families in this area. . . . You know what testimonial advertising is, don't you? Well . . . Educational Enterprises has finally gone into Testimonial Advertising. The families that we are interviewing right now, families like yourselves, that are helping us out, we are paying them very handsomely for their help, not in cash but in the form of merchandise."

After showing them a sample of the "beautiful library," he gets to the heart of the lie, as outlined in the long, memorized speech: "That's right, you would receive this beautiful $489 masterpiece, all twenty volumes within the next two weeks, postage prepaid, as an advertising premium in exchange for your promise to write us a testimonial letter and signing the Owner's Register Card which gives us permission to use your name as a registered owner of the National Encyclopedia." Later in the canned pitch comes the catch: "Gee, I almost forgot. There is one thing I have to make crystal clear to you. We give you the Cadillac so to speak, but we have to draw the line somewhere. We don't give you the Gas and Oil. In other words, you get this complete library within two weeks, but we don't keep it up-to-date for you, too."

The salesman makes it clear they wouldn't want to place a set in the home of an "insincere" person who wouldn't "appreciate" it. There are only two things expected to show appreciation, he explains.

". . . the yearbook service that comes out each year, that adds onto your set, that keeps it up-to-date. Well, we don't give these to you or anyone. You can understand this I'm sure." Farther on, "See these coupons here?

"We have at present over 2,000 experts in every field working in our

Library Research Department in New York City. Anytime something new comes up and you want to know more about it right now, all you would have to do is clip out one of these research coupons and send in a letter with the coupon to our Research Department in New York."

It turns out that the "yearbooks" are priced at $15 each for ten years. The "research coupons" cost $5 apiece, and the customer must buy ten coupons each year for ten years. All of this adds up to $650, but somehow because of "mass production," the company has been able to cut the cost to $335.50—just nine cents a day. The salesman gives the customer a calendar bank in which to deposit his daily dime, and attempts to persuade him to pay it all off in two years instead of ten.

The pitch is peppered throughout with insincerities and lies. On the contract there is no mention of a "free" encyclopedia. The salesman is instructed to write "20 volume encyclopedia" and the price. All of the other is verbal misrepresentation, which is difficult to prove in court. Such words are not binding, but the customer's signature on the contract is.

Aside from harm to the customer, it seems to me reprehensible that grown men are hiring young boys and teaching them to lie with such cynicism and contemptuousness. For many of these young men it is their first introduction to the world of business. The better-educated boys who already have a career planned may come away with a bad taste for business in general. (There were fifteen boys in Hesse's class and how many stayed with it, we don't know. Hesse left after three days and reported several boys had already confessed to him that they didn't "have the stomach for it.")

Other boys may find their lies so successful they make such selling a way of life. The reformed magazine salesman who came to my office said his career started when he took a temporary selling job, pretending he was working his way through college. He intended to stay only three months, but found it so lucrative he stayed fifteen years. He admitted his conscience bothered him in the beginning, but "I got so wound up in making that sale, I got so I didn't notice it."

Perhaps no sales pitch has been around longer than the "fear-sell." Even the rulers of ancient countries were intimidated into buying amulets lest their souls be damned or they suffer a dreadful accident. In today's sophisticated marketplace, peddlers still make fortunes preying on people's fears. One woman wrote me she had four perfectly healthy maple trees felled by a wandering "tree surgeon," who told her they were rotten and could come crashing down on her house. Gangs of salesmen, according to the National Fire Protection Association, are scouring the country, displaying gruesome photographs of families burned to death in home fires. Their object is to sell home fire-alarm systems which are invariably outrageously priced and sometimes worthless.

Every spring, as regularly as the rain, reports the BBB, the phony chimney repairmen show up. They knock off a few bricks and claim the chimney is about to topple, or claim it is clogged and that the whole family is in imminent danger of dying from carbon monoxide poisoning. Some termite inspectors carry bugs which they plant in the wood, and then inform the alarmed homeowner that unless the "termites" are exterminated, the house will quickly deteriorate. Often the salesmen pose as government inspectors. That they extort millions of dollars from frightened Americans is well-documented.

A classic case is that of the Holland Furnace Company, which for thirty years conducted what Consumers Union branded "one of the most pernicious sales rackets in the country." Holland Furnace, based in Holland, Michigan, with 500 offices throughout the country and 5,000 employees, was the leading furnace-replacement firm in the nation. Through its "tear down and scare tactics" it victimized hundreds of thousands of Americans. Misrepresenting themselves as "furnace engineers" and "safety inspectors," the salesmen frequently dismantled a furnace, condemned it as hazardous and refused to reassemble it, stating they didn't want to be "accessories to murder." The salesmen were merciless. In New England, branch salesmen from one office sold an elderly infirm woman nine new furnaces in six years, for a total take of $18,000.

One woman in San Francisco became suspicious after a Holland Furnace salesman condemned her furnace. She called the Better Business Bureau, which dispatched both an inspector from the local Pacific Gas and Electric Company and a Better Business Bureau representative with a tape recorder. The gas inspector pronounced the furnace perfectly safe and in good repair. When the salesman returned to clinch the sale, he unknowingly delivered his pitch both to the woman and into a hidden tape recorder. It went this way:

> . . . the flue pipe instead of taking all of the smoke and fumes up the flue, a good percentage of them are going up in the house. . . . See where she's burnt out over there. . . . that's going right up into your house. . . . The warm air plenum is above here, which means that the smoke and fumes go up in here, and then that fan turns on back there. . . . I'm not saying this to scare you, I'm just saying it to impress you. . . . This is worse than the raw gas, because the raw gas you can smell. This is carbon monoxide. . . . This is no different than if you took the exhaust pipe from your automobile and ran it in here. . . . I would actually be doing you a favor . . . by shutting your furnace off. . . . I'm not doing that to sell you a furnace, I'm just trying to be honest with you. . . . It's not healthy, I would replace it and I would do it now. . . . It's leaking. . . We can allow you $28.50 as junk for that old furnace.

The amazing thing about this fraud, besides the boldness of the company and the size of its loot, is its longevity, which once again painfully illustrates the inefficacy of our present laws to bring deceptive practices to a quick halt. Although victims began complaining about Holland Furnace in the 1930s and the FTC soon after began collecting proof, which is now voluminous, it was not until January 1965 that the company finally was forced to close its doors. The ex-president of the company was sentenced to six months in prison (the first time an official of a major corporation has been held criminally responsible for the misrepresentations of its salesmen), and the corporation was fined $100,000 for violation of a court injunction issued in 1959. The fine reportedly was sufficient to cause bankruptcy. In the meantime, Holland Furnace at the height of its business cost the American public 30 million dollars a year.

If one were writing a textbook on deceptive selling, these five schemes —phony special price, bait and switch, referral selling, the free gimmick and the fear-sell—could be described as the basics of the course. For with a little ingenuity they can be, and are being, applied to the shady salesmanship of any product imaginable, from pots and pans to real estate. The five schemes are used alone or in endless combination with one another and with dozens of other misrepresentations, such as "I'm from the school board to test your child's musical talent"; "Of course you can cancel the contract if you change your mind"; "I'm a veteran just back from Vietnam"; "Our carpeting is cheaper because it is sold in 'factory units' " (a factory unit turns out to be one-third of a yard). "If you don't want the free magazines yourself, we are authorized to donate them for you to the local school; they say they *need* these magazines." "I see that your vacuum sweeper (sewing machine, automobile, washing machine) is completely shot." "You're only signing a receipt," when, in fact, it is a sales contract or promissory note.

In addition to these five basic schemes there are several hundred others. Among the most prevalent, pernicious, and costly are:

*Charity swindles* for nonexistent churches, hospitals, veterans' organizations and so on. This scheme accounts for a 100-million-dollar a year loss to the public.

*Business opportunity rackets.* A person seeking extra income is induced to buy an expensive vending machine with the promise that he can install the machine in a local place of business and collect the proceeds; or a piece of equipment such as a floor polisher with the promise that floor-polishing jobs will be referred to him by the seller. Victims invariably discover that no place of business will take the vending machine and that no jobs are forthcoming.

*Unsolicited merchandise* through the mail. A package containing vitamin capsules, stamps for albums, ties, books arrives, and unless the receiver returns it or pays for it, he is bombarded with dunning letters, the last one threatening a law suit. Some swindlers scan the obituary columns of newspapers and address merchandise to the deceased. His survivors, thinking he ordered the goods, pay for it.

*Phony home improvements.* These swindlers are often fly-by-nights who insist on cash immediately, and for good reason. Their lightning rod "cables" turn out to be silver-painted rope; they resurface driveways by covering them with motor oil; they neglect to mention that when they "paint" a house, they don't use waterproof paint, and with the first rain the paint washes off. For more than thiry years one Irish family known as the "Terrible Williamsons" has worked the country performing phony home-repair jobs. It is said that the clan on the road now numbers at least one hundred.

*Substandard correspondence and vocational schools.* Undoubtedly this is one of the most disheartening rackets of all, for it preys on the aspirations of the elderly and undereducated who are falsely led to believe they can raise their station in life by subscribing to one of these costly substandard courses. The courses purport to teach such occupational skills as motel management, insurance claim adjusting, data processing, telegraphy, how to pass a civil service examination, and how to operate a bulldozer (without ever seeing one). After spending hundreds, sometimes thousands, of dollars on this shabby education, the "graduate" finds that when he goes out to seek a job, he is totally unqualified and no one will hire him.

*Land-fraud sales.* Thousands of persons, many seeking retirement homes or investments, have bought lots, sight unseen, on the basis of glowing brochures or color slides that bore no resemblance to the actual land site. Some of the "developments" were never developed at all and turned out to be in the swamps, in the desert, on the top of mountains, under water and even in the jungles and lava beds of South America.

In late 1966, a company called the Western Growth Capital Corporation, promoting Cohise Country Club Estates in Arizona, came into my state of Washington and persuaded 174 persons, after an elaborate free dinner party and a slide presentation, to invest $350,000 in lots in this development. Contrary to assertions of the "public relations director" who emceed the event, the lots had no gas, electricity, telephone service, or paved roads. The only paved road in the development was a county road leading to the company's sales office. The "PGA-approved nine-hole golf course" was so overgrown, said one investigator, "you would lose your ball on the green." The "well-equipped pro shop with the year-round pro" was an empty shack that was boarded up. The "beautiful blue lake" was an enormous dried-up hole of forty acres. After obtaining signatures on sales and promissory notes, the sales crew promptly moved on to Minnesota and then to Pennsylvania.

The corporation quickly sold the contracts to a bank in Arizona. Just recently, the company was declared bankrupt. Thus, the cheated consumer is totally helpless. The bank in Arizona has already sent stern collection letters to the victims in Washington, demanding its money. And the Washington attorney general's office admits, "We are without any recourse even to stop the bank from enforcing the contracts." These people, a few of whom invested their life savings or sold their homes planning to move to the "promised land," must month by month pay for a practically uninhabitable plot of land that they will probably never see.

Why are we unable to control such deceptive practices and to prevent consumer exploitation? Primarily because our present laws are outmoded and inadequate to deal with the modern complexities of consumer fraud. Most of our laws on dishonest selling were designed long ago to catch and punish a few "hardened criminals" and not to cope with the vast web of subtle deceits and credit merchandising abuses that characterizes the businesses of today's "soft-sell" swindlers. Generally, our legal remedies have two defects: (1) they are ineffective in halting deceptive selling, and (2) they make virtually no provisions for redressing the wrong, whether by freeing the cheated consumer of a fraudulently induced debt or by reimbursing him.

The Federal Trade Commission, as the federal agency primarily responsible for stopping deceptive selling on a national scale, has broad powers and has been effective in curtailing unscrupulous sellers in interstate commerce for half a century. Nevertheless, we cannot depend on the FTC alone to halt all deceptive selling nationwide. Even with an addition in personnel it would still be impossible for the FTC to stop all deceptive selling even within its interstate jurisdiction. And the FTC also has certain limitations in its powers to protect consumers.

As we have seen, the FTC cannot stop deceptive selling operations that limit their activities to intrastate commerce, staying within a state's borders, which is where most such selling occurs. Nor can the FTC in some cases move fast enough to halt the swindlers before they have victimized a number of consumers and accumulated a small fortune. Nor can the FTC act on behalf of an individual consumer; it can move only when a substantial number of Americans have been injured (enough to make an FTC action "in the public interest").

Then, too, the FTC can only compel the offender to stop working his deceptive arts on future customers; it cannot order him to reimburse those whom he has already cheated or to cancel collection of their debts.

The Post Office Department, as the other federal agency most responsible for halting fraudulent and deceptive schemes, also has been remarkably successful within their jurisdiction. But postal officials, too, are hampered in their efforts to control certain types of deceptive selling by mail. Under present law, they often cannot move fast enough to curtail mail-order schemes and sometimes cannot stop them at all. In testifying to this fact before a subcommittee of the House Committee on Post Office and Civil Service in April 1967, Henry B. Montague, chief postal inspector for the Post Office Department, illustrated the difficulty in halting mail-order land-fraud sales:

> The investigation of the Lake Mead Land & Water Company in Arizona began in 1962. Evidence that the desert property was not in fact "an enchanted city in the making"; that the "favorite swimming hole" pictured in the advertising brochure was in truth a cattle-watering pond not even located on the promoter's property; that various springs and wells depicted in the literature were also not located on the property, was not too difficult to ascertain. Proof of intent or personal knowledge on the part of the principal promoter, of course, required considerably more time.
>
> An indictment was returned in October 1963 and conviction resulted in June 1965. Three thousand home- or investment-seeking persons, many of the elderly class, lost an estimated one million dollars before the enterprise was finally stopped through conviction. The promoter continued to receive payments by mail up to the very end.

Even though a scheme is patently false and postal officials know it, they cannot always stop a perpetrator's inflow of mail containing the lucrative rewards of deceit. Postal authorities must stand helpless, witnessing the bilking of the elderly and the hopeful, until it can be proved that the purveyor of falsity *intended* to defraud, which, as Mr. Montague pointed out, takes much longer than just proving untruth by comparing the brochures or advertisements with the lay of the land. Partially as a result of this time lag while investigators try to fathom the state of a man's mind, the forty-nine land-fraud swindlers finally brought to justice were able to accumulate, through a steady flow of mail payments, more than 50 million dollars from an unsuspecting public before they were convicted and their mail was marked "fraudulent; return to sender."

At the state level, officials who attempt to protect consumers are incredibly handicapped by inadequate laws. Although many states have recently passed effective laws and set up machinery to enforce them, the picture of state consumer legislation is, as a whole, dreary indeed. An informal survey by the FTC in June 1967 showed that only nineteen states could be said to have "good" or "excellent" laws prohibiting deceptive selling practices. At least one-third of the states have pitifully weak laws. Effective consumer legislation is especially lacking in Alabama, Arkansas, Indiana, Mississippi, New Hampshire, North Carolina, Ohio, Oklahoma, South Carolina, South Dakota, Tennessee, Texas, Virginia, West Virginia and Wyoming.

In a few states legislation is simply nonexistent. Only a handful of states regulate correspondence schools, fraudulent selling of land or unsolicited merchandise sent through the mails. Only twenty states specifically outlaw bait advertising.

Absence of laws, however, is not the only problem in the states. For as the *Columbia Law Review* has noted, "The states have adopted a staggering number of statutes noteworthy for their ad hoc and piecemeal approach to the problems of advertising control and for the very slight degree to which they are enforced." In truth, all but three states—Arkansas, Delaware and New Mexico—have a "Printer's Ink" statute (named for the advertising magazine of the same name) making it a misdemeanor to make an "untrue, deceptive or misleading" statement with the intent to sell a product.

One would think this law so comprehensive that it would virtually wipe out deceptive advertising in the states. Such is not the case, for the law, broad as it is, contains an insurmountable flaw: it is a *criminal* statute, as are many of the other measures adopted by the states to halt deceptive selling. Under the criminal statute, conviction demands proof beyond a reasonable doubt and carries with it fines, possible jail sentences and the stigma of being branded a criminal.

Since its adoption in 1911, the Printer's Ink statute may have deterred some sellers from deceptive practices, but the number of culprits it has actually brought to justice is infinitesimal. Law enforcement officials overwhelmingly consider the law so unrealistic that they don't attempt to enforce it. A survey by the *Columbia Law Review* in 1956 discovered that during nearly fifty years, only "a handful of prosecutions" had been brought under the Printer's Ink statutes throughout the country. Many attorneys general and county prosecutors freely admitted that they had never tried to enforce it. One reason is that local prosecutors are burdened with trying to halt major felonies such as murder, rape and robbery, and are disinclined to waste their time on such a relatively small "crime" as false advertising or selling. Another reason is that few prosecutors believe they will get a conviction. They have found that juries are hesitant to find a man guilty of a crime for what may merely be "overzealous salesmanship"; consequently, few public officials prosecute.

Two law students at the University of Pennsylvania, investigating the ineffectiveness of consumer legislation, recently found:

> Even when a law enforcement official believes that a particular scheme has been made actionable by statute, he often does not prosecute because of a widely held belief that, except in the most egregious circumstances, fraudulent operators should not be treated like criminals. Lawyers, business leaders and prosecutors have stated that "judges, juries and district attorneys do not like to put businessmen in jail." One district attorney, when asked by the attorney general to prosecute an alleged fraudulent operator, retorted: "I can't even get a conviction

when they stick a gun in somebody's back; how can I get one when they just talk him out of his money?"

Trying to completely control consumer fraud by proving criminality is an outmoded concept. But even if the criminal statutes could be enforced (and New York, for example, has achieved rare success in obtaining convictions), it is doubtful that society's purpose is best served by only putting a swindler behind bars. The sentence is usually short (in Pennsylvania one man who made $300,000 selling fake automobile parts was sentenced to a term of one year), after which the wrongdoer is set free to spend his ill-gotten money, and the cheated consumer, who understandably wants no justice so much as his money back, is left to suffer without restitution.

Additionally, the hit-and-miss proposition of locking up criminals who defraud the public is inefficient in halting consumer fraud on a broad scale. Only one operator can be put out of business at a time, after long, costly court proceedings, while thousands of other gypsters—perhaps associated with the same company or swindle—are allowed to flourish. And even after a short prison term, the ex-convict can start up a new racket, using the same fraudulent techniques, and rob Americans of a fortune, while local authorities once again gear up their machinery to start the slow, painful process of gathering evidence against him on the new charge.

The injured consumer can bring suit himself, but few do. They soon discover that lawyer's fees, court costs and time away from employment will cost more than they can possibly recover. A woman in Ohio, who hired an attorney to keep from losing her $15,000-house because of a home-improvement repairs bill of $7,200, had already paid a legal fee of $1,500 and still did not receive her house back. Under strict legal requirements in most states, the complainant must have an exceptionally good case in order to win; many times it is only his word against that of the shady seller.

Invariably, the victim has also unknowingly, by signing the contract, given away a number of rights of defense and agreed that nothing the seller told him, unless specifically stated in the contract, is binding. When a group of lawyers in Pennsylvania were asked in an informal survey what they would do with a client who had been gypped out of several hundred dollars for carpeting in a "bait and switch" scheme, they unanimously agreed: "Send him home."

Clearly, the weak, inappropriate, poorly enforced, hit-and-miss legislation that is the rule throughout the nation is quite undependable in combating the complexities and size of our present-day consumer deception. In this antiquated system of justice, the dishonest steal quietly off to count their loot, while the injured consumer is sacrificed on the altar of legislative short-sightedness.

# 3

# *The Nature, Impact, and Prosecution of White-Collar Crime*

*Herbert Edelhertz*

## DEFINITION OF WHITE-COLLAR CRIME

The term "white-collar crime" is not subject to any one clear definition. Everyone believes he knows what the term means, but when definitions are compared there are usually sharp divergences as to whether one crime or another comes within the definition.

For the purpose of this paper, the term will be defined as *an illegal act or series of illegal acts committed by nonphysical means and by concealment or guile, to obtain money or property, to avoid the payment or loss of money or property, or to obtain business or personal advantage.*

The definition, in that it hinges on the modifying words "an illegal act or series of illegal acts," does not go to the question whether particular activities should be the subject of criminal proscriptions.

It is a definition which differs markedly from that advanced by Edwin H. Sutherland, who said that ". . . white-collar crime may be defined approximately as a crime committed by a person of respectability and high social status in the course of his occupation." Sutherland introduced this definition with the comment that these white-collar crimes are violations of law by persons in the "upper socio-economic class."

Sutherland's definition is far too restrictive. His view provided a rational basis for the economic determinism which was the underlying theme of this analysis, but did not comprehend the many crimes committed outside one's occupation. Ready examples of crimes falling outside one's occupation would be personal and nonbusiness false income tax returns, fraudulent claims for Social Security benefits, concealing assets in a personal bankruptcy, and use of large-scale buying on credit with no intention or capability to ever pay for purchases. His definition does not take into ac-

From National Institute of Law Enforcement and Criminal Justice, U.S. Department of Justice, Law Enforcement Assistance Administration, May 1970, pp. 3–11, 23–38, 54, 58–60, 63–69.

count crime as a business, such as a planned bankruptcy, or an old fashioned "con game" operated in a business milieu. Though these crimes fall outside Sutherland's definition, they were considered and discussed by him.

Sutherland made a valuable contribution. He illuminated the double standard built into our law enforcement structure and contrasted society's treatment of abusive acts by the well-to-do with law enforcement and penal provisions applicable to abusive acts by those less fortunate or well placed. He forcefully pointed out that our legislation has established a unique legal structure with a complex of administrative proceedings, injunctions, and cease and desist orders to meet common law fraud if committed in a business context, thus largely preempting the field of enforcement and making criminal proceedings unlikely or seemingly inappropriate. He showed how fraudulent sales practices, or sale of drugs by misrepresentations, or patent abuses, can continue through years of administrative and judicial proceedings to a determination which is no more than a slap on the wrist, whereas the less sophisticated thief must face additional criminal charges if he commits further and similar acts in the course of his much briefer and less lucrative activity.

Sutherland was basically concerned with society's disparate approach to the crimes of the respectable and well-to-do on the one hand, and those of the poor and disadvantaged on the other. His definition of white-collar crime concentrated, therefore, on characterizing violators rather than violations. The definition on which this paper is based is, hopefully, a more inclusive one.

White-collar crime is democratic. It can be committed by a bank teller or the head of his institution. The offender can be a high government official with a conflict of interest. He can be the destitute beneficiary of a poverty program who is told to hire a work group and puts fictional workers on the payroll so that he can appropriate their wages. The character of white-collar crime must be found in its modi operandi and its objectives rather [than] in the nature of the offenders.

It is important that in our definitions of crime we concentrate on the nature of the crime rather than on the personal characteristics or status of the criminal. The latter analysis may be relevant and even of primary utility in the design and implementation of specific law enforcement programs or to rehabilitation of offenders. Confusion and discriminatory application of penal sanctions must necessarily flow, however, from personalizing our conceptions of the nature of any one crime or group of crimes.

The above definition is the cornerstone of the following conceptualizations of various aspects of white-collar crime. It is crucial to this discussion of deterrence, investigation, evaluation, prosecution, and sentencing.

## THE IMPACT OF WHITE-COLLAR CRIME

Sutherland published his "White Collar Crime" in 1949, a year already in the buried past. The complexity of our society in the intervening fifth of a century has increased so rapidly that it is difficult to do more than recognize resemblances between the problem he described and that which we face today. He saw the problem as one of victimization and discrimination, valid today as then. More important now, however, is our expanded vulnerability to white-collar crime because of changes in our economic and social environment.

We should not fall into the trap of idealizing the past (as with Rousseau's noble savage), but we can recognize that progress has its harmful side effects. In the white-collar field the basic side effect is the weakening of certain safeguards which were built into the marketing and distribution patterns of an earlier age and which retained much of their vitality only 20 years ago.

Most purchases were once made in stores which were managed and serviced by their individual owners. Owners either lived in the communities which they serviced or had close ties to these communities. They were known to their customers and had to face them after a purchase as well as before. These proprietors competed on the basis of service and reliability and, even though products might be presold by advertising, they would bear the brunt of customer dissatisfaction. Today most consumer goods—food, drugs, appliances—are sold by chains or similar large organizations, and the mobility of their personnel is matched, in part at least, by the mobility of their customers. On the retail level there has developed an essentially faceless transactional environment.

Today transactions are executed or moved by nonpersonal or credit instrumentalities. Retail credit is no longer carried on the books of the retailer, to be financed by retailer bank loans, but is now the subject of highly sophisticated and costly credit transactions involving bank and non-bank credit cards, revolving credit, credit life insurance—all substituting the credit granting and administering entities for the retailer after the sale is made.

The genesis of transactions between businesses, and within businesses, is less the subject of individual decisions and more the result of programed procedures. Thus we now have electronic links, managed by computers. A perpetual inventory system may trigger a purchase order which in turn galvanizes a series of computer-induced stages culminating in an automatically written and signed check to pay for the purchase.

Conflicting objectives internal to business operations multiply exposure to white-collar crimes. Thus manufacturing and sales departments within a company will seek to over-ride the restraints imposed by a credit department with consequent vulnerability to bankruptcy fraud operations. Sales departments will deliberately court risks, as by mailing of unsolicited credit cards, relegating possible fraud losses to the status of costs of doing business as if mere rent or utility charges. This may be an acceptable price to pay for economic growth, but it does invite white-collar crime.

Business planning is more and more keyed to the creation of needs, rather than to discovering or satisfying needs. Thus we have patterns of built-in style obsolescence, in hard goods and soft, and products may also be manufactured with a limited useful life.

Our economy has passed the point where it is geared to meet only the basic and elemental needs of the greater part of our population. The number of "haves" is very high, and large numbers of "have-nots" possess items which generate the desire for similar items on the part of their neighbors. Television exposes even the poorest to an incessant barrage of incitation to consumption of nonnecessities and to the titillation of desires based on nothing more than the exploitation of longing for status, beauty, or virility. The juxtaposition of these desires with our credit economy intensifies the incentive and opportunity for fraud in the marketing of consumer goods and services.

Our social and economic organization exposes us to new species of white-collar crime, having different or mixed objectives. In an earlier age the unlawful or ethically questionable amassing of wealth was characteristically accomplished by bald plunder or seizure of the public domain. "Teapot Dome" was a classic case, as was the land-grant device which provided the capital for building much of this nation's railroad grid. Today such blatant power and property grabs are avoided. The new avenues for creation of wealth often involve tax avoidance (or evasion, which is criminal) to facilitate the accumulation of capital on which further acquisitions of wealth may be based. Tax avoidance or evasion are advantages to be wielded as is the ability to obtain favored treatment by zoning commissions, or special favors in connection with public guarantees of real property loans, or to be free from regulation in the operation of quasi-public utilities. The boundaries of the permissible and the impermissible are not drawn with precision, and perhaps they should not be. But as a consequence substantial loopholes persist, permitting the commission of crimes or acts inconsistent with policy limits set by our society.

The affluence of our society heightens exposure to criminal abuses by fiduciaries, an exposure which was once confined to the wealthy and the upper middle classes. More of us are now beneficiaries of trusts and quasi-trusts managed by the growing fiduciary industry. New targets for crime are the increasing proportion of trusts and estates of middle-class descendants, interests in union and company pension, welfare, and profit-sharing funds, and the broad panoply of mutual funds, investment trusts, credit unions, and investment clubs. . . .

As individuals we are more exposed to abuse. We are more likely to deal with strangers than with those we know (whose blemishes we can assess), and we are more vulnerable than we used to be because we tend to rely more on one another or on protection by government. Those who buy securities are better protected than ever before because of the work of the Securities and Exchange Commission and comparable state agencies, yet are more exposed to the stock fraud artist who deceives the regulatory agency or totally circumvents its supervision. The buyer of food relies on weights and measures marked on prepackaged merchandise, since there is no occasion to look for the thumb on the seller's scale. We find it hard to believe that government food inspectors would permit most unesthetic portions of animals to be ground into our hamburgers or sausages, and are therefore most shocked when sporadic inquiries disclose what we are eating. The physician relies on the vigilance of the Food and Drug Administration, and therefore accepts his education as to prescribable drugs from detail men sent to his office by pharmaceutical manufacturers. The certificates of guarantee which accompany our purchases of appliances and automobiles give us a false sense of security, no matter how often we have been burned in the past. Caveat emptor loses meaning when we buy closed packages.

Technical developments increase our exposure to white-collar crime. A prime objective of computerization is the cutting of labor costs, which means substituting hardware and computer programs for expensive labor. Our experience has given us an extensive fund of knowledge (often imperfect) as to how we can control, audit, and monitor people, but we have only the most elementary knowledge of how to audit computers and those who have learned how to use them. Much thought is being given to methods of coping with computers from a management point of view, i.e., internal controls, but little to audit by outsiders such as regulatory or law enforcement agencies. The search for control procedures is complicated by the accelerating rate at which the computer art is developing, a rate which makes controls obsolete almost as quickly as they are developed. Existing control methodology is not adequate for internal control, or for investigation by investigating agencies, or for regulation by regulatory agencies.

White-collar crime is a low visibility, high impact factor in our society. Because of the changes in the nature of our economic organization, particularly new developments in marketing, distribution, and investment, it is a fair assumption that white-collar crime has increased at a rate which exceeds population growth. Its effects intersect with and interact with other problems of our society, such as poverty and discrimination. It also weighs heavily on the aged who are, in our society, divorced from the homes and community of their children in contrast to most prior human social organization.

The increasing complexity of our society heightens vulnerability because it increases the difficulty of obtaining redress for losses suffered. Legal services are costly, prosecutors and investigators are overburdened, and court calendars are clogged. A victim must measure the time it takes to obtain redress and wonder whether [the major sufferer will not be he,] rather than the target of his complaint.

The prevention, deterrence, investigation, and prosecution of white-collar crime must compete with other interests for allocation of law enforcement dollars, in an atmosphere in which every other national problem is made more serious and more costly of solution by the increasing complexities of our society.

No dollar amount can adequately identify the costs of white-collar crime, though many figures have been used in various studies. Invariably these are projections based on known cases, yet even with highly publicized cases there is no way of truly determining costs to victims and to the public. . . .

White-collar crime, like common crime, can have a serious influence on the social fabric and on the freedom of commercial and interpersonal transactions. Every stock market fraud lessens confidence in the securities market. Every commercial bribe or kickback debases the level of business competition, often forcing other suppliers to join in the practice if they are to survive. The business which accumulates capital to finance expansion by tax evasion places at a disadvantage the competitor who pays his taxes and is compelled to turn to lenders (for operating and expansion capital). The pharmaceutical company which markets a new drug based on fraudulent test results undercuts its competitors who are still marketing the properly tested drugs, and may cause them to adopt similar methods. Competitors who join in a conspiracy to freeze out their competition, or to fix prices, may gravely influence the course of our economy, in addition to harming their competitors and customers. The tax evader adds to the ultimate burden of the man who pays his taxes.

We should take special note of the impact of white-collar crime on the elderly and the poor, especially ghetto residents. These groups are the victims of minor offenses, such as housing violations, and of what we conventionally refer to as "consumer frauds." The impact is self-evident, but there is little comprehension of the outward rippling from consumer frauds on the elderly and the poor.

The very poor, and particularly the destitute elderly, are not profitable targets for those engaged in white-collar criminal activities. They may "pay more," as some surveys have indicated, but they are relatively impervious to the general harassment of process servers and collection agents, whose success is the ultimate reliance and raison d'être of every consumer fraud operation. If a mother on welfare is given a short weight when she buys food, the impact on her family is clear, but the transaction itself is not a vehicle for continued oppression and victimization. . . .

The true and ultimate vulnerability is the possession of an asset which can be lost. Such an asset may be tangible, such as a house, or an intangible such as a job which can be lost or made less desirable if wages are garnisheed, or some relationship which can be exploited by the fraud operator. A surprisingly large number of people living in ghettoes do have something to lose, but unlike the established middle classes the asset in jeopardy is very often the only asset which stands between its owner and utter destitution.

In the case of a home improvement fraud, the fraud operator will solicit a job such as installation of aluminum siding for a house, making misrepresentations as to cost, quality, and credit terms. The victims are often past their prime working years, with perhaps very small savings to piece out the sub-marginal existence afforded by Social Security payments. Such victims have just about worked out their life schemes to avoid becoming public charges in their old age. The monthly payments required are more or less manageable, but the victims do not realize that these installments are largely interest payments on the inflated cost and that the major part of the contract price will be payable immediately following the final monthly payment in what is called a "balloon." The victims also do not understand that their house has been mortgaged to secure the exorbitant cost of the repair or improvement and interest and fees in connection therewith. Nor do they understand that their promissory note and mortgage will be promptly negotiated to a so-called holder in due course who will demand payment even if the work is never done, or never properly done. When the balloon payment is due the victims must refinance and subject themselves to what often is a form of perpetual peonage to finance companies, inevitably resulting in a desperate economic situation with consequent loss of house, savings, and all payments made. The victims are then on welfare or a burden on their children.

Merchandising frauds may have similar impact. The typical case would involve an overpriced television set or furniture, with heavy finance charges. This kind of credit is extended only to those with jobs (to be endangered if wages are garnisheed) or to those whose obligations can be guaranteed by relatives or parents who have jobs or other assets. When installment payments are missed, the entire obligation becomes immediately due and payable, and the victims are faced with the choice of refinancing and assuming even greater obligations, or becoming subject to garnishment procedures which could cost them their jobs. . . .

The social and economic costs of tax violations, self-dealing by corporate employees and bank officials, adulteration or watering of foods and drugs, charity frauds, insurance frauds, price fixing, frauds arising out of government procurement, and abuses of trust are clearly enormous even though not easily measured. If substantial progress can be made in the prevention, deterrence, and successful prosecution of these crimes we may reasonably anticipate substantial benefits to the material and qualitative aspects of our national life. . . .

## DETECTION OF WHITE-COLLAR CRIMES

There are three basic sources of detection. They are: (1) complaints by victims; (2) informants; and (3) affirmative searches for violations by law enforcement agencies.

### Complaints by Victims

When a common crime is committed, the victim immediately knows that something has been done to him. He has been assaulted or robbed or injured in some clearly definable way. He then has the plain option to report the crime to law enforcement authorities or to refrain from doing so. This is not necessarily the case with respect to white-collar crimes in which the victim may never learn he has been victimized, or the realization comes too late to do him any good or too late to be of meaningful assistance to law enforcement authorities. In the case of a charity fraud, where the victim makes a small contribution, it is highly unlikely that he will even take the trouble to think about the possibility of a loss, since his consideration is of a nonmaterial nature without practical consequences except for the remote disallowance of a charity deduction claimed on an income tax return. In the case of a magazine-selling fraud, the salesman "working his way through college" will also falsely represent that the subscriptions offered are at a discount price. In fact the price may well be higher than that available by regular subscription—yet the victim may never know it. The victim is quite likely, especially where small amounts are involved, to attribute his disappointments to factors other than criminality and will simply decide to write off the entire episode as not worth further trouble.

In many instances white-collar crimes are based upon predictable delays in victims' awareness of the fact that they have been defrauded. Arid desert land was sold by mail for millions of dollars, in reliance that very few purchasers would quickly travel from the East to parched areas of Arizona or Nevada to see their expensive oases (which in fact are waterless patches of scrub and sand). Ponzi schemes rely on perpetual delay in victim realization, as do chain referral schemes, work-at-home schemes, fraudulent self-improvement schools, advance fee schemes, and credit card frauds.

There are frauds committed every day, where the victims never learn about the frauds and as a practical matter it is impossible for them to learn. A typical example would be a check kite by an otherwise legitimate businessman who cannot obtain a bank loan but needs operating capital to tide him over his busy season. To obtain $50,000 he may put millions of dollars of checks in circulation between several bank accounts and, if his season goes as planned, he settles up. The banks have, in fact, made a $50,000 loan without interest to one who might be an ineligible credit risk for this amount, and they have been exposed to loss without knowing it. In most cases, these check kites work out, and, although a mail fraud has been committed, law enforcement authorities will never have the violation brought to their attention.

Many white-collar crimes against governments are based on "playing the percentages" that the victim will never know and, if by chance it should find out, will easily be induced to settle. The false entertainment deduction, where the taxpayer expects his claim to be passed without examination, is a good example. Another example of this would be the padding of expenses on cost reimbursable contracts, or "accidental" shifting of costs from work on fixed-cost contracts to those which are cost reimbursable.

Once the victim knows, or suspects that he has been criminally wronged, he must make a decision as to whether he should complain to law enforcement authorities and, then, a second decision as to where he must go to lodge his complaint. This is a crucial stage from the law enforcement point of view for several reasons: (1) if the victim does not complain, a crime will go unheeded and others may similarly suffer; (2) the success of a white-collar criminal prosecution is dependent on a showing of criminal intent, inferable from the circumstances—which often means a showing of similar acts and transactions. The number of complaints will therefore play a key role in the prosecutive evaluation and in the ultimate success of a prosecution; (3) if there are not clear lines for intake of complaints, victims who make the threshold determination to complain may very well cease their efforts after unsuccessful initial attempts to reach appropriate law enforcement officials.

At this point we should recognize that many white-collar crimes are technical and not worthy of serious prosecutive consideration. Our concern that complaints be made and properly received should not be carried so far as to cause us to seek ways to "drum up business." There are more than enough cases in every investigator's office and in every prosecutor's office.

If we assume that appropriate complaints by victims should be encouraged (without attempting to define which complaints are "appropriate") we should also appreciate that victims' confidence in law enforcement is a necessary precondition to the success of the enforcement effort. The law enforcement effort must have credibility. Victims are unlikely to complain if they believe nothing will be done as a result of their complaints. A negative view of the criminal process may stem from prior unsatisfactory personal experience with complaints or from the community reputation of law enforcement agencies. In some way his relationship with the law enforcement authority must benefit a complainant and certainly not hurt him. Consideration must also be given to the interpersonal relationship between the victim and the representative of the appropriate law enforcement agency.

### Informants

Informants are an established detection resource with respect to certain white-collar crimes, such as tax or customs violations where the reward or bounty system is employed. Informants play a role, though a lesser one, with respect to Securities Act violations, banking violations, and frauds against the government, but are practically a nonexistent factor in consumer frauds and con games. Informants are valuable in the investigation of white-collar crimes but, except as indicated above, they are of minimal significance in bringing possible white-collar violations to the attention of investigating or prosecuting agencies in the first instance.

### Affirmative Searches for Violations by Law Enforcement Personnel

Distinctions must be made between classes of white-collar crimes and perpetrators of such crimes in assessing the desirability and cost effectiveness of intensive affirmative searches for violations by law enforcement personnel.

If we use the classifications of white collar crimes advanced above, it will be apparent that there is more likelihood of victim complaints in the cases of personal crimes, abuses of trust, or con games than with respect to business crimes (crimes incidental to and in furtherance of business operations, but not the central purpose of such business operations).

Business crimes, as defined, are carefully contrived in private transactions to avoid total destructive impact on other parties, to only partially affect such transactions, or to appear to be only a matter of degree. In transactions with governmental bodies they are designed to shade liabilities or obtain only incremental profits or advantages, and are extremely surreptitious and sophisticated in implementation.

The most intensive pattern of affirmative searches is to be found in the area of such business crimes. The Antitrust Division of the Department of Justice and the Federal Trade Commission maintain oversight with respect to mergers, trade association activities, and pricing policies of dominant firms in important markets. The Internal Revenue Service and state tax authorities strive to more carefully audit larger returns. The Department of Agriculture and the Food and Drug Administration make qualitative and quantitative examinations of food and drug products. The Securities and Exchange Commission examines new stock issues and monitors over-the-counter and exchange trading. All of these activities have, of course, non-prosecutive objectives, such as collecting tax revenues, civil injunctions, maintenance of qualitative standards of food and drugs on a preventive basis, and protection of the interests of the investing public. Yet, always in the background is the ultimate sanction of criminal prosecution. Agencies operating in the area of business crimes cannot rely on others to give them the information necessary to meet their responsibilities. They must maintain a solid capability to mount and sustain affirmative searches for violations.

In the case of business crimes, the desirability of beefing up affirmative investigative capabilities is self-evident. In other areas, such as consumer frauds, increased investigatory capability is more likely to be utilized in the handling and investigation of complaints which are not being adequately and fully dealt with at the present time. This might be a correct decision, since there are more than enough complaints at the Post Office (for example) to produce a very good payoff in worthwhile consumer fraud cases if the staff of postal inspectors is increased. However, we should ask ourselves the hard question whether this would not result in better protection for certain classes of victims, such as those most prone to make complaints, while more silent sufferers (ghetto residents, or the elderly, or the unknowing victims of charity frauds) are an overlooked or minimized constituency. We must always be careful not to operate on the principle that "only the squeaky wheel gets the grease." However, since investigators of consumer fraud are generally an idealistic lot (though they might well balk at this adjective), it would take but little support and encouragement to make them look up from overloaded complaint desks to give greater attention to criminal abuses which are not the subject of complaints.

## INVESTIGATIONS

The question how investigations can be conducted more efficiently and a listing of all possible investigatory problems are not within the scope of this paper. The varieties of techniques available are infinite, and so are the problems. We should, however, concentrate on a few specific problems of almost universal applicability and on the special problem of ghetto or inner-city investigations.

## Jurisdiction

Most white-collar crimes are violations of laws in multiple jurisdictions, either vertically (state-federal) or horizontally (between states, between jurisdictions in one state, or between jurisdictions in the federal government). This leads to problems of coordination of effort where more than one jurisdiction is fully on the case, or cooperation where one jurisdiction assumes or is ceded the laboring oar, or conflicts, or attempts to avoid responsibility by claiming another jurisdiction has primary responsibility. . . .

## Facilitating Private Aid to Investigators

There is a tradition that governments should run their own investigations, separate and apart from any involvement with interested private parties. It is a good tradition. Any other course would open the door to use of the prosecutive mechanism of government to improper exploitation by private parties. Every prosecutor's office is haunted by the specter of becoming a collection agency for private debts, and it would be unthinkable for public policy on investigative priorities to be determined by private interests willing to pick up the costs. The halls of law enforcement agencies should not be frequented by lobbyists or special pleaders.

Having said this, we should recognize that existing practices implicitly recognize the desirability and even the necessity of private support for the investigative process. Thus a prosecution for fraud on a telephone company in connection with long distance tolls will inevitably be based on investigations by telephone company security departments. The security department of a credit card company will already have completed the major part of the necessary criminal investigation before the matter is turned over to local police or to federal investigators. A bank embezzlement case will necessarily exploit the work of the bank's own auditors. In a bankruptcy fraud, work by creditors' investigators and attorneys often represent the basic case ultimately prosecuted. . . .

## Conflicting Interests of Victims and Private Parties

Since white-collar crimes more often than not deal with deprivations of money or property, the first concern of any victim is restitution rather than punishment. The complaint made by a victim is usually preceded by a failure to obtain such restitution and is in fact triggered by it, but the desire for restitution (even at the cost of denying or minimizing cooperation with the government whose aid has been invoked) continues unabated.

While it may have no legal significance, a civil settlement by a victim or victims during a criminal investigation or prosecution has an almost lethal effect on criminal enforcement. To start with, the dividing line between civil abuse and a criminal violation is often less than clear in the white-collar crime area, and therefore prosecutors and investigators will tend to accept the fact of a settlement as an indication that the civil aspect outweighed the criminal. The investigator (or prosecutor) also knows that the victim will no longer be a wholehearted witness for the prosecution and that any defense counsel worth his salt will find some way to make the jury aware that the case was mooted by civil settlement, even though evidence of such settlement might be inadmissible. Civil settlement may also be pursued as a device to dispose of an issue of fact crucial to criminal prosecution; this is a particularly effective technique where the settlement requires judicial approval (and thus judicial imprimatur). . . .

### Cooperation of Victims and Witnesses

An observer might conclude that victims and witnesses exist only insofar as they are useful to law enforcement authorities, rather than the other way around. This anomaly is not characteristic of the white-collar crime area alone, or even more of a problem in this area than in others. However, in light of [the] greater difficulty of assembling white-collar prosecutions and the larger numbers of victims and witnesses usually involved in any one case, the impact of this problem is greater in the white-collar crime field. . . .

### Benefits of Investigation

No private party or nonpublic body has available to it the evidence-gathering powers of a law enforcement agency. Banks will often give information to an FBI agent, subject only to the condition that subpoena will be subsequently delivered if the data produced will be used in some public way. Individuals will commonly talk to a government investigator or prosecutor in situations where they would not talk to private litigants. Where cooperation with law enforcement agencies is not voluntary, there is available the administrative subpoena, the grand jury subpoena, or the trial subpoena—sometimes backed up by the power to grant immunity from prosecution and thus the ultimate compulsion which overrides even a plea against self-incrimination.

It is therefore completely understandable that victims of white-collar crimes, who are more likely to be pursuing related civil remedies than victims of common crimes, will seek to obtain the benefits of a public investigation. . . .

### Investigative Techniques

White-collar crimes are investigated by all of the usual techniques, plus a few very special ones. The methods employed depend on the agencies, both state and federal, and on prosecutors who often supervise the latter stages of investigations. Underlying government action is, of course, private inquiry (formal or informal, amateurish or professional) which so often precedes the complaint triggering an official investigation.

With a complaint on his desk, the investigator must first determine whether the facts alleged, if supported by legal evidence, would constitute a crime and if so, what crime. He is usually not an attorney. If it would be a crime worthy of prosecution the investigator will interview witnesses and seek to examine pertinent records. If an agency has regulatory or special investigatory powers, it may compel answers or production of records by threat of suspension of business operations, or by subpoena, or both. If there is a refusal to cooperate with a regulatory agency, there may be a grant of immunity. At some point there is a shift in the theater of action to the prosecutor's bailiwick, and an investigation may be continued by a grand jury.

The methods described work very well with respect to the usual run of SEC cases, financial cases, procurement frauds, and similar crimes. In many instances of consumer fraud, or housing maintenance or health offenses on the local level, these methods may not be adequate. They are certainly inconvenient if large numbers of victims are to be interviewed in a consumer fraud case or with respect to wage and hour violations. . . .

## PROSECUTIVE EVALUATIONS

. . . If prosecutive evaluations are mishandled, the consequences may be serious and far-reaching, both to the subjects of evaluation and to the administration of justice:

1. A sense of injustice on the part of those who know they are singled out for prosecution whereas others escape the net after being apprehended.
2. Failure to effectively use prosecutions and investigations for maximum effect in prevention, deterrence, and detection.
3. Blurring of standards for measuring the effectiveness of law enforcement efforts.
4. Vulnerability to disparity in treatment of offenders based on influence or quality of defense counsel.
5. Imposition of the brand of criminality on those who should not have been prosecuted in the first instance, whether they are convicted or found not guilty.
6. Failure to adequately prosecute certain crimes, particularly some white-collar crimes which may have little publicity value or provide for minimal penalties, may discourage enforcement efforts by agencies and investigators. . . .

## PLEAS AND PLEA BARGAINING

White-collar cases are generally characterized by the use of representative charges, in many counts, rather than charges which comprehend the entire range of criminal conduct which is the subject of the indictment. The exception would be the common use of the conspiracy charge, which is an effort to sweep together all the bits and pieces. The fact that white-collar criminal charges are narrow in scope does not mean that a defendant's full range of conduct will not be comprehended on the trial, but it is a reflection of the structured framework of criminal enforcement.

Thus a bank robber will be charged with the bank robbery which resulted in his apprehension, while the white-collar defendant is usually being charged with specific acts which represent points on a line which is a continuum of conduct. A securities promoter may have made 5,000 sales of unregistered stock, but the indictment will charge in 15 counts that he mailed confirmations of purchases, or certificates, to 15 specific customers. There may also be a conspiracy charge if two or more persons were involved in the sale. . . .

Although the use of representative counts in white-collar cases only occasionally has the effect of restricting proof at the trial, it does establish the dimensions of the arena for plea bargaining. The bank robber or burglar has one act to answer for, and his counsel may direct his efforts to negotiating a plea to a lesser-included offense. The white-collar defendant usually must target in on the additional objective of pleading to a lesser number of counts.

The objectives of a plea are therefore several, in white-collar areas:

1. As in all plea bargaining, to restrict the punishment by pleading to lesser offenses or lesser-included offenses.
2. As in all plea bargaining, to restrict the punishment by pleading to the smallest possible number of counts.
3. By minimizing the number of counts to which guilty pleas are entered, to establish a basis for a defense argument on sentencing aimed at narrowing the scope of the overall conduct for which the judge is meting out punishment.
4. By minimizing the number of counts, to limit the extent to which the defendant may be civilly liable to the victims of his conduct.
5. By seeking permission to enter *nolo contendere* pleas, to eliminate civil consequences which might flow from guilty pleas.
6. By seeking permission to enter a *nolo contendere* plea to deter the court from imposing a severe sentence. While the traditional doctrine is that a *nolo* plea is the same as a guilty plea for sentencing purposes, it is plain that courts regard government acquiescence or nominal objection to the proffer of a *nolo* plea as a downgrading of the importance

or true criminal impact of the acts charged in the indictment or information. If the prosecutor genuinely objects, overriding of such an objection by the court will generally be followed by a light or only nominal sentence. . . .

# SENTENCING

There is a general impression that the more serious the white-collar crime, the less severe the sentence. This is part of the folk myth that if one steals it is better to steal big. Part of the rationale for this generalization is that the penalties are no greater, the chances of being caught are less, and operating on a large scale will insure that money is available for hiring [the] most able counsel.

While one should be wary of generalizations, they usually emerge because they are valid most of the time. They fail us when we do not realize that they may not be valid in all situations. This generalization, that it pays to steal big, can be the subject of innumerable illustrations, and also can be countered with a few dramatic opposites.

Assuming the validity of the generalization, the explanation may partially be that those who steal big can afford to hire the best counsel, but this can only be a partial explanation since white-collar crimes generally result in . . . lighter sentences than common crimes, whether the defendants be rich or poor.

Analyses of white-collar crimes and those who commit them may provide us with better explanations for disparities of treatment on sentencing than the simplistic division between the defense resources of the rich and those of the poor. Or, if there be some credit to be given to the rich versus poor explanation, we would probably find that it is only one factor for consideration.

In the analysis of white-collar crimes, supra, four categories were outlined: (1) personal crimes; (2) abuses of trust; (3) business crimes; and (4) con games. Consideration of these categories would make it obvious that, except for the fourth category, con games, the vast majority of defendants would have no criminal records and that the recidivism rate would be almost nonexistent. Sentencing judges would, therefore, have before them (in the first three categories) a defendant with no record, already severely punished by criminal charges because part of business and social milieus in which arrestees or people with records are almost unknown, and with little likelihood of recidivism. This narrows the judge's objectives to two, deterrence and punishment supplementary to that already suffered by the defendant. Under these circumstances it is not surprising that sentences in white-collar cases tend to be lighter in the first three categories, even though the judge's discretion to inflict severe punishment does not differ markedly from that available to him in most non-white-collar cases.

Notwithstanding this apparently rational explanation for presumed judicial leniency in sentencing white-collar criminal defendants guilty of crimes other than con games, two questions remain: (1) as to any specific white-collar crime, are there disparities in sentencing which are not attributable to idiosyncracies of individual judges, but to some more general cause or causes; and (2) do present levels of sentencing in white-collar cases adequately meet the deterrence and punishment objectives which should be considered by judges? This assumes that the problems of correction and rehabilitation are comparatively unimportant in these areas.

In the absence of hard data, the first question can only be answered by reference to impressions gained from observations over a period of time. The impressions of the writer are that, as to embezzlement and misapplication violations by bank personnel, the bank teller is more likely to go to prison than the bank officer or director. With respect to most other violations, the writer has no clear impressions as to disparities of sentencing within violation categories. The writer is of the view, however, that within violation categories the wealthier or better placed subject has a substantially smaller likelihood of being charged or if charged, tried, or if tried, convicted. There would thus be an unrepresentative sampling at the sentencing level even if the disparities at that level were found to be minor.

Deterrence and punitive considerations are not, in the writer's view, given sufficient weight in the sentencing of white-collar criminals. White-collar crimes are not reactive or spontaneous and in most cases they are not the result of irresistible impulses. Sentences will therefore have marked deterrent effect to the extent that they are known. This would be true even for suspended sentences, for the brand of felon is a heavy burden for most men to carry, and the higher the social scale the heavier and more disabling the burden. . . .

In discussing deterrence, one's first inclination is to think of prison. In the white-collar crime area we often deal, however, with corporate defendants. Top management is highly sophisticated in its ability to insulate itself from exposure to prosecution for the crimes it generates and supervises, and the prosecutor is often relegated to charging only the corporation and lower-level officials or employees. Punishment for the corporation can rarely be measured on any scale other than money. Such punishments could be quite meaningful, especially if nondeductible for tax purposes, yet the scale of such penalties bears no true relationship to the conduct on which the prosecution is grounded. The power of the Securities and Exchange Commission to suspend the activity of a broker-dealer for failure to properly supervise its employees provides more meaningful monetary penalties than any fine provided for in our penal codes. Unless such administrative penalty or parallel civil litigation is available, corporate fines are no more than a modest, though somewhat messy, cost of doing business. Fines, at anything like their present levels, constitute neither meaningful punishment for the corporation or wealthy defendant nor deterrence to those tempted to commit similar transgressions.

If punishment is a valid consideration in sentencing, apart from deterrence and rehabilitation, it suffers in this area as compared to non-white-collar crimes. In the abuse of trust and business crimes categories, the crimes are only possible because the violators are given the opportunity to commit crimes, by society, because they have presumably shown themselves worthy. Under these circumstances white-collar violations may well be more reprehensible and more deserving of punishment, if punishment is the sole criterion, than common crimes such as burglary. . . .

## LEGISLATION

There are many inconsistent and anomalous statutory provisions dealing with white-collar crimes, on federal and state levels, which should be thoroughly reviewed. Many of them are being considered on the federal level by the committee presently reviewing the Federal Criminal Code. Particular stress should be given to the feasibility of a number of proposals, the need for which is quite evident in all jurisdictions.

Criminal fines should be raised to levels which realistically punish and realistically deter, and not merely to levels reflecting decreases in the value of the dollar since enactment of the fines presently on our statute books. Fines of merely a few thousand dollars on each count for violations of securities acts or broad-scale consumer frauds or procurement frauds which may have cost the public or the government millions of dollars are poor deterrence and little or no punishment. . . .

Basic inconsistencies in our statutory patterns should be eliminated. One example would be the existence of 18 U.S.C. 215 which makes it a federal misdemeanor for a banker to accept a bribe for granting a loan, while it is not a criminal violation to offer or pay such a bribe. Is it rational to make it a specific federal felony to procure a loan from a federally insured savings and loan association by submission of a false financial statement, but not to proscribe the same abuse of the loan process of a federally insured or chartered commercial bank?

Legislation should be considered as a vehicle for using the criminal process to provide a basis for restitution to victims, whenever they are part of the class victimized by the scheme or pattern of acts charged in the indictment on information.

Consideration should be given to possibilities of injunctive relief, analogous to that which the Securities and Exchange Commission may apply for, either during investigations or between indictment and trial, to protect further victimization of the public. We are all familiar with receiverships and trusteeships to prevent looting of business or wastage of assets on a proper showing of danger or voluntary bankruptcy proceedings. The public as a class of prospective victims should be entitled to the same protection, on a proper showing, where criminal processes, investigatory or prosecutorial, are pending or impending.

Consideration should be given to statutes of general application authorizing investigatory subpoenas on state and federal levels.

On the state and local level the problem is so diverse and amorphous that it is difficult to suggest any simple pattern of legislation. One possible avenue, which would have deterrence value and be punitive in a monetary sense, would be to adopt one of the various existing proposals to create federal rights in consumer fraud cases, which could be the subject of private derivative actions or actions by law enforcement officers in state as well as federal courts.

For criminal law to be an adequate deterrent and remedy in the white-collar criminal field, it must be employed flexibly and with imagination, for the varieties of culpable human behavior in the white-collar area are almost without limit. It would be impossible to create specific statutes to proscribe all such wrongful conduct. . . .

## CONSIDERATION OF SPECIFIC AREAS OF CONCERN

### Implications of the Cashless Society

We must make a start on consideration of the law enforcement implications of the creditless person in the looming cashless, credit card society. . . .

Cash is losing much of its utility as a medium of exchange. For a host of reasons, including crimes, buses and possibly taxis within less than a decade will be charging fares by accepting credit cards pushed into a slot. Bank credit cards have expanded retailer credit from large sales outlets to the neighborhood specialty store, and supermarkets may soon be expected to succumb to this trend.

The expansion of our credit card environment will create broad-scale opportunities for thefts of cards, for disavowals of use by fraudulent reports that cards were stolen, by misuse of restricted cards, and by retailer-facilitated misuse of credit cards.

There should be careful studies, now, of avenues for prevention, deterrence, investigation, and prosecution in the credit card area. Among the matters for consideration should be:

1. Should there not be some control over the distribution of unsolicited credit cards? Should they be permitted? If permitted, should their mailing by certified or registered mail be compulsory?

2. Should identification pictures on credit cards be made compulsory? Or should legislation make the requirement of such pictures a condition of holder liability whenever a lost or stolen credit card is used?

3. What are the technical possibilities in this area? Would it not be desirable to foster uniformity of shape and size of cards, so that service establishments could have a single processing machine for all cards which would be wired to computers which could instantly identify stolen cards or the attempted unauthorized use for prohibited classes of goods or services?

4. Credit cards add a new element to the problem of fraud by computers. Most people tend to accept their bills without checking, as they have a tendency to do with bank statements, merely adjusting for errors. More and more retailers and credit card companies are moving away from submission of duplicate invoices, and substituting coded listings referring to merchandise classifications. This opens the way to frauds by insiders in retail establishments, particularly in billing departments, who may be able to work out methods for thefts of merchandise under this system, and even for compensating if account holders catch the errors in their bills.

5. If we assume that credit cards may well be necessary for those on welfare, the question of control to prevent misuse should be a first priority. Prevention here would be a primary objective.

6. What will be the role of state and local law enforcement authorities in the credit card area? Is the problem itself so vast, with cards becoming more and more national in character, that it should be primarily a federal problem? . . .

### Civil Rights and White-Collar Crime

Under what circumstances should civil rights violations be considered white-collar crimes and punishable as such? This is not an academic question since the tools of white-collar enforcement are both available and applicable to problems of civil rights compliance. Under the federal false statement statute, 18 U.S.C. 1001, it is a felony to make a false statement or to conceal a fact which would be material to the making of an administrative decision or determination. Where statements of compliance with civil rights mandates are required, i.e., by government contractors, false statements would be prosecutable. Where they are not now required, to compel such filings would shift the arena from the regulatory to the criminal area and provide options for increased enforcement. . . .

### Election Laws and Corrupt Practices

This is a complex area with limitless ramifications, criminal, social, and political. Such legislation as exists is still ill suited to achieving reporting and public disclosure on a level which serves to inform the public of the true costs of electing public officials and the equally crucial question of who is paying these costs. The first problem, therefore, is a legislative one, to amend existing statutes, federal and state, to close many obvious loopholes. The second problem is the investigatory and prosecutive one of coordinating election problems with tax enforcement, since all those familiar with the field are quite convinced that many campaign costs such as printing and provision of office space are met by contributions in the form of picking up bills, and end up as deductions on business tax returns.

### Environmental Problems

Enforcement in the environmental field, with respect to air and water pollution and disposition of waste, is necessary if we hope to maintain or improve the quality of life. While there are some petty substantive criminal violations, usually at the level of technical misdemeanors, available as enforcement tools, the primary thrust of enforcement efforts has been to induce compliance by persuasion, conferences, subsidies, and regulatory measures of various kinds.

The pollution of our atmosphere, water, and soil is obviously too great a problem for draconian criminal solutions. Major efforts must be non-criminal, as they are now. But the ultimate sanction, the penal sanction, may be every bit as important in achieving civil compliance in this area as it is in the securities and banking areas, where only a very small portion of entrepreneurial violations ever reach the level of criminal prosecution. The potential is, however, of the utmost importance in meeting the overall regulatory responsibilities of the agencies involved. . . .

### Consumer Protection

Many proposals have been advanced to provide for improved consumer protection. Some provide for new consumer rights and remedies, some for organizational changes to make possible more effective government action. All are directed, at a minimum, to the conversion of technical rights into meaningful and realistic remedies.

Certain problems in this area call for particular attention:

1. Consumer protection is undermined by the "holder in due course" doctrine, which strips a victim of his right to defend or to interpose a set-off when he is sued for payment by one who purchased the right to collect installment payments. It is easy to recommend a statutory elimination of

"holder in due course status" in connection with purchases of goods and services by ultimate consumers, but the existence of mechanisms for legally protected purchases of installment paper is necessary to the maintenance of credit installment sales. Developing new approaches to the "holder in due course" doctrine, new forms of debt instruments, and legislation to reconcile the need for credit-generating mechanisms with consumer protection should be priority objectives for legislators and researchers.

2. Concern for the consumer inspires the structuring of proposals for consumer relief through class actions, restraining orders, and the statutory right to rescind contracts. As such proposals are enacted, they will be evaluated to determine their effectiveness. It is important, however, that there be continuous scrutiny to determine whether criminal sanctions are being used, where available, and whether such sanctions should not be provided for in any new proposed consumer protection legislation. Those who seek to abuse the consumer must be required to recognize that they may face penalties which cannot be mentally assessed as being no more than a supportable cost of doing business.

3. Special consideration should be given to the problem of preventing victimization of the public after an abuse has been brought to the attention of investigative agencies. This is a most difficult problem, since restraining orders and injunctions are not customarily available to law enforcement agencies. Methods must be devised to stop ongoing frauds during state and federal criminal investigation without risking immunity baths, and also without risking irreparable injury to those who may be falsely accused.

### Diversion of Cases to Noncriminal Channels

Truly effective and intelligent prosecutive evaluation would serve to screen out many of the cases which currently clog our courts and prosecutors' offices. The development of effective evaluation procedures may well be hampered by the absence of procedures and standards which offer prosecutors a meaningful alternative when they consider a case which is prosecutable but not truly worthy of prosecution.

Alternative remedies, whether in the form of arbitration or priority civil or civil class actions, would provide many benefits. Victims could obtain faster relief. Perpetrators of fraud would be subject to restraint by the use of legal tools which would not be available if there was to be an impending prosecution. And, most important, our courts and prosecutors would be freed to deal with prosecutions which would provide a more meaningful return because more significant in character and more intensively pursued. . . .

# III

# *Business Deviance in Daily Life*

## INTRODUCTION

This part includes four readings, all original contributions published here for the first time, which analyze business practices and deviance in several settings of daily life. Chapter 4, "Cashing in on Crime," reports Gene Siegel's study of the burglar alarm industry in a large metropolitan community of the Southwest, one known to have experienced one of the most rapidly increasing crime rates in the United States in recent years. Siegel's study shows how this particular industry is the benefactor of the recent crime promotions of the official agencies and mass media and how they utilize lo-balling and fear selling to capitalize on the public's fear of crime, especially burglary.

One noteworthy aspect of Siegel's study is that it reports relatively routine and undramatic business practices, very much like those of many other industries caught in the flux of a rising market situation. While many citizens might view either the burglar alarm selling practices or the interface between this industry and state officialdom as highly deviant, one important aspect of this study is that it clearly shows the burglar alarm salesmen do not see it this way at all. Indeed, most of them view their actions as providing a valuable service to the community.

This point is even further illustrated in the extraordinary contribution by David Altheide, Patricia Adler, Peter Adler, and Duane Altheide, "The Social Meanings of Employee Theft" (Chapter 5). Employee theft is ubiquitous throughout American society. Yet very few employees who possess the insider understandings of such acts perceive them moralistically or legalistically. Unlike the "Operators" described by Frank Gibney in Chapter 1, employees who misappropriate or otherwise use organizational goods and products for nonorganizational purposes think of themselves as respectable, law-abiding citizens. The meanings of employee thefts are tied to the work contexts where such acts occur, and they are often viewed as officially sanctioned compensation or unofficially sanctioned rewards for jobs well done. Such thefts are misunderstood if viewed through the narrow lens of a legalistic point of view. Chapter 5 represents one of the few sociological studies based on systematic observations and careful interviews about actual work practices, and it goes a long way in providing us with an understanding of the meanings of employee theft and its relations to other features of the entire employee–employer work context.

Andrea Fontana's work experiences and field researches in convalescent nursing homes provide the data presented in Chapter 6, "Ripping Off the Elderly." Fontana observed that nursing home operators routinely cut down on the operational and daily living expenses of patient care in order to achieve a greater profit margin from the federal Medicaid program. Such practices not only include financial fraud, but in addition much inhumane and bureaucratized treatment of patients. Fontana's observations tend to support the earlier analysis of Herbert Edelhertz (Chapter 3), which suggested that the poor and the elderly are often those most victimized by business and professional deviance.

Chapter 7 reports Robert Snow's analysis of the complexities involved in the vast land fraud in Arizona during the past decade. The land development and real estate market in Arizona represent a "boom market mentality," according to Snow, which is based on individuals' beliefs in the "greater fool theory." This belief supports the gullibility and acceptability of purchasing land and other forms of real estate at vastly inflated prices in the hope that there will be another "greater fool" who will pay even more in order to "beat inflation" and make a profit on his investment. The land fraud swindles and other high-level financial scams in Arizona involved billions and billions of dollars which were eventually taken by investors. Arizona Attorney General Bruce Babbitt concluded, after years of land fraud investigations, that perhaps *all* real estate transactions of undeveloped land in non-metropolitan Arizona areas involved one or more forms of fraud. The Arizona land fraud swindles involved virtually all aspects of the legitimate business community, including banks, title companies, investment companies, realtors, developers, contractors, advertising men, media, and the corruption of a surprising segment of the local officials and legal community. Many individuals become caught up in the escalating feelings and emotional tenor of the boom market mentality, according to Snow, and such emotions usually preclude attempts at regulation or control of the fraudulent business operations, which may occur only when there is a downturn in the more general economic situation.

# Cashing in on Crime: 4
# A Study of the
# Burglar Alarm Business

Gene G. Siegel

## INTRODUCTION

The classical sociological perspective exemplified by the work of Emile
Durkheim viewed the problem of crime from a consensual model of society. Illegal behavior is considered an "objective" feature of society, indicating the degree of societal integration and anomie. Increases in rates
of rule violations reflect a decrease in social cohesion. Therefore, the actions of social control agents are deemed a natural and necessary response
to crime. To maintain societal integration, illicit behavior has to be
controlled.

The structural-functional view of crime represented in the work of
Robert K. Merton also entails a consensual model of society. The actions
of official agents are assumed to represent a functional response to illegal
behavior tending to control it. It is assumed that law enforcement ex-
ecutors are "disinterested" in the sense that they are not acting on the
basis of their own practical or moral interests. The official definition of
crime is taken for granted and left unquestioned.

The labeling approach to deviant behavior was the first to question
official definitions of crime and deviance. This perspective placed increased
emphasis on the subjective aspects of criminal conceptions, paying particular attention to the perspectives of people defined as deviant. No
longer seeing crime as an objective fact of social life, the labeling approach
stressed the importance of the reactions of control agents:

> Social groups create deviance by making rules whose infraction consti-
> tutes deviance and by applying those rules to particular people and
> labeling them as outsiders. From this point of view, deviance is not a
> quality of the act a person commits, but rather a consequence of the
> application by others of rules and sanctions to an "offender." The de-
> viant is one to whom that label has successfully been applied, deviant
> behavior is behavior that people so label.[1]

I would like to express my gratitude to David L. Altheide, John M. Johnson, and Erdwin
H. Pfuhl, Jr., for their help and guidance during this project.

Taking the labeling point of view one step further, an interrelationship exists between agents of social control and patterns of crime. Jack Douglas (1970) claims that the specific forms of crime patterns are largely a response to official actions, policies, and practices. The interaction between criminal actors and criminal definers is considered crucial for the study of deviance. In short, labeling proponents brought out the relevance of studying "rule makers" and "rule enforcers" and implicated both groups in how crime is defined within a particular society.

The role of vested interests in the crime situation has received a good deal of attention in sociological literature (Quinney, 1970; Taylor, Walton, and Young, 1973; Davis, 1975), as has the influence of interest groups in fostering social problems. Utilizing a social movements perspective to analyze social problems, Armand Mauss (1975) identified six categories of interest groups (psychological, moral, political, economic, occupational, and scientific). While various kinds of interest groups have been identified as having crucial roles in the crime process, there has not been an intensive study of business-economic interest groups supported by the existing crime situation. In addition, very little is known about those persons who are indirectly involved in the situation and have economic considerations.

This paper involves an investigation and analysis of the burglar alarm industry. Over the past few years there has been a steady increase in the rate of burglaries, and the ever-rising crime rate seems to have led many people to invest in personal security in spite of troubled economic times. Security systems and protective services have been termed "virtually recession-proof industries,"[2] and their sales patterns seemingly parallel upsurges in crime.[3] As the incidence of burglary continues to increase, the consumer demand for protection seems to follow. Recent reports have indicated that the rate of growth for alarms has been 15 to 20 percent annually over the past few years. One study showed that sales of all types of protection services totaled over $2 billion last year, up from a little more than $1.5 billion the year before. For the current year, sales are expected to reach in the neighborhood of $3 billion.[4] Thus, public concern for the rising crime problem (Furstenberg, 1971) appears to have major consequences for burglar alarm purchases.[5]

The major alarm firms described in this study are located within a "Sun Belt" urban area. The population base of this city is expanding, and rapid economic development is evident. In 1974, this area had one of the highest crime rates in the nation.[6] For burglary, it ranked third, behind Las Vegas and Daytona Beach, respectively. Between 1973 and 1974, the incidence of known local burglaries rose by almost 6,000 (approximately 30 percent). During this same period, the number of local alarm companies rose from 51 to 71 (approximately a 39 percent increase). The close correspondence of these figures certainly suggests that crime rates have a very influential effect on the establishment of security companies. Where burglary rates rise dramatically, one can also expect to find a rise in burglar alarm enterprises.

At present, concrete data on alarm sales over time are not available from local agencies. However, we can get an indication of how strong the crime–alarm sales interrelationship is through other avenues of information. Recording the number of local alarm firms found in the Yellow Pages from 1966-76 provided a somewhat conservative but accurate gauge of growth. Concurrently, a measure of the upswing in local burglaries was acquired from the *Uniform Crime Reports* for the same ten-year period. Juxtaposing a curve of known burglaries with one of alarm company expansion gives an interesting result.

Observing the two graphs gives us a good indication of the almost parallel relationship between crime rates and the number of home safeguard businesses. As the graph shows, the number of burglaries known to police nearly tripled in this city during this period. Within the same time span, the number of local burglar alarm establishments increased by eight times. In short, the crime predicament has led to a significant growth in the local security industry.

In the past, reports of "scare tactics" have been launched against some alarm company employees. The popular media has reported the presence of "con men" who take advantage of the customer.[7] This study

**Table 1. Changes in Reported Burglaries: 1966–76**

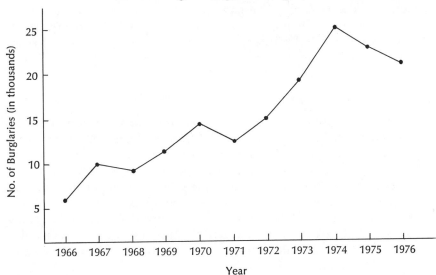

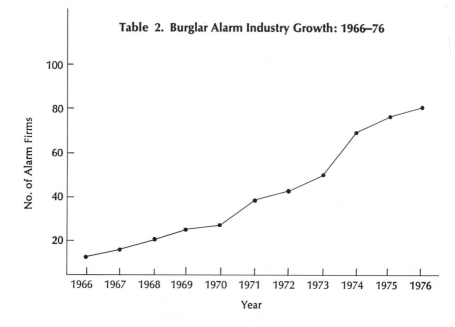

Table 2. Burglar Alarm Industry Growth: 1966–76

attempts to gauge the accuracy of such a perspective. In addition, the contrasting and sometimes conflicting reality perspectives that exist between alarm personnel, alarm consumers, and official agents of social control will be covered as significant elements within the total scheme. By investigating firsthand the major burglar alarm businesses in this city, it is hoped that a clearer picture of the "fear of crime" and its economic implications will emerge. The possibility that security services affect the nature and form of burglary will also be discussed. Furthermore, an interest-based theoretical perspective will be offered as a frame of reference for understanding the burglar alarm phenomenon.

## METHOD OF PROCEDURE

In order to discover which companies were the largest alarm firms in the area, contact was initiated with a member of the local police department with access to business and tax records. Upon receiving this information, the researcher arranged interviews with the firms to discuss the nature of the research. The first interview took place in the spring of 1976, the second interview occurred approximately one month later, and the final contacts occurred in the fall. These interviews involved high-ranking sales managers and/or district representatives of the three largest companies. Permission to conduct the research was initially granted by all three of the establishments.

To more fully grasp the role of fear within the burglar alarm business, the researcher used the technique of participant observation. Essentially, this involved posing as a sales trainee, accompanying burglar personnel on residential and commercial sales calls. The sales representatives of each company expressed no concern over this approach and stated that the observer posed no threat to potential sales. Therefore, "gaining entry" into the situation was not a serious problem for the investigator.

The observer's participation in such calls was intermittent due to time demands and scheduling problems. The majority of visits took place during the spring of 1977. The role of the researcher in these situations was rather passive. After being introduced to the prospective client as a sales trainee, the observer remained silent unless directly questioned. At times, the researcher took notes during the sales call, which, according to the majority of salesmen, was not unusual for a trainee. Following a call, a taped interview was arranged with the salesperson at a convenient location. These interviews primarily involved a recounting of the previous interaction between customer and seller.

Interviews were also engaged between the researcher and five higher ranking company officials (three sales managers, two general managers). These interviews entailed more lengthy discussions of the security industry itself, as well as more detailed information on company policies. In order to investigate the role of financial incentives for buying alarms, interviews were also arranged with representatives of the four major insurance companies in the area. Each of these firms employed a burglary and/or fire underwriter who specialized in evaluating credit rates for alarm systems.

The products handled by the alarm firms ranged from simple buzzer type devices to sophisticated central station "full service" instruments. Each sales employee was fully trained regarding the operation of such devices and had company leaflets explaining the range of services available to the customer. To gain a more basic understanding of the effectiveness of these devices, the researcher consulted written references.[8]

## MAKING THE SALE

The sales process from initiating contact to the final sale involves a multitude of factors. Robert Bogdan (1975) discussed these variables regarding the door-to-door sales approach, and Mark Shafer (1976) outlined the procedures involved in selling vacuum cleaners. While some alarm businesses utilize door-to-door tactics, the overall approach of the companies investigated was not of this type.

The primary means of initiating alarm sales contacts involved phone calls from potential buyers. For the most part, the three alarm firms did not actively utilize phone sales techniques, and the vast majority of residential and commercial appointments stemmed from calls received by alarm companies (all of the sales managers interviewed stated that well over half of their residential and commercial sales contacts resulted from such customer-initiated phone calls). Thus, the first step involved in the alarm sales approach is arranging appointments for face-to-face interaction, primarily through phone calls by the potential buyer to the firm of interest.

Another important factor involved in the sales process is the role of advertising. Local security businesses do not use television or radio advertisements to any great extent—only one burglar alarm firm in the area used television commercials. Each of the observed companies advertised in the print media, most apparently in the Yellow Pages (a fact which attests to the significance of the phone). Clearly, the primary purpose of these ads is to provide the means for customer contacts.

When the frequency of potential buyer call-ins drops below acceptable levels, more direct sales measures have to be taken to promote business. Under these conditions, certain salespersons may employ door-to-door tactics or other more direct approaches. For example, during a "slow week," one in which there are few, if any sales appointments, a sales representative will look over various sources of information on residential and commercial developments (printed information on new homes being built, homes being sold, new office or shopping centers being constructed, and so forth) to establish prospective clients. However, it should be noted that these more direct methods are the exception rather than the norm. They occur only when sales contacts drop below a desirable level.

### The Sales Presentation

Previous analyses of salesman-consumer interactions have incorporated a dramaturgical focus. In his discussion of "strategies of persuasion" employed by sales personnel, Bogdan (1975) relied heavily on the ideas of Erving Goffman (1959). For this paper, such a perspective offers a useful avenue for describing and understanding the alarm sales presentation. The concept of "impression management" appears particularly crucial in this regard.

While the burglar alarm salesman utilizes a number of cues prior to face-to-face contact with the prospective buyer, he usually does not know exactly what will transpire in the customer's home. In approaching a caller, the security representative must be ready to "play it by ear." In other words, the sales pitch largely depends on physical/interactional cues and the client's account. Typically the salesman looks for physical evidence to determine what type of consumer he is confronting. As one company representative reported, these cues can greatly influence the continuance of a presentation: "Initial contact, initial impressions are very vital to whether or not you pursue that sale."

Salesmen also employ middle-class typifications in weighing the relevance of physical criteria. By observing the external conditions of a home, a salesman can achieve a reasonable measure of a potential buyer's financial strength:

> In your initial contact with a person you are trying to determine that [socioeconomic status]; how well do they keep the house up, how well is the lawn mowed, what kind of car do they drive? You don't ask them but you just by observation can tell how well they're fixed financially. Are they basically lazy people, or are they really hurting for money.

Upon entering a residence or business, a salesman must consider a number of variables which play crucial parts in the sales pitch. The first component concerns who is to be dealt with in the situation. Since most residential calls occur in the early morning or afternoon, housewives usually perform the initial consumer role. Apparently, even if the husband and wife are both present for the sales talk, the pitch is often directed toward the married woman's interests. Such an approach seems to have a practical basis in that alarm systems are frequently purchased for the protection of the family. One salesman explained the focus on the wife in terms of typical role expectations within marriage:

> Chances are if you've sold the wife, you've sold the system. The reason people are interested in an alarm is protection. The wife may be home alone at times and feel that an alarm system would protect her. So, the husband would get the system since he is unable to provide the protection he feels she needs. On the other hand, if you sell the husband and not the wife, you may not get the sale. After all, if she feels safe she's not going to try and persuade her husband to invest in security.

The age of the potential buyer is another important part of the sales presentation. The reasons for interest in security seem to differ between age groups. For example, according to one salesman, elderly people in general are more concerned with protecting their property than their persons. In contrast, young people, particularly those couples with young children, tend to be more concerned with personal security. The effect of this on a salesman's presentation is reflected in the type and range of protection offered to the customer. In the first case, the older couple might request protection only for those areas in the house which contain valuables. The younger couple might ask for additional protection for their children.

Once the sales representative has established face-to-face contact with the prospective client, his next job is to find out why this person called.

Talking to the resident or businessman about his reasons for wanting an alarm system serves as an important cue. The sales talk is given direction and focus through the determination of customer needs and/or fears. Often a potential buyer will volunteer this information at the outset of the meeting. When this is not the case, the salesman may ask the interested party what event caused him to call in the first place.

Once the reasons for interest have been disclosed, a salesman can more easily support and maintain the customer's definition of the situation. For example, if an individual has been assaulted during a burglary, the salesman would stress the protective strength of a certain type of security device. As one salesman put it:

> People buy because they have something to protect, to prevent a loss, or they want to protect themselves. . . . And that's what you're after . . . what motivates them, why did they call you in the first place, and then you sell to that.

In identifying client needs and/or fears, the alarm salesman is usually mindful of two chief considerations: the living and residence patterns of the interested party and their past experience (such as previous burglary).

The existence of a wide range of protective services frequently enables alarm companies to tailor units to the requirements of the consumer. A resident who vacations regularly may desire a different form of security from a person who remains at home year-round. For example, those customers who travel often tend to want protection only for their valuables. They are not looking for a system which emphasizes the safety of their persons. On the other hand, a relative "homebody" would probably desire a more wide-ranging system which included maximum personal safeguards. Therefore, a sales agent must find out about the customer's lifestyle when presenting his product.

The second and perhaps most crucial consideration involves the previous experience of the prospective consumer. According to the alarm companies studied, somewhere between 75 and 90 percent of all alarm purchases derive from people who had been burglarized or knew of a burglary in their neighborhood. It is in these instances that the role of fear and/or concern as motivating forces is especially evident.

The most important practical element in the sales presentation is the internal structure of the home. Before an alarm seller can offer a system to a customer he must examine the architecture and construction of the residence. This procedure entails a walk-through of the home, usually with the interested party. The salesperson inspects windows, doors, and walls to determine areas for alarm contacts and wiring. All of the alarm sales agents impressed upon the researcher that certain sophisticated systems could not operate optimally within certain structures. In other words, the inside framework of a home dictates to a significant degree the kind of protective service one offers to a potential buyer. For commercial establishments, a similar examination of the building is undertaken.

Each alarm salesman brings his own unique style to the sales exchange situation. Some sales agents are verbally aggressive while others lean toward a more passive approach. Overall, however, there are two types of sales methodology which became clear in the research. One mode of operation involves accentuating and supporting the client's fears (I will refer to this as the "fear accentuation" approach). The other type[9] steers away from customer-fear and stresses the protective advantages of the alarm system (I will refer to this as the "aura of protection" approach). It should be noted that these two kinds of approaches are not necessarily mutually exclusive. In fact, the majority of sales visits contained a combination of them. However, the distinction is made here for analytical purposes.

As stated earlier, one of the primary components of alarm selling is the ability of the salesman to tie into the customer's situation. One way of accomplishing this is to systematically reinforce the circumstances of a particular client. This often entails a degree of emotive reassurance and concern for the customer's plight. One salesman explained the process in this way: "If they [the burglars] did come in and happened to kick the dog and broke his leg, you feel sorry for the dog right away, . . . if she's frightened, you get frightened right along with her."

These factors are particularly important for sales agents who employ the fear accentuation approach in interactions with prospective buyers.

### Fear Accentuation

While posing as a sales trainee, it became increasingly clear that alarm salesmen "preying" upon unwary consumers were generally the exception rather than the rule. For the most part, active fear-inducing tactics seem to have fallen by the wayside. Within the local alarm business, only one of the smaller companies was suspected of employing high-pressure tactics in its residential market. None of the alarm personnel I interacted with displayed such aggressive techniques. Interestingly enough, all of the companies observed expressed confidence in the lack of necessity for using such methods. All of the sales managers pointed out that sufficient fear and concern already exists among the public. However, while the lack of necessity for high-pressure sales seems evident, the specific tactics employed by alarm salesmen in general are dependent on situations.

The fear accentuation approach is a more subtle means of fostering an atmosphere conducive to an alarm purchase. Rather than forcibly imposing the notion of a rampaging "crime menace" on the customer, a salesman of this type plays a more affective-supportive role. While this method lacks the intensity of scare tactics, it is nonetheless every bit, if not more, effective for sales. Of prime importance in this mode of operation is the revelation (by the customer) of the event(s) which led to contact with the security company. Once a potential buyer expresses his or her fears, the sales agent selectively influences the situation in order to reinforce the need for alarm services. For example, during one visit a young woman revealed a "traumatic event" which had happened to her a few days earlier. In reference to this event the salesman later remarked:

> It's a good idea to help them relive that experience as much as you possibly can. . . . I listened to her story and encouraged her to tell me what had happened because that alarm system has to be designed to prevent that thing from happening again.

On other visits this salesman stated that there were a number of ways in which he could impress the consumer with the need for protection. For example, telling stories about previously unprotected and victimized citizens aids in the creation of an atmosphere of need: "There's a dozen stories that I could tell relative to most any circumstances that could have happened."

In short, then, the fear accentuation approach involves (1) revelation and identification of fears, (2) reconstruction of the client's "traumatic event," and (3) impressing the "need" for protection (e.g., through storytelling). If a sales agent can adeptly manage these tactics, he is very likely to make his sale, even if other companies underbid his price. As one salesman put it: "He [the customer] is probably gonna check out another bidder to see if you're competitive, but the fear alone overrides the price." Overall, this method maintains and supports the existing fears of the customer.

### Aura of Protection

In contrast to the subtle techniques of the fear accentuator, a salesman of the second type stresses the protective strong points of burglar alarm systems. The advantages of certain devices are the central point of a protective sales pitch. A successful salesman using this approach is able to incorporate verbal and nonverbal reinforcement to convince a customer to buy. A good example of this occurred during a residential sales call one morning:

> *Customer:* I have a brother-in-law in Connecticut who had an alarm. He forgot to turn it on one night. Two black boys broke in and hit him on the head—and gave him a concussion—they thought he was going to the phone.
> *Salesman:* (shakes head, takes deep breath).
> *Customer:* They really cleaned him out in spite of the alarm.

*Salesman:* Yes. That's really a shame (shakes head). . . . With your system we will have switches located wherever you need them.

While the fear accentuator relies heavily on a more cognitive-affective performance, the protective salesman enhances his pitch with a more rationalistic appeal. For these representatives, an alarm purchase implies safety above all else. One salesman explained this idea as follows:

I don't sell alarms on price, you got to sell them the protection they need and I think price should be secondary, I really do. If price is a factor and if it's a very big thing in their mind, then definitely it should come into play and you don't sell as much sophisticated equipment since these alarms are very expandable—we can always add to them down the road. If they need something just to satisfy insurance requirements, that's fine. I'll be happy to close it. But in my proposal I will put that this is the type of system that was recommended and I suggest that they put this in later on.

In general, the protective salesman tries to avoid purely emotional appeals. The sales goal in this approach is to try to get the client to draw rational conclusions from his experiences. One salesman expressed a distaste for fear tactics and pointed out that fear alone may not be the reason people buy alarms:

I don't feel that at all, no. I think there's a concern, I don't think people are afraid. . . . I don't think they have 17 locks on their doors. And if they are, I try to diminish it in my selling because I don't think that's healthy, you know, to have a fear. To be using the alarm system to hide and be in kind of a prison. I don't think it's healthy and I try not to. . . . I know some people are paranoid and they want to have pretty much a fortress. I've sold some [laugh] that you couldn't sneeze in the place without the alarm going off. But I don't think that the major fear is there . . . in general, I don't. And I hope it doesn't get that bad.

In brief, then, the aura of protection presentation involves: (1) a focus on the "best" type of protective device for the consumer, (2) a more rationalistic appeal, and (3) an overall emphasis on safety rather than fear. Again, it should be mentioned that despite the apparent distinguishing characteristics of these two types of sales pitches, the method practiced by a salesman is often contingent on the circumstances he finds himself in and how the *clients* define them.

### Closing the Sale

Once the sales pitch has been given and a customer shows an intent to purchase, the final process of alarm sales goes into motion. At this juncture, a relatively uniform approach occurs in getting the client to fill out a contract for service. Needless to say, to get the potential customer to "sign on the dotted line," the sale presentation must be effective and convincing.

The center of attention during a sales closure is the merging of alarm company and alarm customer interests. The client must realize and accept the fact that his home or business is optimally protected. He must also be made aware of his responsibilities in helping the system to work properly. The alarm company must demonstrate its protective capacity to the buyer while at the same time educating him on how the security device operates. The firm must also weigh the potential liabilities of servicing a particular customer (e.g., possible false alarm hazards).

In those instances where a possible buyer remains uncertain regarding protective services (e.g., for economic reasons), further persuasive techniques are needed. For example, a salesman might offer a base rate on an alarm system in order to quell financial concerns. Then, once the deal has been completed, the salesman might call back to the buyer to inform him of additional services he should invest in (such as guard protection). For the most part, though, closing an alarm sale hinges on the ability of the sales agent to create and foster a favorable impression of protection.

## SECURITY ENGINEERS

One of the more important elements of impression management conducted by alarm salesmen lies in the term "security engineer." Alarm sellers in general prefer this more dignified term which they feel aptly describes the role they play. In viewing himself as a security engineer, the alarm company employee adds legitimacy and authority to his performance. As Goffman points out, social actors vary in the degree to which they believe in their own performances:

> At one extreme, one finds that the performer can be fully taken in by his own act; he can be sincerely convinced that the impression of reality which he stages is the real reality. When his audience is also convinced in this way about the show he puts on . . . then for the moment at least, only the sociologist or the socially disgruntled will have any doubts about the "realness" of what is presented.[10]

The technical training of security engineers is a crucial part of the sales initiation process. Each prospective engineer undergoes substantial education regarding burglary protection equipment. The practical basis for such a background is clear: employees must have an understanding of security devices in order to deal with curious customers. More significant, however, is the fact that such technical expertise enables alarm sellers to perceive themselves as something above common salesmen. Consequently, the security engineer creates an aura of "expertness" in the sales encounter.

In accordance with the self-perceived role of expert, protection engineers tend to view the security realm as an exclusive arena for their talents. It is argued that the only real means of attaining safety is through the guidance of proficient professionals. Such a stance calls attention to the increasing tendency of alarm consumers to install their own equipment—a practice which, needless to say, diverts a sizable number of buyers from the major security companies. Therefore, when constructing a reality of protection, the security engineer must claim knowledge far beyond that of the layman.

The role of security engineer is further amplified by the criminal conceptions of alarm salesmen. The importance of such ideas cannot be underestimated as Quinney forcefully notes:

> Conceptions of crime—the subjective aspect of the social reality of crime —are constructed with intentions, not merely to satisfy the imagination. We end up with some realities rather than others for good reason— because someone has something to protect. That protection can be achieved by the perpetuation of a certain view of reality. Realities are, then, the most subtle and insidious of our forms of social control. No weapon is stronger than the control of one's world of reality. It is the control of one's mind.[11]

By playing the part of security engineer, the saleman gives additional weight to the creation and/or support of a particular conception of crime.

### The Security Engineer as Criminologist

The alarm salesman not only commands technical expertise but also has an abundance of criminal knowledge at his disposal. The *Uniform Crime Reports* dispensed annually by the Federal Bureau of Investigation are readily available to security firms. The official data are well-advertised, and each salesman utilizes burglary statistics when the need arises. Along similar lines, many alarm sellers tend to view crime from a rather positivistic-objectivistic standpoint.[12] Rather than critically examining the phenomena of crime, security engineers explain deviant actions by attending to the causes of burglary. One alarm salesman offered an explanation which closely resembles Sutherland's differential association approach to criminal behavior:

> Today, right now, I really believe that four out of five of them [burglaries] are caused by peer pressure. . . . The kids are led into it and they are constantly leading other kids. I don't mean just kids but they start out in the sixth, seventh, and eighth grade and as they progress . . . they're

having more of this demand thrust on them by the people they associate with.

Another salesman offered an interesting combination of physical types, drug abuse, and family problems in explaining burglary:

> If you're a jock you don't get involved in that. If you're a long-hair, you're a good potential candidate to end up in this particular realm [burglary]. Now I think the drugs, particularly marijuana, have an awful lot to do with it. . . . I think a lot of these kids . . . have not had a happy relationship at home. And not necessarily an unhappy type of situation, but the child abuse thing when they're in their infancy, and there's an insecure relationship and they find a basic friendship with these other long-hairs who, on the other . . . I said long-hair but, that particular cover they can identify with. . . . There is a feeling of belonging which they don't feel in their family relationship.

In short, then, the position of security engineer entails technical and criminological abilities. By skillfully employing his exclusive knowledge, the security engineer constructs an atmosphere of increased legitimacy. His expertness is not questioned and the assumptions underlying his performance are not brought to task. By once again referring to Quinney we can begin to see the implications of such a state of affairs:

> By constructing a reality that we are all to believe in, those in positions of power legitimize their authority. That which is believed to be true, to be the "real" nature of things, is good in itself. It is right simply because it is, and is not to be questioned or refuted. Believing is accepting. Hence, the reality of crime that is constructed for all of us by those in a position of power is the reality we tend to accept as our own. By doing so, we grant those in power the authority to carry out the actions that best promote their interests.[13]

## BURGLAR ALARMS AS CRIME-FIGHTERS: THE FALSE ALARM PROBLEM

> Just having the alarm will deter crime if not completely eliminate it. And that's documented also; it's in the newspapers, it's in crime reports, there's been a lot of studies in areas that determine the number of burglaries that happen overall; how many happen in homes with alarms, how many happen in homes with operation identification stickers; and they find that the homes with the alarms seem to get less attempts . . . to break in.

The most evident contradiction to the official line on protective service involves the disproportionate incidence of false alarms. False warnings have been a most troublesome part of the security industry since its inception:

False alarms have always been a problem with burglary protection devices, so much of a problem that many police departments have banned the popular automatic dialer system that directly alerted the police switchboard when it sensed something wrong. But much of today's alarm equipment is designed not to send a silent distress signal to a central station but to activate bells, sirens, or lights at the home to frighten intruders away.[14]

In questioning the security company representatives on this topic, the reported incidence of false alarms ranges from 75 to 90 percent of all alarms sounded. The local police department also conveyed an inordinately high figure (between 80 and 99 percent). Such circumstances seem to directly challenge the true effectivness of alarm devices in the crime-preventing process.

The effects of such a high frequency of false alarms can be wide-ranging. Public nuisances are created when loud alarms resound throughout a neighborhood during late evening hours. Often, the result of such disturbances is the creation of city ordinances restricting the use of loud burglar alarms. One local ordinance involves fines of up to 150 dollars for alarm subscribers who fail to control their devices.

The magnitude of false alarms has greatly affected the response of law enforcement officials. Obviously, a substantial degree of manpower and time is wasted when investigating such calls. Also, if mistaken alarms occur consistently, law enforcement agents may hesitate or totally ignore cries for help. As one law enforcement officer put it:

The danger in all this is the old business about crying wolf. . . . Our officers, knowing ninety-nine percent are going to be false alarms, can develop a lax mental attitude. We hope they're going to be alert, but the volume and frequency of false alarms may lull them into letting their guard down.[15]

The scope of the false alarm dilemma may also adversely affect the response of security company officials. In one particular case, a local woman lost almost $200,000 in valuables when an alarm firm she employed failed to summon police.[16] In both situations, we see clearly the potentially confounding effects alarms can have upon law enforcement practices.

The extremity of this situation would logically seem to lead to a marked potential conflict between police and security representatives. For example, one security company employee argued that in some cases "the worst advice [for security equipment] can come from police. . . . They are largely unfamiliar with the product and lack the technical know-how." On the other hand, one police officer emphasized caution concerning the effectiveness of alarms: "Alarms can fail you, and I don't think they should ever be installed to replace good locks or lighting."

Despite such potential antagonism, relatively little disaccord seems to exist between the two groups. On both a national and a local level, the need for protective devices is espoused by police and security agents alike. Police see a definite need for residential and commercial burglar alarms, albeit different opinions exist over what type of system works best. Some feel that apprehension should be the primary goal of protective instruments, advocating the use of silent alarms. Others feel that audible alarms provide a very effective means of deterrence. In brief, despite the false alarm problem, official law enforcement agents still feel that burglar alarms function to prevent crime.

### Who's at Fault?

The alarm companies contend that nearly all false alarms are customer initiated. The expertise of security engineers and alarm installers is not questioned, and equipment malfunction is not deemed an important cause in this regard. According to one local representative, there are three major sources of false warnings: (1) "accidents" (caused by subscriber mistakes, humidity, electrical problems, CB radios, etc.), (2) "lack of knowledge" (particularly evident in commercial establishments where, for example, night workers are not informed that a system is operating), and (3) "do-it-yourselfers" (referring to those errors made by consumers when installing protective units or buying faulty equipment). Consequently, both alarm companies and police have resorted to various tactics (e.g., reeducation of customer, frequent call-backs, computer checks) in order to make customers more aware of the false alarm problem.[17]

In spite of the purported attempts to decrease the incidence of false alarms, the indication is that erroneous calls will continue to plague the industry in the future. During one particular interview, a security engineer remarked that present efforts to prevent false alarms had lowered the rate approximately 85 percent (a figure that has not been substantiated by local police studying the problem). Another company representative argued that a current ordinance devised to improve the situation was "ridiculous," since false alarms are bound to continue due to the forgetfulness and ignorance of customers. Nevertheless, the future for alarm sales seems brighter than ever.

The continued existence of a disproportionate percentage of false alarms seems inevitable when viewing the trends of the alarm business. While the extent of growth for the burglar alarm industry is hard to determine precisely, police in some locations estimate that approximately one in five homes in the more affluent neighborhoods are "protected."[18] As more and more security devices are put into operation, the chances for a future increase in erroneous calls are enhanced. Considering the amount of police or guard time that might be spent attending to such calls, the future success of burglar alarms in the "fight against crime" is indeed problematic.

## BURGLAR ALARMS AND SOCIAL CONTROL

Recent writings on crime seem to reflect a general trend toward positivistic modes of criminology. These prominent criminologists emphasize the importance of studying crime from a "social defense" position. In other words, crime should be conceived as a definite threat to social order. In examining the expansion of the burglar alarm industry, we can see that a social defense perspective can be a misleading road to follow.

Legal policy in America also seems headed in the direction of a social defense outlook. Recently, for example, the attorney general of the United States called for mandatory prison sentences for violent offenders and habitual criminals. The movement away from rehabilitative-treatment modes of social control has been steadily gaining strength, and such a trend can be expected to continue. Therefore, it appears that further development of sophisticated preventive-punitive methods of crime control will be instituted. It is the position of this report that the sharp rise in alarm sales may be construed as one component of this general trend—that is, the increased usage of advanced protective services points to a potentially wide-range current of increased social control.

Earlier, I briefly touched upon the present status of the security industry. It will be recalled that the alarm business as a whole is in the midst of a substantial rise in sales and profits. Alarm companies are beginning to enter into large-scale agreements with major residential contractors in order to get hold of the vast home market. And, if present conditions continue to spiral upward, burglar alarms may assume a role similar to other common household appliances. As one salesman predicted:

> *Researcher:* Should everyone have a burglar alarm?
> *Salesman:* I think so. I feel a burglar alarm is a deterrent to crime and someone is gonna go down the street and hit someone that doesn't have one. So if everyone has one it's obviously got to be a major factor—this guy's gonna have to take a little bigger risk, a little bigger gamble to break into a house to get something. So, sure . . . and I think it's probably down the road, . . . we are looking at burglar alarms being wired into homes as electrical wiring is. I think it's going to be here in the near future.

In short, the continued growth of the security business has definite implications for the control of crime. Such implications, however, are more problematic than appears at first glance.

Altheide posited the following hypothesis in his paper on formal security procedures:

A hypothesis worthy of investigation posits a relationship between increased security in retail stores and an increase in street crimes such as muggings. The security may dissuade some persons from risking a burglary, but not robbery; when stores and apartments are harder to rip off, unarmed and frightened pedestrians may well be more inviting.[19]

The problem raised here involves the possibility that, because of protective devices which deter burglary, previously nonviolent individuals may resort to more aggressive means of attaining their objectives. Looking once again at the *Uniform Crime Report* of 1975, we find that 57 percent of all recorded unlawful entries were committed by juveniles. It is clear that the majority of burglaries involve young persons acting in a nonviolent manner.[20] This being the case, the problem articulated by Altheide becomes extremely important. Could it be that by increasing the efficacy and use of security devices, we are also increasing the probability of violent encounters?

The sore spots of security have potentially severe implications for the amateur burglar. If we continue along the present line of argument, it becomes evident that widespread security measures may have disruptive effects on the amateur's role. Thus, the increased employment of security aids and guards may increase the likelihood of force or violence occurring in residential or commercial intrusion. Taking it one step further, if a burglar is discovered in the act, his or her only recourse for escape may be to employ violent tactics. For some burglars, alarms may have a deterrent effect. For others, the protective system may actually increase the chances for more violent actions.

On the other side of the burglary coin lies the professional. This entrepreneur of crime utilizes more sophisticated techniques in order to reach his or her goal. Altheide notes that certain professionals may even employ those instruments devised for protection.

Could it be that security procedures discourage some kinds of untoward acts, e.g., malicious destruction, but not carefully planned burglaries? If so, what good is formal security when professional burglars can take advantage of the procedures designed to stop them? Relatedly, would these professionals be even better at their craft without such precautions?[21]

The queries raised in this instance highlight a significant trouble spot for security services. By taking for granted the preventive function of burglar alarms, we fail to acknowledge the ways in which such services can be manipulated. For example, earlier I mentioned the existence of "con men" who pose as security engineers. One salesman echoed this common concern:

Very few times has anyone ever asked me to show identification. And I think this could be a major problem and I imagine it is going on now today. . . . Where this is how people are getting into people's homes and surveying them and so forth. I am convinced, taking it one step further, that most serious burglaries occur by someone who has been in that house at one point or another.

While no specific data exist regarding the role of prior knowledge in serious burglaries, the gist of the above statement is clear. As long as alarm salesmen operate in a big residential market, certain dishonest characters may play the part of security engineer to plan large-scale burglaries. In this way, burglar alarm protection may, in fact, serve the interests of the professional thief:

> . . . experienced burglars and confidence men and women often rely on the secured members' acceptance of control and assurance of safety. The professional can more easily fulfill his purpose without arousing suspicion when the secured assumed that presence implies acceptance. However, if security procedures are not relied on, or if people lose confidence in their efficacy, then more citizens may become suspicious to the point of personally guarding their property and carrying firearms. Now the trespasser can depend less on stealth and cunning in utilizing security procedures, but must rely more on force which, like the amateur, increases the chances of getting caught, if not physically injured. The implication is that security procedures will impede, but seldom stop, a professional who can see beyond formal security's symbolic shield. Most important, perhaps, is that crafty use of security permits the professional to do his work without personal contact or use of force.[22]

Whether or not burglar alarm protection somehow leads to a rise in violent encounters is a debatable issue (subject to empirical validation). Nevertheless, it is one area that needs to be carefully investigated. Burglary, for the most part, is a crime with economic underpinnings. While some offenders steal for "kicks," others may steal out of necessity or desire. The problems raised by Altheide should alert us to the possibility that security devices may have undesirable consequences of their own. The continued meteoric growth of the security industry may, in the long run, lead to a transformation in the nature of burglary.

## CONCLUSION

The continued elevation in burglar alarm purchases depends heavily on public knowledge of crime. Earlier it was noted that the security engineer's primary role is to heighten a client's awareness through selective reinforcement. Communicating the official law and order reality to consumers perpetuates a concern for protection. While the techniques used by most alarm salesmen are not high-pressured, the efficacy of their tactics is underscored by a rising law and order mentality. Public opinion polls and current sales trends in the security business point to the validity of such a conclusion.

The rising demand for protection has definitive implications for law enforcement practices. The enormity of the false alarm dilemma continues unabated, and the persistence of an extremely high level of erroneous calls seems likely. If this occurs, the cooperation between police and security companies may become increasingly strained. Ironically, police efforts to spread public awareness of the "burglary problem" may, in fact, accelerate such a condition.

The widening forms of protective services in the United States reflect an overall movement toward stronger social control. Dispersing sophisticated security equipment to an expanding market may, in effect, alter the ways in which burglars operate. If we assume that burglar alarms possess a true deterrent value, we must also look for possible undesirable side effects (e.g., a rise in street crimes). The fact that the vast majority of services are distributed among the higher social classes points to the class basis of crime control. (For example, by "protecting" only middle- and upper-class neighborhoods is it possible that lower-class area burglaries will subsequently mushroom?)

We must recognize that legal officials are not the only group with vested interests in the crime problem. Private business groups must also be studied to ascertain their influence on law enforcement. A symbiotic relationships exists between the burglar alarm industry and official control agents. Their mutual use of crime rates and crime-fighting procedures attests to such a connection. Thus, in order to more firmly grasp the reasons for our present-day law and order psychology, economic interests must not be ignored. Clinging to the official ideology of regulatory agents will prevent a critical examination of this predicament.

## NOTES

1. Howard S. Becker, *Outsiders: Studies in the Sociology of Deviance* (New York: The Free Press, 1963), p. 9.
2. *Business Week,* 20 June 1976, pp. 112–14.
3. *Christian Science Monitor,* 16 March 1976, p. 11.
4. *Phoenix Gazette,* 18 May 1977, p. A–14.
5. *Time,* May 24, 1971, pp. 80–82.
6. FBI *Uniform Crime Reports,* 1974.
7. *Business Week,* 20 June 1976, p. 112.
8. *Consumer Reports,* February 1977, pp. 71–77.
9. The identification of "types" of sales presentations should be understood in the Weberian sense.
10. Erving Goffman, *The Presentation of Self in Everyday Life* (Garden City, N.Y.: Doubleday, 1959), p. 17.
11. Richard Quinney, *The Social Reality of Crime* (Boston: Little, Brown, 1970), p. 303.
12. It should be noted here that it is not the purpose of this paper to describe the

criminal attitudes of all security personnel. Such a project is well beyond the scope of this paper.

13. Quinney, *The Social Reality of Crime.*
14. *National Observer,* 8 May 1976, p. 9.
15. *Ibid.*
16. *Phoenix Gazette,* 1 June 1976, p. B–1.
17. A special program in Des Moines, Iowa, enabled alarm dialers to tie into a special phone at police headquarters. During the month of February, the phone rang 175 times —all were false alarms. During a six-month period there were only 17 valid calls out of a total of 1,078! (*National Observer,* 8 May 1976, p. 9.)
18. *Ibid.*
19. David L. Altheide, "The Irony of Security," *Urban Life* 4, 2 (July 1975): 194.
20. Burglary is officially defined as a nonviolent act. The *Uniform Crime Report,* 1975, gives the following definition: ". . . the unlawful entry of a structure to commit a felony or theft. The use of force to gain entry is not required to classify the crime as a burglary" (pp. 27–28).
21. Altheide, "The Irony of Security," p. 193.
22. *Ibid.,* pp. 193–94.

# REFERENCES

Altheide, David L. "The Irony of Security." *Urban Life* 4, 2 (July 1975): 179–96.

Becker, Howard S. *Outsiders: Studies in the Sociology of Deviance.* New York: The Free Press, 1963.

Block, Richard L. "Fear of Crime and Fear of the Police." *Social Problems* 19 (Summer 1971): 91–100.

Bogdan, Robert and Steven J. Taylor. *Introduction to Qualitative Research Methods: A Phenomenological Approach to the Social Sciences.* New York: John Wiley & Sons, 1975.

Davis, Nanette J. *Sociological Constructions of Deviance: Perspectives and Issues in the Field.* Dubuque, Iowa: Wm. C. Brown Company, 1975.

Douglas, Jack D. *American Social Order: Social Rules in a Pluralistic Society.* New York: The Free Press, 1971.

————, ed. *Crime and Justice in American Society.* Indianapolis, Ind.: Bobbs-Merrill, 1971.

————. *Investigative Social Research: Individual and Team Field Research.* Beverly Hills, Calif.: Sage Publications, 1976.

Furstenberg, Frank F. "Public Reaction to Crime in the Streets." *The American Scholar* 40 (Autumn 1971): 601–10.

Goffman, Erving. *The Presentation of Self in Everyday Life.* Garden City, N.Y.: Doubleday, 1959.

Johnson, John M. *Doing Field Research.* New York: The Free Press, 1975.

Lotz, Roy. "Is Public Anxiety over Crime Rational?" Unpublished paper, 1976.

Mauss, Armand L. *Social Problems as Social Movements.* Philadelphia: J. B. Lippincott Company, 1975.

Quinney, Richard. *The Social Reality of Crime.* Boston: Little, Brown, 1970.

Schur, Edwin M. *Labeling Deviant Behavior: Its Sociological Implications.* New York: Harper & Row, 1971.

Shafer, Mark G. "Situational Staging and Context Manipulation." Unpublished Paper, 1976.

Taylor, Ian, Paul Walton, and Jock Young. *The New Criminology: For a Social Theory of Deviance.* New York: Harper & Row, 1973.

Wilson, James Q. *Thinking about Crime.* New York: Basic Books, 1975.

# 5

# *The Social Meanings of Employee Theft*

*David L. Altheide, Patricia A. Adler, Peter Adler, Duane A. Altheide*

Millions of people steal billions of dollars worth of merchandise annually from the businesses and organizations where they work. These are not the "street criminals" whose immoral behavior is presented daily by the news media as a "menace" to society, property, and safety. Nor are they like the wheelers and dealers who pull off lucrative stock frauds, land swindles, bank swindles, or "paper" insurance capers. The people focused on in this essay are predominantly solid, respectable citizens who pay taxes, root for major league stars, believe in the "American way of life" and the virtues of hard work and honesty, and are quickly angered by the thought of welfare chiselers, street hoodlums, and the permissiveness and immorality which they believe is upsetting an established social order. Moreover, few of these people regard themselves as thieves, even though it is estimated that as many as 50 percent of the nation's work force steals (Lipman, 1973). While no one really knows the dollar amount that is taken in cash and property annually, in 1973 the FBI estimated the value at 15 billion dollars. This figure is even more fascinating when compared to the estimated 1 billion dollars lost to street crime in the same year.

Many paradoxes surround employee theft. For one thing, why so much theft occurs while income and purchasing power continue to rise is unclear. The increased amount of formal security does not make much difference; nor do ubiquitous threats of prosecution. Finally, people continue to steal even though public pronouncements—and public support—of law and order efforts increase.

This essay addresses these paradoxes. Drawing on previously published accounts of employee theft, security, historical treatments of work-related activities, and personal experiences and interviews with some three dozen persons in various parts of the United States, we offer a rather different appraisal of the employee theft situation. Our research indicates that the significance of employee theft is part of the total work context and cannot be understood by simply imposing legalistic definitions or by adopting the perspective of the employer. Our aim is to focus on the perspective of workers in order to further understand the rationale and justifications for what millions of people are doing: taking money and merchandise that officially does not belong to them but they nevertheless feel entitled to.

## WHAT IS EMPLOYEE THEFT?

The term "white-collar crime" is broadly used today in reference to illegal or deviant behavior on the part of "business persons." Often the entire labor force is subsumed under this title, from corporate owners to blue-collar and unskilled workers. Coined by E. H. Sutherland (1949), this term initially focused exclusively on business managers and executives who violated laws and regulations *on behalf of their corporations*. Our concern here falls outside this strict usage, portraying employee thieves as " 'enemies within' who surreptitiously steal the assets of the organization and make no contribution to the economic health of the business concern" (Gibbons, 1968:314). Thus, the wider definition of this behavior includes: *pilfering* (stealing in small quantities, petty theft); *chiseling* (a euphemism for cheating or swindling, often in minor quantities [Smigel and Ross, 1970]); and *embezzlement* (destruction or fraudulent appropriation of another's money or merchandise which had been entrusted to one's care). Universal in all types of behavior is the subject's employment: the subject must have a job in order to steal from an employer.

## HOW SOCIOLOGISTS VIEW THEFT: EMPIRICAL STUDIES

Despite the enormity of employee theft, few sociologists have carefully examined it. The major scrutiny of this phenomenon, studied from a legalistic and preventive point of view, has been carried out by security agents (see Curtis, 1960; Hemphill, 1971, 1975). In addition to Donald Cressey's (1953) study of embezzlers—a unique type of employee theft—Melville Dalton (1959), Alvin Gouldner (1954), and Donald Horning (1970) provide the best insights into the foundations of this activity. Brief discussions of the latter three follow.

### Men Who Manage

Melville Dalton (1959) examined how managing was performed by all levels of supervisors in three chemical plants. A career as a research chemist, combined with a sociological perspective, enabled Dalton to observe systematically the relationships among management strata (executives, foremen, staff specialists, and supervisors) and analyze the complex inter-action between formal and informal means of achieving desired ends and rewarding good work. It is particularly within this last area that our interest lies.

Dalton noted that a considerable amount of time, materials, and labor were being allocated to tasks other than the production of goods. He first viewed these misappropriations, strictly forbidden both socially and le-gally, as theft. A depth involvement in the plant initiated a reevaluation; these usages were conceived as forms of unofficial reward and perquisites to management.

Extra benefits were permitted as normal allowances or special bonuses for performance, allocated on an individual or group basis. Items were manufactured, for example, from plant materials by employees working on company time, for most executive managers and retired officials. First, when a person performed extraordinarily in his official and unofficial du-ties, he was rewarded specifically by accomplishment. Upon reaching a certain level, what once was considered a reward became an expected privilege of seniority and rank, which could then be allocated judiciously to subordinates.

Dalton suggests a continuum for evaluating the merit and type of ex-tra-salarial payment. Clearly, theft that is unapproved and unknown to management is the extreme nonlegitimate form of reward (e.g., falsifica-tion of production or time-card records). In contrast is officially sanctioned compensation for top executives through other than direct monetary means (e.g., company automobiles, accommodations, and expense accounts). Be-tween these extremes lies an uncertain gray area of varying degrees of legitimacy: favors and perquisites granted for no obvious service; orga-nized pilfering rights (paid "frolics," picnics, conventions, and trips); use of plant facilities under a community relations guise or no pretext what-soever; a license for lifting plant property that is tied to rank; expense ac-count padding and even the very existence of expense accounts.

Thus, at the executive level, various forms of misappropriations abound, each of which can be deemed illegal yet never subject to judicial action. Rather, these *potentially categorized thefts* are treated as side-payments, so that the boundary between what is honest and dishonest be-comes problematic to insiders as well as outsiders. Institutionalized actions such as these were tolerated by the executives, Dalton argued, because the practical considerations involved were too complicated for any formal system to handle.

This perceived need for flexibility created a situation in which a clear line could no longer be drawn between improper usurpations of company goods and services (theft) and permissible allocation of materials with the intent of producing executive loyalty and morale (rewards). A fusion of feeling to strict theory was noted in all cases by Dalton as the most functional managerial alternative.

### Patterns of Industrial Bureaucracy

A similar study, of a gypsum factory, was undertaken by Alvin Gouldner in 1954, using a team of graduate student researchers. Conducting informal interviews, they sought information pertaining to a Weberian theme: what is the nature of bureaucracy? Gouldner's concern in this work is the transition from a traditional management structure to a rational-legal one.

Our area of interest lies in the beginning of the study, during the former administration. This stage resembles the situation described by Dalton: a loose and friendly place characterized by paternalistic relations. Located in a rural farm setting, close ties existed between supervisors and workers. When interviewed, miners and surfacemen expressed satisfaction with their jobs, giving descriptions of what Gouldner was to call the "indulgency pattern." Workers perceived their bosses as lenient ("they ain't very strict"), allowing the men to operate at their own pace, relax when so desired, and punch in early or out late to earn overtime hours. Company tools could be taken home for personal projects, private possessions repaired on company time and machinery, and reasonable amounts of raw materials and gypsum board freely taken for personal use.

The result of such treatment was a group of loyal, motivated, satisfied, trusting, and trustable employees. Although Gouldner does not specify as much, one would speculate that workers' identification with the plant precluded any noticeable employee theft or destruction of company property.

With the advent of the new plant manager, the indulgency pattern was replaced with the criterion of efficiency. Bureaucratic rules and regulations were established, transforming friendly relations between strata into the impersonality of red tape. The previous leniencies were discontinued and perquisites of the job denied. Knowledge of human nature suggests that these men would not suddenly be satisfied with less than they had been receiving and would therefore turn to other means of obtaining these perquisites—employee theft.

The indulgency phase of this factory is similar to the informal reward system of Dalton's chemical plants. Salaries are supplemented by nontaxable allowances of goods and services, unquestionably costly to top ownership, but valuable in the long run. In a naive attempt to raise profits and efficiency, an inpersonal formal bureaucracy was instituted replacing the earlier situation. Security experts decry such transformations as open invitations to employee theft. The main message of these professionals is: pay your employees a good living wage or your niggardliness will cause them to embezzle; ascertain their personal problems and treat them decently or your indifference and ignorance will cause them to steal. Gouldner's gypsum factory provides a prime example of a trend in many industrial settings today: traditional, personal modes of management and leadership are being replaced with rational-legal, machine-like organizations.

### Blue-Collar Theft

Donald Horning's (1970) study of a midwestern TV plant introduced some refreshingly creative interpretive dimensions into the arena of employee poaching. He sought, first, to clarify his scope of interest and narrow it considerably from the broad, vague concept of white-collar crime. To this end he defined blue-collar theft as "the illegal or unauthorized utilization of facilities or removal and conversion to one's own use of company property or personal property located on the plant premises by nonsalaried personnel employed in the plant."

Conducting semistructured interviews with a stratified sample of 88 men, Horning focused on conceptions of property ownership within the plant. Clear-cut cases where items definitely belonged to the company or to private individuals existed, but as these distinctions became fuzzier on other objects a nebulous residual category of uncertain ownership appeared. Distinct examples of this latter type of property could be found, mostly scrap and consumed materials, but a less clearly defined melange of items could also be characterized as being of uncertain ownership. A continuum thus emerged with the definite private and company property at each extreme, clearly uncertain property in the center, and a fluid and negotiable gray area in between.

The result of such a tripartite division was that property of uncertain ownership could be semi-legitimately picked up and taken by the men. This action was sanctioned by their work group mores as long as such "claiming" remained within tolerable limits of size and quantity. Notions of victimization involved a bipartite division: the company suffered losses from company property and individuals were damaged through theft of personal property. Consequently, filching property of uncertain ownership was perceived as a victimless crime.

Items in the nebulous range were not permanently affixed to this group but could be recalled by company attention to certain ownership status. Any loose system of inventory imposed to control the flow of goods immediately bestowed company property rank on such merchandise. Thus, uncertainty categorization was inversely related to managerial regulation of materials.

Probing further into workers' attitudes toward theft, Horning discovered that almost half the individuals did not view their activities as deviant. In some cases workers' identification with the company was so strong that theft was considered taking from themselves. Most saw it as collecting unwanted and unowned articles. For those who acknowledged their own or other's removal of goods from company premises, around three-quarters had no feelings of guilt. Horning concluded that work groups form mores which specify what kind of object removal is acceptable. Those who remain within these bounds are protected by the group norms, but those who deviate are liable to pangs of conscience. The work group folkways served to limit most pilfering to a relatively harmless degree (for those who adhered), in accord with the production aspirations of management and the desire to maintain the status quo: a relaxed working environment where modest amounts of appropriation are tolerated.

The present study of employee theft remains consistent with the general findings noted above, especially those of Dalton and Horning. We also seek to relate theft to working behavior, but emphasize even more the relevance of group norms and work situations to what employees actually do and how they feel (see Douglas and Johnson, 1977).

## THE SOCIAL CONTEXT OF EMPLOYEE THEFT

All employee theft is not the same. People have different reasons and justifications for taking money and, more typically, merchandise which does not belong to them. Moreover, a vast amount of theft is probably done indirectly through such means as "discounts," "loans," and acquiring "damaged goods." Our research suggests that the various reasons people have for taking things not officially theirs are grounded in general contexts: (1) the history of employer-employee work relations and the way these are translated into each individual's early on-the-job experience; (2) a ubiquitous belief throughout our society in the equality of people and the implications this has for situationally breaching the subordinate-superordinate relationships in the complex division of labor of most work settings; (3) trans-situational constant loyalty to work groups, standards of legitimacy, and fair play; and (4) culturally acceptable vocabularies of motives to legitimize and neutralize what one takes and widespread beliefs about the "objective" meanings of theft and deviance. Each of these contexts for theft will be elaborated and illustrated with specific examples drawn mainly from eight informants who worked in various occupations in different parts of the continental United States during the last decade. Once these important meanings of theft are clarified, the reason formal security is generally ineffective in curtailing work-related theft will become clear.

### Work History and Worker Experience

According to some scholars, workers have been accustomed to obtaining at least part of their wages "in kind" (see Ditton, 1977). Simply stated, wages in kind means that workers expect extras to supplement their objective dollar or material earnings. This was especially true in agrarian seventeenth-century England. After noting that the same legal (or common) rights were available for fuel, fowl, carts, and clay, Jason Ditton (1977:40-41) observes:

> Taken together they supply the means whereby the system of cultivation was maintained, the wants of the tenants other than those met by the product of the arable and the meadows were supplied, and full use made both of the waste and of the land in cultivation at such time as the crops were not in the ground . . . the extended package of common rights not only cemented feudalist and community ties . . . it also made a significant material contribution to the domestic and household budgets of the tenants. Domestic consumption was guaranteed either directly from cultivation, or indirectly from the exercise of right.

This situation changed with the enactment of the Acts of Enclosure, which fundamentally altered the definition of property and, by implication, the rights of those who owned it and those who merely worked it. The overall impact was to define as "criminal" what had previously been custom; to treat "common" as bad; to justify incarceration and persecution of those who dared to "criminalize" the newly defined property through trespass and poaching. As property became more scarce, and rights more precise, the category of poor people grew, many eventually seeking jobs in the urban areas. The long-range effects of this process were of no minor consequence for our present discussion.

> Of crucial interest here, is that this process released into urban life a working population not only used to receiving part of their "wages" in kind . . . but also one still stinging from the effects of the abrupt and cruel negation of those practices in the countryside. As one might expect, and empirical evidence supports, *a major source of irritation to factory owners who took on such "idle" rural labors was their penchant for making off with parts of the workplace or the fruits of their labor there, in addition to their wages* (Ditton, 1977:43) (Emphasis added).

However, the redefinition of land and rights was not completely categorical, because the transition from reciprocal feudal labor obligations to contractual ones was informed by the realization that some sort of in-kind payment does generate a greater commitment to a particular employer. Such "perks" were sanctionable supplements to the wages of a selected few, while those persons not honored by particular occupations and/or not favored by their employers would be accused of pilferage and, more recently, theft. But the line between the two is not as clear in practice as in intent. For one thing, some jobs have built in perks, such as expense accounts, while other jobs have informal perks, such as theft of one loaf of bread per day by employees of a bread factory. In the former case, a bit of extravagance is expected, while in the latter case it may be prosecutable. Thus, between "wage-perks" and "wage-theft" there emerged a rather ambiguous area of "pilferage," an offense without a legal definition. As Ditton (1977:49) observes:

> Occupational theft is either proceeded against as "theft," or is proceeded against because it is defined as a "perk." *This* is the paradox of wage-pilferage systems. Whether or not the theft in question is defined as "theft" or as "just a perk" will depend upon quite arbitrary, extraneous and non-specifiable dictates of those in control . . . that meaning [pilferer] is decided by others, after the action has objectively occurred.

The above remarks regarding the history of wages, pilferage, and theft can be useful in clarifying some aspects of employee theft. Rather than merely looking toward the employee as the culprit, who, if caught, will be punished, the foregoing analysis suggests interaction among employer privileges, the work setting, and employees. For example, Dalton's (1959) study of two chemical manufacturing companies shows that "unofficial rewards" are quicker and more convenient to dispense than promotions. This reward structure is maintained through shared understandings of "reasonable" extra benefits. If these expectations are violated, then the environment is ripe for a new definition to emerge, namely, "employee theft." But even in the latter case, the employers may encourage theft while simultaneously condemning it. The crucial difference is the relative power of the worker to control his work setting and, by implication, the definition of what he is entitled to. Elliot Liebow's (1967:38-39) account of how unskilled streetcorner men may be paid $35 per week and then assumed to steal another $35 illustrates the point that the collusion is more implicit, and certainly less friendly, than in the case noted by Dalton.

> The employer is not in wage-theft collusion with the employee. . . . Were he to have caught Tonk in the act of stealing, he would, of course, have fired him from the job and perhaps called the police as well. . . . The employer knowingly provides the conditions which entice (force) the employee to steal the unpaid value of his labor, but at the same time, he punishes him for theft if he catches him doing it.

The major difference, then, between an expense account and the acquisition of wages-in-kind through rule violation is the criterion of legitimacy. One informant who worked for a large copper company (CC) explained how theft was legitimized, and even encouraged, by the bosses.

> The first thing when I got there, I heard a lot of talk about government jobs. People would laugh and smirk. . . . What government jobs were, they had nothing to do with the government, but people would ask for stuff . . . ask the foreman for stuff, and he would tell a boiler-maker to

make something, and the guy would get it. . . . Mostly people around in the community who were fairly high up in the hierarchy. . . . The first thing that I did was to weld some pipes together for the county sheriff's house . . . they wrote it off by charging it to the smelter. That is pretty interesting, you know, because that is the guy [the sheriff] that I used to look up to, and here he's ripping off the company. . . . I saw it as a ripoff; the other guys saw it as a government job; he's the sheriff, he deserves that. . . .

The connection between employer and employee definitions of appropriateness and ownership is more evident when the former clearly approves illegitimate acts among the latter. This is especially true when the victim is the customer. Sam Ruddy's (1977) study of the organization of a dog racing track shows that the management was continually aware that employees were violating company policy, and making a profit from their deviations. For example, two sisters who sold reserve seats on a first-come, first-served basis would hold onto choice tickets and inflate the prices for last-minute arrivals. Similarly, the reservationists would sell tickets to early arrivers who had no reservations but were "good tippers." This often created problems when the reservation holders would arrive a bit later, only to find that their seats were taken. Other employees would usually be blamed for the "foul up." This practice had been occurring for nearly eight years, and periodically the management would ritually "chew out" the reservationists. However, since the reservationists were loyal to the company and could be trusted to competently perform their duties and always be at work, their rule violations were tolerated. Moreover, it is important to note that such practices would have been less common if the public who purchased illegitimate reservations with extra "tips" did not approve of such practices in this particular situation. Most of the patrons at the track, like their co-conspirators throughout society, simply deduce that such practices occur and that employees can render any organization vulnerable. Similarly, supervisors of bread truck drivers who were collecting "tips" from customers often unofficially condoned the practice. One informant speculated that one reason supervisors were not "hard-assed" about the "price irregularities" was that they shared sentiments about the relatively low benefits of the job.

If you figure it out, we're making less than $2 an hour. It is hard work, dirty, lots of pressures, traffic, and it wasn't the best job in the world if you didn't have these fringe benefits, so how are they going to keep people if they put too much pressure on them, if they don't let you have this extra? So there is also incentive for them to go along with it.

Wages-in-kind, or extras to which one feels entitled, are not only part of our cultural history; they are also part of a vast number of people's early socialization experience into the world of work. Since many of the people one works with are already involved in some sort of direct theft, this process becomes normal and routine. More commonly, however, a new worker learns that his or her effort and time on the job should be self-regulated according to group standards which may clash with the employer's ideals. To do otherwise is to be called a "rate buster," a "brown noser," an "ass kisser," and other derogatory names. Most importantly, these terms mark off group boundaries; colleagues are supposed to be more important to a worker than a boss or employer who seeks to regulate all of them. Many researchers have found that group norms limit output. One study indicated that anyone who did not perform adequately was labeled a "chiseler" (see Homans, 1950). An informant who began his work career in a copper plant had to learn this: "I was pretty much of a deviant because I was this ideological college student. . . . I was slowly indoctrinated, and if I had stayed up there another two years, I would have probably been doing the same stuff. . . . I went up there ready to work, and I was working my ass off, and they were laughing at me."

A similar situation was reported by one of the researchers. After a young worker was hired by a family friend, he was told that his new boss expected him to work hard, not waste time, and set an example around the plant. The young man did just that. He spent time cleaning up when fellow workers were "taking a break," and when everything was clean, he would run errands and do one of a hundred little things that any worker knows are unnecessary. After he worked this way for several hours, one of the older and more experienced workers explained to the novice that all this "shit" was unnecessary and, most important, made the rest of them look bad since they appeared to be just standing around in contrast to the busy new hiree. When the first warning to "cool it" was not heeded, this same veteran threatened to "knock the shit" out of the eager beaver. It was then that the young man understood.

The above examples illustrate that while some workers may attach certain moral meanings to "doing a good job," their more experienced co-workers have other priorities and meanings of labor. This is especially true with time and "taking breaks," and any effort by management to push the workers harder is bound to be met with resentment and ingenious ways of combating this requirement. One worker for a large store, RIPCITY, explained how management would be cooled out.

The managers didn't like the free time most lease personnel had. In electronics we always watched television. We would just stand around or else sit in our sound room watching television. We even constructed a speaker which we mounted in our sound room and plugged the other end into a television in the television section. This way we could sit down and have a coke or snack or whatever, and never miss what was going on the television. . . . Managers were also irritated because we would eat snacks and drink cokes in our sound room. . . . Our luxuries also caused some jealousy among other employees because of our "easy" jobs. . . . When we didn't have a potential customer we would just fuck off. . . . The managers tried to thwart us but to no avail. . . . [But] when we were in the process of planning a rip-off in our department, we would try not to agitate the managers.

The belief that management did not really care about the workers, but were more interested in their careers and commissions, was further supported by the seemingly indiscriminate laying off and transferring of employees to another store. This general attitude weighed heavily in the situated decision to "rip-off" a couple of chain saws.

It almost became a game. We hated the new store, we hated the guys who would come over and bug us, they took away our TV, just totally pissed off about it. So here were these two chain saws, and we figured we'll get these out of here; it will make the store managers look bad. You had all these bosses and they all wanted to exert their authority in one way or another, so they were constantly looking over you, checking over you, acting like they were very distrustful of you . . . there was the big window where 1 and 2's offices are, and they can see over the whole store . . . so they were up there doing their office work and they would constantly watch your behavior.

One way of monitoring the salespersons at this particular store was to check on them with "shoppers," persons who pretended to be customers but would carefully note every detail of the sales staff and file a report on them. The same employee explained what she or her coworkers thought about these "shoppers" and what measures could be taken to protect themselves.

[The employees] don't like them. . . . They see it as kind of conniving, that the people don't trust you, that the bosses don't trust you. . . . They used to get real up tight about it, because they could predict that every two or three months it was time to start watching out for the shoppers . . . they purchase small things, so you could kind of watch for those people.

Another reason socialization into the work experience promotes the wages-in-kind notion is even more practical. Not only is agreement to "go along with the way things are done around here" related to employee theft, but often the test of individual membership is one's willingness to cover or protect unofficial acts by one's coworkers. One example is "Lew's" experience as a bread truck driver in New York City. Eager to get along with his coworkers and determined to succeed in this new job, Lew carefully noted how to make deliveries, keep records, and interact with customers. He also learned that with the periodic mistakes in giving owners credit for stale goods, merchandise would have to be made up out of his own pocket. That was part of company policy. The not infrequent occurrence of "coming up short" cut deeply into an already depressed wage, but he just thought that over a period of time fewer mistakes would occur, and things would get better. They did not.

> It was easy to lose money. You come home and you tell your wife I was short two bucks today; she passes it off. You come back another time and you're short, and she says, you know, you're going to have to quit the job . . . if this is a trend, we can't live on $80 a week if you're bringing home a hundred, and if you have to pay out $10 or $20 a week just to work there, you need another job. And you know, you start looking around, and for my education there was not that many alternatives. . . . When it really hits you hard . . . is when you come up $8 short and you look for an hour (for the mistake) and you're in a panic you're losing time and you want to go home, and you can't find it, that's when you start saying, "well shit, I've got to make this up."

Lew eventually did figure out how to do it. During the five years he worked with the bread company he cleared more than $25,000 above his normal salary. This tidy bonus was a product of long-term involvement with veteran drivers who had mastered the techniques of padding bills, duplicating bills, "shoplifting" or removing merchandise just placed in a store, and other procedures. He explained:

> In the early days you always appeared to make it look like a mistake. You would go in—I would call it shoplifting—put your stuff away and when nobody was looking, put it back on the rack and go sell it to somebody else. . . . On one route I had fruit slices and fruit bars; fruit bars were .47¢ and fruit slices ran .12¢ each, and you could lay them flat underneath a box. . . . I must have sold some of them three or four hundred times, they were so beat up. . . . They had no selling date because of all the preservatives so if I couldn't take them out one day, I would take them out another day.

Not only were the wages of theft extremely good for his more affluent lifestyle, but they were also ritualistically and symbolically tied to becoming a successful employee, one who gets along well. For one thing, he discovered that his coworkers expected him to charge what they charged customers; to do otherwise would alert customers to a discrepancy which in turn might lead them to more carefully watch the regular driver. Lew explained how he in turn helped socialize other new drivers: "So the customers would not detect that I was different, I would tell him how to do various stores . . . the ones that were good for me, I wanted to make sure that he didn't screw them up. . . ."

But it is not always easy to socialize somebody into a job who is unwilling to go along with the practical problems. Lew explained how he came to educate novices.

> A good example was when I had my route, when I was stealing about $40 a day. I got a new "swing man" [a substitute] and I am breaking him in. I can't steal if I don't know who he is. . . . The consideration I have to operate with is that if he does not operate the same way I do, then it might expose me. . . . So you feel him out, you ask him if he is making enough money, how many kids you got, etc., and then you might intimate that you steal. . . . You might say, one of the problems you're going to have here is coming up short of money, but there's ways to avoid it. That's the critical point.

Our informant verified the importance of checking out new workers in order to make sure they are "okay."

> When my manager told the other personnel I was a nice guy and I was O.K. (that is, I would never snitch on someone) I was automatically taken in on some capers. Getting behind the scenes like this without anyone knowing who you are would take a long time. This is because no one likes to do some act which could get them fired, in front of a stranger or someone you didn't know very well.

The above examples, and others that will follow, suggest that being a competent worker is difficult because of the need for artful reconciliation between often conflicting demands—those of the employer and one's fellow employees. Over a period of time, however, and as a person obtains more work experience, the dilemma is less noticeable and is likely to arise only in moments of reflection. Just as work experience promotes job efficiency and expertise, it also teaches workers how to evaluate their work situation as they follow the unstated, but very real, rules about "getting along."

### Belief in the Equality of Workers and Employers

Any worker's socialization into the world of work will be influenced by the prevailing standards of his or her prework experience, as well as the standards of the work group that is entered. The latter will be dealt with in the next section, but the present focus is on the impact of the value of equality on work situations.

It is commonplace for employees, like street criminals, to steal for greed and fun; those cases do not require a lot of explaining. However, it is also true that many employees steal for revenge and dignity. They see their wages-in-kind as not only something they are entitled to, but also as a way of "getting back" at a boss or supervisor who made an unkind remark or, probably more common, insisted that a worker show up for overtime. Indeed, workers will even resort to sabotage in order "to show that bastard that he can't talk to me that way." One informant told about a custodian who shoved his broom through a box of expensive dishes "to teach the management for not giving him a day off." Other incidents occurred in RIPCITY which led employees to "get back."

> The detached or superior attitudes of RIPCITY managers actually triggered some thefts. For instance, after a clean-up boy was lectured on the correct way to mop floors, the boy took several books to show the manager he was not to be belittled. Now the books were not made known to the manager, but were shown to friends with a story of how he showed the manager. . . . These types of thefts also occurred when the employees felt they had been screwed out of something. For instance, one employee took a shirt from men's wear because he didn't get time and a half for working a Sunday.

The source of worker resentment is, ironically, the cultural value of equality and the existence of differential rewards (e.g., income and prestige) for those persons regarded as the most competent, responsible, and trustworthy. In the work context, this means that employers and supervisors are given more authority and the concomitant increments in income and prestige. It also means that the people who, in a given work setting, make the most money, have the most authority, and often are presumed to do the least amount of work are the same people who give orders to their "subordinates." One assistant parts manager who sold stolen auto parts to coworkers and customers felt this way. According to an informant, "He was in the position, 'I've been here eight years . . . the old owner just puts the shits to me, he doesn't pay me shit, you know. I am working down here nearly 60 hours a week, and the manager don't do shit; I am doing all his work; he is on a free ride.' "

Individual worker resentment is less evident if he or she believes the superordinate person (boss or supervisor) is deserving of this power and/or does not abuse it. However, this is seldom the case since too many daily experiences—in a variety of different jobs—convince workers that "a suck system is operating" whereby a few people obtain their positions through personal political efforts and not some objective standard of competence. As one worker at a truck-stop in the northwestern United States put it, "around here, it is not who you know, but who you blow." The sexual connotation is not accidental since this worker, like many others, believes that supervisors and bosses could only get where they are by humiliating themselves before management. One logical extension of this mode of thinking is that any supervisor is likely to be seen as a "kiss ass," or "brown noser," terms obviously demeaning of anyone who would stoop so low. Indeed, the idea of anyone engaging in "brown nosing" is often regarded as symbolic of their substantial self and as an explanation for the treatment of subordinates. Our informant in RIPCITY and his coworkers could artfully derogate the management who engaged in such practice and simultaneously take advantage of it for "ripping off."

> The managers went so much by the book, and were so detached from the personnel, that they actually encouraged stealing. The managers had such set routines that it was easy to spot them and work around them. Although there were three offices upstairs, the managers always talked and discussed matters in the grill. . . . The topics were varied but most of these meetings were nothing more than "brownnosing sessions." Well, when all managers, or just even two, are in the grill it's rip city. It's time for the employees to rip items off without fear of a manager walking up on them in the middle of the heist.

Americans are especially susceptible to resentment toward superiors since part of the cultural myth is that one's social standing is a direct reflection of one's effort and talent. Relatedly, individual success is presumed to be at least partially indicated by occupational success. The major practical problem with this ideal is that it is impossible for everyone to "succeed" by reaching the top; there are more climbers than there are rungs to climb. This fear of failure—that is, relative to others—is a source of repression and scapegoating. Stated differently, workers who must take orders often find themselves in the same cognitive situation as oppressed minority groups or even dominant group members who believe their disadvantage is caused by some conniving ethnic group, such as "the Jews." Just as the literature in the field of race and ethnic relations reflects both the widespread application of group blame for seemingly unrelated problems, including the stigmatizing stereotypes, the nature of worker and employee relations reflects the impact and negotiation of the meanings of subordination in a social and cultural context of "equality of opportunity." In brief, then, many Americans do not like the idea of being subordinate, and they resist it even more when, in the day-to-day rituals of interaction, they are often reminded that the words and actions of some person(s) influences their lives more than the converse. When our informant who worked for a large copper company was asked if the employees, who stole a lot of material despite their relatively high wages ($8 to $10 an hour), were loyal, he replied:

> Not outwardly. Everybody is pretty pissed off most of the time. There is loyalty. I think to be a salaried employee you have to be loyal. Those guys in management have to be loyal, and everybody else has to be unloyal. That is just the way it is. A lot of people bitched all the time. They felt that CC had complete control over them. One guy told me—the guy who searched my lunch box, and I didn't think he could do it—he told me flat out that CC can do whatever they want to. And I said

"bullshit," you know, I got pretty heated. I don't like to be told what I can do and what I can't. . . . That's the way people feel.

The cultural context of the meaning of equality, along with concrete experience about the revulsion at being subordinate to another, can give rise to *situated* acts of resentment. This becomes even more likely when it is noted that workers have family and friends who are also likely to resent subordinate relations with employers. These people are often a significant audience for a worker to symbolically liberate himself from the "bullshit" by "beating the system." This can be done by extracting wages-in-kind through merchandise, obtaining gifts and/or favors for friends and relatives, or simply goofing off, obtaining extra overtime, and the like. One informant explained why well-paid copper workers would routinely take tools and other materials. "It was like, well, they would come off the job with all kinds of garbage on them, like acid had got on their shirt or something, and would say, 'I'll take this wrench. I mean they owe it to me.' Or, 'I've stayed in this shitty town for seven years; they owe it to me.'"

The major importance of such acts is their symbolic value of showing that there are many players in the game of power and prestige besides the bosses, who are perceived as wanting to run things.

The importance of not being "put down" or not appreciated was evident in several of our interviews. While we do not mean to imply that resentment and revenge are the only reasons people steal, our data suggest that commitment to certain individual employers can make a large difference. One worker, "Tara," had been employed in two record stores; one she stole from and the other she did not. She explained why she removed an average of 15 albums a night for several months.

I stole there all the time, towards the end I did, just because I didn't like him at all. . . . It wasn't the money, because I could have gotten a raise. Just, I would do things and there was never any appreciation, so I didn't want to give out any more. . . . He didn't give anything at all. He acted like everything was expected of you. Like, I worked very hard and I never got anything, not even a thank you or something. That's how most of them felt. They just didn't like him; he just wasn't a good person.

Even after she quit the job, she returned to steal records.

I still go back and steal. . . . I know the people, and he's not there, so they just let me take them . . . about five albums twice a month . . . about once a week for tapes.

The other record store was different, however.

Working for them, you just didn't want to steal; there was no reason

to . . . you liked to work there. It was like, if you wanted an album
that bad you could just ask the manager and he would have given it to
you. . . . They would do anything you wanted. If you wanted a raise,
they'd get one for you, and you could take off any time.

Another experienced young employee felt that getting along well with
one's boss, plus worker satisfaction, was more important than wages.

Then, again, I have known guys who work at some places where they are
really satisfied with their job, and the guy they work for is really super—
like at the racquet ball courts. They don't get paid much, but the benefits
are really good, they can come in and play for free. There's lots of wearing apparel, racquets, and things like this, but I have never known of
anyone to steal anything from that place. . . . They told me that they
would buy things for me with their discount, but all they have is praise
for what happens. The main guy comes in, takes them out to big steak
dinners, is really super nice to them. They feel privileged to have such
a good job. That is a very unique place. . . . I used to work with a guy
in another place who was a big thief at the grocery store. . . . We used
to help each other out taking liquor and things, so I just kind of casually
brought it up that I needed some new shirts, some new shorts, so he
said I can sell them to you for a discount but I can't really steal them
. . . it's not that he is afraid of getting caught because he is the only
one there at night . . . and on inventory they would never know when
they were sold. He feels that he would really hurt the guy if he did this,
and he doesn't want to do it; he feels a sense of pride.

This informant, who was quite adept at recruiting people to assist
him in periodic rip-offs, was convinced that a bad feeling about one's job
and how superordinates treated workers was essential for a commitment
to "rip them off."

That's more or less what I look for, like when I need somebody to help
me [steal]. If you find a person the day before who was really pissed
off, and they're more than ready, e.g., 'yeah, I want to teach these guys
a lesson,' . . . it is just that they feel good inside.

The significance of theft as a symbol of personal control is perhaps
best understood as an occupational version of being "cool." In popular
usage, to be cool is to be above the humdrum of everyday activities, especially the problems that potentially plague us all (see Lyman and Scott,
1970). This includes authority. The more general value of being cool is
that it reflects self-control and an extraordinary ability to define one's activity and concerns regardless of the situation. To be flustered, confused,
and subservient to another is the opposite of cool. We know of dozens of
examples where workers took merchandise and/or services as a way of
demonstrating to their significant others (e.g., family, friends, and cowork-

ers) that they were in control of the situation and themselves. One of our informants enjoys instructing family members on the varieties of theft and shows little sympathy for anyone who suffers a "guilty conscience" from such activities. Another informant explained how her father encouraged theft.

> I used to steal for my dad because he is into music and he didn't have money for an album so I would steal for him. . . . The first time I did he asked if I could get an album for him. I said I didn't have any money, and he said "neither do I." And he goes, "could you get it anyway" . . . that surprised me. So I just came home with the album and he said, "good, you got it."

The emphasis given to the audience a worker is concerned with suggests that employee theft is not purely utilitarian in an economic sense. People do not steal just because they do not make enough money; they steal because of what it means to do so. One informant told us about an entire copper town in Arizona operated by a large company. Residents of this town work in either the mine or the mill and make excellent wages, usually in excess of eight dollars an hour. But they take a lot of merchandise, too. As one worker put it, "I've given [this company] ten years of my life; I think I deserve a little bonus." Most of his friends shared this sentiment, and their homes and garages reflected it. Many have welding shops and complete automobile tool sets, compliments of the company. So rampant is the practice of "taking something home" that tools are replaced in pairs, "one for the job and one for me." The most extreme example our informant knew about was one worker who took home a new eight-cylinder automobile engine!

Knowledge of such spectacular heists is shared among workers, who may then expand their own "reasonable limits" on what one can legitimately get away with. Legitimate here means one thing to management but something else to the workers. The former bread truck driver put it this way.

> The stealing was blatant. . . . A lot of people weren't bashful about it at all. They didn't say, look, you've got to steal from the grocer; they'd say, look, you've got to start "clipping," you've got to start "hitting" them. . . . People used to feel you out and as soon as they find out you're *legitimate* and they ask you a few questions and determine your personality, they'd say, look, the only way you're going to make it is if you make some off the grocer.

A worker for the copper company was also aware of the flexible norms of legitimacy.

> One guy told me in all seriousness, "I think everybody steals." . . . He said "in one way or another, even if you are just sitting down on the

job, you're stealing." There was even a quota. Some stupid guy figured out how much workers were taking, something like $300 a year. Some guys said, "I'm behind schedule, hell, there's only three months left in the year and I don't have my $300!"

A good example of how worker practices influence fellow workers is the way employees take advantage of overtime. One informant who studied detectives in an eastern city noted that some of these men nearly doubled their salaries with overtime payments, while most increased it by approximately one fourth. Most important, a large portion of this extra time was not necessary to do their work but was selectively taken by extending an assignment. When superiors periodically urge employees to reduce overtime or, in some cases, prohibit future overtime—that is, proclaim that it will not be compensated—then detectives and other employees may react by work "slowdowns." In practical terms this means that arrests and actual police work will stop two hours or so before the end of a shift because the resulting paper work could extend beyond a regular eight-hour work day into uncompensated overtime. Indeed, one informant who worked as a security officer for a large chain store explained that experienced guards seldom apprehend a shoplifter during the last two or three hours of their shifts; to do so is to "contribute your own time," since the paper work and follow up take so long.

In sum, workers are not powerless or unaware of the important distinctions between them and their bosses. However, on-the-job experience plus growing up in a cultural milieu that emphasizes success based on ability promote an orientation toward situated symbolic and financial victories.

### Work Group Loyalty

Previous pages have noted some of the cultural content which infuses work in our society, especially an orientation toward employee theft. This section focuses on the somewhat ironic role of the employee work group in both promoting and limiting the nature and extreme of employee theft. It is ironic because, on the one hand, employees have many incentives for various forms of theft while, on the other hand, only a few of these are taken advantage of, and the extent of such theft is remarkably limited compared to what it could be.

An employee in a men's clothing store reflected on this possibility; he had purchased several pairs of shoes on a special discount for his friends.

When I think about it . . . I could have stolen so much merchandise because I was in that store so many evenings by myself, and the only thing that I ever did was buy things at a discount for my friends. . . . I never ripped anything off, but a lot of people did and the opportunities were really there.

The significance of group norm pressures on behavior have been noted in several decades of research in the social sciences, although its meaning for employee theft has consistently been overlooked (see Smigel and Ross, 1970). As noted previously, one becomes a worker by becoming acquainted with technique, skills, and such, as well as a vocabulary and orientation. Anyone who has ever worked on any kind of job realizes the importance of getting along with one's fellows. Our point is simply that employee theft is one part of this process. Not only does one learn how and what to steal, but one is also expected to participate in the theft directly, or indirectly by not informing on one's friends. The man referred to earlier who worked for the large copper company could recall only one person who didn't steal. "I knew one guy who didn't take anything. He was kind of religious, and everybody made fun of him." But in most cases the employees simply work together. An informant with experience in "getting along with" coworkers in a supermarket explained.

> Cashiers would say, "I am kind of hungry," and ask a box boy to check the shelves to see if anything is SPOILED. New guys would say, gee uh, I couldn't find anything, but experienced guys would know that you find something, and rip, here's one, and you take it up front and you eat half of it, and then you take the other half back to the spoil shelf so the store gets credit for it. . . . When you did take your break it was very common to pick out whatever you wanted.

The same informant, working in another store, found a similar situation occurring.

> Most everyone working at the store occasionally took candy or cookies which had been opened or torn accidentally. Most of the time the thief tore open the packages himself and then placed the blame on some asshole customer. This is a common joke and always good for a few laughs. One point that must be made is that the bag must be left on the shelf and the thief just grabs a handful and walks off. . . . The gentlemen in receiving always seem to have a battered box of milky ways or crunch bars laying around. If management asked what happened, they say the box fell off the shelf or something. Now these boxes are actually battered open for realism. I was present (and helped) with two accidental batterings. The boxes are dropped, thrown, kicked, and hit with mops or brooms till a corner or side is split open and the goodies fall out. Usually around 4 bars (good ones) are taken out and then the box is placed in the stock room shelves. These bars are not for everyone, for if management discovers a half empty box, surely they will put 2 and 2 together. This is why usually only 4 bars are taken out of each box.

In this case, the store really does not lose anything since it gets "credit" from the manufacturer and inventories will balance. However, in other cases the store is the loser, inventories will not account for the items, and shoplifters may be blamed for this shrinkage. The supermarket veteran again supplies the example.

> One thing that was very common was for people to pitch in and get one receipt for .45¢ or whatever, and a different night each person would do it, and say "do you want my receipt for your break?" So if someone comes back and asks if you have a receipt for that chicken or whatever, you can show them. So what happens is that five employees would have chicken that day for the price of one.

In some cases supervisors, especially if they are former workers, will share the perspective and sentiments of their new charges. John Bradford's (1976) study of post office workers illustrates supervisory support of "killing time." Postal workers who deliver mail jealously guard preferred routes. All routes are designated as taking a certain amount of time to complete, but if the supervisory people believe a route can be completed more quickly, it may be lengthened. Seldom do postal workers require the allotted time to do their work, and on most days they can complete their mail delivery in half or three-fourths of the time allotted. They may simply go slower, or they may change clothes and frequent a massage parlor, bar, play cards, go home and sleep, watch girls, or engage in a host of other activities. Supervisors realize this and often share the postman's perspective, since they know that on some days the mail is heavier and these letter carriers have to "really hump." Nevertheless, postal regulations prohibit featherbedding, and supervisors are continually urged to take stock of route additions and deletions in order to make the entire operation more efficient. However, when novice substitutes complete the route in less time than is "officially allotted" and broadcast their accomplishment to coworkers, supervisors seldom change the route or castigate the regular delivery person for going too slow. In several cases observed by Bradford, supervisors gave the braggart substitute a "shit work assignment" to keep him busy so that he "would learn his lesson" to never return to the substation before he "should be finished." In one case, a veteran letter carrier who returned from a vacation threatened to break the novice's legs if he ever again "ran through my route and makes me look bad." Such informal control is recognized and condoned by many supervisors. As the bread truck driver who cleared thousands of dollars in "tips" put it: "The supervisors had to know. . . . Like when I was a swingman, the supervisor told me that one of the grocers thought I was stealing from him . . . he is telling me to not do it again—not from this guy."

An employee for a large chain store learned that management condoned "good deals" by marking down merchandise. After noting that two stock boys had been caught for stealing, she talked about how most other rule violations seemed to be rationalized:

Like one time I had cleaned up the entire back room, and there was a lot of damaged merchandise and opened packages, and I put all that to one side. One of the bosses came in the next day and commented on how nice the stock room looked, and thanks for doing it, and so forth, and I told him where all the damaged stuff was, and among it was some diapers. My sister was expecting a baby and I said gosh, I would sure like to have these diapers . . . he said, "okay . . . we'll just charge her ten cents for them, so she has a sales receipt, put them in a bag, and put some tape on it so she can get out the back door." *So, to me that was kind of stealing because they had the plastic, but the manager okayed it. . . . Now that went on in managing all the time.*

Not only would management at this store permit employees to obtain extras, but they would produce "damaged merchandise" for their own benefit as well.

Pillows, great big stuffed pillows in the domestic department, we put this stuff on the back shelf in the stock room, where it was dusty, the kind of things you should cover up. You know, I think everybody knows that, commonsense. It would get dirty, and a few months later (someone would say) well, gee these things are dirty, we can't sell them; mark them down to, maybe ninety-nine cents. *The manager would have to okay it, and the manager would go up and purchase three.*

Supervisors and coworkers set standards of acceptable rule violations and, conversely, establish limits beyond which one must not go. For example, cashiers in supermarkets could take advantage of their position by letting friends take out large purchases. But, according to one informant, this is rare, since it might become too obvious to managers, and if someone were caught, all cashiers would be more carefully watched. However, small items are allowed to pass. An informant explained:

What the cashiers had going was they would send in a son or somebody —and we used to do it for each other, and when I worked the cash register I would do it for other guys—they would come up with some stuff that they were buying for their Mom or whoever, and say "I need some extra cash. Can you make it a little short?" So you would shove the stuff down the counter, charging them one price while throwing down four or five items. . . . Nobody really took advantage of it; it was used mostly with a small number of items.

Similarly, in a truck stop it was understood that selected individuals —not employed by the truck stop—could work on their cars at certain times, when no "prick bosses" were around. But it was also understood that this should not be done too frequently or the shift boss could get in trouble. When this occurred, the "official rules" would have to be temporarily enforced and certain other privileges would be suspended. Similarly, workers knew that materials such as oil and small items like nuts and screws could be taken home for private use, but larger items like batteries and tires should not be "ripped off" because they would be missed, and all employees would be suspected. The net result would be fewer freedoms and less opportunity to take advantage of an otherwise vulnerable situation. "Tara's" experience in removing record albums from the record store illustrates the taken-for-granted limits on the nature and extent of successful theft.

> Like he [manager] was into jazz, and a lot of the jazz albums you wouldn't take because he knew exactly what was in the jazz section, so if you wanted to take jazz it would have to be something real new and that you had a lot of.

The work group simultaneously promotes and limits employee theft in another way. Supervisory personnel realize that worker compliance is more likely to be obtained by keeping a low profile and providing workers with unofficial bonuses in the form of extra break time and services and/or merchandise. As workers pass through employment careers, they realize that there are always ways to get around the rules and honor requests for small favors, but the most successful supervisors are able to define what wages-in-kind will keep worker loyalty. If one's subordinates are not supportive, then jobs will not be done or they will be done strictly "by the book," which, as any worker knows, is but another way of violating good faith and "showing them" who really runs things. With few exceptions, working "by the book" means going slower and often less competently. The net effect of "being a good guy" to one's charges in order to get the job done is meeting rather vague expectations about "taking it easy" and providing the favors mentioned above. This is particularly true on unpopular shifts like "graveyard," which, according to numerous informants, appears to be a quasi-institutionalized time for employee theft. For example, in service station jobs and all-night restaurants, fewer customers must be served so there is usually more lax time. Although employees have duties to perform, usually clean-up, it is commonly understood that working the late hour entitles them to a few more privileges than the day shift. An informant who worked for a large supermarket described some of the extra privileges that accompanied working late.

> When we used to stock, we used to work late. If you were working in the milk section there was all this orange juice and stuff; what you'd do is gulp down about half of it and take it back and fill it up with water and then put it back on the shelf. . . . Everyone used to do that. . . . The produce was always eaten, especially on late night shifts where there was only one manager, and everyone else was in a different area. . . .

They would just eat what they wanted. . . . A lot of times you might want to eat something from a jar or bottle. After you'd eat it, you'd break the bottle . . . you'd save the lid to let the store get credit for it.

The work group also restricts and limits theft by defining what can be taken and from whom. Other researchers have noted, for example, that some employees learn that certain materials, for example, "scrap," are available to take since "it does not belong to anybody" (see Smigel and Ross, 1970). Workers in large companies are probably also more prone to removing merchandise because they understand how items are marked up and have witnessed many instances of customers being "ripped off" by the company. An informant who took auto parts from the company he worked for and sold them to customers for a large discount explained:

When I got the sense that there was a 50% mark up from wholesale to retail, and then you think, well they'll sell this to me for wholesale, and you think they're only paying me $2.30 an hour, and I am selling several thousand dollars of this stuff a month, and I am only making a few hundred; hell, I'll just take this damn thing. Why should I have to pay half price for it?

Fellow workers not only teach an employee how to obtain wages-in-kind, but are also often accomplices. This was true at RIPCITY.

One department had 3 people working in it: myself, Bill, and the manager. . . . We were all members of the same health club and spent lots of our free time with each other. Since we were all good friends we could help each other. Often we would confer with each other on the best way to steal something. By working together we lessened the possibilities of getting caught and acquired many items which took two people to help steal.

Indeed, it is difficult in most jobs to successfully obtain large "extras" without the cooperation and assistance of others. An informant who stole more than $1,000 worth of merchandise from a music store explained how friendship and being a "good person" exacts a price, while also providing rewards.

The first time I ever went in, I had just started playing with his band, and I told him I needed a cymbal, and he said, come in and see me and we'll work out a deal. So while we were there, I bought a large cymbal and a smaller one. He sold me the larger one for a discount anyway and then he slipped the other one underneath it, so I was buying two for less than the price of one. And then he just threw a stand in too, and so I owed him a favor. . . . If I had said "no, I am not going to help you," you feel kind of guilty . . . it is usually expected that if someone does you a favor that they will ask you to do something back. As a matter of fact, when he first said it, he said, "I might need your help later in getting something for myself," and so I said, sure.

One's work and ethical autonomy is also shaped by the division of labor in a setting; specialization demands cooperation if a worker's opportunities for theft are not to be limited by his/her particular job. The way employees at a large auto dealership cooperated illustrates this.

> People did different things. See, I didn't do oil changes so I didn't get oil, but guys on the other side would, so I would ask them for oil, and they'd say, "well yeah, I need some moulding for the side of my truck," and since I was doing the moulding, I would go up and ask for 25 feet and probably use only about 15, so no one is really paying for it except the boss.

And there are occasions when reciprocal relationships prompt "gift giving" between employees. An informant with a large chain store explained:

> The Jewelry Department is where large items start getting taken. The manager of this department could not be swayed into any shady deal. However, the sales girls were very willing. One girl became a very good friend and we often shared many coffee breaks. Although she refused to steal for herself, she would steal for a friend or else ask you to steal something for her. This particular lease department had its own cash register so this made things somewhat easier. Instead of actually stealing something outright, you could buy it for a reduced price. Sam bought a $50 watch for $7. I purchased a $35 turquoise choker for $5. Then we would walk out of the store with a receipt and the merchandise in a brown bag. Since this particular girl took inventory for jewelry, she took care of the missing volume. She never did explain how she did it, and when I inquired about it she just said, "don't worry, I won't get in trouble." When our department closed down and we went to the other store, we exchanged "gifts" with her. I was given a $50 turquoise ring; Sam received a $35 ring, and we gave her an $80 AM-FM portable cassette player. All of these "gifts" were stolen from our respective departments. These "gifts" were going away presents to each other. The rings were handed out over the counter to us and her radio was taken out by me by saying it was going to the repair shop.

We have stressed the situated nature of theft; it is controlled and regulated in most cases by the people who do it. Management often mistakenly assumes that few employees take things or take advantage of their job situations for personal gain because they fear getting caught. While this is true in some situations, our informants were almost unanimous in their disregard for security procedures. The reason is simple—they understood how security worked and could easily circumvent the rules. This could be done by simply knowing when guards go on break or ways to get merchandise out the doors unseen. However, the most common way employees could beat security was to use the rules for their own purposes. One informant who was involved in removing more than $6,000 worth of merchandise within a six-month period explained how this could be done.

Another problem which had to be worked around was security. The store had four security guards or personnel. These people were also looked upon as "jokes." The security personnel were primarily concerned with catching shop-lifting customers. Most of their time was spent behind two way mirrors with binoculars observing shoppers. So in reality while the security personnel caught a customer concealing a pair of pants in her purse, and employee was smuggling four pairs of levis out the front door. Security was concerned with shoppers on the floor while all employee thefts usually occurred in stock rooms. That is, the items were taken or concealed in stock rooms until a favorable time to take them out.

This store required that only packages with sales receipts be permitted to leave, therefore, guards looked for receipts as signs of legitimate purchases. The informant continued:

Once the records were back in our department, the problem now was getting them out of the store. There were several ways this was done. The most common way was to smuggle them out with some item which had been paid for. For instance, if a friend came in . . . you would ask them if they would take some albums out. If they said yes (90% say yes) you put about 5 albums in the bottom of their stereo box. You then pack the stereo in again and tape the box shut. The friend is then given something taken, like a record cleaner or extra speaker wire for the favor he is doing you. Then after work you go pick up your albums and help the friend set up his stereo. One thing we always made sure of was that the friend was a fairly good one . . . we didn't want someone stealing our albums! Another way was to have a friend or roommate come in. Then you would ring up $2 or $3 at our cash register, then pack 25 albums in a paper bag. You then staple the receipt on the bag and staple the bag shut. The friend then pays the $2 or $3 and walks out. Then you would give the friend around 7 or 8 albums and you keep 15. With this process we always had between 5-30 albums going out a month. Some months saw only a few going out while 1 or 2 months were major hauls. The largest haul ever on albums occurred when the manager of my department, Doug, bought two large speakers. . . . We figured they would check inside the boxes on the way out since we were employees, so we removed the backs of the speakers and put 25 albums in the back of one and 30 in the other one. We then screwed the backs on again and packed them in their cardboard packing boxes. When taking the boxes out, they weren't opened by security. Consequently 55 albums went out the front door under their noses.

Another way to steal involved "trade ins."

> The most common way we employed to steal from our department was
> the use of trade ins. We would write up the sales ticket in a fictitious
> name. We would write up the equipment we wanted at a low price.
> Then we would write "less trade in" and subtract that amount from the
> already low price. We would never write what was traded in on the
> ticket. In reality nothing was traded. In this manner it was possible to
> pay $200 for $800 of equipment, with the extra $600 written off as a trade
> in. . . . Sometimes items were actually traded in and later sold. . . . For
> instance I traded in two of my speakers for $400 on an amplifier. The
> speakers were actually worth about $150. Then I sold them to my
> brother for $75. Everyone got a fantastic deal except for my company
> which got a royal fucking over. To add to the injury, I also got $1.75 in
> commission for the sale to my brother.

Inventories could also be altered to cover up losses. This aspect of
overcoming security checks is even more effective if the thieves take the
inventory.

> An inventory of large items was to be taken every week. This was also
> gotten around. We would hide some equipment and not put it on the
> inventory. The inventories were called in on the phone, so we took the
> inventories and just reported to the main office what we had. If no one
> called later asking about the equipment, we kept it off the inventory for
> 6 weeks.

On another occasion, our informant was transferred to another store.
The new boss requested that the informant and his manager report early
to take an inventory audit. In our informant's words:

> This prompted us to hide 1 turntable, 2 tape recorders, one 8-track
> player, and an expensive dust cover in the ceiling of our sound room.
> The ceiling was of the hanging variety so we removed one of the slabs
> and set our equipment up there. This merchandise would not be counted
> and if discovered missing, would be blamed on the previous crew,
> which had been laid off.

The stashed merchandise was then taken out through previously described
methods.

Still another way to effectively use the security precautions to one's
advantage is with cash register tapes. These tapes provided management
with an "objective" record of cash transactions through a particular department. Indeed, this is why few employees will remove cash from the
till; it is wiser to remove merchandise, especially if a similar amount of
money is registered as having been taken in with your department. This
is why each department has its cash register. However, the same "objective" record can be used to cover wages-in-kind.

We also used the advantage of our cash register. Our register was to be used only to ring up items from our electronics department. So anything that went through our department register was for our sales. Whenever we rang up the record or shoe sales, the few dollars was to our credit. We went further than this, however; we told good friends that if they would bring something from another department, we would sell it to them for ½ price. . . . One reason we did this only for friends was these items could not be returned or refunded. Since they were rung through our register, it had our code number on the sales receipt. So if the items were brought back the refund clerk, who was also a security guard, would notice that we rang up another department's merchandise, and we could have been fired. By employing this method we could add perhaps another $30 to our monthly record.

These extra dollars, then, could be used to cover up previous thefts. By implication, if more money was rung through the department's till, it would appear as if X dollars worth of merchandise had been sold. In turn, this meant that the employees in that department could remove this for their own benefit; their problem was to get it out of the store, but once it was gone it would not be officially missed.

The use of inventory and cash register tapes to help control employee theft not only promoted it, as seen above, but actually encouraged theft from other departments to cover someone's losses. The same informant explained:

Our largest inventory boost occurred during the Christmas holidays. The television department also handled small radios and cassette recorders. Both departments handled Panasonic recorders. . . . The television department had about 100 of these recorders stacked up in a display on the floor. During the rush hours we would go over and take a few recorders and then sell them through our department. Also, if a customer brought one over and asked "Can I pay for this here?" the answer was a resounding yes. We were not worried about returns because we handled these recorders in our department also. About 15 recorders were sold in this manner. At $40 a recorder, we easily added close to $600 to our inventory. This covered almost all of the shady deals we had done with trade ins and anything left over was dealt with as shrinkage.

This method of using the cash register tapes to steal is further buttressed when the cunning employee who checks the tapes is actually involved in pirating another department's credit for his own uses. An informant who worked in a clothing store told us how he accepted items for sale and refund from "baby wear" and rang them up on his register. Not surprisingly, soon "baby wear" was showing discrepancies between cash flow and merchandise, and store security began patrolling the area in order to catch shady "baby wear" employees.

Despite the importance of inventory as a potential source of trouble, our informants agreed that there were various ways to cover up discrepancies, especially if one knew they were occurring. The bread truck driver who earned extra "tips" illustrates this.

> Strange, when I stole, my accuracy improved. I kept a record of how much I took. It might be thirty cents in this store, $2 here, but I kept a record and I'd normally know, say, I should have $28 today or $32 extra. . . . You're working in a psychological pressure; you have to be very careful that you appear to be honest; you have to be accurate.

Likewise, our informant at the large chain store was a bit surprised by how well things worked out in the various departments, including the ones he stole from.

> We never really worried about how the different departments would explain their inventory losses. Clothing wear departments usually explained their losses through shrinkage which usually meant that shoplifters had gotten their stuff. I never found out how the hardware department explained the loss of the two chain saws, which we removed. I think that most department managers tend to cover up their losses, because no one ever came around asking questions about this and that. I figure when some department starts losing cases of merchandise that they know it isn't customers taking it. I think most department managers don't want to admit that they have "lost" several hundred dollars in merchandise. So consequently, they tell no one and I think they cover it up by changing their inventory sheets or some other way.

In short, by appearing to be "normal" and by following the rules, employees could effectively use the rules of security and their coworkers' notions of "normal procedure" to their own advantage (see Altheide, 1975). Indeed, anyone who was not accepted as legitimately engaged in an activity could not steal because he would be watched too closely. The bread truck driver provided a good example.

> We would never keep blacks and Puerto Ricans . . . there was always the assumption that blacks wouldn't work, and the thing that I felt was that the difficulty blacks had was that they couldn't afford to keep the job because they couldn't steal. There was an assumption on the part of grocers that blacks would steal, so they would watch them closer.

The previous examples of the impact of coworkers on individual theft and the way informed employees can ironically use a store's security operations for their own benefit are by no means definitive. We are certain that there are other ingenious devices and ploys routinely invoked by creative workers seeking part of their wages in-kind. Our emphasis has been on the reciprocal relationship between opportunity and hazard, on the one hand, and permissiveness and forbearance, on the other. All coexist in the drama of social life and can be viewed as an essential part of the competent employee's perspective. A rhetoric and vocabulary is still another relevant component of the modern worker's orientation to partaking in situated official and unofficial wages-in-kind.

### Justifications and Awareness of "Real" Crime

The three previous sections focused on the general cultural context for employee theft, as well as the specific work group standards, norms, and moralities. While these comments can be seen as at least a partial explanation for the meaning of wages-in-kind from the employees' viewpoint, it is also important to clarify what they compare their activities to and why they often do not see their work-related theft as "real theft." From the perspective we have chosen to study employee theft, it is unrealistic and invalid to argue that the workers of America are "really stealing" even though they do not admit it. We take their definitions seriously and also ask what they might mean by theft, crime, and related terms (see Cressey, 1953). Our interviews and experiences suggest that workers may compare their activities with what they understand as the activities of people they believe to be the "real thieves," although the comments that follow are largely suggestive and demand further investigation.

As has been previously noted in the literature on employee theft, many workers feel they are stealing from no one since corporations are mere legal entities and not individuals. This is an important distinction, as we shall see, since many of the same workers are angered by street criminals robbing specific victims or even small stores where the victims are identifiable; the consequences of theft can be objectively seen. According to a man who worked for an auto dealer, "Most of the people I worked with don't want to rip off the average Joe American, like themselves. If they can fuck this company up, they're just damn happy. . . . This is right." And the bread truck driver essentially agreed.

> Well, Safeway, or a chain store, you just didn't care because you know that you are not stealing from somebody personal; you know they are going to make it up, but when you're stealing from an individual grocery, you have some compunction about it. . . . The unfortunate part about it is that the people you'd rather steal from first are some of the chain stores, and they're successful because they're son-of-a-bitches . . . they are the most careful, they watch you.

Few Americans would condone theft in the abstract. However, many people are willing to take advantage of "bargains" made possible by employee cunning. The man who worked for the auto dealership explained:

> The main thing I did was find the customer, the buyer. Then I went to the assistant parts manager . . . he would take parts out the back door or whatever he wanted . . . so people who knew I was installing acces-

sories would ask me if I could put, say, a radio in their car, would ask how much it would cost. So usually we would quote them a price of half price of what they could buy one for, and people were really satisfied. . . . For some people I did complete jobs. I put moulding on at their homes that was all stolen, or roof racks . . . the mechanics would do work at home on other cars . . . but there would always be a price, but you could double the money that you paid for it. For example . . . if I told them I would install one for $50, I would go to the manager's home, and he would sell me one he had stolen for $25; he'd make $25 and I would make $25, which was more than I got for installing them legit.

This experience of support and acceptance, common in many work contexts, not only normalizes employee theft, but also permits workers to distinguish between their actions and those of "real criminals." The bread truck driver-informant noted that his coworkers would be outraged if they were robbed at gunpoint. In his words, "All those thieves are the most pious, church going, upright citizens, and condemn all those individuals down in the jungle."

Indeed, most of our informants seldom considered the question of whether or not they were "really" thieves; they just did what others in the same situation did. It was normal and routine. For example, from a worker's perspective, it would be easy to normalize theft which is as rampant as suggested by our informant employed by an auto dealership.

After a while I was getting parts from the real peons, the parts runners. . . . They thought they were getting such a raw deal (in terms of wages). I would say, "Hey listen, I've got a guy who wants a radio," and they would undersell the assistant parts manager . . . it was like 3 or 4 guys were competing with each other on a scale. . . . The assistant manager didn't know the other guys were stealing, but they knew he was . . . and they knew his price.

The crucial importance of understanding workers in a situation to unravel the social meanings of employee theft is further illustrated when the situation changes. Three of our informants reported shifts in thinking about wages-in-kind when they became bosses, entrepreneurs, and employers.

Other aspects of the employee's selective perception may be a widespread understanding of who the "real criminals" are and the problem of "street crime." It is our impression that few, if any, of our informants equated news stories about "crime in the streets" and a decline in "law and order" with what they were doing as employees occasionally exacting wages-in-kind. To the contrary, most were critical of liberal politicians and others who were accused of "pampering criminals" and "hand-cuffing the police." This was especially true of worker opinions on burglaries and armed robberies. In listening to these employees during various periods of observation, it was clear that the "crime problem" was "out there" and created by "others." In short, most of the employees who extracted wages-in-kind were less than tolerant of law violations.

A major reason these people take the positions they do on "law and order" can be traced to popular notions about criminals and the vocabulary used to describe them. "Street criminals" are covered in the newspapers and on TV news; employee thieves seldom are (see Altheide, 1976). The former are also the subject of many popular "cops and robbers" TV programs, while regular workers seldom are shown violating rules. Moreover, there is a widespread belief that criminals are irresponsible, if not lazy; our mass media depictions, along with the "folk concepts" (see Turner, 1957) we learn at our mother's knees, suggest that crime and other forms of deviancy occur because an individual does not have a job, is bored, or is not constrained by the norms and rules which bind the rest of us into a solid social unit. The context in which these messages are presented also suggests that criminals are those persons who have contact with law enforcement officers and threaten private property. Studies by George Gerbner (1976) and his associates indicate that heavy TV viewers derive unrealistic images of social problems, trust and fear, and the relative proportion of people in the occupation of law enforcement.

Relatedly, workers seldom hear politicians and other spokespersons who capture TV and news coverage berating workers for "stealing the country blind." To the contrary, most politicians support unions, which often promote employee theft by making it difficult to fire workers for rule violations. Their targets of attack are influenced by their beliefs that the audience hearing and reading their words will share a common conception of the "enemy." Thus, the street criminals become the obvious target and, by implication, a distant comparison group for workers.

Still another factor that seems to play a role in employees' reluctance to consider themselves criminal is a popular image of who steals and what is taken. The most spectacular news reports of theft, burglary, and robbery almost always involve private property. For example, in the looting that occurred during the blackout in New York in July 1977, most of the losses occurred among small shop owners employing few people. The emphasis on the personal loss of these owners conveys a strong sense of victimization —"How could anyone do this?" Compare such a view to how a worker in an auto dealership took car radios.

> A lot of times, some cars would come in with a radio already in them, and you were supposed to remove the old one and replace it with a new one. . . . You would take that out and were supposed to take that back

up to parts. We would take it out and install a new one, and leave the old one back on our bench. If someone called for it, we'd take it up; if not, take it home. After two days no one would ask about it.

Conversely, most employees do not see a victim, since they usually work for a "company"; if they can see an individual bearing the immediate loss, theft may occur anyway, especially if the individual is disliked and believed to "have it coming." Since the major part of employee theft is done gradually and within group standards, there is widespread belief that major losses will not occur. As an employee in a large discount store described "mark downs":

Sure I think stealing was rationalized in that way. Just by the way they'd put stuff away. They'd see some clothing they liked, particularly in the ladies department, and they'd put it away in the backroom in a spot that wouldn't be noticeable, and they'd wait until mark down came. It might get dusty, it might dirty and you could mark it down to $.99 because you were an employee, you could let your layaways go, or because you were an employee you could truly put something on layaway, and wait for it to be marked down.

The consequences of theft for the company may occur only subtly, if at all. These considerations imply that the recent New York looting may actually promote more support for employee theft, since the workers will have even more reason to see the "awful problems" and threats to society brought on by "those animals"—the true criminals. In this way, a worker's own activities become even more normalized and within the bounds of common decency and law.

## SUMMARY AND CONCLUSIONS

This essay began by taking seriously workers' claims about wages-in-kind and theft. We believe that employee theft cannot adequately be explained by adopting the standpoint of management and jurisprudence and defining theft in some objective and context-free situation. While much research needs to be carried out to test and further refine the conceptual framework we have set forth, our involvements with informants in various jobs in various parts of the country suggest that employee theft is imbued with meanings appropriate to certain situations.

Our study suggests more than it proves. Specifically, we note that there is a long tradition for workers accepting and actually expecting wages-in-kind; there is also a long tradition for employers to provide extra "perks" in the form of bonuses or special privileges. The significance of the widespread acceptance and support of wages-in-kind appears to be the bedrock for many workers' expectations that unemployment insurance is a right and should be taken advantage of at every opportunity (Graves, 1977).

Second, the commitment to equality of opportunity, and especially succeeding within this opportunity structure, creates a context of meaning for individual identity. While one must work for a living, one need not accept the definition of his or her worth as indicated by the task or occupation; one can maintain a private meaning of self, including being "cool," "not someone's lacky," and "my own man/woman." Part of this creative synthesis of low job status with personal regard is accomplished through worker theft. In this case, goods are dispensed to friends, taken home, or services are taken advantage of for their symbolic worth and not just because of greed.

Third, the pressures of work group norms and standards can both promote and limit theft. Since this and other research (see Altheide, 1975) suggests that formal security is singularly ineffective against clever employees in most settings, *we tentatively conclude that work groups are the singularly most inhibiting forces in an employer's arsenal against theft.*

Finally, the workers pursue their tasks and collect their wages-in-kind as part of a general life scheme that makes sense to them. Seldom do workers see themselves as criminals or threats to morality and social order. Criminals reported on in the mass media, including those whose actions produce objective losses and suffering to other honest, hard-working people, are perceived as targets of blame. This general cultural view is given more support by politicians and others who speak in the name of society as they castigate all those who violate law and order. And the workers of our society are among their most steadfast supporters.

## REFERENCES

Altheide, David L. *Creating Reality: How TV News Distorts Events.* Beverly Hills, Calif.: Sage Publications, 1976.
———. "The Irony of Security." *Urban Life* 4 (July 1975): 179–96.
Bradford, John A. "A General Perspective on Job Satisfaction: The Relationship between Job Satisfaction, and Sociological, Psychological and Cultural Variables." Ph. D. diss., Department of Sociology, University of Calif., San Diego, 1976.
Cressey, Donald. *Other People's Money.* New York: The Free Press, 1953.
Curtis, S. J. *Modern Retail Security.* Springfield, Ill.: Charles C Thomas, 1960.
Dalton, Melville. *Men Who Manage.* New York: John Wiley & Sons, 1959.
Douglas, Jack D., and John M. Johnson, eds. *Existential Sociology.* New York: Cambridge University Press, 1977.
Ditton, Jason. "Perks, Pilferage, and the Fiddle: The Historical Structure of Invisible Wages." *Theory and Society* 4 (1977): 39–71.
Federal Bureau of Investigation. *Crime in the United States.* Washington, D.C.: U. S. Government Printing Office, 1973.
Gerbner, George, and Larry Gross. "The Scary World of TV's Heavy Viewer." *Psychology Today* (April 1976): 41 ff.
Gibbons, Don C. *Society, Crime and Criminal Careers.* Englewood Cliffs, N.J.: Prentice-Hall, 1968.
Gouldner, Alvin. *Patterns of Industrial Bureaucracy.* New York: The Free Press, 1954.

Graves, K. Kane. "The Social Construction of Eligibility: Working the Unemployment System." Masters paper, Department of Sociology, Arizona State University, 1977.

Hemphill, Charles. *Security for Business and Industry.* Homewood, Ill.: Dow-Jones, 1971.

————, and Thomas Hemphill. *The Secure Company.* Homewood, Ill.: Dow-Jones, 1975.

Homans, George C. *The Human Group.* New York: Harcourt, Brace and World, 1950.

Horning, Donald N. M. "Blue-Collar Theft: Conceptions of Property Attitudes toward Pilfering and Work Group Norms in a Modern Industrial Plant." In Erwin O. Smigel and H. Laurence Ross, eds. *Crime against Bureaucracy.* New York: Van Nostrand Reinhold, 1970.

Liebow, Elliot. *Tally's Corner.* Boston: Little, Brown, 1967.

Lipman, Mark. *Stealing.* New York: Harper's Magazine Press, 1973.

Lyman, Stanford M., and Marvin B. Scott. *A Sociology of the Absurd.* New York: Appleton-Century-Crofts, 1970.

Ruddy, Samuel L. "Nights at the Races: Employee Theft and Organizational Viability." Masters paper, Department of Sociology, Arizona State University, 1977.

Smigel, Erwin O., and H. Laurence Ross. *Crime Against Bureaucracy.* New York: Van Nostrand Reinhold, 1970.

Sutherland, Edwin. *White Collar Crime.* New York: Dryden, 1949.

Turner, Ralph. "The Normative Coherence of Folk Concepts." Research Studies of the State College of Washington 25 (1957): 127–36.

# 6

# Ripping off the Elderly: Inside the Nursing Home

*Andrea Fontana*

There is an animal reek here which keeps me awake at night with horror that mankind should be like it. . . .

> T. E. Lawrence
> The Royal Air Force

## THE ELDERLY AS A COMMODITY

To grow old gracefully and enjoy the golden years of retirement may be the new American dream of a rapidly aging nation.[1] As the babies of yesteryear's boom become streaked with silver hair, they face the twilight of their lives. Most of them manage very nicely. Their hearts grow nostalgic at the beat of yesterday's music and wrinkles map their faces as they battle against sagging bodies; but the annuities accumulated with the savings and that bit of property along the coast keep them going to face that next trip to Hawaii.

For some, the golden years are just that—a bit tarnished perhaps, but the mellow color of aged wheat nonetheless. For others, over a million of them,[2] old age is grim. The gold is not in their future. Instead, they are the golden fleece attracting hordes of profiteers and unscrupulous adventurers: these are convalescent patients in nursing homes.

They are the victims of the American way of life. In other countries such as Sweden and Denmark[3] there is a concerted effort to keep old people in their own homes as long as possible. Various kinds of help are provided to this end: home visits by nurses and therapists, day care, meal services. Apartment complexes for the aged form independent units with medical care, cafeterias, and so on; nursing homes are the last resort.

In the United States the outlook is different. Where can an old person go when, because of waning strength, his or her physical well-being requires assistance from others? There are many who could carry on alone with a limited amount of assistance, but where can this help be gotten? The United States is geared toward institutionalization of troublesome individuals,[4] and fading old people are no exception:[5] they are institutionalized in what are commonly known as convalescent centers. But no one really convalesces, for the illness is terminal: old age. These places are holding pens for those with whom we no longer wish to share our society.

There is more. Having removed the waning elderly from sight, we are not content to leave it at that. We ruthlessly exploit them. Most of them are alone and their closest relative and source of support is the government, especially Medicaid. Medicaid has become a cornucopia dispensing greater and greater benefits to everyone with an interest in pursuing home care. Medicaid spending has increased from $1.5 billion in 1966 to $15 billion in 1976. People over the age of 65 constitute 23.5 percent of individuals eligible for medicaid, and they receive 38.7 percent of all medicaid funds. In 1975 skilled nursing home services received 22 percent of the total medicaid pie, while the doctors' slice was 11 percent.[6]

Today there are about 378,000 physicians in the United States, 250,000 of whom (about two-thirds) participate in the Medicare and Medicaid programs. In 1974 and 1975, 365 doctors received $100,000 or more from Medicaid, while another 247 squeezed Medicare for similar amounts. First prize goes to a Dr. William Triebel of New York, who in 1975 received $785,114.08 in Medicaid payments.[7]

The drug industry doesn't fall far behind physicians, with over $200 million in Medicare funds spent yearly on drugs for nursing homes. A large part of this money, roughly 40 percent, is spent on sedatives or tranquilizers. Thorazine becomes the magic potion to keep aged patients calm and serene, or, if you prefer, in a state of idiotic stupor. The nursing home industry demands its share of the pie, which is about $3.5 billion in annual revenue, three-fourths of which is taxpayers' money funneled into the industry through the government.[8]

The fraud is colossal, ranging from kickbacks from pharmaceutical concerns to the dubious practice of supposedly "throwing away" medicines ordered and only partially used for a patient who died, lest they contaminate other patients.[9] Doctors engage in "gang visits."[10] They walk through a nursing home a couple of times a month and bill Medicaid for each patient in their care whom they supposedly had visited.

One wonders if even a bureaucratically-entangled government such as ours can so easily be ripped off. In fact, Medicaid attempts to limit the profit in nursing homes. For example, in the state of Nevada (where part of this study was conducted), 35 percent of the Medicaid total budget, or about $6 million, is spent on nursing homes,[11] with the average cost per patient around $780 per month.[12]

Cost of living is high; in Nevada the daily cost per patient ranges between $20 and $30 a day.[13] A random survey of ten Southern California nursing homes found an average cost of $22.50 per patient per day.[14] And the cost for decent nursing care is, in fact, much higher. This researcher found that the cheapest of the nursing homes surveyed ($8 a day) was a large private house in which six patients shared each room. The only recreation available was a vintage television set. The staff was comprised of one live-in registered nurse, who was so ancient she could have easily been mistaken for a patient.

Medicaid sets the profit incentive at only $1 per patient per day.[15] Given the small margin of profit, the nursing home operators cut down on the cost of running a nursing home and charge Medicaid for the full amount, thus realizing a tidy, if not quite legal, profit. Of course, elderly patients lose their individuality and are seen as money to be gained. For instance, patients can be fed inexpensive, low-quality items while Medicaid is billed for higher grade food.[16] An extra body means an extra payment by the government, and tales not unlike those of shanghaied sailors in old England are heard among the patients.

Skimming the costs is not the only rip-off to which convalescent patients are subjected. Other malfeasances are perpetrated against the elderly, ending in the final rip-off of their humanity as they become mere objects in a world of greed and cruelty. Rather than enumerate these deeds, let us step inside a nursing home for a while and see a typical example in the making of ripping off the elderly.

## NORMALIZING DEVIANCE

Uncovering rip-offs in a convalescent center is not the easiest of sociological tasks. The findings reported in this essay took many hours of persistent field work by this researcher, serving as a janitor for a convalescent center in Southern California.[17] The administrator and the nursing staff were aware of the study being conducted and allowed informal access to all medical records. The hidden personal secrets of patients held no sanctity for the staff. However, financial records were never disclosed to me, and even the slightest hint of financial matters on my part drew icy stares from the administrator. The hidden financial secrets of the owner were sacred for the staff.

Generally the quality of convalescent centers varies inversely with their proximity to a large city. The greater the distance from governmental inspectors, the less likely one is to find a sparkling convalescent center.[18] My center was a fair distance from the metropolis; it wasn't Auschwitz, but it tried hard.

The center was a locked-door facility, in which a number of patients were officially defined as suffering from mental illness.[19] The others were only guilty of being old, frail, and unloved by relatives. But this was enough to have them locked away, depriving them of open spaces, company, and human dignity.

Rip-offs in the center went far beyond financial misappropriations; the operator and the staff ripped the self out of patients by stripping whatever life existed under those hazy eyes and gnarled bodies.

The center exhibited many forms of deviance, which were perpetrated by individual members of the organization but were really done for and normalized in the name of the organization. The goal of the center, a typical one in this respect,[20] was to provide a smooth-running schedule and flow of work, minimizing disturbances and avoiding trouble. What constituted disturbances and trouble was defined by the staff. Hence many deviant acts perpetrated by patients on other patients or by staff members on patients were handled to minimize their hindrance to the running of the organization. Often these acts were normalized in order to avoid stopping the center's smoothly flowing machine. Therefore if Maria, a wiry old patient, fell heavily to the ground after having been pumped full of thorazine, the incident was dismissed as the result of an obfuscated mind and a deteriorated body.

Rule-keeping was the formal rationale in running the organization, and under this aegis all rules could be informally broken in order to maintain order. Drugs were the main tools for enforcing control over the patients. Medications were prescribed by the physician on an "as needed" basis, thus leaving the decision on their administration to the nurse in charge who, in turn, relied on the aides' suggestions about the patients' behavior. If old Bill had enough of being tied in his wheelchair to the corridor railing (a measure aimed at keeping order) and began to yell at the top of his lungs (an order-disrupting event), then he could be viewed as expressing violent behavior and given another dose of thorazine. This would "officially" calm his nerves and keep his mouth shut.

Thus drugs permitted the staff to eliminate informally problems of officially-defined disruptive behavior, even if the behavior was a "normal" reaction to a situation.[21] But there were other problems that should not even have existed officially—for instance, sexual problems. Convalescent centers, so goes the myth, should not have to worry about sexual promiscuity, since patients are too old and feeble to express any interest in such affairs. Therefore, when sexual problems arose at the center, they were treated as if they did not exist. Nobody must have told big John that he was too old to be interested in sex since he kept walking around with his fly open showing hints of physical delights to whomever was willing to watch. Nurses aides laughed at him, or, if the registered nurse or administrator were around (making the situation potentially troublesome), they merely zipped his pants up. But big John was persistent and somehow convinced Thelma, another patient, to perform fellatio on him. They were caught in the act and quickly separated, amidst laughter. Thelma couldn't speak as a result of an operation, thus no one asked or even considered that perhaps she might have been an unwilling partner.

Or take the time when Wanda, an aide in her mid-fifties, took a fancy to George. George was a patient, but he was younger than Wanda. He was a tall, good-looking black man. Unfortunately, his penchant for drinking had aged him prematurely, and his mental state made him appear to be drunk all the time. Thus there was no noticeable change in his behavior when Wanda began to supply him with bottles of aftershave lotion to drink in exchange for sexual favors. The affair would have dragged on forever since Wanda, as well as the other aides, was practically unchecked in dealing with the patients. But the local drugstore clerk became suspicious at the enormous quantities of aftershave lotion she purchased. His suspicion led to the discovery of the affair. Wanda is gone now, and George still wanders about hazily, perhaps unaware that his body had been used and demeaned for her lusty whims.

Violence wasn't as easily normalized as sex, but the staff managed to do it. Minor things, like hair-pulling or punching, were routine. But violence took more severe forms. Raging violence could not be ignored and had to be subdued with massive shots of thorazine. Verbal violence could be disregarded. Streams of invectives were dismissed with a shrug of the shoulders. Cruel violence was the worst, and it was ignored. At times, some of the stronger or more lucid patients took advantage of others, whose minds and bodies had given way in the onslaught of time and illness. Thus daily harassment became a mere routine which would not be disturbed, since both the harasser and the harassee became quietly set in their roles and no one upset the order of the ward. To maintain order, the staff allowed patients to be teased and condoned behavior which brutalized the weak.

Destructive violence occurred only once during the study, but it was enough. Our funny, beloved old John was the protagonist. The supporting cast was Gary, his thin old roommate who had relinquished rational life for a cloudy world of his own in which no one bothered him and he bothered no one. Gary became the victim of John's suppressed sexual passions rejected or thwarted by everyone in the center. In the quiet of the night and sleepy ignorance of the orderlies, a brutal sexual attack took place, with the attacker raging dementedly and the other, the victim, meekly vanquished. In the macabre ordeal one died and the other was quickly dispatched to a different facility. Order and tranquility reigned in the convalescent center the next day.

A fleeting but important figure in our story was the man in white.

The doctor came rarely; when he did he was swarmed by eager nurses, but barely seen by needy patients. The fact was that the physician could only bill Medicaid twice monthly for each patient, which tended to limit his visits to twice a month on a regular basis.

The physician in his white coat might as well have been a ghost, so rarely was he seen. Even the nurses, in spite of their acceptance of order above care, rules above compassion, became enraged at the physician. For instance, when old Mary contracted pneumonia and her lungs were drowning in their own secretion, the helpless nurse called the doctor. "He told us to watch her," she said, "but all we could do was to watch her die." Or take the time surly old Jim lost his battle with the Grim Reaper. It happened at about 2 A.M., and the young nurse, horrified, prepared a body not yet officially sanctioned as dead. The mortician came unobtrusively on her call and carried old Jim to the morgue. All along, closely guarded by tacit rules, the official arbiter of death slept, his white coat resting nearby.

In its earnest concern for rule-keeping, the staff maintained a tight lid on the patients. Unfortunately, stressing the routinization of the work schedule led the staff to view patients as "work objects."[22] Thus the patient's individuality was sacrificed, once more in the name of the organization.

There was usually a minimal number of aides on the ward, and in order to meet administrative demands the aides would accomplish their daily assignments as quickly as possible. But old patients' bodies are not equipped for speed. Thus it became quicker and easier to bathe a patient rather than let him or her bathe alone: the turnover in the bathroom kept the desired rhythm. The patient was scrubbed, washed, turned over, rinsed —and the aides were ready for the next patient.

Feeding the patients followed the same course. In the rushed meal hour, food was shoved down open mouths or splattered on closed mouths as the aides carried on without missing a beat. The aides broke the rules concerning good care, but it mattered little to them since the goal of efficiency was seemingly more important.

Finally, deviance in the center assumed the obvious form of petty financial misappropriations—petty in nature, but lucrative for the owner. Aides cost money, and skimping on aides increases profits. As long as one can account for the number of "care hours per patient" demanded by Medicaid, who is going to know what kind of care the patients are getting? For example, patients were fed three times a day: breakfast, lunch, and dinner. The meals were compressed in time so that the day staff could take care of them. Patients were abruptly awakened at 5:30 A.M. so that they would be chirpy and ready to eat at breakfast time: 8:00 A.M. Patients were also rushed through an early dinner to fit into the day shift's time. They were ready for bed at 5:30 P.M., leaving the skeletal night crew with a minimal care function.[23]

The center had an emergency room which supposedly was kept vacant for emergencies such as a dying patient or a contagious illness. But business was good and the extra bed meant extra money, so the emergency room became an additional room for a patient.

What about emergencies? They were redefined to be handled routinely, such as when Linda, a new patient, was found to have lice in her hair. The aides kept it quiet, washed her hair, fed her in her room, and assigned her to room with Angie, who spent most of her days wandering along the corridors anyway.

Administration of patients' money provided another way to rip them off. Of course money was administered "for the good of the patients," who were mentally incompetent to handle their own finances. At least that was the account provided by the administrator when I asked why old Jim was always begging for dimes while hovering around the coin-operated soft drink machine. This seemed strange since I knew Medicaid provided each patient with $25 a month for small personal expenses. What I didn't know was that Jim never saw that money, "lest he guzzle soda pop after soda pop until the money is gone," as the administrator put it. But the money was gone anyway. Since most patients were the wards of the government in one fashion or another, when they died there were no relatives claiming their few possessions. This led to another rip-off. Medicaid allotted $15 a month as a clothing allowance for the patients. But, perhaps believing the old myth that old age is a second childhood, the staff handed down clothing to the patients, the clothing of those who no longer needed them in their eternal rest. And the clothing allowance? All I know is that it wasn't handed down along with the old clothing.

## DEVIANTS AND VICTIMS

Nursing homes are a marvelous breeding ground for business deviance. There is a group, the staff, that holds the power to define the situation for all concerned in the home.[24] Therefore, patients' actions can be seen as deviant if they disturb the smooth organizational flow. Otherwise actions can be normalized by constructing various accounts which make them plausible. At the same time the staff can engage in actions which deviate from the official goal of the institution to care for the elderly. These actions are unchecked by outsiders and are acceptable to both new and old staff members who live in a world which stresses efficient operation at minimal cost, thus justifying their behavior vis-à-vis the patients.

The patients, who in reality are victims of this system, are considered deviants. They are deviants if they are senile (a definition which allows the home to obtain extra money from Medicaid); they are deviant if they are restless (agitated behavior); they are deviant if they are moody (manic-depressive behavior); and they are deviant if they are angry (hostile behavior).

Ironically the patients come to believe the staff and they, too, view other patients as deviants.[25] They end up alone—alone since they isolate themselves from other patients; alone since they are overlooked by a staff that has no time for them.

Convalescent patients are indeed the victims of the American way of life. In a society which stresses organizational efficiency and lucrative gain, these old people become commodities. They are used as unwilling tools by others to exploit the government and are the source of a multimillion dollar trade: they become the golden fleece. But they themselves are ripped off in the process—their freedom, individuality, and dignity are taken away.

## NOTES

1. "The Graying of America," *Newsweek,* February 28, 1977, pp. 50–55.
2. Mary Adelaide Mendelson, *Tender Loving Greed* (New York: Vintage Books, 1974).
3. Ralph Nader, *Old Age, the Last Segregation,* Project Director Claire Townsend (New York: Bantam Books, 1970).
4. Philip Slater, *The Pursuit of Loneliness* (Boston: Beacon, 1970).
5. Andrea Fontana, *The Last Frontier* (Beverly Hills, Calif.: Sage Publications, 1977).
6. Special Committee on Aging, U. S. Senate, "Fraud and Abuse among Practitioners Participating in the Medicaid Program" (Washington, D.C.: U. S. Government Printing Office, 1976), pp. 5–6.
7. *Ibid.,* p. 23.
8. Mendelson, *Tender Loving Greed.*
9. This information was gained in a conversation with a governmental official in charge of nursing homes inspections in a western state.
10. See Mendelson, *Tender Loving Greed.*
11. Legislative Commission of the Legislative Counsel Bureau, state of Nevada, "Skilled Nursing Facilities and Problems of the Aged and Aging," Bulletin No. 77–7, p. 8.
12. *Ibid.,* p. 17.
13. *Ibid.,* p. 41.
14. Fontana, unpublished field notes, 1975.
15. Legislative Commission, "Skilled Nursing Facilities," p. 34.
16. See Mendelson, *Tender Loving Greed.*
17. Fontana, *The Last Frontier.*
18. See note 9.
19. See, among others, Thomas J. Scheff, *Being Mentally Ill* (Chicago: Aldine, 1966).
20. See, for instance, Abraham Blumberg, *Criminal Justice* (Chicago: Quadrangle, 1967).
21. Erving Goffman, *Asylums* (Garden City, N.Y.: Anchor, 1971).
22. Barney Glaser and Anselm Strauss, *Awareness of Dying* (Chicago: Aldine, 1965).
23. For similar findings see Mendelson, *Tender Loving Greed.*
24. For a theoretical discussion of this point, see Alfred Schutz, "On Multiple Realities," in *Collected Papers I* (The Hague, Neth.: Martinus Nijhoff, 1971).
25. See Fontana, "Growing Old Between Walls," in *The Last Frontier.*

# 7

# The Golden Fleece: Arizona Land Fraud

Robert P. Snow

Speaking to Arizona police officers in 1977, Dr. Leon Beene, a former Arizona legislative land fraud researcher, stated, "I can't believe the job of stopping economic crime is ever going to get done."[1] Echoing this sentiment, Duane J. Kingsbury, head of Yavapai County's special Land Fraud Task Force, stated, "We're going to be faced with a land fraud problem for a long period of time." Yavapai County currently has 351 approved subdivisions, comprising 62,000 lots which cover 53,480 acres. Most of these subdivisions lie fallow through abandonment or bankruptcy.

Despite this pessimism, special training programs have been developed and new laws have been enacted in Arizona aimed at curbing land fraud and other white-collar crimes. In 1977 the Arizona legislature passed a fairly tough law regulating the development and sale of subdivided land. Developers are now required to provide the State Real Estate Commission with a financial profile of the company, a bankruptcy and criminal history of company personnel, and obtain clearance for advertising campaigns. Brokers and salesmen must meet more stringent licensing requirements, including fingerprinting. Developments must provide permanent access to the property, a detailed program for development and sale of lots, and recordable deeds for purchasers. Violations may result in imprisonment for up to five years on each count. A law with teeth is new for Arizona. During the past two decades Arizona has experienced one of the greatest land booms and fraud actions since the Oklahoma land rush. The snake oil charletons of land speculation promised a dream come true in the great Southwest, with a homesite at Cochise Park, Verde Lakes, Lake Mead Rancheros, Queen Creek, and countless other places. Clean air, continual sun, improved lots, and friendly western neighbors were waiting at the home of your choice. Low down payment and easy terms, but act fast. Don't let the chance of a lifetime pass you by.

From the late fifties to the mid-seventies people from all parts of the country bought a share in the big land boom. Everything from the giant developments of Fountain Hills near Phoenix to miniature mobile home parks have been part of the action. As a business phenomenon, the land business has been a billion dollar industry on both sides of the law. As a sociological phenomenon land development has gone from a boom market mentality of quick profit and buyer beware to the current approach of caution and control. What happened over this period was not so much crime followed by exposure and cleanup as a change in the meanings or definition of the situation applied by businessmen, consumers, media, and justice officials to the land development business. Once everyone was "on the make" or "on the take." Today its go slow and tighten the regulations.

## THE LAND BOOM MENTALITY

Prior to World War II, Phoenix was a medium-size town engaged in citrus and cotton production with a few light industries. Following the war and the development of air conditioning, the metro area mushroomed to its present sprawling million and a quarter inhabitants. The rapid growth of Phoenix during the fifties and sixties proved that many people were anxious to get a piece of the old western casual lifestyle. Southern California was filling up and Arizona was now the new frontier. Elbowroom, clean air, old western conservative ideals, and the casual, comfortable life were evident to all who visited. With the early success of Del Webb's Sun City, the word spread and the boom was on.

One factor that fueled the boom was a scarcity psychology. Private land and water are not abundant in Arizona. The federal government controls most of the land through forest and agricultural districts and Indian reservations. Water is abundant in only a few areas. With water and land scarce, it was obvious to the smart investor that land value would be at a premium. If a land developer promised clear title and water, it was not difficult to convince the prospective buyer to act fast. Land developers could do just that, as laws governing the requirements for subdivisions including title and water guarantees were either ambiguous and easy to manipulate or nonexistent. It was relatively easy to buy a cheap parcel of desert or marginal high country and draw up a brochure promising the development of a retirement community or recreational village. The retirement home or mountain cabin was affordable to an affluent buyer market. More importantly, the purchase of land represented a safe speculation investment. It was obvious to anyone that land values in Arizona would skyrocket. A scarce commodity and an affluent investor were prime ingredients for a boom mentality.

As a form of business deviance, the land phenomenon operated for nearly 15 years as a boom market. The mentality of a boom market is basically one of "the greater fool theory." Make the plunge because there will always be someone to sell to at a handsome profit. Throughout our history we have had many boom periods with the same business mentality —everyone is fair game. Its as American as apple pie and Chevrolet. Only in periods of tight money or a monopolistic market has consumer fraud been taken seriously, and then only by a minority.

With a boom mentality, few people really worried about whether the promises of developers would be fulfilled rapidly. Eventually the land was bound to develop. For most investors the attitude was to get in on what appeared to be the ground floor. Banks and title companies, investment groups and single investors, realtors, contractors, advertising specialists, and of course the super con men all wheeled and dealed to the tune of the big boom. While not all land developments were pie in the sky operations, the majority have gone sour. Even the successful giants, Lake Havasu City and Fountain Hills, have slowed markedly and are in financial trouble. A few years ago it was hard to find any serious questioning of the business tactics or investment future of these developments. Everyone seemed to be in on the action. Today the situation is reversed.

During the boom period, the practices of many developers varied from simple misrepresentation to clear-cut fraud in the sale of securities. These practices may be classified within six categories: deceptive sales techniques; delay or default on development promises; sale of unowned land; multiple sale of the same property; selling buyer contracts or mortgages with intent to defraud; and the proliferation of companies to generate and milk huge profits. These activities were all practiced on a fairly large scale during the boom period. When violations became flagrant and regulatory agencies were asked to act, the legal process somehow became lethargic or inactive. Corruption of officials was an easy step in the boom market mentality. As one nameless person stated in a news report, "Its surprising how cheaply these officials were bought. There was big money to be made."[2]

In the mid-seventies several things happened to bring an end to the boom mentality. The economy slumped badly and investment money became scarce. At the same time lot owners were either ready to build on their homesite or they tried to sell. In either case many people became aware that they had bought a pig-in-a-poke. Big investors were burned badly in the bankruptcy of a number of development companies. Consumer complaints mounted to over 2,000 a year in 1975 and 1976. Suits increased, grand jury investigations were opened, and Federal Trade Commission hearings were held. At the same time the violent death of several land fraud figures willing to testify in grand jury investigations attracted public attention. The boom mentality was over and a different set of norms emerged. By the end of 1976 business, legal, and lay people alike were at least publicly outraged over the practices of land developers.

## THE LAND DEVELOPMENT BUSINESS

Most land development companies were formed as corporations or trusts. These firms obtained investment capital through a blind trust operation in which all investment beneficiaries could hide their identity from all but the Internal Revenue Service and the U.S. Attorney General (through court order).[3] Investors with a public image to protect, such as a bank, or underworld figures could invest with impunity. This business stimulus was critical to developers who intended to defraud. In addition to blind trusts, the corporation and real estate laws worked to the benefit of the developer. There was no requirement to post bond to guarantee development capital. Approval of a particular subdivision was simply a matter of filing a plat map with the county recorder. To sell lots, all an individual had to do was obtain a real estate license, which was an easy task during the boom period. Proof of water on the subdivision consisted only of a statement that it was available. Proof of the potency or longevity of the water source was not required. As for electrical power, in many cases it was nonexistent.

The common procedure for a development firm was to buy a tract of land and subdivide it into lots of various sizes, depending on the intended use. Desert ranches normally were 40 acres, while mountain cabin sites could be smaller than a city residential lot. A promotional map would be drawn with roads, lots, and recreational facilities. On the actual site, some developers failed even to stake the lots. At best roads might be bulldozed and street signs with charming names erected. The market value of lots was set at a level of what it could bring in a developed state. This inflated level was sometimes 100 times greater than its value in an undeveloped state. Cochise College Park in remote southeastern Arizona was valued at $70 per one-third acre but sold for up to $7,000 during the sales campaign. For many of these developments the land is still in a raw state and investors may never have a usable piece of property.

To obtain land for subdivision, a typical practice was to buy land from a rancher at twice its value. The developer would then obtain a local engineer, real estate agent, and lawyers to do the preparation work and create local influence. With local business in on the action, there was rarely a problem in convincing local authorities to support the subdivision.

The sales campaign was conducted by phone, mail, and media advertisements enticing buyers to the familiar sales dinner. At these presentations the buyer would be paired off with a single salesman in a one-to-one, grab-you-by-the-collar relationship. With the help of cocktails, a media blitz, and canned sales routines, the buyer was at their mercy. A few shills were usually present to heighten the emotional excitement. After swallowing the false promise to cancel or buy back the property at no loss, the pigeon would plunk down 10-20 percent and agree to pay off the balance in easy long-term installments. Contracts were rarely read and usually ambiguous regarding such things as improvements. Buyers often did not receive proof of ownership, and developers neglected to record the transaction with the county or state agencies. Since most buyers were thinking long-term investment, there was little to be cautious about. From the buyer's standpoint, what could possibly go wrong with an investment in land?

Involvement of the business community in this enterprise was extensive. Bankers and investors would bankroll a developer using the potential sales and/or value of the land as collateral. Investors would be further enticed with discount prices on choice property. Large ads were placed in all forms of media and it might be safe to assume that media personalities received fringe benefits for their endorsements. Realtors and attorneys purchased package deals and subcontracted. Contractors would be promised considerable business once the development began to take shape. Small businessmen bought lots on the promise of choice locations for their businesses. The action was heavy and big money was at stake.

During the late sixties and early seventies there was a flurry of activity. People in Arizona, the Midwest, and Northeast were constantly bombarded with major media campaigns, mailed brochures, and phone solicitation. From 1970-72 it seemed that our family received at least one phone call or mailing a day on a land deal. On a visit to the local shopping center a beautiful girl would hand you a ticket to be redeemed at a sales presentation for some trinket. Phone boiler-rooms operated constantly, offering everything from green stamps to free gasoline. For the big developments there were charter flights from major Midwest and Eastern cities. Gimmicks such as moving the London Bridge to Lake Havasu City and building the world's tallest fountain at Fountain Hills were very impressive.

During this period there was virtually no mention in the media of possible misrepresentation or fraud. Banks and loan companies advertised low interest rates for that mountain retreat or retirement home. The slogan was, act now and inflation would cover your purchase price in a few short years. Given the amount of advertising and the lack of contrary evidence, some people including myself began to feel guilty for not making an investment. In fact, had I not gone heavily into debt to purchase a home in 1970, I might have made the plunge. With the scarcity psychology in full swing, the temptation was high.

## LAND FRAUD PRACTICES

Sales deception is the most commonly understood form of land fraud. Morton Paulson in *The Great Land Hustle* quotes a newspaper ad for Lake Mead Rancheros: "The Rancheros are livable now. . . . You can own a king-sized western estate with roads and electricity, water and phones available. . . . Build now and move in."[4] Actually a bulldozer cut scars across the desert for roads. Power and phone lines were six miles away, and the nearest water was from a coin-operated pump 12 miles distant. Stonewood Ranch, a 4,000-acre barren tract near the petrified forest, was completely sold out in 40-acre parcels before anyone discovered there was no access to the property. A railroad and the federal government owned the land surrounding Stonewood. A retired army officer from Minnesota bought property at Stonewood with the intention of building a 90-unit motel. To this day all he has at Stonewood is a lot of sand.

Sales deception is executed by the fast-talking, hard-sell salesman. Large firms schooled their salesmen with canned speeches designed to meet every contingency. Horizon Corporation of Tucson, which was charged in 1977 by the Federal Trade Commission with misrepresentation, allegedly instructed its salesmen to talk the customer into submission through baffling contradiction and confusing information. Their tactics included the promise of a refund if not satisfied, resale at a profit guaranteed, the false impression of a feverish sales rate, and testimonials. Each question of objection from a customer was to be countered with a high-pressure pitch until the person, in an exhausted and bewildered state, signed the contract. While federal and state law allows a person six months to view remote property before a contract is binding, few people knew of the law or bothered to exercise their right. Horizon Corp. circumvented the "show me before I buy" axiom by flying prospective buyers over development areas. At Horizon's Whispering Ranch some 60 miles northwest of Sun City, buyers were first shown Sun City by air and then the general area of Whispering Ranch. If desert like Sun City could bloom, then why not Whispering Ranch? After all, Arizona was the fastest growing state in the union at that time. To sweeten the deal, Horizon salesmen allegedly gave the impression that Knotts Berry Farm was planning to build a branch near Whispering Ranch. While the 19,000-acre development was sold out in 1976, the property as of July 1977 has yet to be staked and no water or electricity is available. One well driller said a well would cost between $4,000 and $9,000, with no guarantee of water. Local real estate brokers say the land is good only for cattle grazing and is not in the path of urban development in the foreseeable future.

Reneging on promised improvements is also a common form of land fraud. Some firms operated on a hit and run procedure by selling out the subdivision fast and then abandoning the venture. With no records of sale on file with the county or state, the culprits could disappear with little or no trace. Since many of the buyers would not discover the fraud for several years, there was little risk to the swindler. To make the scam a little more official, one procedure was to fake a federal closure. Several cars would arrive at the subdivision headquarters with people posing as federal agents. Employees would be told to close the operation and vacate. Naive county officials would accept the matter and think no more about it. Other more lucrative and larger scale developments would proceed at a snail's pace until the last dollar could be squeezed from the operation. At this point the firm would transfer funds through loans to other companies and file bankruptcy. The bankruptcy procedure was sometimes lucrative for court-appointed trustees and attorneys who could take the remaining funds for receivership administration. While bankruptcy and receivership was not a direct payoff, it surely helped to mask the original fraud. It is conceivable that attorneys could wait like ambulance chasers for firms to go bankrupt and then move in to feast on the remains.

Apparently it was generally accepted in the business community that making improvements in subdivisions would be a slow process. Most firms depended on down payments and continuing monthly installments for improvement capital. Since several years' accumulation might be necessary before enough capital would be available, it might be unreasonable to assume a firm should make good on improvement promises until four or more years. Whether or not this was an informal guiding norm for regulatory agencies such as the Real Estate Commission, we do know that in many cases from five to ten or more years went by before consumer complaints were brought to the public's attention. Arizona developments such as Chino Meadows, Verde Lakes, Montezuma Lakes, and many others never provided the paved roads, clubhouse, water, and sewer lines promised in the original sale. When complaints were made to regulatory authorities, the consumer was advised to keep making payments.

In Chino Meadows near Prescott, a subdivision operated by Consolidated Mortgage, lot buyers were promised every city comfort, including an artificial lake. After it became apparent that Consolidated would not meet its obligations, the lot owners filed a complaint with the state attorney general. Owners were informed in a letter from Assistant Attorney General Robert Blakey, Jr., that payments must continue or owners could lose their entire investment. The letter went on to state that a steady cash flow was necessary for the company to make the improvements. Complaints to HUD resulted in the advice to stop payment for default by the developer. This was countered by another letter from the state attorney general suggesting, but not legally advising, that payments continue. An interesting addition to this story is that eventually Consolidated Mortgage was investigated by the Attorney General's Office and Robert Blakey, Jr., was given the job of rehabilitating the firm. Consolidated Mortgage is now defunct and, according to Mr. Blakey, the improvements were never made.[5]

Nearly every city in Arizona has a development of some kind in a raw or semideveloped state. The absurdity of street signs and bulldozed paths amid sage brush, tumbleweed, and scrub pine is mute testimony to the land boom mentality. The ratio of subdivision lots per capita in counties such as Mohave, Yavapai, Cochise, and others is more than two to one. Most of these subdivisions will never be developed.

Another land fraud practice is the sale of property not owned by the selling firm. Most cases of selling unowned land were by firms who claimed they intended to acquire the land once enough money was generated in down payments. At Verde Lakes, Consolidated Mortgage promised lot owners communal ownership in a clubhouse. However, the owners discovered that the land to be used was public and controlled by the U.S. Forest Service. Representative Sam Steiger of the district in which Verde Lakes was located was persuaded to use his influence to obtain a land swap for the property in question. Near Snowflake, Arizona, a now defunct land firm sold 45 lots on property owned by the state. After the lots were sold, the firm petitioned the state Land Selection Board (consisting of the governor, attorney general, and land commissioner) requesting a swap. Precedence for this type of deal had been set by at least one previous state administration and the present governor was reported to be reluctant to violate that precedent.

In addition to the land swap practice, Arizona has a land lease law which enables an individual or firm to lease public land for grazing purposes. If persons holding the lease make capital improvements on the land, they may request the state to sell the land in open bidding. If the state agrees, the persons making the capital improvements must receive fair compensation prior to the bidding. Therein lies the catch. Persons making the improvements have the inside track, since they may be the only ones who know the value of the improvements, the new value of the land, and have the ability to come up with the capital to reimburse for the improvements (essentially paying yourself back). With this inside information, the leaseholder can outbid the competition and sock it to the public. One realtor confided that at least one racetrack near Phoenix was acquired in this fashion. Allegedly, various public officials have also fared very well through this scheme. While all of this is perfectly legal, it certainly is not open-market, free competition.

A practice similar to the sale of unowned property is the sale of the same lot to more than one buyer. The logic of this transaction is clear. If a firm never intends to develop the land, then why not sell the same lot to several people that are unlikely to ever meet? Since most people bought for long-term investment purposes, they would not discover multiple ownership until years later. By this time the swindlers could cover their trail. In 1977 Combined Equity Assurance Corporation of Phoenix (defunct since 1974) was indicted for multiple sale of lots in Concho Lakelands in Yavapai County. Cochise College Park worked a scam by making lulling payments to contract holders on contracts that had been voided by purchasers. These lots were resold, creating the impression of booming sales and huge capital assets. While Cochise College Park had 6,000 to 7,000 real lots to sell, it actually sold 9,000 installment contracts, swindling lot buyers and investors of 40 million dollars from 1967 to 1974.[6]

While it may appear that the Cochise College Park practice of making lulling payments on voided purchases was self-defeating, it actually resulted in huge profits. The real money in land fraud was not made by selling land, but by the sale of mortgages or installment contracts. Coined the great "paper caper" by the IRE (Investigative Reporters and Editors) reports,[7] the operation consists of the perfectly legal practice of selling buyer contracts to investors such as banks, title companies, and individual investors. According to Burton Lewkowitz, executive vice-president of the Arizona Realtors Association, "the real fraud was not in land, but in selling contracts. Land simply served as a vehicle for generating paper."[8] The procedure was to sell a lot on installment. The installment contract was then sold without recourse, meaning the collection of the debt was the sole responsibility of the investor holding the note. With the developing firm free of responsibility, they could manipulate in a variety of ways. As mentioned previously, the developing firm often enhanced their position by issuing a nonrecordable deed to the buyer. After the contract was signed, the developer would give the buyer a photocopy of the deed, which is not legal proof of ownership, and, in turn, these sales were not recorded with the county or state recorder. Consequently, the only proof of a sale of real property was in the hands of the developer. With lot owners and investors scattered all over the country, most of these paper capers did not come to light until years later.

Contracts were sold to a variety of investors, large and small, in package deals and single contracts. Large investors, including banks and title companies, were enticed by package deals at discounts of up to 75 percent of the contract value. High interest rates stimulated the sale of contracts, especially to the small investor, with salesmen hawking these in a fly-by-night grift. It is estimated that investors were bilked of over a billion dollars, collectively, during the boom period. Some large banks and title companies absorbed the loss to avoid bad publicity. Small investors did not fare as well, being forced to rely on regulatory agencies or expensive lawsuits. In 1977 a group of Nebraska investors filed suit against Pioneer

National Trust Co. of Tucson, charging that in 1971 they were sold worthless contracts in a development called Apple Valley. They requested a jury trial in Lincoln.

Given the lucrative paper caper scam, a number of firms fattened the grift through an operation called "fenceposting." The term was coined in Arizona and refers to the practice of slipping bogus contracts into package deals along with legitimate contracts. The bogus contracts could have forged names drawn from the phone book or people who agreed to sign a contract but had no intention of ever making payments. Since the person signing the contract did not hold a recordable deed, a default of contract was an easy matter. Given the extreme attractiveness of discounted package deals, investors should have suspected that part of the package was rotten or that developers never intended to fulfill improvement promises. Perhaps even partial payment on contracts was incentive enough. Perhaps operating in a blind trust—protection from public scrutiny—afforded large investors the incentive to take a chance. Whatever the specific motive, few complaints were made during the boom period. The potential for big bucks loomed large.

The final category in this description is the proliferation of companies or formation of offspring companies from the original developing firm. This process generates from the selling of paper. The strategy is to form an initial development firm and sell lots. Members of the original company then form a second company as an investment or trust firm. A number of options affording big money are now available. The investment firm could buy contracts from the developing firm, collect payments, and allow the developing firm to file for bankruptcy and avoid the improvement expenses. In another option, loans could be made from one company to the other. Since this is essentially borrowing from oneself, no collateral was at stake. The firm standing to benefit the most from bankruptcy would then file, or the money could simply be moved along from one company to another, one step ahead of creditors and prosecution.

Ned Warren, Sr., the reputed "Godfather of Arizona Land Fraud," formed an extensive series of companies over a 15-year period. In each case he would sell a company to associates but be retained as a highly paid consultant. In this fashion he is alleged to have masterminded a vast multimillion-dollar operation in Arizona. During the period 1961 to 1977 Warren operated with impunity, and yet in a fairly open fashion. His list of credits is long and impressive, including Great Southwest Land and Cattle, Cochise Park, Lake Montezuma, Verde Lakes, Prescott Valley, Queen Creek, Consolidated Mortgage, Advance Realty, and others. Another con artist, Harvey Neal Kramer, acquired a controlling interest in nearly a score of Arizona corporations. One by one the firms would be looted and liquidated, with profits shuffled along a chain of firms ending with Kingston Land and Cattle Company. Kingston is headquartered on Grand Cayman Island, where federal authorities have been denied access to the corporation records.

## CONTROL AND CORRUPTION OF REGULATORY AGENCIES

The various forms of land fraud described above are difficult to maintain over a long period without some form of official complicity. While the boom market mentality will tolerate some unethical practices, it cannot account for repeated flagrant violations of the law. Corruption of public officials is the obvious means of avoiding prosecution.

Control of legal and regulatory agencies was apparently one of Ned Warren, Sr.'s, specialties. According to a copyrighted story by the IRE, Warren learned the ropes from Nathan Voloshen, a master influence peddler in Washington during the sixties. Voloshen's basic premise was: "If you control the party machinery—party officials and key contributors —you essentially control the government, because the party runs the elected officials."[9] One of Warren's methods was to acquire politicians as business associates. Two democratic national committeemen were partners with Warren at separate times.[10] Key officials in and contributors to the state Republican and Democratic parties were within Warren's web of influence. Even Senator Barry Goldwater once wrote a letter on Senate stationery promoting the sale of Arizona land to American servicemen in Southeast Asia. It was this land deal that recently forced Warren to plead guilty to charges of grand theft.

The key public official for Warren and others over the years was State Real Estate Commissioner J. Fred Talley. According to an IRE story, Talley was receiving up to $10,000 a month in payoffs from various land companies. Half of the $10,000 supposedly went to a higher state official. The same IRE story told of Sunday afternoon parties held by Talley for the loyal employees of the Real Estate Commission which were attended by Warren and associates. An informant stated: "Old Fred, he was king of the kings at the parties. He sat there and everybody was paying attention to him and he was good ol' Talley, our good ol' buddy . . . love this guy . . . they had Talley so buttered up." Even Talley's son Fred, Jr., worked as a sales manager in the Warren-run Diamond Valley operation.[11] Over the years Talley apparently was enormously helpful to Warren and others, enabling them to head off consumer complaints and avoid legal entanglements. When the police informed the commission of their intention to raid Great Southwest and seize the books, Talley sent his men there first, and it took a court order to get the Great Southwest books from him. Other stories tell of companies being tipped off in advance of impending inspections, enabling the firms to get things in order for a good show.

During Talley's tenure, there were numerous consumer complaints that apparently went unanswered. Dr. Leon Beene, who claimed he was pressured into resigning from his investigative position with the legislature on land fraud, said that he "got sick" from reading letters of complaints from defrauded land buyers. "If you want to get angry," said Beene, "read the Real Estate Department complaints."[12] In addition to unanswered complaints, it was also apparent that checks into the background of applicants for real estate licenses were cursory at best. In the case of convicted felon Harvey Neal Kramer, the *Arizona Republic* published a story in 1973 disclosing that he was operating an illegal pyramid sales scheme in Georgia. At that time Kramer already had been convicted of a crime in Indiana. Despite this disclosure, Kramer was subsequently granted a real estate license that was valid as of July 1977.[13] After receiving his license, Kramer worked for Horizon Corp., which is currently charged with sales misrepresentations by the Federal Trade Commission.[14]

In addition to regulatory agencies, Warren and others had considerable clout with the judicial system. From the state attorneys general to county attorneys and superior court there were numerous actions that proved favorable to Warren and other land firms during the boom period. Prosecution evidence was lost, cases were dismissed, complaints were not acted on, and even after guilty verdicts were obtained the sentences in some cases seem out of line. Warren himself appeared to be immune to the law, but then, as Maricopa County Attorney Moise Berger said in a reported conversation to a Phoenix police detective, "The Goddam lid is on the son-of-a-bitch."[15]

## END OF THE LAND BOOM

By 1974 the economy was in the midst of what appeared to be a long-term slump. Money was tight and loans were being called in on everything that seemed the least bit tenuous. In Arizona money was especially tight on anything concerned with construction, such as retirement or vacation homes. People who had bought land were now taking a hard look at the value of their investments. Lot owners who were fighting developers over delays in improvements and those attempting to receive compensation for fraudulent schemes were now panicked. The boom mentality had vanished.

Serious investigations of land values and the defaulting of numerous development companies brought consumer complaints to a record 2,000 a year between 1974 and 1976. People demanded and began to receive assistance from federal agencies, who in turn put pressure on state agencies.

The bribery hearing of J. Fred Talley in 1974 was only the beginning. Public arousal brought a change of state administration in 1974. Promises of clean government fell on receptive ears. In the business community an unusual group was formed called the Phoenix Forty. Consisting of 40 of the business elite in the Phoenix area, this group made several public statements about the state of crime, especially white-collar crime, in Arizona. It was obvious the business community felt a need to alter its public image. This group was instrumental in forcing out the county attorney on the basis that he failed to do his job (followed the dismissal of charges against Ned Warren, Sr.). Regulatory agencies and the judicial system responded with investigations and indictments. Naturally the media followed the cases with a newfound zeal.

With former public officials and fraudulent land operators now facing the real possibility of prison terms, the situation grew tense and violence erupted. Edward Lazar, a former business partner of Ned Warren, Sr., was shot to death in a parking lot the day before he was to testify before a grand jury. Another Warren associate, subsequently found guilty in a land fraud case, was sent to prison where he was killed by inmates. Other Warren associates died mysteriously, and yet no proof seemed to exist of Warren's guilt. Then on June 13, 1976, Don Bolles, an investigative reporter for the *Arizona Republic,* was murdered by a bomb placed under his car. While the Bolles murder probably has no direct relation to land fraud, it served to blow off the lid that County Attorney Berger had previously spoken of. During the next year accounts of an incredible web of white-collar crime emerged.

## SUMMARY AND CONCLUSIONS

The elder Marshall Field once remarked that "Buying real estate is not only the best way, the quickest way and the safest way, but the only way to become wealthy."[16] Belief in this motto is perhaps the cornerstone of American middle-class economics. Most of us middle-income folk know the only way we will beat inflation is to invest wisely in real estate. Therefore, it is no surprise that whenever a new real estate market opens there are plenty of eager participants. Florida, Southern California, Colorado, and Arizona are the most recent bonanzas. These boom markets all seem to share the same economics mentality: a scarcity psychology involving a rare commodity in high demand; the social-psychological factor of a business identity involving shrewdness and a willingness to take a risk; access to the market by anyone with a small amount of capital; acceptance of a buyer beware attitude; and a significant degree of ambiguity in the overall rules of the game, allowing for wide latitude in manipulation by all participants.

In Arizona during the sixties and early seventies, the scarcity psychology syndrome was at a high pitch. With private land, water, and electricity at a premium, the average investor knew that land values were bound to skyrocket in rapidly growing southwest desert. Phoenix residents have seen their property values double and triple in the past 10-15 years. Sun City has become a thriving retirement community. If it could happen in Phoenix and Sun City, then why not in other areas of the state? This belief led hundreds of thousands of people to make land investments in Arizona over the past two decades.

The business identity of shrewdness and risk-taking is a deep-seated American characteristic. Bend an elbow at the corner tavern and a day laborer will tell you about the fantastic deal he got on an old car that he will fix up and sell at a profit. The stock market, house trading, buying antiques are all part of this business identity we hold dear. Applying this attitude to the land speculation sales pitch was a sure winner for Arizona subdivision developers. The salesman supplied the shrewdness rationale and the buyer added the excitement of investment risk, or the excitement of adventure in eventually packing up and moving to that desert retirement home.

Access to the real estate market during the sixties and early seventies was easy for most middle-class Americans. It was an affluent period for most of us. Inflation had not yet taken its big bite, jobs were fairly secure, automobiles were still cheap, and the horizon looked fairly bright. The kids were raising hell about Vietnam, but that would pass, and even they were having a fair amount of fun at their game of revolution. Thinking of a retirement home, a vacation retreat, or investment property was realistic for the majority. Consequently the land salesman had no trouble enticing prospective buyers to sales dinners and the like.

The fourth point in the boom mentality is the acceptance of a buyer beware attitude by both seller and buyer. Boom markets generally involve a new product or idea. For the businessman it involves the attitude of exploitation, that is, work the market for all it's worth before the craze levels off or dies out. For the buyer it involves the philosophy of "he who hesitates is lost" and the acceptance of taking a risk. The buyer understands that things are moving so fast that it is not prudent to cover all the angles before making the plunge. This factor enables developers to sell subdivision lots in barren Arizona regions without fear of the customer reading the fine print or asking to see a property report before signing the contract.

The last factor in the boom mentality concerns the degree of ambiguity in the rules covering both business and consumer activity. For the land developer, the laws in Arizona were either vague and without teeth or nonexistent. On the legal side of the problem, developers could sell land in marginal areas and make grandiose promises about the future without fear of legal reprisal. The moral side of the issue could simply be left in a state of ambiguity. After all, cities in Arizona and elsewhere had been started from scratch and succeeded. All it took was commitment and industry on the part of residents. Given the affluent market, the buyer beware attitude, and the notion that buyers were also a greedy lot, why raise an issue of morality or business ethics? The lack of tight regulations and well-defined norms of land development seemed to dictate a business ethic of exploitation. Therefore, the business community seemed to invoke the axiom "whatever the market will bear," and the market was wide open. On the consumer's side, the ambiguity was basically the same. There was a commodity to be consumed for profit and security. Very little negative evidence on the soundness of these investments seemed to exist. Arizona was definitely growing at an enormous rate. Therefore, anything was possible—the sky might be the limit. In short, the ambiguity factor was the vacuum that enabled the business community and the consumer to wheel and deal according to "the greater fool theory."

The greater fool theory is based on the premise that in a boom market a buyer can always be found at a profit. Consequently, the business community was fairly eager to participate in land development. Investment capital, trust operations, legal services, advertising, and construction were profitably involved during the boom period. When various practices such as misrepresentation, reneging on promised improvements, and selling bogus paper became evident, the reaction in the business community was to handle it as a civil matter and not criminal activity. Traditionally white-collar crime such as embezzelment is handled "in house." The consumer is left to seek redress through regulatory agencies. The land market, being a highly profitable venture, was not to be disrupted. Regarding consumer complaints, businessmen also used the rationalization that many of these people were just as greedy as the con artist and got what they deserved. The definition of the situation in the business community was that almost everything and everyone was fair game. Also, this was still the old West where the rule that everyone is responsible for his own actions could be invoked.

For regulatory agencies there was considerable ambiguity in the law and the administration of justice. It was difficult to develop a solid case for fraud, and even when a case was made, the sentence was only a fine (except for federal convictions). What remained for the regulatory agencies was the ability to apply pressure through harassment. This form of power could enable regulatory agencies to get in on the action (receive payoffs), but not to close down the operations. Given the amount of money being generated by land speculation, one can argue that it might have been foolhardy to clean house. In any case, it seems plausible that many people both inside and outside the legitimate business community had a stake in the corruption of public officials.[17]

By 1974 the situation began to change dramatically. The economic slump forced businessmen and consumers alike to reevaluate their investments. The greater fool theory was no longer tenable for land development. Buyers were not easy to find, consumer complaints mounted, and the business community began to speak out. Apparently investment firms, contractors, and trust companies could no longer handle various frauds as civil matters. Increased pressure on the regulatory agencies forced the exposure of corruption. In 1974 hearings on bribery charges against Real Estate Commissioner J. Fred Talley were conducted. Talley resigned and died before formal criminal charges were made, but a picture of criminal fraud was beginning to emerge. What once was defined as normal business, such as discounts, rebates, gifts, shrewd sales, was now being defined as bribery and fraud. Essentially, boom market definitions were being replaced by public "ideal ethics." The public began to demand and receive criminal investigations rather than civil redress.

Free of local constraints, federal agencies such as the Federal Trade Commission began investigations and hearings on the interstate sale of phony contracts. Federal and local grand jury hearings were held. Violence erupted with the death of several land fraud figures and ending with the murder of investigative reporter Don Bolles in June of 1976. The public's immediate reaction (via media stories) was that land fraud was the motive for Bolles's murder. While this scenario has since been discarded, it served to stimulate public outrage against the land development business. Investigations into various land fraud practices were now top media stories.

The death of Bolles became a national story, and accounts of Arizona land fraud appeared in the nation's leading newspapers and magazines. In the aftermath a group of investigative reporters called the IRE was formed and came to Phoenix to investigate white-collar crime. What unfolded was a shocking web of crime involving public figures and known mobsters engaged in gambling, narcotics, prostitution, and land fraud. While the local business and political community was chagrined and reacted negatively to the IRE's activity, the situation may actually have benefitted their position. Business and government now blamed organized crime for land fraud and made a public demonstration of cleaning house. During late 1976 and 1977 blind trusts were outlawed, a new criminal code was proposed, and tougher real estate laws on subdivisions were enacted. The business community was now applying a new set of definitions to land development—that of caution and regulation.

Commenting on the land boom and resulting fraudulent activity Burton Lewkowitz of the Arizona Realtor's Association stated:

If the professional association had been in control of the land development business the fraud would not have occurred. The difference
between a realtor belonging to the Realtor's Association and someone
who simply has a license to sell real estate is one of professional ethics
and control.[18]

While this statement accurately reflects the attitude of realtors today, it
does not account for what happened during the boom period. One may
well ask, where was the Association when the fraud was in full swing? It
seems that at best the Realtor's Association did not have much influence
on the regulatory agencies or the political/legal process until the mid-
seventies. In the past several years that situation has reversed, and the Association has led the fight for tougher laws and more effective regulation
of real estate development. But this has all occurred after the public and
the business community turned from a boom market mentality to a more
cautious approach in land speculation and development. What the realtors
seem to be saying now is we want to regulate and control so as not to kill
the golden goose. In sociological terms, a new definition of the situation
has emerged.

## NOTES

1. *Arizona Republic* (Phoenix), 26 June 1977.
2. *Arizona Daily Star* (Tucson), 23 March 1977.
3. In 1976 the Arizona legislature outlawed the formation of blind trusts and ordered all trusts opened to the public.
4. Morton C. Paulson, *The Great Land Hustle* (Chicago: Henry Regnery Company, 1972), p. 56.
5. *Arizona Republic,* 5 December 1976.
6. *Ibid.,* 25 June 1977.
7. Investigative Reporters and Editors (IRE) were a group of newspapermen that in-vestigated crime in Arizona and wrote a series of syndicated articles that appeared in various newspapers throughout the country during the spring of 1977.
8. Personal interview, June 1977.
9. *Arizona Daily Star,* 24 March 1977.
10. Lee Ackerman and Dr. John Kruglick, both former Democratic national committee-men, were associated with Western Growth and Capital and Prescott Valley, respectively.
11. *Arizona Daily Star,* 24 March 1977.
12. *Arizona Republic,* 26 June 1977.
13. Kramer's license was suspended by the Real Estate Commission in July 1977 when it was discovered (after compliance with the fingerprint law) that he had been convicted of theft in 1973. Given the *Arizona Republic* story, what was a fact in 1977 apparently was not in 1973.
14. *Arizona Republic,* 19 June 1977.
15. IRE, *Arizona Daily Star,* 25 March 1977.
16. Paulson, *The Great Land Hustle,* p. 102.
17. According to an *Arizona Republic* story (7/18/77) elected regulatory officials from the Corporation Commission to superior court judges have for many years received up to one-third of their campaign funds from the industries they regulate. Some regulatory officials see nothing wrong in this practice. As Ernest Garfield, corporation commissioner, states, "Its my judgment that no one is going to buy me for a campaign contribution."

Yet Commissioner Garfield also stated that elected officials such as himself often solicit contributions from the firms they regulate. In defense he stated, "That is all perfectly legal." Speaking for the regulated companies, a former board chairman of a major utility company said, "I never felt these contributions were in exchange for favors." Nevertheless, one commission source estimated that "on a good week more than $100 worth of freebies would exchange hands" between agency personnel and executives of regulated companies.

18. Personal interview, June 1977.

# IV

# Securities Frauds, Price-Fixing, and High-Level Financial Scams

## INTRODUCTION

Part IV includes three chapters which analyze the secret world of securities frauds, price-fixing, and other high-level financial wheelings and dealings. While it is always preferable to have first-hand observational accounts of all kinds of deviant actions and practices, this is typically impossible to obtain for such high-level financial transactions. We have therefore tried to include three of the very best analyses done by those who possess the inside information and technical knowledge needed to understand such activities. In Chapter 8 William E. Blundell, one of the editors for the *Wall Street Journal* and author of many excellent articles on business activities, presents an in-depth account of Equity Funding, perhaps one of the largest securities and investment frauds ever perpetrated on the American public, eventually involving losses of somewhere between two and three billion dollars, more than the total losses of *all* street crime in the United States for one year. Like the generally booming economic climate needed to sustain the vast land fraud practices in Arizona, as described by Robert Snow in the last chapter, Equity Funding emerged and survived for over a decade (1960-73) partly because of the optimistic economic situation and the greed which typically sustains it. The "Equity Funding Concept" involved a combined life insurance and (mutual funded) investment "package," sold to investors with a new twist on the old theme of "getting something for nothing." By the time this huge financial empire crumbled, millions of investors lost billions of dollars. As William Blundell points out, the victims tended to be "the little people who bleed and suffer for months and years and perhaps the rest of their lives. In this sense the toll taken by Equity Funding was one of the most horrible of any modern crime." As with most business and securities crimes, the Equity Funding conspirators, if convicted, received relatively light fines and sentences when compared to their "street crime" counterparts.

Some of the reasons for this are presented in Chapter 9, "Wall Street Flouts the Law" by Christopher Elias, which shows the interface between the Wall Street financial experts and those mandated to control their actions, especially the Securities and Exchange Commission. Elias argues that Wall Street financial institutions routinely violate the laws and regulations set up to protect investors' interests and officials commonly prefer to look the other way, except of course in those situations which gain media attention or publicity, when the officials have to denounce the immoral and illegal dealings of their erstwhile "colleagues."

In "The Business of Buying Friends" (Chapter 10) by Jim Hougan, we are given a detailed account of the massive bribes, kickbacks, and other financial shennanigans of Lockheed Aircraft Corporation, America's largest defense multinational. While Hougan argues that the multi-billion dollar business transactions involving contracts for aircraft can only take place in the context of a near-perfect symbiosis between national political officials and the corrupt business leaders, increasingly our largest multinational corporations operate with many of the privileges of sovereign states, difficult if not actually impossible to control.

# 8

# *Equity Funding: "I Did It for the Jollies"*

*William E. Blundell*

If Beacon Street in Boston has the aroma of Old Money and Wall Street is redolent of Big Money, then there hangs over the Avenue of the Stars the crisp, raw smell of New Money. This singular boulevard bisects a commercial, residential, business, and entertainment complex in Los Angeles known as Century City. Designed as a self-contained urban tomorrowland, it is as pretty and patterned as the architects' drawings; amid the song of fountains and the flutter of flags, office towers rise sleekly from lawns banked with flowers. It all looks rather too good to be true. The same could have been said of its most notorious tenant, Equity Funding Corporation of America.

Equity Funding was an "idea company." In the soaring sixties, when it went public and became a hot stock, an idea was all you really needed. Carloads of hungry money poured into anything with certain buzz words in the corporate title: computer, systems, micro-this or -that. Sometimes it didn't matter what the company actually *did*. The grandly titled Performance Systems Inc. peddled fried chicken, and not very good fried chicken at that.

Century City was and is a lodestone for idea companies, the hot young lawyers who serve them, the consultants, the guys with a gimmick. Far down Wilshire Boulevard in the old downtown area, the big conservative banks, oil companies, and other long-entrenched businesses soberly managed their assets to minimize the chance of loss. But out on the West Side, in Century City and adjacent Beverly Hills, the swingers clustered.

They managed assets to maximize the chance for profit. If that often did not materialize, if, distressingly, a shortsighted world was not ready for solar toilets or hamster tax-shelters or a particular synergistic miniconglomerate—well, it was not their own money the idea men were playing with. Tough luck, suckers.

There has never been a shortage of the latter among the residents of the West Side, which may house more *nouveaux riches* per acre than any place outside the Middle East. These self-made men, their fortunes just beginning to bloom, their backgrounds in finance sketchy, are eager to listen to those who have new ideas on how to make their money grow fast. In such a deep pool of capital thick with such fat fish, sharks are inevitable. So the West Side has had more than its share of business scandals and failures in recent years, with investors disconsolately picking their way through the ruins of bombed-out tax shelters, unstrung conglomerates, collapsed brokerages, and commodity options schemes blown to bits.

But the biggest explosion was that of Equity Funding. The company fit its surroundings perfectly: it was big, new, aggressive, obsessed with rapid growth, and it pushed an idea that gave it powerful investor appeal. This was the so-called Equity Funding concept.

In its execution, a purchaser first bought from an Equity Funding salesman a life-insurance policy and some mutual-fund shares. He paid for the shares, but then left them with the company, which used them as collateral for a loan it gave him to pay his policy premium. This procedure was followed for ten years, the company expanding its loan year by year to pay the annual policy premium, the insured buying, year by year, enough additional fund shares to keep his expanding loan collateralized. At the end of ten years the program was to end. The insured would pay off his loan and interest (usually with some of his fund shares). He would keep the rest of his shares and an insurance policy with cash value. He would have beaten the game, gotten something for nothing.

That assumes, of course, that the mutual fund shares were growing in value. Little was said about what would happen in a prolonged market slump, which would leave the insured with a capital loss on his shares, the loan to repay, and the interest. But in those bullish times no one appreciated that eventuality.

At first, Equity Funding was just an agency, selling policies and mutual funds underwritten and sponsored by other firms. But you didn't get to be a hot stock by just tending to your knitting, and beginning in 1967, three years after going public, the company started swallowing up all manner of other concerns in the carnivorous fashion of the day—winding up, by mid-1972, the owner of three insurance companies of its own, mutual-fund management and sales operations, savings-and-loan associations, real-estate companies, oil and gas concessions, a cattle-breeding outfit, and a Bahamian bank.

Wow, said Wall Street. Along the way Equity Funding became the fastest-growing financial-services concern on Fortune's list. The year it went public it earned a measly $390,000 on revenues of $2.9 million; when the roof caved in it was ready to report earnings for 1972 of $22.6 million on revenues of $152.6 million. It listed assets approaching $750 million and a net worth of $143.4 million.

Or so the company said. The whole thing was a mirage, and in a few short weeks in the spring of 1973 Equity Funding, as everyone had known it, simply disappeared. Subsequent investigation disclosed that since it had gone public it had *never* made any money. Its earnings all those years were fake. Its assets were bloated and its liabilities hidden. The money it had raised from bank loans and debenture offerings had been soaked up in covering its real losses. It had created out of thin air $2 billion worth of insurance that its agents had never written—and then resold it for cash to trusting reinsurers. It had gulled some of its auditors and suborned others, who then conspired with it in a swindle that lasted almost a decade. "Why did you do it, for God's sake, why?" an anguished banker asked one of the executive ringleaders. He looked at the banker and said, "I did it for the jollies."

That was not an entirely facetious answer. The methodology of the fraud at Equity Funding and its tremendous impact on various institutions has been dissected by financial writers. But there has been baffled silence on a central question—what possessed men, some of them professionals in specialties with clearly defined codes of ethics, men whose prior brushes with the law had amounted to traffic violations, to do what they did?

Twenty employees and two outside auditors of the company were indicted on federal charges in the case, including the chairman and president, several executive vice-presidents, and a clutch of vice-presidents and other managers. In the course of the fraud, these ordinary suburbanites, these guys next door, had engaged in lying, forgery, counterfeiting, bugging, embezzlement, and multiple forms of fraud that had victimized thousands of unwary people, costing them hundreds of millions of dollars.

But the criminals were victims too, sucked into a vortex they did not have the strength or the will to escape. Gradually, the conspiracy of which they were a part seemed to take on a life of its own and grew so enormous, so voracious, that it made vassals even of the men who had designed it and thought they were its masters. They could not halt it. By then, some had been so transformed by it that they did not care; they had grown to enjoy their bondage, and thus knew true evil. They were, in an awful sense, doing it for the jollies.

It is easy to label their motives. Money? Certainly with some it was very important. But it is also true that many of the conspirators got absolutely nothing out of the scheme and didn't ask to; they cheerfully slaved 80 hours a week to enrich their superiors and in the end went down clutching worthless company stock. Corporate loyalty? Some of that, yes—but for others it was a joke. One defendant hated corporate life and the values it represented to him. Others felt they owed nothing at all to Equity Funding as a corporation.

So labels say little. But there is a lesson. Corporations can and do create a moral tone that powerfully influences the thinking, conduct, values, and even the personalities of the people who work for them. This tone is set by the men who run the company, and their corruption can quickly corrupt all else. A startling thing about Equity Funding is how rarely one finds, in a cast of characters big enough to make a war movie, a man who said, "No, I won't do that. It's wrong." As for the majority who were sucked in and drowned, their motives were many and fixed. The important thing is that the fraud unerringly pressed upon their weaknesses, some of which they were unaware of at the time, and quickly overthrew them almost before they realized what had happened.

It all began, as Equity Funding itself began, with the enigmatic but menacing figure of Stanley Goldblum, a founder and chief executive of the company until the fraud was uncovered. Goldblum was one of five men who started Equity Funding in 1960. There was bickering, there were buyouts, and soon only two were left, Goldblum and Michael Riordan. Both had been salesmen, Goldblum in life insurance and Riordan a wholesaler in mutual funds, but there all similarity ended.

Riordan went to Cornell, came from money, and moved through life on wheels greased by it and by his own huge Irish expansiveness. He cut across all class lines. If Wall Street investment bankers and lawyers were his friends, so were denizens of the Manhattan bars where he drank the nights away. He loved parties, 100-mph spins in his Lincoln, a turn of the cards. Riordan's magnetism rose naturally from sheer warmth and unbounded enthusiasm. He wanted to smell the flowers while he could, and there was hardly a bouquet that went untested when he was on the scene.

Goldblum was his polar opposite. His father was a jeweler of small means, and Goldblum's dream of becoming a physician was stifled. Dropping out of UCLA short of his degree, he got a job hauling scrap. Later he would join his father-in-law in the meat-packing business, shoving tons of beef around every day, making sausage, just to earn a buck. It wasn't until 1955, when he was 28, that he turned to life insurance, eventually joining the partnership that evolved into Equity Funding.

He became a millionaire before he was 40, but money did not warm him. By all accounts, he was extraordinarily quick and shrewd, but aloof, hard, and curt with subordinates. His private life remained private. He was no bon vivant. While Riordan partied, Goldblum sweated in his $100,000 gym, behind his house, a silent man, pumping iron, maintaining an awesome physique; at six feet, two inches, 235 pounds of bone and muscle, he was physically intimidating. His eyes were chilly, and high cheekbones gave his face an Oriental cast. He had a cold, commanding manner that oozed power. Always seizing an initiative, giving the orders, dominating every meeting, he was as much emperor as chief executive.

It was not easy to talk to such a man, especially if you were several rungs below him on the corporate ladder. Goldblum knew it. He had a dark sense of humor, sometimes exercised at his own expense. He once characterized himself as "an imposing figure, a threatening authority figure. I'm not a gregarious fellow."

Most people mired in the fraud couldn't bring themselves to complain to Goldblum. Says one conspirator, a lowly vice-president:

> I never went up top. You looked at Goldblum and you knew you'd never get anywhere with him. He was such a grim man; I never saw him smile but once. That was when we were bugging the offices that the regulators were using for the audit of the company's books. Goldblum said, "If they catch you, tell them the bad guys over there (waving to the offices of some executive vice-presidents) told you to do it.

Gary Beckerman, a young manager involved in a counterfeiting scheme, asked for a vacation. "You're going to stay," said Goldblum flatly. "I don't know why I didn't up and leave anyway," Beckerman recalls. "If it had been anyone else I would have said, 'kiss my ass!' But Goldblum had this tremendous presence. . . ."

For all their differences, Goldblum and Riordan were close. The latter was almost certainly an architect of the early stages of the fraud, but his precise responsibility will probably never be fixed; he died in an uniquely Los Angeles fashion in 1969, when a mudslide triggered by heavy rains rolled down a hillside and through the wall of his canyon home, smothering him. Stanley Goldblum took the Riordan family into his house. "He was the greatest guy I ever met," said Goldblum, and years afterward, when his ornate office was seized upon disclosure of the fraud, only one personal thing would be found in it—a photograph of Mike Riordan.

If Riordan helped design the fraud, Goldblum played the major part in nourishing it into the devouring thing it eventually became. Riordan, as chairman, dealt with the sales force and with banks and Wall Street. Goldblum, the president, ran the internal affairs of the company—"the bookkeeper in the background," as he has been called. In late 1964, just after Equity Funding went public, the bookkeeper took what was probably the first step into the moras.

He told Jerome Evans, then Equity Funding's treasurer, to post as income money that the company hadn't yet received—commissions, he told Evans, that were due the company from brokerage firms involved in transactions with Equity Funding. Because it would have been improper to list these "give up" commissions as such, Evans was told that he should post them in the books as ordinary commissions received on the sales of mutual fund-life insurance packages.

There weren't any commissions. This was the beginning of what has been called the "funding fraud." The funding concept, under which a buyer of the mutual fund-insurance package was granted loans on his shares to pay his policy premiums, yielded income to the company in several ways. The company got commissions on the sale of the funds and the insurance, and interest on the loan. It then paid out part of this income in commissions to the individual agents who did the actual selling and in interest on the money it had to borrow itself to extend the policyholder loans. What was left was profit. Now what if the company claimed phony commission income? First, its revenues would look larger than they really were. Second, net income, or profit, could be similarly inflated at an even greater rate, since there were no real agents' commissions and other expenses to pay. Third, phony assets could be added to the books in the form of "loans receivable" from phony borrowers.

All the scheme required were complaisant outside auditors, which Equity Funding had in men from Wolfson, Weiner and Company; the sabotage of the internal auditing function, easily accomplished by simple neglect; and the knowledge of the few people who actually made false entries and ordered them. Only those who needed to know needed to be told. With hardly more than a few pencil strokes, the company could be made to look bigger, more efficient, and more financially stable than it was.

Evans posted phony figures in the books at the end of 1964 and waited for the cash to come in. It didn't. Evans asked about it, and Goldblum assured him it was coming; meanwhile, there were even more "give up" commissions for Evans to put on the books for the first quarter. Reluctantly, Evans did so. Strand after fine strand, for quarter after quarter, the web was cast over Evans until, in time, he found he could not resist at all. By now he knew there were no real commissions coming; Goldblum knew he knew, and the pretense was dropped. Year after year, Evans doctored the books at Goldblum's order. The president no longer even bothered to give Evans a commission figure—just an earnings-per-share target that Evans was to meet. The arithmetic was up to Evans.

The steady upward march of the company's reported earnings, revenues, and assets impressed Wall Street. Equity Funding's stock soared.

That was the purpose of the fraud. Goldblum had founder's shares in the company, as did Riordan, and both got rich. Goldblum was to make $5 million in stock; Riordan and his estate, $19 million. Beyond that, a high stock price was necessary to motivate Equity Funding's army of salesmen, lured to the company in part by a generous stock incentive program. And the bloated stock and asset figures were the keystone in Equity Funding's success in acquiring other companies in exchange for stock, in floating bond offerings, and in otherwise borrowing money.

The treatment of Evans by Goldblum; the encouragement to do what seemed at first a little thing, for a plausible reason; then the request to do it again and yet again, until finally there was no excuse, just an assumption that the subordinate was now firmly enmeshed in the conspiracy, run through the Equity Funding tale. "Nothing was ever laid out completely to me," says Larry Collins, a former officer jailed for his part. "It all evolved in little bits and pieces, gradually; it took a long time before it finally hit you that you were committing a crime. 'Don't worry,' they said. That's what they *always* said at Equity Funding. 'Don't worry.'"

Evans kept plugging in phony figures and, year by year, sweated out the annual audits; certainly the auditors were complaisant, but still they needed certain assurances, even if these were lies, to justify the skewed figures they were reviewing. Early in 1969, just after Riordan died, and shortly after Evans himself had a heart attack, Evans could face it no longer. One day he left the office, packed his bags and drove aimlessly around the country for six weeks. He never returned to the company.

By now, after five years of falsification, Equity Funding's books were horribly distorted; assets in "funded loans receivable" were so bloated that it was nearly impossible to cover up the enormous discrepancy between the phony figure and the real. The audit of 1968 results was beginning, and the conspirators had lost Riordan and Evans.

The difficulties at Equity Funding were compounded by the arrival there of a couple of honest men. One was Harry Watkins, inexplicably assigned by the auditors to coordinate the 1968 audit. The other was a financial man, John Templeton, hired as controller by Equity Funding in late 1968 and later asked to take over Evans' audit chores after Evans disappeared.

Templeton just couldn't find any real evidence that Equity Funding had the $36 million in funded loans receivable that the books said it had. Then Harry Watkins did something that other members of his firm evidently had never bothered to do before. He pressed for the evidence, demanding a list of all those policyholders with funded loans outstanding so he could verify that they really had borrowed and owed the money. A computer run totaled their debts; the money due Equity Funding amounted to just $7.6 million.

This touched off a desperate scramble by the conspirators to somehow explain nearly $30 million in ephemeral assets. Goldblum gave Templeton the old story about the receipt of brokerage-house commissions concealed as ordinary commissions on funded programs and posted as loans receivable on the books. Fine, said Templeton; explain that to the auditor. No, said Goldblum.

At Goldblum's direction, Templeton then started on a course of justification, adding terminated loans, new business, and other dubious entries to try to cover the discrepancy. At this point, he too was in danger of being sucked in. The troublesome Watkins was whisked off the audit entirely and a more reasonable bean counter substituted. Templeton stood alone and under great pressure.

However, none of the coverups completely succeeded, and Goldblum himself finally had to trot out the tall tale about commissions for the auditors. He added that Riordan, who had just died, had been the only man who kept track of these commissions, and the total was now lost. The auditors bought this remarkable story and the "evidence" that Templeton reluctantly compiled to verify the claimed $36 million in loans receivable. That evidence was a pastiche of lies and exaggerations, some of them impossible on their face.

By the close of the audit, Templeton was convinced that the figures were ridiculous, but he told no one. Then he was asked to sign a form S-1, an official registration statement filed with the Securities and Exchange Commission, that included the bogus 1968 financial figures. It is a crime knowingly to certify a false SEC statement. For Templeton, the situation became drastic.

In a roomful of his superiors and corporate attorneys, he refused to sign, and left. Someone else signed. A week later, he was called to Goldblum's office. There, Templeton blurted out his suspicion that there was fraud. Goldblum's almond-shaped eyes regarded him coldly. "When are you going to forget all this shit and get to work?" the harsh voice asked.

"Never," said Templeton, and walked out.

Later the same day, Goldblum called him back in and offered him a raise and promotion. Templeton wavered: here was a chance to get places fast, make big money. Would Goldblum sweeten the pot with more cash, maybe grant Templeton stock options? Sure, said Goldblum. The controller succumbed.

However, he was still deeply disturbed. Ambition at war with conscience, Templeton talked with his wife. One night very soon after that, he went into Goldblum's empty office and left a letter of resignation on the massive, spotless desk. He walked away, one of the few men at Equity Funding who had been exposed to complicity in the fraud and then struggled free of it.

"Never underestimate Goldblum," said Rodney Loeb, general counsel of Equity Funding then and now, and uninvolved in the fraud. "He was a cold man, but a damn good psychologist. He knew just how far to push people and just when to give them a pat on the back. He'd say, 'Give that guy two attaboys and he'll do fine,' and he'd be right." Goldblum even had "attaboy" certificates printed to award to deserving employees.

Templeton's successor as controller was a former auditor, Samuel Lowell, a round, soft dumpling of a man who loved rich living and tournament bridge. His highest qualification for the job, however, lay in his disregard for the niceties his predecessor had observed. Quickly becoming acquainted with the fraud, he fell into it with no discernible struggle and became one of its key operators; before long he was executive vice-president for finance and operations, one of Goldblum's closer associates and a principal juggler of the books.

Among other things, Lowell helped in the foreign phase, one of the most ludicrous aspects of the whole conspiracy. Through a series of deals involving shell corporations, phony notes signed by fictitious people like "Dr. Heinrich Wangerhof" and "Alphonso Perez da Silva" (names invented by Goldblum and Lowell), the conspirators tried to raise cash abroad in the form of loans.

The loans never would be recorded as liabilities. The proceeds would be used as "free credits" to reduce the outrageously large funded-loan figures swelling on the books and to meet operating expenses. Though the figures showed it was making money, the company all along was losing heavily, and salaries, rents, agents' commissions, vendors, all had to be paid in hard dollars. The foreign operations also served as a maze in which to generate and conceal more bogus income.

Overall, the whole foreign venture was more trouble than it was worth and only betrayed the amateurish fumbling of its perpetrators. The apogee was reached in 1970 when they tried to swindle the Pope in the purchase of a rundown Rome spaghetti factory, 93 percent of which was owned by the Holy See. They bought it for a song and got the promise of a $5 million loan at low interest to renovate the place, plus another $1.2 million in loan money up front. The latter they quickly shunted into Equity Funding's coffers and, through a complicated series of maneuvers, repatriated most of the rest of the loan, the proceeds of which were to have stayed in Italy to pay for renovation work. The company then went about mismanaging the pasta plant, losing hundreds of thousands of dollars before it was able to unload it. Italian authorities launched criminal investigations centering on the loans, and Equity Funding had to repay them. The whole thing was a typical bungle. With fine scorn, the report of Equity Funding's trustee in bankruptcy concludes that the conspirators "became entranced by a romantic self-image as captains of international business and finance."

While all this was going on, Equity Funding was getting deeper into the business of underwriting insurance. The company's first acquisition, in 1967, was Presidential Life Insurance Company of Illinois, a smallish insurer that was quickly renamed Equity Funding Life Insurance Company (EFLIC) and moved to Los Angeles. With Presidential, Equity Funding purchased the services of its 30-year-old general counsel, Fred Levin.

Almost immediately, Levin was named president of EFLIC and became an executive vice-president of the parent company in charge of all insurance and marketing operations. (Equity Funding later purchased two other insurers, both untouched by the fraud.) Before long Levin would replace Lowell as Goldblum's right hand, and would corrupt EFLIC thoroughly. He did so with such charm that to this day most of the people he sucked in feel kindly toward him. Many detested Lowell—and at least one referred to him as a "pompous ass"—but they still call Levin "Freddie."

If Levin was a corrupter, he was also corrupted, the victim of a mass of insecurities whose cumulative effect was to drive him unmercifully to achieve. He climbed for the sake of climbing, a mountaineer on a slope whose summit he could never reach or even see. Conscience, a moral structure, anything that might stand in the way, was ground to rubble by this remorseless need to achieve. He was Sammy Glick with warmth.

Like Goldblum, Levin was a Jew, but a practicing, Orthodox Jew. As the son of a poor kosher butcher in Chicago, Levin, like his new boss, had to make his own success and did. President of this class and that student council, a brilliant student in Hebrew theology, an honor student in law school, a bright, energetic young lawyer, he pushed and strove. "I always used everything I had," he says.

So Levin became Goldblum's protege. The chief executive unbuttoned himself more with Levin, and to some extent Lowell, than with anyone else at the company, cracking jokes and holding long, easy conversations. Levin loved it, loved going to Goldblum's house with Lowell, staying up till midnight hatching new plots. He basked in the radiance of Goldblum's regard.

By his own account, he desperately needed that regard. As a boy he remembered his father pacing the floor night after night, harried by fear that his little shop—"a disgusting business," Levin calls it—would fail, that he could not handle the work. Levin was embarrassed by his father's ignorance of English and slipped books under his pillow at night. He was shamed by what he saw as his father's weakness and frightened by it. Once, says Levin, his father tried to overdose on pills and had to be taken to the hospital. "Another time," he recalls, "I caught him in front of the oven with the gas on."

There was no warmth between them. Gnawed by his anxieties, the elder Levin had no time for his son. "I could never figure out why he didn't play with me, like the other fathers. . . . I remember him as a weak man," Levin says. Freddie Levin would be as different from his father as he could. He would put a world between himself and the butcher shop and that weak and worried man, endlessly pacing the floors at night while the boy listened.

And so it happened. Levin rose, earning a reputation as an honest, diligent young attorney at the Illinois state insurance department, getting hired in 1964 as assistant vice-president and general counsel of Presidential when still in his mid-twenties. He worshiped his boss—"I was like his child"—sopping up the attention and affection he never had as a child. In 1968, he became the boss. At 30 he was, he says, the youngest president of any large life-insurance company in the United States. "A real ego trip," Levin says.

Goldblum had made it so. His new young president owed him a lot and knew it. There was a stronger bond. "Maybe I saw Stanley as the father I'd never had," Levin says. "I really liked the guy and felt he liked me. He epitomized everything I ever wanted. He had a big house in Beverly Hills and drove a maroon Rolls-Royce. We were both from the ghetto and worked our way out." Levin was later to do anything necessary to keep the regard and affection of this man Goldblum, who was many things but who certainly was not weak.

But Goldblum's affection alone was not enough, not nearly. Levin had to get it from everywhere he could. "Fred mother-henned everyone in sight," says general counsel Loeb, who saw him often.

> He gave off warmth, because he needed the adulation that came back to him in return. One year, on his birthday, he must have gotten thirty or forty presents from the sales force. He brought me in and waved his arm around and said, "Look at that! Look at how those guys love me." And he kept all that stuff in his office for ten days.

In time Loeb, who was fond of Levin, would wonder whether the young executive had the emotional stability to handle his job. Once Levin rode with Loeb in a limousine after a meeting with officers of Bankers National Life Insurance Company, which Equity Funding purchased in 1971. Levin had been at his best, asking penetrating questions, holding forth at length on insurance matters and Equity Funding's handling of its business, loosening things up with jokes. In the car he was euphoric to the edge of mania. "Those people loved me!" he said. "Didn't I wow them? Didn't I have them eating out of my hand?"

Loeb was told that Levin was certainly up to his job, a brilliant executive who just happened to have "insecurity problems." Don't worry about it, Loeb was told. Still, Loeb did worry. He would sit in meetings with Levin, watching the dark-haired, bespectacled young man gnaw on his fingernails until they were bloody.

On taking over Presidential, Levin surrounded himself with the brightest young executives he could find. He wanted subordinates who were under 30, younger than himself. He wanted the respect and affection from junior men that he himself had been giving to his seniors. For a man like Levin, giving orders to an older man would be difficult. And how much love, warmth, and loyalty could he expect from such a subordinate?

His recruiting was successful. Not long after he took over he was encircled by youngsters. One of them was Lawrence Grey Collins, then 29, who joined EFLIC as an underwriting manager in 1968. "I was happy where I was before," Collins recalls,

> and I didn't want to make a change. Fred asked me out to dinner and I said what the hell, why not listen anyway? So I took my wife along —she's my business manager—and Levin was just a hell of a salesman. He could make you believe things were going to happen, and he told me he was going to make a giant out of the company. This appealed to me and I signed on.

Collins got $15,000, a $3,000 increase from his previous salary. Soon he would become a vice-president in charge of all underwriting, and eventually he would earn $30,000 a year and a stock bonus. Collins still felt that much of the time he was underpaid, and he was right. It was a small price to pay for his soul.

Only a few months after Collins came aboard, Levin ordered him to Chicago to sack about 30 employees on the underwriting staff. All the work was being transferred to Los Angeles, and Levin wanted fresh faces, hired locally. Quiet and conservative, Collins was ill-suited for hatchet work, and he quailed. "I could hardly face up to it," he recalls. "It was so shitty, right before Christmas. I had my assistant do most of it. This gave me my first inkling that maybe they might someday be just as cold-blooded with me."

Collins had caught his first glimpse of something cold and ugly that lay under Levin's warmth and candor. Levin did not quail at firing people, far from it; he sometimes seemed to get a perverse joy in it, and he made it a game. Once, when he and another Equity Funding executive went to New Jersey to fire a flock of Bankers National Life employees, Levin toyed with the idea of leaking word that if an employee were summoned to the unmarked office he, Levin, would occupy, the employee would be sacked; but if sent to the colleague's office, the employee would be praised and retained. Then, Levin suggested, the two of them should switch offices, and employees expecting rewards would be fired, and those expecting firing would be rewarded. Levin did drop the cruel hoax. But on another occasion, he told a Bankers executive that a new man was joining the firm. "In whose capacity?" the executive asked. "Yours," Levin said, brutally and truthfully.

No one saw this ugliness at first. EFLIC was humming, relocating and restaffing. By all accounts, it was a grand place to work, completely unlike the tightly ordered, dull gray world of most insurance companies. James Banks, a 29-year-old lawyer who was hired by Levin in 1968 as counsel and assistant secretary at EFLIC, remembers it fondly.

"The appeal of EFLIC at first was the same thing that kept me there till the end," he says.

> Levin's ability to galvanize and lead people was remarkable. The management at EFLIC was a nucleus of young guys intensely loyal to Fred. He promised a lot and delivered a lot. He made it a company with no hours. No one chewed you out for coming in late, and no one patted you on the head for working overtime. It was your time and your company, and there was no rigid hierarchy.

The youth movement overcame EFLIC and the parent Equity Funding as well. Lowell, moving up to an executive vice-presidency at 30, took on a young assistant named Michael Sultan. Later, as controller, Sultan would serve as Lowell's rubber stamp—writing the figures on phony transactions and doctoring the books at the boss's order. Art Lewis, a brilliant young actuary who became a primary cog in the conspiracy, signed on. So did Lloyd Edens, EFLIC treasurer, later vice-president of the parent company. All were on the near side of 30. And, like many other colleagues just a few years older, they shared a common fate.

All of them would go to jail.

The stress placed upon youth in this management cadre struck some of its former cadremen as an important factor in the success of the fraud. "We were all just crazy, punk kids, really," said Larry Collins. "Our people were easily led: we were too young to have developed mature ethical judgments. I have to wonder if the youth movement wasn't deliberate: In the Army, it's always the young troopers you get to do your killing."

But back then, it wasn't the Army; it was Camelot. There was Levin, giving everybody strokes and getting them in return from his young Turks. Lawyer Banks was caught up in the freewheeling approach and impressed by the glamour of it all.

"If there was a problem, you got on an airplane and you went and solved it," he recalled. Banks, a Canadian newly naturalized as an American, had worked as an obscure tax specialist, the stuffiest of fields, in one of the stuffiest big old-line law firms in Los Angeles. Now he was somebody.

"I would go to all the meetings and conventions and bask in all the compliments we were getting on our growth," he said. "The travel, the compliments—it was all pretty appealing. EFLIC was like the new little kid on the block, trying to make a name for himself. The company was terribly PR conscious, terribly sensitive to how others regarded it."

But at the top of the Equity Funding pyramid, there was trouble. Goldblum kept demanding that earnings per share grow year by year and quarter by quarter; the stock price had to be supported. But as we have seen, the books were a shambles, the foreign fraud was a botch, and there was simply not enough real cash coming in.

Still, no one outside suspected a thing. Wall Street, in the throes of the final surge of the bull market of the sixties, had put a value of $80 a share on Equity Funding stock in 1969. If you wanted to buy the company for cash on the counter, you would have had to pay about $420 million for its 5.2 million shares of stock; when it had gone public only five years before, it had sold a modest 100,000 shares at only $6 apiece.

But to keep the ball rolling, the company had to have cash to pay its bills. Conventional debt financing was a limited answer. Equity Funding already was borrowing heavily and there were two problems with that; you had to pay interest, and sooner or later you had to pay off the principal. For a company whose real operations were actually losing money all along, the disadvantages in honest borrowing were obvious.

So the management decided to steal. There was no comprehensive plan. Like everything else, this aspect of the fraud, in the words of Equity Funding's trustee, developed in a "helter-skelter, hand-to-mouth" fashion and was preceded by the usual rain dance of rationale, justification, and circumlocution.

It was a matter of putting a tentative toe in the water, then wading a little deeper—and finally swimming for your life. The full weight of this part of the fraud fell on Fred Levin and his men at EFLIC.

By now Levin knew about the funding operation. His friend Lowell had told him and Levin's first reaction was, "Hey, Sam—that's *your* problem." But when his turn came, there was no way Levin could thus dismiss Stanley Goldblum.

In 1963, when Equity Funding was just an agency selling insurance policies underwritten by others, it made a pact with Pennsylvania Life Company. In it, Equity Funding agreed, with two minor exceptions, to sell only insurance underwritten by Penn Life, and the latter agreed that only Equity Funding would be its agent in peddling life insurance in conjunction with mutual-fund shares. But Equity Funding's hunger for growth soon left it dissatisfied: the selling part of the insurance business isn't nearly as profitable as the underwriting of coverage, and Equity Funding consequently bought Presidential (later EFLIC). But it was still bound by the Penn Life pact. To get out of it, Equity Funding had to promise that it would resell Penn Life some of the insurance that EFLIC would write—$250 million worth (in face amount) in the 1968-70 period.

This was what the industry calls a reinsurance treaty. It has its legitimate uses. A company may be short of operating cash or the required assets to back the sale of more policies. By selling some off to another insurer, it gets the cash it needs. The buying company is responsible for maintaining the cash reserves to back up the insurance policies it has agreed to underwrite; in return, it should get the lion's share of future premiums.

The policyholder never knows that he has been bartered away to somebody else. The seller company remains responsible for all the bookkeeping and records on the policy and still does all the billing, collecting, and communicating with the insured. The seller also gets to count the policies it has sold as insurance in force, even though the buyer counts them too.

Reinsurance is one of the most poorly regulated activities in an industry where regulation is often abysmally bad anyway. It is largely a gentleman's agreement: the buyer gets from the seller not the actual policies themselves, but just a printout of numbers and other bare data on the policies—premium, type of insurance, and so on. Ordinarily, he simply takes it for granted that he is being dealt with honestly.

When a selling company cedes a policy, it will turn over the annual premium to the buyer. The latter pays the seller an initial amount greater than that premium. This reflects reimbursement of the seller's sales expense and a cut of the profit that accrues when the policy has remained in force for some years.

In its reinsurance deals, Equity Funding got 180 to 190 percent. For every $100 in premium it turned over, essentially, it was getting a quick gross profit in cash of $80 to $90; the long-term profit would go to the reinsurance company that bought the premiums.

After making its deal with Penn Life, a wildly optimistic Equity Funding management also entered into reinsurance agreements with several other concerns. Everyone just assumed that Equity Funding's hot-shot salesmen would drum up enough new life insurance business to meet the Penn Life commitment and more, but early in 1968 it was apparent that they weren't going to come close. This would be embarrassing to a company that was tooting its own trumpet within the industry and up and down Wall Street.

It would also be expensive. Equity Funding's stock might be seriously affected. In addition, the company might also lose an increasingly valuable Penn Life stock option given it as an inducement for sales back in 1965, exercisable now only if the company was able to meet the terms of its Penn Life reinsurance treaty. What to do?

In 1968, the company stuck its corporate toe in the water by issuing what it called "special-class" insurance to its own salesmen and employees. At first, they'd be given a big inducement, a 50 percent reduction in the first year's premium, to sign up for coverage on themselves, their wives, children, cousins, great-aunts, and any other relatives they could scrape up. As fast as the business was written it would be dealt off to Penn Life, which would not be told of its "special-class" nature.

Then Equity Funding added another inducement. It gave insurance away, completely forgiving the first-year premium. Employees jumped at it, loading up on $50,000 policies for themselves and wives and $25,000 on each of their children, and the business was force-fed to an unsuspecting Penn Life.

The "special class" was, of course, garbage. It would lapse at a sky-high rate the second year, because employees would then have to pay premiums they couldn't have afforded in the first place. The buyer, Penn Life, would be stuck. No one cried about that, says a former EFLIC executive. "People would laugh out loud about it," he said. "They thought it was funny as hell to jab another company that way."

Equity Funding's director of communications and advertising, Gary Beckerman, had a pretty good idea that the special-class business was, to say the least, sharp dealing. But like so many others, the young PR-marketing man rationalized it. "I asked myself, 'Is it honorable?' No. 'Who's hurt?' The reinsurers. 'Is the reinsurer a big boy?' You bet. In the end, I certainly wasn't enthusiastic about it, but it didn't seem worth quitting for. 'Let the country club boys fight it out,' I said, 'I'm just taking my pictures and putting out my releases.'" Beckerman signed his mother up for the special-class coverage. She flunked the physical.

Among the Levin cadre at EFLIC, the special-class ploy went down without anyone gagging. At this stage, anything that helped EFLIC was applauded as inherently desirable. Already, the difference between honest achievement and a reputation founded on lies was blurred; before long it would disappear entirely, and the conspirators would wallow in self-delusion so acute that it bordered on clinical psychosis.

"I had a tremendous amount of corporate loyalty then," said Jim Banks, EFLIC's young counsel. "The company was like your family, like the Mafia. When you spoke you fell into phrases like 'the company and I' and 'me and the company.' You might criticize something internally, but you would never, never badmouth the company to outsiders."

Levin, who hadn't yet taken over EFLIC, had only a peripheral part in the early "special-class" scheme, which would continue in 1969 and 1970. But in 1969 he was called on to pay his dues. The men at the top concluded that the potential for special class was too limited to help the company meet the Penn Life quota that year, the company's earnings target, or its need for cash. So Levin and his men designed and operated the so-called "pending business" caper to supplement it.

In this scheme, policies that had been applied for but not yet granted, were recorded as if they were in force and the premiums paid. Then they were sold to Penn Life and others for cash. "Stanley and I came to accept that others were doing the same thing," says Levin. " 'Everybody does it,' we said. But we weren't taking into account the scale of the thing." Up to $750,000 in premiums were sold.

Pending business is also garbage. A high percentage of applications never became policies: applicants strong-armed into applying by salesmen often change their minds, and others can't pass the physical examination, credit check, or other screening measures. The "policies" sold on these dropouts are thus entirely bogus. The company had moved from the resale of real insurance on real people, to insurance of dubious worth on its own employees, to fake insurance on real people. The next step was only natural—fake insurance written on fake people.

In the summer of 1970, the conspirators decided to take that fateful step which has given the most notoriety to the Equity Funding case. They would insure phantoms.

The year 1970 was shaping up as rotten. The company had just made another costly error in judgment dictated by the swollen corporate ego, moving from a Beverly Hills location into its luxurious and expensive new quarters in Century City, quickly dubbed "the Taj Mahal." Though the young managers around Levin at EFLIC fancied themselves part of a "hot" company, the hard fact was that the sales force—upon which everything really depended—was falling on its face.

It wasn't all their fault: a recession was dampening new sales and causing policyholders in existing funded programs to drop out as the value of their mutual fund shares fell. Flying high at more than $80 just the year before, Equity Funding's own stock had been clawed in the bear market and had slipped to a historic low of $12. Goldblum was edgy.

The conspirators were also grappling with one of the boomerang effects of reinsuring the special-class and pending business. As expected, special-class policies were lapsing in wholesale lots. Employees were unwilling or unable to pay their full premiums in the second year, and many of the pending policies were never issued. Penn Life smelled a rat and demanded additional reinsurance—but insurance that would stick.

To keep enough business on the books to lull the reinsurers, Equity Funding had to pay the second-year premiums on a sizeable proportion of the garbage. To get the money, and to feed more operating cash into what essentially was an insolvent firm, Goldblum, Levin, Art Lewis, and a couple of others felt they had to traffic in phantoms.

This was more than just colossal chutzpah. According to the rules of math, it was suicidal. The company would get a lot of up-front cash when it sold policies, but then would have to hand over all subsequent premiums to the reinsurer for years afterward. Since there would be no live premium payers, the company would have to come up with the money itself. The more it sold in one year, the greater the sum it would have to pay the next. It would have to geometrically increase bogus sales year by year just to stay even.

The actuaries, CPAs, and insurance experts involved should have seen this and probably did, but by now everyone was out of touch with reality. Levin recalls convincing himself that he could work the company out of the fraud, that it was only a temporary expedient. "I thought I was Superman," says Levin, who had never before failed at anything.

Even deep into the insurance fraud, the conspirators would refuse to acknowledge its criminality. It was just a way to borrow money interest-free; a loan, as it were, that would be repaid when Equity Funding realized its manifest destiny and started *really* to outsell everyone else in the industry. So the managers said, often enough to persuade themselves.

That they were felons was too much to face squarely, too much for men who, by and large, still regarded themselves as decent, law-abiding citizens. Young Gary Beckerman, the PR-marketing man, was called into Goldblum's office in 1972 and asked to help in the counterfeiting of $100 million in corporate bonds needed to give EFLIC some "assets" it was supposed to have but didn't. "I couldn't, didn't, ever use the word counterfeiting, even to myself," he recalls. "I couldn't have it in my vocabulary. I couldn't apply it to myself." Overpowered by Goldblum, Beckerman went along. Others who did the same found it just as difficult to use words like fraud and forgery.

In late 1970, the company began selling its first blocks of bogus policies, dummied up from altered versions of real ones in force. At the end of the year its reported sales were staggering. EFLIC had almost tripled its insurance in force within 12 months, writing a total of nearly 19,000 policies with a face amount of more than $828 million. The industry was agog. The conspirators loved it.

Jim Banks says:

> Levin would take enormous pride in having the rest of the industry praise us. I'd come back from meetings and conventions, and he'd always ask what they were saying about us. I'd tell him they were full of admiration for our growth, and he'd just beam. And so would I, so would I. Both of us knew that half or more of the business was fake, but we were honestly, really *proud* anyway. God, what a crazy thing, what self-delusion! When we passed $1 billion in force we took out big ads, and we were proud of them, too.

Lies had become truth; pipedreams, reality. Nasty problems, however, intruded on the dreamers. For one thing, EFLIC was being audited not by good old Wolfson Weiner, who handled the parent company, but by Haskins & Sells. As a matter of course, these auditors would ask for policy files to check against a sampling of the policy numbers EFLIC claimed to have in force. And the many phantom policyholders had no files.

What the conspirators did, in the main, was wait for the auditors to request certain policy files and then, at night-time, "fraud parties" feverishly forged sets of files for delivery to the auditors. This involved filling out medical forms, policy applications, credit checks, and other documentation for each policy issued. Later, when the bogus policies were created in huge numbers, a separate "mass marketing" office staffed by young women would whip out forged documents in assembly-line fashion.

When lawyer Banks first was asked to help out at the "parties," he says, it was like "someone asking you to help move a sofa from here to there. I didn't think anything of it; it was something the company needed done, that's all."

Banks' loyalty had lulled his conscience. That loyalty, he feels now, stemmed from gratitude. In his previous job, working as a tax drudge for the starchy Los Angeles law firm, he was waiting to pass the California bar examination and get a job with more pay and more status at the same firm. He passed the examination, but the job offer he got was disappointing.

Banks had gone to law school in his native Canada. The school had little luster. "I saw that the people the firm was hiring came from the prestigious U.S. schools," Banks says. "I just wasn't in the club." Bearing those scars of rejection, he left for Equity Funding. "I had a lack of confidence," he says. "Deep down, I thought I would never be able to make it if I went into practice for myself, so I felt I owed a lot to the company that had taken me in." Later, he proved himself wrong. Waiting to be indicted, he started his own law practice, and earned about as much from it as he had earned at Equity Funding.

Underwriter Collins was sucked into the forgery for different reasons. Unlike some of the others, he wasn't power-mad, nor was he lusting after high position and a six-figure salary. His profile at the parent company was low—"sort of a Clark Kent," said one executive—and he was seldom seen there. His idea of success was a decent, interesting job that would allow his family to live comfortably, not sumptuously; about $30,000 a year would do it, he figured. He also had no particular loyalty to Equity Funding per se and had been sufficiently upset at EFLIC's sales of garbage to reinsurers to complain to Levin and threaten to quit.

Collins, too, had his insecurities and weaknesses. He had never finished college, and at EFLIC he was in fast company. "I always felt I had to make up for my lack of a degree by sheer effort. I worked my tail off," he says.

A man who labors that hard is usually proud of his work and that of his subordinates, and Collins was. His professionalism was offended by the mess the other conspirators were making of the policy files; as chief under-writer, that was *his* field. Even now there is a hint of outrage in his voice at the sloppy work his colleagues were doing.

"They were just botching it," he complains. "They would have got-ten caught without me. They *needed* me; I knew those files and I knew what was supposed to be in them."

Finally, Collins was an eminently agreeable man. He tried to put him-self in Levin's shoes, giving careful consideration to the argument that the bogus business was a distasteful but only temporary measure, that it would all be cleaned up and no one would be hurt. In the end, he became a forger too.

"I know I should have just quit on the spot," he says. "My assistant would have, no doubt about it; he was a black-and-white man. I'm very much afraid that I was a shades-of-gray man. . . ."

So it rolled out, cascades of computer printouts laden with phony pol-icies, earnings still rising. A pharaoh perched on the twenty-eighth floor, the top of his Century City headquarters, Goldblum curtly gave his orders. The princelings dancing attendance on him passed the word down to over-seers like Banks and Collins directing the serfs who were building Gold-blum's treasure city.

The chief executive, and to a lesser extent the princelings, were the only people benefiting hugely. They had the really big salaries, stock bonuses, entertainment allowances, and perquisites. The lower-level con-spirators were rewarded more generously than their honest colleagues, but not by much. Basically, they were putting their necks in the noose to enrich Stanley Goldblum, the principal stockholder. Despite this, at first none of these ill-rewarded overseers even looked up from his desk, not even Col-lins. By now, he knew that what he was doing was criminal, and he knew his world would be shattered by any disclosure of the scandal.

He was terribly afraid, but kept plowing blindly on, out of some mistaken notion of loyalty. "If I'd had the brains," he marvels, "I would have said, 'What the hell are we doing? The guys upstairs are raping us.' " But though he threatened to quit several times, Collins could not break away.

The fraud was dragging more bodies into its vortex. One belonged to Alan Green, a 24-year-old trainee working for chief actuary Art Lewis, de-scribed by one conspirator as "a brilliant man with a truly sinister mind." Early in 1972, Lewis invited Green to his home for drinks and dinner; they both got drunk and Lewis spilled the crucial elements of the insurance fraud to his young assistant, asking him to help program phony policies into the data-processing system.

Lewis probably didn't realize it, but he could not have picked a more likely recruit for the fraud. "My first reaction was surprise but not shock," Green admits.

> I thought to myself, "Far out! This is really something." And I was flattered that I was being asked in. Lewis said that he and Edens specifically were trying to become more important within the company, and the way they were doing it was to build up the size of EFLIC. "We're on a power trip," he said.

Green himself was on no power trip. He considered corporate life a hideous bore and he rejected its values. He was little interested in money; his payoff for joining the fraud was a raise that amounted to a grand total of $600 before he quit to roam about the country in a van. The only thing that personally interested him in the fraud was an opportunity to do computer programming. He thought that might be intellectually stimulating.

There was something else. Nonconformist as he was in many areas, Green still retained much of the good soldier, and his new assignment was partly just a matter of obeying orders. "I've noticed since then that my attitude toward my superiors has always been one of respect and a little fear," he says. "It's been my attitude toward my teachers, toward my bosses, toward my supervisor in prison. That was part of it."

And Green also, by his own account, had a definite criminal tendency. "I was—am—a self-centered person," he observes. "The foremost thing on my mind was whether or not this thing was right for me—not other people, me. If I'd thought there was a big chance I'd be caught, I wouldn't have done it. But I didn't see myself getting indicted. I should have known better."

Indeed. Green, a good student, used to cheat on tests anyway. He always got caught. As a child, he stole things. He got caught. After he left Equity Funding, he drifted into a job at a bookstore, and found a way to steal. Nailed again, he was fired.

Green signed on without giving a thought to the morality of the thing. The day after his talk with Lewis he was helping forge policy files. It amused him. One corporation's ripping off others tickled his sense of irony, as it did that of some other participants. "Party is a good term for it," he says. "There was a lot of hilarity. Everybody wanted to be the doctor." Between parties, Green programmed the phony business into the computer. Iconoclastic, drugged with LSD much of the time, he certainly was one of the most offbeat of the fraud participants.

Phantom policyholders have one unhappy attribute, aside from their absolute inability to pay their own insurance premiums. They live forever, and thus owe premiums forever, unless you can murder them. In 1971, Equity Funding began to murder its phantoms. It started filing forged death claims with reinsurers who had purchased the bogus policies. The reinsurers would forward the insurance payoff to Equity Funding. Having no widow or orphan to turn the money over to, the company kept it. The scheme accelerated vastly in 1972, and early in 1973 Levin decided to kill $10 million worth of phantom policyholders. He was finally persuaded that this genocide surely would be remarked by the reinsurers; $3 million or so seemed more reasonable.

Banks was a principal architect and operator of the death-claim procedure, and before long he was diverting some of the proceeds into his own pocket. How could Banks, the company loyalist, do it? The atmosphere at EFLIC and the parent company was changing. A moral infection had become gangrenous, and Levin was removed from day-to-day contact with his followers, spending most of his time above them on the twenty-eighth floor.

That the underlings were risking their freedom for the men on that floor and getting little for it became apparent at last. Morale plunged. Greed and fear took over. Gradually the company was riddled with subcells of conspirators and lone-wolf operators stealing everything they could while there was still something left to steal.

First Banks, then Edens, Lewis, and another employee, were taking death-claim money for themselves from reinsurers. Then they took it from EFLIC itself. Then they stole checks. Another subcell rigged the computer to pay its members unauthorized commissions. A lone wolf tried to make off with the cash values of lapsed policies. The executives were running wild; one triple-billed his expense accounts, another had the company pay for his divorce, another furnished a girlfriend's apartment, courtesy of Equity Funding.

"There wasn't any talk of corporate loyalty anymore," says Banks. "Nobody cared, there wasn't a shred of morality left. The whole structure was rotten to the core." Earlier, when Frank Majerus, EFLIC's controller, became deeply troubled by the fraud and consulted his minister, he was told to get out of the company; when he gave this news to his colleagues, he was derided. "When Majerus said that, well, we just roared," Banks says. "It seemed so laughable then. It was only much later we realized how lucky he'd been to have someone help pull him out of it." Majerus finally did quit and escaped jail.

Few were that fortunate. The fraud had slowly been isolating the conspirators, cutting them off from friends, churches, and even their own wives.

"The company, the fraud, was taking the place of the marital relationship," says Banks. Always close to his wife, they temporarily drifted apart during the period of the swindle. Terrie Collins complained that Larry was never at home; where *was* he all those nights? It took a lot of convincing to prove to her that he was indeed putting in 80 hours a week in Goldblum's vineyard. A former deacon in his church, Collins could not spare the time for it anymore and Levin, the Orthodox Jew, was neglecting temple. Disclosure of the fraud would shatter Levin's marriage entirely.

Collins, on the thin edge now, looked for someone to tell who could give him objective advice. There was no one, no family close by, no friends who weren't in the insurance business. He was alone.

He could discuss it with none of his subordinates, instinctively knowing it might be fatal to expose them to the corruption of the fraud. He did not want them to drink from the same cup that had already poisoned him. So he lied to them or told them nothing. Once he deliberately passed over for promotion a man he knew had a good outside offer, thus forcing him away from Equity Funding. The man was hurt—until the scandal broke. He then thanked Collins for his kindness.

By late 1972, the dread that the whole thing could blow anytime was pervasive. Caught by Goldblum and Levin in the embezzlement scheme, Banks and others were told to repay the money and some were given stock bonuses to help them do so. Goldblum, said Banks, appealed to them to stay and "save the stockholders."

It didn't escape their attention that this really meant, in large part, "save Goldblum." But they knew there were thousands of other people involved, too. Their own careers and the security of their families were also on the line. Alan Green says: "The one thing they couldn't afford to do then was just stop."

The younger executives, however, did get a grudging commitment from Goldblum to at least try to put on the brakes. Thus was born "Project Z," the ineffectual attempt to gradually get out of the bogus insurance spiral before it was too late. One of the first moves was an attempt to slash company costs deeply, and it proved to be the final, fatal error.

One of those let go in early 1973 for economy reasons was Ronald Secrist, who knew of the fraud and had been a minor participant in it at one time, and who had been packed off to work at Bankers Life when he became queasy. Smarting at his dismissal, Secrist got himself another job and then made a couple of phone calls, one to a rumpled, inquisitive little securities analyst named Ray Dirks, a specialist in insurance stocks, and the other to insurance regulators.

There had been suspicion and minor leaks before, but for the first time the code of *omerta* that had kept present and former employees from talking had been breached in a significant way. This silence of almost nine years had its roots in fear; by and large, the people who had any concrete, first-hand knowledge of the fraud were people who already had been soiled by it. If they talked, they feared, they would find themselves in trouble immediately.

Others knew of the fraud, but all their knowledge was hearsay. They had heard oblique references to what was going on or specifics about one area of the fraud. But they themselves had seen nothing and done nothing; they could not be absolutely certain. Still others had seen or done some minor things they considered improper or unusual, but had been boxed off from information about the entire nature of the conspiracy; all they would have to talk about were what appeared to be minor improprieties. So, until Secrist, there was silence.

In mid-March of 1973, insurance examiners for the states of California and Illinois (the official home state of Presidential, then EFLIC) suddenly appeared at EFLIC's offices. They said it was a routine triennial audit. It was actually a surprise audit aimed at verifying Secrist's information.

Meanwhile, Dirks had tipped the *Wall Street Journal* to Secrist's allegations and was poking into some dark corners himself. Informants began to surface and in late March began to talk to the SEC as well as the *Journal*. On Wall Street, big institutions alerted by Dirks began to sell, and soon big blocks of Equity Funding stock were being tossed down the street like so many white-hot cannonballs. Prices on the stock fell from the twenties into the low teens in days. Trading was halted. Rumors spread; Equity Funding denied them all.

The conspirators were overwhelmed by shock and panic. Lewis broke out in a severe skin rash. His hands trembling, Collins would look in the mirror in the morning and feel a sick dread at the very thought of going to the job he had once enjoyed so much. "It was a nightmare," he says. "We were trapped inside a volcano. We could have talked, spilled the whole thing, but we would have blown up with everyone else. It was just too late." Banks, anesthetized all this time, finally sensed that he had an excellent chance of going to jail. A couple of months before, when he had thought of leaving the company, he had for the first time analyzed what he'd been doing. "I knew then I had confused the illegal part of the company's business with the legal," he says. "There were two channels; one open, honest, regular, the other secretive, illegal, both going on at the same time. I had never separated the two. When you sign on, I told myself, you agree to do the company's business. This was part of the business of the company and I did it." Toward the end, Banks says, he was spending 80 percent to 90 percent of a crushing work week in the dark waters of that second channel. Then Levin asked him to do one final fraudulent thing, and he told his boss to go to hell. But it was too late for him anyway.

In a last attempt to block discovery of the fraud, Goldblum ordered the bugging of the company offices that had been loaned to the insurance examiners, hoping to ferret out their plans. Collins assisted in this ("good old Larry, always ready to help out," he recalls bitterly), stringing wires into the listening post—Goldblum's bathroom. Banks helped too ("morally, it was hideous"), and one day found himself sitting on Goldblum's toilet, listening to the examiners talk while the chief executive coolly entertained company in his office next door.

By Friday, March 30, the examiners had not yet found the bogus policies. But Illinois authorities did discover that $24 million in bonds, the lion's share of EFLIC's claimed assets, had never existed (the plan to use some of the counterfeit bonds never worked; the printing job was bad). The next day, Illinois moved to seize the company and found California had already done so Friday night.

Rodney Loeb, the general counsel, was thunderstruck when it became clear to him that the worst of the rumors, and more, were probably true. Loeb concedes he himself was no businessman—"all I ever wanted to be was a good lawyer"—and he had never dreamed that Goldblum could be involved. In matters involving securities law, Goldblum had ordered that Equity Funding be beyond reproach. Loeb had hired a tough little SEC lawyer named Larry Williams as chief of compliance, and together, at Goldblum's urging, they prepared guidelines for the conduct of the company's securities salesmen that both considered airtight.

Goldblum was the chairman of a district committee of the National Association of Securities Dealers. When he returned from meetings where unethical sales practices were discussed, Loeb recalled, "he always wanted to know, 'Could it happen here? I don't want it to ever happen,' and Larry and I would work on it."

Once, an Equity Funding salesman peddled a funding package, which takes ten years to mature, to an 87-year-old woman. Williams recommended a stiff punishment, a suspension for 60 days. But Goldblum, outraged, said, "Hell no! We're going to fire the son of a bitch right now!" And they did.

Could this man have pulled off one of the hugest, most audacious frauds in the history of American business? Loeb couldn't believe it—until, that week before the fall, Goldblum hired a lawyer who told him to plead the Fifth Amendment if called before the SEC and advised that his princelings hire themselves the best criminal counsel they could.

Loeb, as secretary of Equity Funding, called an emergency meeting of the board over that fateful last weekend. There was shouting and tumult when Goldblum refused to answer some point-blank questions about what had gone on. His resignation was forced out of him, and after he vainly tried to get severance pay and a $200-a-day consulting post, he, Levin, and Lowell were ordered off the premises.

The next day, April 2, 1973, the *Wall Street Journal* broke the story on its front page and Equity Funding blew to pieces. Its offices around the country were paralyzed, telephones shut down. Creditors descended on it in swarms; so did policyholders and securities holders. Loeb and another uninvolved executive vice-president, Herbert Glaser, were trying to run the company, and it fell to Loeb that Monday to fire the other principal conspirators. Some of them demanded consulting posts, too, on the ground that they were the only ones who could run the company. So far had delusion gone. Loeb offered to throw them out the window.

Mickey Sultan, Lowell's young assistant and rubber-stamp, was different. Getting word later that day from the authorities that he was apparently involved and should be fired, Loeb was pained. He had always liked Sultan. He told him gently, and Sultan only said: "It's all right, Rodney. I understand."

Shortly afterward, Loeb had a chance meeting with Sultan in the company parking garage. "He looked at me and broke down and cried," says Loeb. "I gave him a handkerchief and told him, 'Don't cry. What's done is done; it's over.' And he said, 'Rodney, I'm so sorry to have done this to you, to the others, to have fooled everyone.'"

Nothing short of bankruptcy proceedings could save what was left of the company. On Wednesday, April 4, after helping to prepare the petition that would be accepted by the court the next day, the general counsel went home and sat on the edge of his bed.

He had come to Equity Funding from a job at Commonwealth United Corporation, another Beverly Hills hot-air balloon that had fallen under the weight of its own debentures. Now this. Loeb began to weep. It was the first time his wife had ever seen him cry.

Within three days of the *Journal* story, more than $10 billion worth of civil lawsuits from courts across the country had rained down on Equity Funding and its officers and directors, innocent and guilty alike. Those suits are still pending.

Stripped of most of their executive staff, both EFLIC and the parent firm were in absolute chaos. The SEC recruited and the court approved a trustee to run Equity Funding under protection of Chapter 10 of the Bankruptcy Act. It was the biggest fraud-induced Chapter 10 proceeding in American business history.

Over months of investigation, the whole sorry story squeezed into the light. Of $3.2 billion in life insurance EFLIC had purportedly written, about two-thirds was pulled out of thin air. Later, the company would be ordered dismantled, and its flesh-and-blood policyholders entrusted to a subsidiary untarred by the fraud.

The parent company, which was supposed to have a net worth of over

$143 million, didn't have a net worth at all; whacking down those impossibly bloated assets and adding real but undisclosed liabilities to the books, the trustee found it actually had liabilities that exceeded its assets by more than $40 million. Equity Funding was worse than broke and had been for a long time. Only borrowed and stolen money had kept it going.

For the army of creditors and securities holders, there was precious little. After selling off everything he could, trustee Robert Loeffler would eventually come up with a reorganization plan, now moving toward execution, for a new company centered on the two untouched insurance subsidiaries. In this proposed replay of the miracle of loaves and fishes, the banks and other senior, secured creditors would get some cash and notes payable from the income of the new company. All other claimants would have to settle for new stock in this new company, of undetermined market value.

The common stockholders of Equity Funding would get new shares, worth about 12 cents for each dollar of loss. It isn't much, but then neither was Equity Funding. Trustee Loeffler says the whole story of the fraud reminds him very much of *Alice in Wonderland,* a favorite of his when he was a boy.

Society treats the stock swindler with a tolerance that borders on admiration. The absence of violence in his particular crime tends to defuse antagonism, for one thing. For another, there is a sneaking delight in all of us at seeing someone outwit the system, however short-lived his success.

The courts reflect this. Dragged before the bar, the stock-fraud artist cuts an appealing figure; well-dressed, well-barbered, well-spoken, represented by the ablest counsel stolen money can buy, he is the embodiment of contrition. This is clearly no surly felon menacing the public safety, but a fellow country-club member who in a moment of weakness strayed from the path and now knows it. Give him a light sentence.

But if punishment is in any way connected with the sheer bulk of suffering that the criminal caused, justice simply isn't being done in many cases. The victims of a major stock fraud may run well into the thousands, and most are not fat cats who can write it off, hop a train for Scarsdale, and forget it over cocktails. They are little people who bleed and suffer for months and years and perhaps the rest of their lives. In this sense the toll taken by Equity Funding was one of the most horrible of any modern crime.

The day that the news of the fraud broke, Equity Funding stock that had been worth almost $300 million in market value at the beginning of the year was worth zero. The company's bonds and warrants were also suddenly worthless. Among the little people there was consternation, then numbness, and finally a sick pain as the impact of what had happened seeped through. A year after the fraud was unmasked, it was still ruining lives.

On that first anniversary, a 74-year-old widow named Peggy Rahn was sitting in her tiny New York apartment, looking at her bankbook. It said she had $900 left in the world. Her Social Security payments weren't quite enough to cover her rent. Gainfully employed for 55 years, always proudly self-sufficient, she was being inexorably pushed toward the welfare rolls. "Every day I wake up and wonder what will happen to me," she said. She wishes she had never ever heard of Equity Funding Corporation of America, in which she invested $7,000—almost all of the money she had.

With the sudden losses came shame and attempts at secrecy so that loved ones would not learn of what happened and begin to fear for the future. Across the Hudson from Mrs. Rahn's apartment in New York, a New Jersey shopkeeper in failing health yearned for retirement but was still dragging himself to work; his wife and son could not understand why. Self-employed, ineligible for Social Security, he had put more than $25,000, the bulk of his life savings, into Equity Funding securities. His wife and son did not know the company had blown up, and he was hiding it from them. "I don't know how much longer I can do it, but I have to," he said, weeping. "How can I ever tell my wife I lost most of the money we were going to retire on? I don't know what it will do to her, and I'll die of shame."

At the same time, in a small town in Nebraska, a college student who badly needed medical care his parents could not afford had hit on a way to get the needed money. He would sock it into Equity Funding, a hot growth stock. He invested the day before trading was halted. His parents, who borrowed on their home to put up the capital for him, were trying not to let him see how terribly worried they were. His medical treatments were, of course, delayed.

Lynbrook Larry, a retiree, was raging at the regulators. "Where were the men who were supposed to look out for us little people?" he asked. Larry, who went down with $21,000 worth of securities, told his wife but not his friends. "Nobody knows the trouble we're having. Nobody can," he whispered. "It would kill my wife if they knew; she'd commit suicide or something."

There are others, a far greater number, who were victimized and will never know it. They are the potential beneficiaries of various trusts, pension funds, and endowments stuck with Equity Funding securities.

To the gentlemen overseeing these mountains of money, the losses they faced were piddling. Princeton University's endowment fund had $1.3 million in Equity Funding, it's true, but it also had about $500 million in things that didn't go broke.

The State Teachers Retirement Fund of Ohio would barely notice a

$10.8 million loss. And a $50,000 loss to the trust providing income to the Laughlin Children's Center in Pittsburgh, which treats youngsters with learning disabilities, wasn't fatal.

That is one way to look at it. But it remains that to the extent these investments are losses, the beneficiaries of these funds will be the poorer. The $50,000 was a third of the annual operating budget of the children's center. At the many colleges holding Equity Funding, losses can be translated into faculty salaries and student scholarships. Just how many people will ultimately lose in the Equity Funding debacle, then, will never be known.

Among the hardest-hit groups were the present and former employees of Equity Funding who were innocent of wrongdoing in the fraud. The company's collapse cost most of them their jobs, and the nature of its failure made it difficult for them to find new ones. Other companies were understanding and sympathetic; and in the end, they decided they didn't want the words "Equity Funding" in their personnel records.

General counsel Rodney Loeb and his chief of compliance, Larry Williams, were badly scorched. Just before trading was stopped, Williams urged his brother to invest heavily in Equity Funding stock on behalf of their father. Goldblum had sworn up and down to Williams that absolutely nothing was wrong, so that made the stock a real buy.

Loeb was stuck with $75,000 in loans he had made in order to pay taxes on his stock bonuses. The stock itself was collateral and now its price, in those last days, was dropping steeply. We want to sell you out, the bank said, but Loeb couldn't allow it; under securities law he was an insider, and his right to dispose of stock was limited. After the debacle the bank got nasty, and Loeb had to give it a second mortgage on his home, refinance his first mortgage, sell some possessions, and borrow from his family.

He got the debt down to $55,000, and the bank then gave him more time to pay this off. Loeb told his son in New York that he could no longer help him financially. His wife didn't buy a dress and he didn't buy a suit. After two years of pounding and grinding, the tab is now down to about $30,000.

When the scandal exploded in his face, Loeb felt the deepest humiliation. "I avoided every place where I'd be in contact with other lawyers," he recalls. "I felt I would never be able to hold up my head again. People certainly would have snickered behind my back and said, '*Sure*, he didn't know.'" This feeling has largely disappeared and Loeb believes he has reestablished himself now in his profession.

But he adds: "It's still painful to face the only two alternatives to the question of how this could have gone on for so long without the general counsel knowing. Either I was very stupid or very naive, or both."

For the conspirators themselves, the span of more than two years between exposure of the fraud and their sentencing seemed interminable. Larry Collins was broke and had to borrow $5,000 from his mother to pay a lawyer. He fell ill with suspected lung cancer that turned out to be something else, and his wife Terrie had to go in for psychiatric counseling. Fred Levin sold Mazda automobiles for a while and then sank into lethargy, passing endless days reading every word of the *Wall Street Journal* and talking to people on the phone. He and his management cadre were cooperating fully with the investigators. Stanley Goldblum wasn't talking.

Jim Banks remembers sitting in front of his television set, watching a parade of young presidential aides baring their souls at the Watergate hearings. "I listened to those underlings," he says,

> and I found myself sympathizing with them and nodding when they talked. They did what they did in the name of national security, invoked by the President of the United States. Now, my president was just this shithead over in Beverly Hills, I know, but he had us do things in the name of corporate well-being. That was pretty powerful stuff for me then.

The indictments came in November 1973. Eighteen of the men who were charged eventually pleaded guilty. Of the company executives, only Goldblum held out, and even he decided to plead guilty shortly after his trial began in October 1974, following damaging testimony against him by Jerry Evans. Shortly afterward, auditors who had been indicted were convicted after a lengthy trial.

In the spring of 1975 the sentences came down. U.S. Attorney William Keller personally pleaded in court for a 20-year sentence for Stanley Goldblum as a deterrent to white-collar crime and a fitting punishment. The judge gave him eight years.

Among the others, Levin and Lowell got five years each and Lewis, Edens, and Banks, three. Smith, Sultan, and Collins got two years. Green got a two-year suspended sentence; but he had to serve three months, and he was put on probation for three years. Jerry Evans got a year's suspended sentence and probation. Gary Beckerman got two years, suspended, and probation. The accountants later got two-year suspended sentences, three months of actual jail time, and four years probation. They also were required to do 2,000 hours of charity work.

As Levin waited for the day when he would enter prison, he was tormented by dreams. In one he relived a real experience, when a good friend in the securities business who had recently suffered a heart attack told him, only days before trading halted, that he had bought $100,000 worth of Equity Funding stock. "I believe in you," he told Levin, who knew the man must have gone in debt to make the purchase. "I wanted to tell him to sell right away, but I couldn't, I couldn't," says Levin. "Only his firm and another brokerage house were keeping the stock afloat." The only time Levin has seen or talked to his friend since are in those recurring dreams.

In other dreams he saw the faces of old people, stockholders, who came to Presidential Life when Equity Funding was going to buy it for stock. They wanted more dividends. "Don't worry," Levin would say in his dreams, "Your stock is going to be replaced by the stock of a wonder growth company." Sometimes, Levin says, he woke in a cold sweat.

Through it all, he could not actually cry over what had happened. But a friend tells how Levin would sit for hours in front of his TV set, watching the old movies of which he is so fond. Then, during the sad parts, he would weep.

The flower fields of Lompoc, California, lie in rainbow bands across a little valley that opens to the sea. The air is heavy with floral perfumes and the tang of the Pacific. About 160 miles north of Century City, Lompoc might as well be on Mars, so far removed is it in spirit and pace from the mindless hustle of the metropolis to the south. Here they raise flowers to make money, or they work at what the Bureau of Prisons calls the "Correctional Facility," a prim euphemism for the federal penitentiary and camp. Petunias are big business here but so is punishment.

If you have to go to jail the camp is not a bad jail to go to. Guards are unarmed, there are trees and lawns, a gym, even a scruffy athletic field and golf course. Khaki-clad inmates look like privates stuck in some boondocks post run by a commanding officer who has let discipline slip a bit.

There are hard cases in the nearby prison, but the camp itself houses gentler felons—bewildered wetbacks and a conglomeration of white-collar criminals. There are bank tellers who withdrew from other people's accounts, bush-league mail fraud artists, politicians who couldn't get their hands out of the cash register in time, perjurers, and a clutch of people who used to work for Equity Funding.

Alan Green, the programmer who plugged the phony policies into EFLIC's computer, likes it here. He has had time to get acquainted with himself and has found there is much he never realized.

He has no remorse over the legions of swindled investors and the others marked by the scandal. "Equity Funding was only one example of a widespread disease," he says. "In that light, what was so wrong with what I was doing? It was only what many others were doing. I didn't see any responsibility on my part for the investors and the others and I don't blame myself now—that just wouldn't do me a bit of good."

But out of sheer self-interest, Green has spent a lot of time thinking about how to avoid what could be called the Finger of God, the force that always seems to come down out of the clouds and squash him whenever he has done something wrong. Internal mechanisms—a sense of morality, a code of ethics—don't mean much to Green. But the seeming inevitability of punishment does.

"The primary thing with me is still what is going to be best for me. I certainly don't want to go to jail again," he says. "Now I'm able to see in myself that criminal tendency to always try to get something for nothing. All the times I tried I was caught. Now that I know I have this tendency, I can control it."

But what if the opportunity to commit a criminal act came again, another chance to get something for nothing, and this time it was *absolutely certain* that Green *couldn't* be caught? A hypothetical question, certainly, but Green considers it seriously. "I think," he says carefully, "that would have to depend on the specific situation."

If Green is reasonably content here, assessing himself while assembling furniture in the prison factory, for others the experience is nearly unbearable. They suffer from the common but debilitating disease of most men in captivity, "slow time." Every tick of the clock is separated by a gulf from the next; each hour flows as slowly as syrup. And, for all the little niceties of the camp, for all the lack of walls and watchtowers, they are keenly conscious that they have no freedom.

"They try hard here," Larry Collins sighs, "but you can't forget you're in the joint." He passes the time on a landscape crew whose foreman amuses them with tales of *mafiosi*, politicos, and businessmen he has had pulling weeds and clipping shrubs under his direction. Collins, like others, lives mainly for visits from his wife, and in the long spaces between, he thinks of why this happened to him.

"I kick myself for being weak," he says.

> I never was a real yes man. But I was weak. I still consider myself honest, but I went along with it. I must have *wanted* to believe the things they were telling me. You have to worry about your sense of ethics, of morality, when this happens. I'm a very adaptable person, good old Larry, always ready to listen to the other guy's arguments, and to weigh his point of view. And that's what got me in here.

Jim Banks is resigned to Lompoc. Of his being here, he says, "There are good reasons. I stole a lot of money." But his helplessness to ease the strain on his wife and family constantly discourages him. He may have got what was coming to him, but they are suffering more. "I have three children," he says. "One has a stuttering problem that has gotten much worse. Another is a daughter who was always cheerful, outgoing. Now she's withdrawn into herself. I've got to believe it's because of what's happened, not having her father there."

A lawyer, Banks expects to be disbarred. He isn't quite sure what he will do when he leaves Lompoc, but he has one idea.

"There are a lot of people out there in a lot of companies who will do what I did at Equity Funding," he says.

> Somebody has to tell them about priorities, somebody has to tell them what a company and a career mean in the scheme of things, and what place a man's family has. I've been there; I could counsel them. And the first thing I'd say is, "If it happens, don't think you can stop anytime. You aren't going to be strong enough to extricate yourself. You're going to need help."

A guard reminds him that his time is up. He walks across a parking lot and a strip of lawn to the waiting prison barracks.

Is Banks still deluding himself, disguising himself in the company of a herd of thousands or hundreds of thousands of young businessmen who he would have you believe are just as vulnerable to criminality as he was?

Not long ago, an assistant professor of management at the University of Georgia, Archie Carroll, made a survey of some 240 business executives that provides a clue to an answer. Most of the people who responded were middle and lower managers who were insidiously threatened by the expectations of their superiors.

Did they feel under pressure to compromise their personal standards to meet company goals? Sixty-five percent said yes. The lower in the corporate pecking order, the stronger the feeling became; 84 percent of the lower-level managers reported it. Could the respondents conceive of a situation where the managers of the company were ethical men but so demanding of results that there would be compromises of conscience and morality? Yes, said more than 78 percent.

This question was not asked, but it is a natural one: Now what if the chief executive is a Stanley Goldblum, a powerful presence, a dark god on the twenty-eighth floor, who not only wants the bottom line to look good but who prescribes criminal measures to make it so? If the millions of white-collar spear carriers in American business feel threatened by the very authority structure in which they labor, the answer seems clear.

At Ohio State University, Professor Frederick Sturdivant was teaching a class in business ethics. He laid out the Equity Funding case to his students and asked them what they would do had they worked at the company. Even knowing the denouement, an alarming number said they would be, as the professor put it, "good Germans." They would go along.

# 9

# *Wall Street Flouts the Law*

*Christopher Elias*

In the 1930s a cowboy movie sheriff named Tom Mix rode to fame astride his "wonder horse," Tony. He rounded up crooks, who were often portrayed as a town's financial leaders, and he uttered such words as, "Straight shooters always win; lawbreakers always lose." Inevitably, Tom Mix proved his point in each picture. As the straight shooter and the honest lawman, he always got his lawbreaker.

But Tom Mix, the cowboy sheriff, never had to ply his trade in Wall Street, a community where straight shooters do not abound and lawbreakers have a strange immunity from prosecution.

It might be that some of the immunity exists because modern lawmen and prosecutors find the jargon, the techniques of finance, and the secrecy of Wall Street impenetrable. Indeed, it is not always easy to determine when a Wall Streeter is breaking the law, even when the sleuths know their way around . . . For example, . . . the SEC was for years unable to get a look at Wall Street's books because the firms simply refused to show them to anyone, especially to the SEC. Yet all the time the SEC had the requisite authority. It simply refused to assert its authority.

Defiance, however, has been merely a symptom of the real problem of enforcing the law in Wall Street, for as long as there has been a Street, authorities of all kinds—in the exchanges, the regulatory agencies, the local and federal administrations—have shown a profound reluctance to initiate actions. Indeed, Wall Street's history is filled with stories of the failure of officials at all levels to act. Entire legislatures have been bought off, as have mayors, councilmen, judges, and policemen. For example, Cornelius Vanderbilt and Daniel Drew each bribed New York's entire Common Council of Aldermen, including the infamous Boss Tweed, in their fight to control New York City's Harlem Railroad; they bribed the New York State legislature as well. In his fight with Drew, Vanderbilt even bribed a New York judge and got him to issue an injunction against the directors

From Christopher Elias, *Fleecing the Lambs*. Chicago: Henry Regnery, Inc., 1971, pp. 203-16. Reprinted by permission.

of the Erie Railroad forbidding them to repay a $3.5 million loan to Drew.

On the federal level, Wall Street has had unusual influence with presidents, especially the Republican presidents of the 1920s who undoubtedly administered their office with blinkers on so far as Wall Street was concerned. The excesses of those years, as we have seen, were extreme. Wall Street also had unusual influence with President Roosevelt, who appointed Joseph P. Kennedy, one of the all-time great speculators, to head the SEC, and with President Nixon, who has adopted a blinkers-on attitude reminiscent of the presidents of the 1920s. As a result of its influence at all levels, the Street too often successfully has intimidated its opponents, and from this sort of success has grown a feeling among its members that they are immune from the laws that other men must live under. Even when blatant skullduggery has been unearthed and there was no way to avoid a hearing, trial, or other adjudication, the punishments meted out to the guilty have been as ineffectual as no punishments at all.

For example, in December 1970, the SEC, the New York Stock Exchange, and the American Stock Exchange almost simultaneously charged Kleiner, Bell & Company, a Beverly Hills firm, its president, Bert S. Kleiner (one of Martin Mayer's "new breed on Wall Street"), and a vice-president, Ralph J. Shapiro, with a long list of violations of federal securities laws and Exchange rules. Kleiner, Bell had recommended to investors that they buy the stock of a conglomerate, Commonwealth United Corporation, while all the while the firm itself was selling the stock on the basis of inside information. During 1968 and part of 1969, Commonwealth United stock had risen sharply, but unknown to investors the company was expected to lose $61 million in 1969 alone. (Kleiner once told Mayer, "I'm just trying to make money.")

This particular complaint originated with the American Stock Exchange. But official trouble over Commonwealth United for Kleiner, Bell had come up before. In October, 1969, the SEC charged that a registration statement and proxy material issued by Commonwealth United were false and misleading since they did not disclose the close relationship between Kleiner, Bell and Commonwealth United. The SEC also found that Kleiner, Bell had mixed customers' fully paid for securities with securities it used to secure the firm's debts. In fact, the New York Stock Exchange charged that Kleiner, Bell had improperly "used $889,285 of customer securities for collateral." Further, said the Exchange, Bert Kleiner and Ralph Shapiro had "improperly been reporting restricted securities for inclusion in the firm's capital and that this had assisted the firm in not reporting a violation of capital requirements from January, 1970."

Getting customers to buy while insiders were selling and using customers' securities as collateral for their own debts were only part of the charges. The SEC charged that in 1968 Kleiner, Bell manipulated the price of Omega Equities stock by bidding for it and then purchasing it at increasingly higher prices. All the time Kleiner, Bell was making its sham transactions it was recommending to its customers that they buy Omega shares. It was a very old ploy and one the SEC said violated the antifraud provisions of federal securities laws.

Despite the number and seriousness of the charges, *no one* involved ever came to trial. Kleiner, Bell as a firm and Bert Kleiner and Ralph Shapiro as individuals consented to the findings of the SEC and the exchanges without admitting anything. The penalties they accepted were the revocation of Kleiner, Bell's registration as a broker-dealer and the barring of Kleiner and Shapiro from association with any securities broker-dealer. The exchanges expelled the firm and the two men from membership or from association "in any capacity with any member or member organizations" of the exchanges. As is often the case, Kleiner, Bell stayed in business, not as a brokerage house, but in its investment banking capacity.

As for the individual investors Kleiner, Bell had been telling to buy Commonwealth United and Omega Equities, they took their losses. It may be that the exchanges, the SEC, and law enforcement agencies felt the same way about them as Bert Kleiner did when he said:

> They are a new breed of wealthy men, still unused to what they have. They don't have the concept of conserving capital. They've tasted it. They went to Las Vegas and lost $17,000, paid $15,000 to $20,000 for a painting. So they'll put up $50,000. Maybe they'll lose it, but maybe they'll make a million.

The truth is that the customers themselves feel a lot differently. Until the advent in recent years of class action damage suits, which can be initiated by individuals in *everyone's* interest, investors have been relatively helpless, and Wall Street has never been truly taken to task on behalf of individual investors. It was always the outsiders that the guns were aimed at—the corporations issuing stock, the corporate raiders, the common thieves who stole securities, and even employees of Wall Street firms. In August 1970, however, when the Exchange decided it would not reimburse the customers of three insolvent firms—First Devonshire of Boston, Charles Plohn & Company of New York, and Robinson & Company of Philadelphia—lawsuits brought by some of the victimized customers reversed the Exchange's view. Indeed, the Exchange itself is a defendant in a $3 billion suit brought by the National Shareholders Association, an organization of small investors formed in July 1970 that opposes the Exchange's fixed commission structure. In a suit brought in Federal District Court in New York, the association said the nation's investors had been damaged to the extent of $500 million by the fixed commissions naming, in addition to the Exchange, the American Stock Exchange, the Association of Stock Exchange

Firms, and the brokerage houses of Merrill Lynch, Bache & Company, Walston & Company, Paine, Webber, Jackson & Curtis, and F. I. duPont, Glore Forgan & Company.

There have been a few times when Wall Street has done more than slap the wrists of its élite, and investors have not had to do the job that assigned regulators should be doing. But any observer or chronicler of such exceptional periods—which is what they were—would do well to look beneath the surface. Vigorous prosecution has come about almost only when the Street has feared that inaction would result in the loss of a privilege or a prerogative, or worse, result in action by an angry Congress.

Thus in December 1961, Edward T. McCormick, president of the American Stock Exchange (and a former SEC commissioner), was forced to resign by the Amex board of governors following the ouster of Gerard A. Re and Gerard F. Re, a father-and-son specialist team in the firm of Re, Re & Sagarese, who had been found by the SEC to be guilty of manipulation of stock prices and of fraud. McCormick, who had made personal stock transactions through the Res, might still have escaped punishment but for the fact that the SEC had also found that the self-regulatory process had failed abysmally during McCormick's presidency. The two factors were just too much, and a reluctant Amex board was forced to get rid of the embarrassment they were confronted with, especially since Congress had commissioned William T. Cary, the newly arrived chairman of the SEC, to embark on a Special Study that would result in 1964 in amendments to the securities act.

Of course, the classic case that demonstrates Wall Street's willingness to throw its own to the wolves if it feels threatened is that of Richard Whitney, president of the New York Stock Exchange during most of the 1930s. As we have seen, Whitney, who in 1938 was sentenced to a ten-year term in Sing Sing prison for appropriating the securities of customers, was as much a victim as his customers, ending up in prison not so much because he had taken their securities as because he was in the way. He was a leader of the old guard opposed to a faction led by William McChesney Martin that was prepared to introduce administrative reforms demanded by Congress. Whitney had been appropriating his customers' securities since 1926, and his need for funds had been well known in Wall Street since he was a consistent borrower. Two months after he was exposed in 1938, he was in jail. One month later the reforms were passed, for in the aftermath of the scandal, opposition crumbled.

The fact is that Wall Street has never really felt that the appropriation of its customers' securities is a crime. It has always intermingled its own with its customers.' Thus, despite the fact that McDonnell & Company took securities it was holding in safekeeping for customers—actually stole them, forging the necessary signatures—and even accepted payment, as scores of Street firms did in the late 1960s, for securities purchased by customers knowing it would be unable to deliver those securities (another grounds for action), there is *no* public record available to suggest that the house was ever charged. Instead, the penalties levied on the firm and its principals by a paternal Stock Exchange amounted to liquidating the company and using Exchange funds to return money and securities due McDonnell's customers. It was a little like allowing bank robbers, upon their capture, to go free if their parents gave back the money they stole. Tom Mix, of course, never would have held still for such practices.

At the SEC a decision in April 1970 merely barred McDonnell's chairman, T. Murray McDonnell, from assuming any material or supervisory job with a securities firm without prior SEC approval. Yet that approval is no more than anyone else must get. In another exercise in futility the SEC revoked the license of McDonnell & Company as a broker and dealer in securities. Like Merrill Lynch, the firm consented to the SEC sanctions without prejudice, as did T. Murray McDonnell, who consented to findings that he merely failed to exercise the type of supervision that would have prevented violations of antifraud regulations of the Securities Act. Specifically, he had failed to advise stock buyers of the "true condition" of the firm's fouled up back office, its books, and its records. The SEC said that he also had failed to tell customers of the firm's failure to comply with financial requirements and of "large operating losses" experienced by the firm between September and December of 1968.

There is strong reason to believe that Wall Street breaks the laws on a widespread basis, but modern crime-busters prefer to look the other way. The records may be buried in both the Exchange's and the SEC's files or even in the files of elected prosecutors, but the inferences of widespread abuse are plain enough. They showed up early in 1971, for example, when the SEC began forcing Wall Street firms to file weekly, instead of annual, financial reports. They showed up, too, when the SEC's investigators insisted on personally counting the securities the firms were holding in safekeeping for others, then comparing the count with the figures shown on the books. Hints of wrongdoing were implied when the SEC began requiring brokers for the first time to maintain a capital reserve against money that customers left on deposit with them. Clearly, unless there had been abuses throughout the industry and violations of fiduciary responsibilities, no such measures would have had to be taken. Nor would the Stock Exchange have accepted them.

The new "hard" stance of the SEC simply represents after-the-fact correction of lawbreaking routines. In April 1971, the SEC decided that Goodbody & Company, a firm married to Merrill Lynch in a shotgun wedding demanded by the Stock Exchange, should not be permitted to keep its license as a broker-dealer. Like McDonnell, Goodbody had not kept its records straight. The penalty, slight though it was, came *after* Goodbody had become a part of Merrill Lynch and, thus, no longer really existed.

The reluctance to prosecute the men and firms at the top in Wall Street is not confined to regulatory bodies such as the Exchange and the SEC. The most serious and famed crime-busters, those elected by the people or appointed by the federal government, show a marked tendency to avoid running down high-level crime in the Street. The late Tom Dewey, for example, was undoubtedly New York's most successful crime-buster. But Tom Dewey pursued what is euphemistically called "organized crime," members of the Mafia and waterfront murderers. New York's very respected district attorney William Hogan has not made his reputation by digging away at Wall Street, although clearly there has been enough reason to begin an investigation. Nor has New York State's respected attorney general, Louis Lefkowitz, initiated actions against any Wall Street principals, although he and his staff consistently develop surveys of wrongdoing. At the Stock Exchange, in fact, Lefkowitz is considered a friend.

Even the U.S. Attorney in New York, Whitney North Seymour, Jr., has seen no reason to look into Wall Street at high managerial levels, although his office on Foley Square is only a few short blocks from the Street. Of more interest to him, apparently, is the run-of-the-mill kind of thief. An inquiry in the summer of 1970, a period when Wall Street's insolvencies were at their peak, showed that the typical wrong-doer being pursued by the U.S. Attorney's office was hardly in the big leagues of crime. In a Tom Mix scenario he might have been one of the thugs working for the crooked banker.

The U.S. Attorney's files showed, for example, that for transporting about 7,100 shares of stock between Newark, New Jersey, and New York City in the summer of 1968, two men, Edward J. Farris and Joseph M. Mainer, received the following sentences after being prosecuted vigorously: Mainer was given one year each on three counts of an indictment, or a total of three years to be served concurrently; Farris was sentenced to 18 months on each of three counts, the sentences also to be served concurrently. A third man, William P. Petracca, who was not captured until March 1969, was found guilty on two counts and sentenced to concurrent terms of five years on each. The presiding judge, noting that Petracca was very young, placed him on probation with the requirement that he go back to school or go to work.

Whether the sentences seem unduly harsh is not the issue. They may well be typical of sentences most people would receive upon being successfully prosecuted for comparable crimes. The issue is whether the machinations of *all* Wall Streeters should not be approached with equitable treatment in mind. It might even be considered reasonable that when guilt is established in the case of Wall Street principals the penalties ought to be greater, for a greater degree of trust is involved. Brokers are permitted by the Federal Reserve, for example, to borrow the funds of customers, interest-free, to lend to other customers, at high rates of interest. Brokers also may keep the securities of customers in safekeeping, though not without the express consent of those customers and not without segregating the securities from their own. Other laws require brokers if they are privy to inside information to divulge that information on an equitable basis.

Time and again, brokers have ignored the responsibilities that go with such privileges—as in the case of McDonnell & Company, Merrill Lynch, Kleiner, Bell, and a long, long list of others. Indeed, the extent of brokers' failures and the many times they ignore the laws, as shown by the near-daily accounts of SEC investigations, suggest strongly that harsher penalties are needed. The facts also suggest that the Exchange's regulatory practices are sadly deficient. When it was granted the privilege of self-regulation by the Securities Act of 1934, the Exchange agreed, in turn, to make the Act work and to make it work in the public interest. That was its part of the deal. Yet all too often its actions have abrogated that agreement, as a look at the mood of the Justice Department suggests.

In the eyes of the trust busters, the New York Stock Exchange is a lawful monopolist entitled to fix prices and to control 80 percent of the securities market. The basis for this view is the Securities Exchange Act of 1934 and an opinion of the U.S. Supreme Court, which heard an antitrust suit brought against the Exchange. The Court determined that the Act, though not saying so specifically, implied that the Exchange was entitled to some degree of antitrust repeal. The degree of repeal was clearly limited, however. The Court said: "Repeal is to be regarded as implied only if *necessary* to make the Securities Act work, and even then only to the minimum extent necessary."

In the years since it was granted regulatory power, the Exchange frequently has tried to broaden that implied repeal of the antitrust laws to its maximum reach—not necessarily to make the Securities Act work but to benefit its insider members. As a result it has run afoul of the Justice Department, which has often had to point out to the Exchange that it is a public institution, not a private club conducting its affairs only in accordance with the interests of its members.

One recent occurrence came late in 1969 when the Exchange decided that its members needed to sell stock in themselves to the public if they were to survive. There were twenty-two conditions in the proposals the Exchange put before the SEC. Practically all of them were written to limit sharply the control and influence of investors and to permit those already in control to stay in control.

At the Justice Department, which had been asked by the SEC to comment, the proposals were tested against the Supreme Court edict. Were they necessary to achieve some legitimate goal of the Securities Exchange Act of 1934? Or were they designed to keep outsiders out? "The SEC," said the Justice Department in a memo signed by Richard W. McLaren, assistant attorney general, and three other attorneys in the department, "should carefully distinguish between proposals which actually broaden the Stock Exchange membership base and those which only benefit the existing members by permitting them to go public. The former are more likely to meet the requirements of the Exchange Act and the antitrust laws." Later in the memo, the trust busters said that there was "a strong inference that the limitations were primarily designed to exclude institutional investors from membership."

The Exchange maintained, of course, that its proposals fell within the scope of the Exchange's right of self-regulation, and, further, that they were necessary to carry out the purposes of the Securities Act. Then it really fired both barrels. The Exchange counsel, a prestigious lower Manhattan firm, Milbank, Tweed, Hadley & McCloy, asserted that there could be no antitrust liability because the proposals were subject to the SEC's powers of review. As might be expected, the Justice Department denied such a motion. Congress, it said, provided general antitrust exemption only when there was comprehensive economic regulation, including authority over rates, marketing areas, and extent of service as in the transportation industry. The Congress expressly provided antitrust exemption for companies whose actions had the approval of their regulatory agency. The SEC, however, was not charged with comprehensive economic supervision of Wall Street.

Despite its opinions that the Exchange has run the securities industry at times for its members' exclusive benefit, no one can say that the Justice Department has taken the Exchange and Wall Street to task. The Department's dealings with the Exchange are a dialogue—no more—intended to raise little more than an illusion of activity. There can be no question that the Justice Department is basically friendly toward the Street. It has initiated few actions and excuses its lack of activity by saying it does not wish to "intrude" on the SEC.

The Department of Justice did nothing, for example, when Merrill Lynch acquired Goodbody & Company, when the Exchange forced a whole string of mergers in 1970, and when the Street's odd-lot firms, already reduced to two, merged into one in 1970, thereby eliminating all competition. In contrast, the Justice Department has been vigorous in its pursuit of antitrust violations among U.S. corporations, so vigorous in fact that its chief, Richard McLaren, was attacked by a former chief, Lee Loevingers, for breaking up corporate mergers that did not restrain competition at all but in McLaren's view merely had the "potential" to do so.

As a result of the Department's less-than-vigorous law enforcement in Wall Street, antitrust actions there invariably stem from civil suits filed by shareowners or by firms that have been blocked by the Exchange from doing business.

A few years ago a number of shareholders in the Lehman Corporation and other mutual funds brought a class action suit against the Exchange and four member firms. The suit asked treble damages, charging that the Exchange and the firms had engaged in a coercive conspiracy, fixing minimum uniform rates of brokerage commissions and applying those rates in violation of the Sherman Antitrust Act. Since the Securities Act of 1934 did not expressly grant immunity from the antitrust laws, the suing shareholders claimed the Exchange had no immunity. The courts admitted that though there was no express exemption, a repeal of the antitrust laws, as determined by the Supreme Court, did exist. The mutual fund shareholders left the New York District Court after being told that the antitrust laws were inapplicable.

In recent years, however, there has been reason to believe the Exchange and its member firms are not as immune to antitrust laws as they have always thought they were. The issue now is restraint of trade, and the plaintiffs—though not in court—are a group of Wall Street firms doing business independent of the Exchange: Weeden & Company, which makes markets in Exchange-listed stocks; the First Boston Corporation, a large underwriter; and M. A. Schapiro & Company, a firm that was for years an independent dealer in bank stocks.

As far back as 1964 the M. A. Schapiro firm charged that an Exchange rule (number 394) prohibiting members from trading with nonmembers in stocks listed on the Exchange was in restraint of trade. By forcing member firms to deal only with each other, the Exchange assured that most trading in a stock would remain within its own preserves, that is, the floor of the Stock Exchange and the specialists stationed there. Once an issue was listed, member firms could not trade in it except with other members. In the case of Schapiro, the rule was more than disadvantageous—it was disastrous. A major market maker in bank stocks for years, the firm became a direct victim of the Exchange's rule when bank after bank was listed on the Exchange in the late 1960s.

Whether it was the case of Schapiro or the combined complaints of other firms operating in the so-called third market—Weeden, First Boston, and a host of lesser lights—the Justice Department early in 1971 called for the abolition of rule 394. This move strikes at the heart of the private club, for it clearly suggests that the Exchange has been in restraint of trade. By the spring of the year, the Exchange was close to striking down the rule. With rule 394 gone, member firms would be free to deal with just about anyone—and a membership on the Exchange would carry far less value. Indeed, much of the Exchange's power would disappear.

For investors, the results of the abolition of rule 394 could be extraordinarily advantageous. Though member firms are required under Exchange rules to buy or sell stocks at the best price, the best price has not always been that found at the Exchange. Indeed, the third market only grew because it could make a better deal for its customers—generally institutions. The third market's growth is, perhaps, the strongest indicator that the Exchange has become a fat, immovable monopoly in which competition has largely disappeared, as indicated by the lack of competitive prices for stocks. If this is so, then immunization from antitrust laws no longer shields an institution theoretically acting in the public interest but in actuality acting first in its members' interests. Not only should the laws of antitrust be applied to the institution itself, but the common law should be applied to the members and principals of the Street as well—and vigorously. Then, we would see changes.

# 10

# *The Business of Buying Friends*

*Jim Hougan*

*That was in another Country:*
*And, besides, the Wench is dead.*
  Christopher Marlowe, *The Jew of Malta*

When Daniel J. Haughton came before the Senate's microphones in September of [1975], humiliation and loss impended. Summoned there as the Lockheed Corporation's chairman of the board, Haughton knew that his testimony was likely to prove catastrophic—not only to his reputation, but to the firm as well.

To most of the members and staff of the Subcommittee on Multinational Corporations, it was apparent that Haughton's organization had been up to no good. If preliminary reports and investigations could be believed, Lockheed had invaded the treasuries of a dozen nations, helped to corrupt the political processes of both hemispheres, deceived the taxpayer, destabilized the governments of three allies, undermined NATO, subverted the marketplace, boosted inflation, and prompted a series of newspaper sensations that appeared to have resulted in suicides as far apart as Tokyo and L.A.

In hearing rooms accustomed to pleas of the Fifth Amendment by witnesses with paper bags over their heads, Haughton made a disquieting appearance. Because he and his organization had not, apparently, broken any American laws in the United States, Haughton and his attorneys insisted that he'd done nothing *wrong*. Sen. Joseph Biden (among others) took issue with this, commenting:

> Your concept of morality is very intriguing. . . . The chairman [Sen. Frank Church] has said we have got to search for a way out of this. I am not sure I want to look with you for a way out, to be perfectly blunt about it. . . . In my mind, you may have corrupted the system completely.

Senator Biden was not alone in his despair of arriving at a clear view or a way out. Just as he threw up his hands in frustration, so did the press. For more than a year the subcommittee had been engaged in a series of investigations into the corrupt practices of American corporations operating abroad. With lunar regularity, silver-haired barons of commerce arrived in Washington under subpoena, shot their cuffs, swore to God, and reluctantly confirmed the pattern of bribery and intrigue revealed by the subcommittee's staff. Daylong affairs, the hearings were predictably sensational. In the matter of the Lockheed Corporation alone, the missing principals included: the prince of the Netherlands, a French socialite known as "Paris popette," a chorus of dead Luftwaffe pilots, a former Spanish priest on the Hong Kong–Tokyo currency run, various heroes of the European Resistance, the Japanese general who conceived the attack on Pearl Harbor, a survivor of Nazi medical experiments, former Manchurian spies, and a pro-Fascist samurai with bags of industrial diamonds and ties to both the Ginza mob and the Rev. Sun Myung Moon— not to mention an assortment of Ivy League bag-men, Swiss gnomes, Arab sheikhs, and Third World generals linked invisibly to one another by a sirocco of numbered accounts, conduits, and dummy corporations.

It was too much to handle in two days of hearings, and reporters' jobs were made harder, rather than easier, by the release, *en bloc,* of several hundred pages of relevant documents. Included among them were checks, contracts, audit reports, memos, letters, Telexes, receipts, and scrawled notes—many of them censored and all of them couched in double-talk of one kind or another. The lawyer's recondite phrase. The spy's allusion. The bag-man's euphemism. And just plain code. The material was impossible to interpret on a short deadline, and its publication in full was absurd to contemplate.

In the absence of indictments, the shortage of time, the interest of space, and the prevailing confusion, the story tended to be reduced to a single headline: WOGS TAKE BRIBES. Which was hardly news. However awkward it might seem that American firms should have had to indulge in the greasy activities described, the consensus appeared to be that perfidy and corruption are genetically entrenched aboard, and thus the price of doing business there. American corporations are not alone in paying bribes: the French arms industry and Japanese ship-building concerns are frequently cited as being among the most ruthless practitioners of "black salesmanship." Lockheed's bribes (and Northrop's and Exxon's, and those of some 200 other American firms) were reimbursable, added on to the cost of every commodity sold. And so the money did not come out of "our" pockets, but "theirs." Indeed, by including bribes and kickbacks in the cost of manufacture and overhead, the net profit—figured by adding a fixed percentage of the product's total cost to the final sales price—was actually *larger* than it would have been if no improper payments had been made. The joke, you see, was on "them."

Americans were not, therefore, particularly sympathetic to what they regarded as the pieties of the Subcommittee on Multinational Corporations. Common sense, reinforced by a measure of postwar xenophobia, suggested that kickbacks were commonplace and even essential to doing business abroad. Once again, it seemed, Washington politicians and the press were embarrassing respected Americans to no worthwhile end, expecting Uncle Sam to compete with one hand tied behind his back.

Enormous pressure was brought to bear. Employees and stockholders of the firms under investigation wrote furious letters to Congress complaining that the "Church circus" threatened their jobs, their unearned income, and the American economy itself. Secretary of State Henry Kissinger implied that the subcommittee threatened national security by its revelations, embarrassing America's best friends, and creating unprecedented opportunities for Communist gains in national elections the world over. And there was pressure from abroad, too. Foreign industrialists, politicians, military leaders—whole governments—pushed every lever at their disposal to block the wash of bad news. From Japan, an organization of kamikaze enthusiasts, calling itself "Chrysanthemum in Water," swore to assassinate the entire subcommittee and its staff for the offense it had given to their homeland.

All of this made it difficult to discuss certain aspects of the affair. For instance, the subcommittee's search into the slush funds and conduits of Lockheed et al. was part of a continuing investigation into the general nature and impact of multinational corporations. Earlier efforts in this area had provided insights into the machinations of ITT and the International Petroleum Cartel, their relationships to the intelligence community, corrupt practices, financial power, and roles in sundry coups d'état. The issues raised by these investigations—matters that went to the heart of political and economic control in the twentieth century—were far larger than any single contract or sale of arms. And yet the subcommittee was forced to deal in specifics: bearer checks, bank transfers, and telegrams from Beirut.

The hearings of which Lockheed and Northrop became the subjects began with a suggestion from the Watergate Special Prosecutor's Office: there seemed to be a lot of unexplained money floating around in the Alps, Bahamas, and Makasar Strait—why didn't the subcommittee look into it? The most recent scandals, then, were a financial extension of the political debacle of Watergate: not only had corporate slush funds, laundered abroad, been used to fund Nixon's presidency, but the relationship between the White House and the multinationals was central to the whole affair. The two existed in near-perfect symbiosis, forming an ecosystem of high-altitude corruption.

And there were other issues, too. For one thing, corporations found to be making "improper payments" were not (as they tried to suggest) competing exclusively against corrupt foreign firms, but against honest American ones as well. Diverting contracts from American competitors with superior products, they deprived stockholders of other firms and, in some instances, weakened the military capability of American allies. Moreover, in making *value* a tertiary criterion of the marketplace, they compelled their competitors to emulate their illicit practices abroad. Northrop's corruption, for example, was a direct, *defensive* response to Lockheed's. Thus, as if by a variation of Gresham's law, bad business drove out the good.

There was also the issue of national security. Needing to pay off only the most respected and influential—NATO generals, defense ministers, and heads of state—the multinationals achieved with ease what hostile intelligence services had been endeavoring to accomplish for decades. Bribing and kicking back, the industrial giants rendered their beneficiaries susceptible to every sort of blackmail.

In addition there was the question of "self-service" kickbacks. With their conduits and dummy corporations receding into the jurisdictional fogs of Liechtenstein and Panama, it was impossible to tell where the American money actually went. The impression conveyed to the public is that it went abroad. To foreigners. In fact, some of it may have stuck to American palms, and subcommittee lawyers privately suspect—but have not proven—that a portion of the kickbacks paid to foreigners were, in turn, punted toward the numbered accounts of American executives.

There are even more basic issues. Jack Blum, formerly of the subcommittee's staff, remembers a conversation with Swiss air attachés. Looking out at the peaceful expanse of the Swiss cantons, a countryside redolent with neutrality, he set the generals back with a basic question. "Why does Switzerland need fighter jets?" he asked. It took a few minutes and a few phone calls for the answer to come back, and even then it was in the form of another question. It was: "To protect the valleys?" Switzerland, of course, can afford its lethal toys, but other countries cannot. The point was made by Senator Church while questioning Lockheed's international sales chief, William Cowden. Noting that Lockheed paid kickbacks even in the absence of competition he asked why. "Because," Cowden said, "we are frequently competing, not necessarily with another airplane just like ours, but we are competing for the sales dollars that would be spent on something else."

"Such as Kellogg's Corn Flakes," Church replied. "I mean, what you are really saying there is if we don't get their dollars, they might spend them for something unrelated to aircraft. . . . If you don't pay commissions they might buy food."

Whether the product is heroin or fighter jets, the result is often the same: profits that corrupt and, not occasionally, impoverish. Similarly, there has been osmosis between the CIA and the multinationals, with each making use of the facilities, methods, and personnel of the other. In this connection, it's been pointed out that "aggressive, expansionist societies have the best organized intelligence systems."[1] True of countries, it is also true of corporations.

## THE OLD GANG DE CAUSIBUS

The Lockheed Corporation is the largest defense contractor of the most heavily armed superpower in the history of the world. With about 60,000 employees, an equal number of stockholders, and contracts in the billions, it produces passenger jets, cargo jets, fighter jets, patrol planes, helicopters, missiles, armored cars, submarines, satellite systems, computer wares, rocket motors, ground sensor devices, bulk tankers, and a whole lot more—most of it classified and all of it expensive.

The firm's sales to foreign countries are a relatively small, but not insignificant, part of the country's overall balance of trade—and a key to whatever financial success Lockheed can have. In the past, that success has been considerable. It was Lockheed, for instance, that put the Luftwaffe back in the air following World War II, flogging 900 Starfighter jets to the fledgling West German Air Force. That sale proved strategic to the company's subsequent growth because it led, rather directly, to the sale of still more Starfighters to the other NATO countries and Japan. Accomplishing this rearmament at a time when European industry was still rebuilding from the war meant that Lockheed's only competition came from other American companies. This, however, did not stop the firm from engaging in certain "business unorthodoxies." According to Ernest Hauser, an international arms merchant whose Lockheed journals have caused him to be dubbed "the diary man," the firm awarded $12 million to West Germany's ultraconservative Christian Social Union. The money, Hauser claims, was paid to the party's right-wing leader, Franz-Josef Strauss, to influence the 1961 Starfighter transactions. Former West German Defense Minister Strauss denies the allegation: Defense Ministry files pertaining to the Starfighter deal have mysteriously "disappeared." Strauss, however, has an allegation of his own: according to him, West German Chancellor Helmut Schmidt offered Prince Bernhard of the Netherlands $40 million in the early 1970s if the prince would urge the Dutch to purchase F-14 Cobras from the Northrop Corporation. (Schmidt denies the accusation.) A former Lockheed representative in Europe, Hauser also alleges princely greed, insisting that under-the-table Lockheed payments in excess of $1 million were paid to Bernhard in the early Sixties.

Heir to the principality of Germany's Lippe-Biesterfeld, Bernhard was an early member of the Hitler Youth Movement and an employee of the I. G. Farben combine. The prince, however, became a hero of the Dutch Resistance shortly after his wedding to Juliana (heiress to the House of Orange, future queen, and perhaps the world's richest woman). Taking an active role in Europe's reconstruction, he joined the boards of more than 300 corporations. Despite the evidence of his wealth, it's widely believed that Bernhard accepted the million-dollar Lockheed bribe and used the money to support his illegitimate daughter and her mother, "Paris popette," in France.

Hauser's accusations against the prince, while convincing in many details, have yet to be proven. Lockheed officials admit that some of the money was paid, but their European capo, an American expatriate named Fred Meuser, claims to have pocketed the bribe himself (thereby echoing an alibi put forward by another agent in behalf of an Arab prince). An investigative council of "three wise men," appointed by the Dutch, has issued an ambiguous report on the matter, simultaneously chastising and acquitting Bernhard in the name of reasonable doubt.

The Starfighter affair is an especially sensitive one. A financial bonanza, the plane was less successful in a military sense. An "unforgiving" bird at best, the jet became positively dangerous when its European purchasers converted it from a "single-mission" fighter to a "multiple-mission" aircraft. Loading it down with a vast array of special equipment, the plane was brought to the very edge of its capabilities. Getting it there was a notoriously profitable business for Lockheed and its agents, since commissions on the additional equipment and replacement parts were often two and three times as high as those on the original sale. It seemed to many, therefore, that the agents made a financial killing when the plane was rendered into a kind of time bomb.[2]

Amid all the denials, one hardly knows whom to believe. Mechanisms for paying the bribes were deliberately established in such a way that the payments could never be uncovered or, failing that, would allow the recipient room for "plausible denial." Moreover, many of the agents were themselves quite devious, in some cases peddling influence they didn't have, pocketing kickbacks intended for others, making pacts with competitors, and "discounting" their own contracts to third parties. "Double agents" were commonplace, especially at Lockheed.

Lockheed's financial success was, in any case, a temporary affair. While it organized a worldwide private intelligence network of considerable competence, the firm suffered ghastly setbacks on its domestic front. The C-5A cargo jet, developed for the Defense Department, incurred enormous cost overruns at precisely the time that the profitable air war in Indochina was coming to an end. A few years earlier, Lockheed might have persuaded federal officials of the need to have the government absorb the overruns; in 1970, however, the Pentagon was on the defensive both at home *and* abroad. Against its will, the Defense Department was forced to make Lockheed foot the bill for its excesses. In February 1971 the firm consented to absorb $200 million in overruns, making dire prophecies even as it acquiesced. Two days later, the prophecies began to come true. Rolls Royce, supplier of engines for the C-5A, announced that it would go into receivership. With this catastrophe compounding its own troubles, Lockheed predicted its financial suicide—unless . . .

Unless Congress agreed to provide a $250-million loan guarantee.

The proposal outraged principled liberals and conservatives alike, but received powerful support from President Nixon and then Secretary of the Treasury John B. Connally. With overt appeals to Congress, and personal phone calls at the last minute, Nixon and Connally bullied the legislative branch for what many regarded as "corporate welfare." By a 49-48 vote (in which souls were reported lost), the Senate, wracked with filibuster, agreed to insure the loan for a period of two years (extensions were subsequently granted) and Lockheed was restored to grace. Not that the firm had been idle.

In Europe, the Orient, the Mideast, Indonesia, and Latin America, Lockheed's "foreign intrigue channels" were ablaze with activity. Following an unrecorded tête-à-tête between President Nixon and Japanese Prime Minister Takuei Tanaka in Hawaii [August 31 to September 1, 1972] it was agreed that Japan should buy at least $320 million in civil aircraft from an American firm, the purchase to take place within two years. In less than two months All-Nippon Airways signed a $400 million contract for twenty-one Lockheed Tristars, thereby fulfilling a major part of the bargain with Japan. Within those same two months, between the summit talks and November 7, 1972 (Election Day), exactly 1 billion yen ($2.7 million) was delivered in 15 bags to Yoshio Kodama, Lockheed's secret agent in Japan.

In mid-1975 the Subcommittee on Multinational Corporations revealed the pattern of bribery abroad and subpoenaed Lockheed executives. A few days later, Robert N. Waters, Lockheed's treasurer, was found shot to death, an apparent suicide. While the firm swore to resist demands for its confidential records, the oath was soon declared inoperative by the apparently mistaken arrival of those records in the subcommittee's offices. The effect was immediate and violent. "Undiagnosed" ailments placed prospective witnesses in hospital suites where, incommunicado, they recovered with uncommon slowness. In Italy, various agents and executives disappeared across the Swiss border. Meanwhile, leads contained in the

Lockheed documents sent subcommittee agents on a Lindblad's tour of world finance: to mansions and castles in the Black Forest, to tropical bars, basements in Tokyo, vaults in Hong Kong, and penthouses in Rome. Occasionally they found what they sought; more often they did not. In Japan an obscure young fanatic obsessed with his country's honor and memories of the "divine wind" became an overnight celebrity when he carried out a kamikaze attack on the mansion of Yoshio Kodama. This attempt at restoring Japanese "face," however, was seriously compromised when local newspapers filled their front pages with stills from the young man's appearances in pornographic films. (Kodama survived and remains too ill to testify.)

Despite months of investigation by teams of lawyers, auditors, accountants, and the world press, efforts that yielded the testimony of more than 100 witnesses from a dozen nations, and the accumulation of documents that came to be measured by the linear foot—despite all this, the expenditure of a small fortune, and the interventions of all three branches of government, little was resolved. A $1.3 billion Lockheed contract with Japan was canceled, $3 billion in other contracts was jeopardized, and at least one government was demanding some of its money back on an earlier deal. Daniel J. Haughton retired from Lockheed with a $750,000 pension. Former Prime Minister Takuei Tanaka was charged with corruption and jailed. Legislation that might have regulated or eliminated corporate bribery drowned in parliamentary compromise. As for the Subcommittee on Multinational Corporations and its repertory company of investigators, it was recently incorporated into a larger unit of the Senate, restricted by orders that its staff should not investigate specific corporations.

What follows, then, is a narrative of the sort which the subcommittee is now forbidden to embark upon. It is an attempt to illuminate the texture and extent of corporate intrigue as it occurred, and, insofar as possible, to do so in the words of the principals themselves. Relying upon documents delivered into the public domain by the Senate, the narrative intends to explain rather than to expose. While it concentrates upon Lockheed and its agents, moving from country to country and deal to deal, its concern rests not with the corrupting influence of a single corporation but with the *phenomenon* of multinational intrigues. With counterparts deriving from a dozen nations, Lockheed is in no way unique. As the economic instrument of its owners and managers, the firm enjoys a kind of jurisdictional immunity common to all multinationals. That immunity, however, imposes a logic of its own upon the multinationals, a calculus that inclines the firm's executives toward the maximization of profits by any means. Lockheed and its doppelgängers from Europe, Africa, and Japan are representative of a phenomenon that's been gathering force since the Second World War: the establishment of a multinational raj whose borders are marked, not by the static positions of rivers and mountains, but by the flow and transfer of accumulated capital. It is a renaissance of sorts.

## FRAGMENTS OF RUIN

Telex, 9-6-68, from Lockheed officer to executives in the firm's Georgia headquarters:

> Rush   Rush   Rush
> Reference: *Zephyr Locust*
> The Milan meeting September Fourth with *Locust,* ———, and Snyder addressed itself to delicate and sticky issues; . . . it is quite apparent that *Locust's* past and current performance in keeping ——— happy remains effective—remembering that ——— is one of the key people we must satisfy with not only what we do, but also with how we do it (and "who we send to do it"). . . . I feel *Caviar* can do business the *Zephyr* way . . . and at the same time make less agonizing the obtaining of future *Zephyr* business, which is not limited by aye good margin to defense hardware and services. The foregoing thoughts are just that and not intended as aye white (or even dirty cream) paper. End. Jackman/ Paris. (I've made some minor changes in the telegram's punctuation so that its text might be intelligible.)

The use of codes (and distribution designators which serve to "classify" internal documents) have become commonplace at many multinational corporations—as have paper shredders, phone scramblers, burn bags, and a host of eavesdropping and countermeasures equipment with such exotic names as "cloaks" and "slaves." In the above telegram, a substitution code is used wherein "Zephyr" means Saudi Arabia, "Caviar" is the Lockheed Aircraft Corporation, and "Locust" refers to a consultant.

Another telegram, whose subject is the addition of 1 percent to an agent's existing commission, suggests that countermeasures equipment may indeed be necessary.

> You are authorized to [offer] it to party concerned, but only thru [consultant]. You may be pressured to make d-i-r-e-c-t arrangement but do not repeat not do so. Have information that [code] has been b-r-o-k-e-n in [Saudi Arabia] so handle this accordingly.[3]

The "information" apparently came from a Lockheed agent, Adnan Khashoggi. A portly and balding Arab sophisticate, Khashoggi compares himself to J. P. Morgan and presides over an empire that includes more than 50 companies, ranging from banks in California to ships in Indonesia, a meat-packing plant in Brazil, and a Paris fashion house called Jungle Jap. Traveling the world in his own Boeing 727, Khashoggi was paid $106 million by the Lockheed Corporation between 1970 and 1975; during the same period he represented the Northrop Corporation, billing it more than $100 million for his services as a go-between. A friend of Richard Nixon's (and a contributor to his campaign), Khashoggi served as intermediary between the White House and the late King Faisal during the 1973 Mideast War. In a 1972 cable from Beirut, a Lockheed executive reports:

> Impossible submit daily status due security. Khashoggi suspects customer knows code.[4]

The "customer," of course, was Saudi Arabia.

That Nixon should have used Khashoggi as a confidential agent is strange in view of the Arab's disfavor with the since-murdered king. Faisal was reportedly upset by Khashoggi's ostentation, "corrupting influence," and methods of doing business. A Lockheed letter suggests that the king had good reason to be suspicious:

> During a recent conference in New York with Adnan Khashoggi, he requested that any and all communications touching upon commissions, however innocuous they might seem to the sender, be sent solely to his representative:
>
> > Gerard Boissier
> > 2 Place du Port
> > Geneva, Switzerland
>
> and that mail should be used, rather than Telex. He begged that no mention of any commissions ever be sent to either Beirut or Saudi Arabia.[5]

Obviously, Khashoggi feared that electronic communications to Beirut or Saudi Arabia might be intercepted. The subsequent use of Telex to convey sensitive messages concerning commissions implies that codes began to be used after the above letter was written. The distrust is not difficult to understand.

Memorandum from J. A. Davidson to William Cowden, November 25, 1969:

> A decree by the Saudi Arabian Council of Ministers requires a clause in all contracts specifying that no agent has been paid to secure the sale of the equipment in question. This decree further specifies that if any agent fees have been paid, the price to the Kingdom must be reduced by a corresponding amount. It is my understanding that LAS [Lockheed Aircraft Services] has accepted this as a necessary part of the risk in doing business in Saudi Arabia. They have signed, and are now negotiating to sign, contracts with such a statement included, but with full intention of paying our representative his usual fees.

The clause forbidding agents, however, became the subject of a public ritual. When contracts were signed in Saudi Arabia, the seller would be asked aloud if he had employed an agent in the country. So that the deception could be carried forward *without actually lying,* Khashoggi promised to be out of the country whenever such ceremonies were held.

The distrust was not a simple matter confined to the relationship between governments and manufacturers; there was at least as much suspicion between the manufacturers and their own agents—as well as conflicts between the agents themselves. Referring to a "marketing contingency fund . . . used by the Consultant for 'under the table' compensation to Saudi officials," a memo notes: "We really have no way of knowing if the so-called 'under the table' compensation is ever disbursed to Saudi officials or stops at our Consultant's bank account."[6] Not that they actually wanted to know: so long as they remained unwitting, they could not be "held accountable" in either the literal or the figurative sense.

Had Lockheed really wanted to know where the money went, it could probably have figured it out by following the checks that it issued—though this might well have required the services of three lawyers and a wall of concave mirrors. Any such inquiry would have touched upon the firm's use of what it called "subsidiaries of the first and second tier"—Lockheed entities of substance and conduits that existed only on paper for the purposes of tax avoidance. For instance, rather than paying Khashoggi directly, a "second-tier" subsidiary based in Geneva would employ the "marketing services" of a subsidiary on the "first tier," based in California. In its turn, the California firm would "subcontract" all or most of those services to Khashoggi's Triad Corporation.

Upon effecting a sale, Triad would bill its California employer; this firm would then dun its Swiss subsidiary. This jurisdictional stratagem resulted in a decided tax advantage for Lockheed: because the highly profitable Saudi Arabian contracts were signed with the Swiss firm, monies paid by it to the entity in California reduced the former's tax liability in Switzerland. For its part, "California" would show no profit on its putative marketing services, having paid to Khashoggi an amount equal to that which had been paid to it by "Switzerland." The only losers on the deal were taxpayers everywhere. U.S. taxpayers lost because profitable foreign contracts were routed to a Swiss-based vehicle subject to taxes that are much lower than those ordinarily paid in the U.S. Swiss taxpayers lost because the dummy in their midst rerouted some of those profits to the U.S.—where, of course, they were "offset" by equal payments to Khashoggi's Triad Establishment.

Following the money, then, it moved from King Faisal in Arabia to Lockheed in Switzerland, *from Lockheed* in Switzerland *to Lockheed* in

California, from Lockheed in California to Khashoggi in Switzerland. As you see, there's a little "loop" in the middle of the transaction, a seemingly extraneous curlicue that is, in fact, potentially worth millions in tax advantages.

Khashoggi's own maneuvers were no less interesting than Lockheed's. While his ALNASR Trading and Industrial Corporation served as the Riyadh-based beachhead for his efforts in Saudi Arabia, the Triad Financial Establishment was the vehicle through which Khashoggi signed his contracts with Lockheed. Incorporated in the postal enclave of Vaduz, Liechtenstein, Triad's operational center appeared to be in Beirut, Lebanon, while communications pertaining to commissions were routed through Khashoggi's representative, Gerard Boissier, in Geneva. This diversification was further obscured by the legal nature of his agreements with Lockheed. A 1967 "Consultant Agreement," for instance, provides that:

> In consideration of services . . . furnished by [the Triad Financial Establishment, or "Consultant"] . . . , Lockheed shall pay . . . compensation in accordance with the following rates:

| Product | Percentage of Selling Price |
|---|---|
| New Model C-130 Military Airplanes | 2% |
| New Commercial Hercules and Military C-130 Spare Parts and Ground Support Equipment | 2% |

It is, by any standards, a modest commission (though potentially quite lucrative). On the same day that the above contract was signed, however, three secret "letter agreements" were prepared, "supplementing" the commissions established in the original contract. The first such letter agreement provided for additional commissions of 5 percent and 13 percent, respectively, on the selling price of C-130s and related equipment. The second letter agreement stated that "Lockheed agrees to pay to Consultant . . . a special fee in the amount of $41,000 for each such [C-130] airplane for which Lockheed is paid the full contract price of $2,670,000." The third letter agreement doubled and tripled commissions agreed upon for the sale of *commercial* aircraft to Saudi Arabia. Thus Khashoggi's commissions amounted to as much as 16 percent, and in no instance went lower than 7 percent of the sales price. Even with these amounts, plus subsequent "incentives" and contingency funds, things did not always go smoothly in the wadis.

RUSH   RUSH   RUSH
Strongly suspect machinery stalled for lack of grease Stop. Is former air attache really pushing query? Urge you insist agent make move now to keep log rolling Stop. . . .[7]

An earlier memorandum marked "Confidential," reports:

1. —— is completely disenchanted with Adnan Khashoggi. He indicated that he never received the $150,000 that was agreed to between Max, Adnan and —— during their Paris meeting last year. He further indicated a dislike of Adnan and said while he likes Adil (Khashoggi, Adnan's brother) he is unwilling to deal with him because of his distrust of Adnan.

2. At the moment all LAIAG programs are in the "deep freeze. . . ."

3. . . . The reason for 2 . . . is 1, above.

4. —— showed Harley (Snyder) his statements on total payments made to LAIAG. He said he cannot understand why Adnan says that he (Adnan) has not received any money in view of these payments. —— statement to Harley was that he feels Adnan is lying to him.

5. ——indicated that he was told by Adnan that Adnan is only getting 2% commission.

Because Saudi officials were angered by the slowness with which Khashoggi made payments and by their distrust of him, they prevailed upon Lockheed to compel Khashoggi to make a formal assignment of portions of his commissions to various numbered accounts at Geneva's Credit Suisse. Effectively, this meant that Lockheed was responsible for making *direct* payments to such corporate dummies as the Lauvier and Cantona "Establishments." Incorporated in Vaduz, Liechtenstein, both "firms" seem to have played a purely passive role in Lockheed's affairs. Such "assignments," however, did not always diminish Khashoggi's own receipts. Viz.:

This will confirm that Triad Financial Establishment irrevocably commits . . . to Cantona Establishment . . . a portion of its marketing fees equivalent to one percent of the contract price. . . . Such . . . assignment to Cantona Establishment is contingent upon . . . [Lockheed's] increasing Triad's marketing fees . . . by one percent of contract price.

Other payments received by Khashoggi, including $400,000 earmarked by Lockheed as a "special adjustment," were disguised and added to subsequent contracts with Saudi Arabia, so that Lockheed's agent was always reimbursed.

"Reimbursed," that is, on the dubious assumption that he actually made the payments that he claims to have made. As a memo quoted earlier reported: [Lockheed officials] really have no way of knowing if the so-called 'under the table' compensation is ever disbursed to Saudi officials or stops at [Khashoggi's] bank account." The direct "assignments" of cash to the accounts of Cantona and Lauvier were apparently earmarked for third parties, but there is no way to be certain what happened to all or a part of this money. There is, however, an internal Lockheed memorandum that clarifies the nature of one such assignment and provides a remarkable insight into Khashoggi's astuteness.

Memorandum dated January 22, 1974:

A proposal for the sale of ten C-130H aircraft was presented to ———— on November 14, 1973. These aircraft were priced at $6.3 million each, which sum included the normal commissions plus $200,000 of "negotiating money." This $200,000 was included in the price at the insistence of A.K. [Adnan Khashoggi] and, in theory, can be committed by A.K. and/or the Gelac [Lockheed's Georgia plant] salesman for a price reduction or by A.K. alone for under the table payoffs. For this particular deal A.K. has taken the position that all negotiating money not negotiated away would go to TRIAD as a bonus. P.K. [other Lockheed memoranda make it clear that "P.K." refers to Prince Khalid] had been told by A.K. of this "bonus" arrangement. However, A.K. told P.K. there was $150,000 rather than the actual [amount].

———— on November 28 insisted that our price of $6.3 million (per plane) was too high. . . .

Over the phone from Beirut, Temp Walker received approval . . . to reduce the price of the aircraft to $6.1 million, if necessary to get a quick decision from ————. . . .

A.K. was told of the decision to go to $6.1 million, if necessary, thereby giving up all of the negotiating money. A.K. agreed . . . , but asked Temp to hold out . . . as long as possible.

Temp Walker met with ————, Gen. ————, Dorm Viers and Sal Aswaad at 9 a.m., December 1. ———— accepted our latest schedule, but insisted he must have a price reduction. After about two hours of negotiating, Temp Walker agreed to reduce the price to $6.2 million . . . The contract was signed . . .

On December 3, P.K. sent word to Temp Walker that he desired a meeting. Temp met with P.K. at . . . P.K.'s villa. P.K. was upset that Temp had given away $100,000 of the negotiating money. . . . P.K. then informed Temp that he and A.K. had formed a new company (SAVERIA) to market all C-130s in Saudi Arabia. P.K. said the split was to be 60% for A.K. and 40% for P.K. He then asked if there was a letter in Lockheed explaining this new company. Temp knew nothing of this and told P.K. so. . . .

P.K. then stated he had reason to believe the total commission paid by Lockheed was about 8% plus the negotiating money. . . . P.K. (repeatedly) asked Temp to assure that P.K.'s 40% share would meet or exceed $175,000. He implied he had a commitment of $125,000 to ———— and needed to know. Temp again repeated he did not know, whereupon P.K. asked Temp to make an estimate, hinting that he could still influence ———— to delay the contract should Temp refuse.

Temp thereupon did a rough calculation and told P.K. that if the 8%

was correct and the 60–40 split was correct, he would be in good shape. Based on a rough calculation, 40% of the supposed 8% would be about $225,000.

(Breaking into the memo: had Temp thought about it, he would have recalled P.K.'s allusion to his $125,000 debt to ————. That debt was P.K.'s justification for needing to realize at least $175,000 from the sale. The point is that P.K. incorrectly believed that the commissions to be paid would equal 8 percent of the cost of *a single aircraft*—plus the entirety of the bonus money attaching to *each* of the aircraft. Thus, receiving 40 percent of 8 percent of $6.2 million, P.K. would easily realize his goal of at least $175,000—but the real dough, so far as he was mistakenly concerned, rested with the $150,000 per plane "bonus." This money, if not "negotiated away," would provide him with an additional $60,000 for each plane sold, or an "extra" $600,000 on the deal. The commission itself, incorrectly thought to equal no more than a small percentage of a single plane's cost, was potentially less than one-third of the money P.K. might reap through the bonus. By "negotiating away" $100,000 of the supposed $150,000 bonus, Temp seemed to have reduced P.K.'s bonus share from $600,000 to a mere $200,000. Predictably, the prince was furious. And Temp, of course, was confused, incorrectly assuming that P.K. had a commitment to ———— of $125,000 *per plane,* whereas, in fact, it appears to have been a simple, one-time debt. Had Temp understood that, he would have told P.K. that his 40 percent of 8 percent, plus remaining bonus, would amount to more than $2.25 million on the deal— about three times the amount envisioned in his wildest dreams.) Following this confusing session in the prince's villa, the memorandum continues:

Temp Walker, D. O. Wood, Ned Ridings and Lew Lauler [Lauler was Khashoggi's "man in Beirut" at the Triad offices] met with A.K. in Beirut to resolve the flap caused by P.K. phoning Lew Lauler and asking for an accounting. A.K. did not seem particularly disturbed for he apparently guessed that P.K. was talking about a *total payment* to P.K. of about $275,000 and that P.K. would be overjoyed when he actually got more. A story was developed to present to P.K. which would support the actual split A.K. intended to make with P.K.

Under the SAVERIA company, A.K. has told P.K. that the total commission paid by Lockheed is 3% of the sales price plus 50% of any negotiating monies remaining. A.K. and P.K. split this 60%–40%.

On December 10 in Riyadh [those who'd met earlier in Beirut] met with P.K. to settle matters. It soon became evident that P.K. was not upset over the percentage commission, 3% of the total contract being much more than P.K. had expected, but was *very upset* over Temp giving up "his" negotiating money unnecessarily. . . . To further complicate matters, A.K. had told P.K. there was $150,000 negotiating money rather than the actual $200,000. It was finally agreed by D. O. Wood that P.K.

would receive his commission (through SAVERIA Co.) as though Temp had not negotiated away $100,000. [Memorandum dated January 22, 1974.]

Poor Temp. How could he have explained to P.K. that the "negotiating money" was mere peanuts, placed in the contract as a sop to Arab haggling, and *meant* to be bargained away? As for Khashoggi, he must have seemed both a genius and a benefactor to P.K., having negotiated a deal with Lockheed that provided Saveria Establishment with 3 percent of $62 million rather than 8 percent of a mere $6.2 million. And, as for P.K., he undoubtedly regarded himself as quite the wily Arab, forcing the decadent Americans to cave in to demands for the replacement of "his share" of the $100,000 in mad money.

Adnan Khashoggi was far from Lockheed's only agent, and Saudi Arabia was certainly not its only customer. In Italy, for instance, Lockheed's marketing of the C-130 transport required substantial contributions to Christian Democrats and a host of government ministers. Ovidio Lefebvre, a rich and obviously well-connected attorney in Rome, served as the aircraft firm's local "cut-out," making "direct payments" and channeling larger sums through a variety of conduits and fronts with such names as the Ikaria Establishment (of Liechtenstein) and the Temperate Zone Research Foundation (of Panama and Geneva). Competing against a Franco-Germanic consortium known for its unholy pragmatism in matters economic, Lockheed agents feared for their lives. In a letter from the Grand Hotel in Rome, Lockheed attorney Roger Smith writes (to Charles Valentine, director of contracts) on March 28, 1969:

Please accept my apologies for addressing you on scratch paper and in my execrable handwriting, but I am in no position to disclose to local Third Persons the contents hereof. . . .

Please hold onto your seat, as what follows may be a shocker to you. . . . Ovidio Lefebvre states that Gelac . . . must be prepared to go as high as $120,000 *per airplane* for the cumshaw pot. He hopes it will be less . . . but says that such is a nasty part of life in the arena in which we are trying to offset the same type tactics by a combination (this time) of both the French and the Germans. (In the last go-round, the French beat us single-handedly.)

Furthermore, he said that, unlike in the P-3 matter, there will not again be a face-to-face negotiation between a representative of the "party" and Lockheed representatives, but that he will be told, probably, by the Antelope Cobbler (get out your little black book—mine is dated October 15, 1965)[9] just how much the "party" demands.

Further, there will be the Cobbler himself, and Pun, and various others. . . .

In this connection, he insists that he will only give names and figures to one person. . . . He says he wishes it to be me. . . . If you want it to be someone else, then it must be someone who will be able to be here in person when needed since he will not put any of the information in the mails. If I get the information I would propose to seal it up and deliver it, so sealed, to our Paris lawyer for safe-keeping, with instructions to deliver it to the President of Lockheed in the event of my death, disability, or disappearance. He said he wanted it to be me . . . because I am a lawyer. (Doesn't that just make you available as a repository for guilty knowledge??) . . .

I hope you keep this letter on a *very* strict need-to-know basis with respect to your compatriots. As for the compensation to Third Persons part, we are dealing with dynamite that could blow Lockheed right out of Italy with terrible repercussions.

The nature of that "dynamite" is spelled out in an unsigned Lockheed memorandum entitled "Italian C-130 Contract Problems." Discussing delays in the payment of "commissions and fees," the memo acknowledges the fact that "the delay . . . is damaging our Corporate image with key personnel in the *Ministry of Defense* and in other Italian Government circles." (Italicized portions supplied from censored documents by the Subcommittee on Multinational Corporations.) Recapitulating previous payments, the memo reports that $78,000 was paid to "the *previous Minister* and certain members of his team, who are now in the *Ministry* and will review the contract. We have recently agreed to an additional payment for special compensation to the *Minister* for his activities in connection with the price increase that was negotiated in December."

Listing $1,680,000 in "Promotional Expenses," the memo notes that "More than 85% of this is for the *Minister's* political party." Despite the Italian bureaucracy, the memo says, the contract has progressed "in record time." Nevertheless,

The Defense Minister is . . . suspicious that the reason for our lack of action is that we are merely waiting for a government change so no payment to his party will be necessary. . . . The Minister's current position is that he will not process the contract further until the second ($575,000) payment is made to him. He feels that this is his last really effective pressure point, and apparently he intends to use it.

Foreseeing a cumulative cash investment of $7.8 million in the program over the next four months, the memo urges immediate payment to the Minister despite Lockheed's worsening cash-flow problems. "With the known instability of the Italian Government," it says, "we consider it imperative to assure that the contract is firmed up as soon as possible. The last thing we want is a new government and a new set of players at this stage of the game, and this possibility is getting stronger all the time, according to *Lefebvre*."

The procedure of describing bribes, kickbacks, and commissions as "promotional expenses" seems to be a standard one. "Thanks for your

Telex . . . concerning Dural Payments. . . . Invoices covering both extraordinary and normal expenses . . . and quote publicity expenses . . . breakdown as follows" (June 1975 Lockheed Telex). The "quote publicity expenses" are then shown to exceed "normal expenses" by a factor of three. The semantic issue was important, not only from a tax perspective, but in terms of who footed the bill. "I understand you . . . planned to review present outstanding invoices to separate the true quote extraordinary unquote expenses from the gifts. I assumed that [Dural] was going to be asked to swallow the latter and we pay only the former" (May 1, 1973, Telex from Lockheed's Allen Meyer).

"Dural" is Nezih Dural, Lockheed's agent in Ankara, Turkey. Distrusted by Lockheed ("It is disturbing to contemplate the possibility that Nezih is racking us a bit"[10]), Dural was subjected to closer scrutiny than most agents: over his protests, for instance, he was made to explain expenses involving thousands of dollars—which, as it turned out, had been spent in nightclubs and at Disneyland. And he differed from some other agents in other ways as well: he was, for example, provided a budget for industrial espionage. "Mr. Dural has now advised me . . . that the requirements to establish firm competitive data intelligence will require an expenditure of . . . $5,000 per month. . . . The intelligence data . . . [are] required to enable us to know what the competition is doing."[11] Apparently, the intelligence effort was successful. In a letter to Lockheed's Beirut representative, Dural mentions the budget for spookery and reminds his contact that "I brought a nice package present to Burbank. I am sure that you will have heard about this package."[12] Four months later, following a sale of Starfighters to Turkey, an interdepartmental communication orders the issuance of "a commission check to Nezih Dural . . . in the amount of $240,000." "When this check is ready," the IDC continues, "it will be delivered to the Geneva office, where it will be held for Dural."[13]

How Lockheed selected its agents is no secret: the firm simply hired the most politically and socially influential people it could find.

Letter from N. S. Orwat to M. M. Egan, entitled "Discussion with Vice-Admiral Heinz Kuhnle, Chief of the German Navy," July 9, 1973:

> Margaret and I were invited to dinner in Düsseldorf by [Lockheed consultant Christian] Steinrucke. As you know, Steinrucke has a rather magnificent home . . . and entertains in what might moderately be termed the grand old style. Certainly the dinner . . . for 16 people was as splendidly presented and served as any I have attended in Europe. I am told—and I can believe it!—that Germans seldom turn down a dinner invitation from the Steinruckes.
>
> At dinner were Dr. and Mrs. Mommsen (he was Defense Minister Schmidt's Deputy in the Ministry of Defense . . . and is now head of Thyssen, one of Germany's largest companies), several other top indus-

trialists, a high official from the Finance Ministry, and Vice Admiral Kuhnle, Chief of the German Navy, and Mrs. Kuhnle.

After dinner, I was able to have a private talk in the garden with Admiral Kuhnle. He had visited the U.S. a short time ago as the guest of Admiral Zumwalt. Bud is a classmate of mine from the National War College, which helped to establish the basis for a friendly conversation.

Kuhnle is a great admirer of Zumwalt and went on at some length about his admirable qualities, notably his ability in the face of a restricted Defense Budget to get more than his fair share. . . . This permitted me to inquire about Kuhnle's own budgetary problems. They are severe. . . .

When I inquired about the S-3, he seemed nonplussed. Either he did not know anything about the S-3, or he knew just enough to be danger-ous. . . . I could not press the point because the time had come to join the other guests.

I was impressed once again . . . with the political, military, financial and industrial associations that Steinrucke has in high circles. . . . I am confident that Steinrucke could be helpful to us by putting us in touch— under favorable circumstances—with the type of people to whom we would wish to communicate.

The S-3A is an antisubmarine aircraft of which Kuhnle, as head of the German Navy, should have known. His host, Steinrucke, was Lock-heed's agent in selling the plane and, according to his contract, stood to make "$100,000 per S-3A sold to the German Navy, for the first 15 aircraft only. Additional sales will be subject to new commission negotiations."[14] And, while it may be true that Steinrucke entertained "in what might moderately be termed the grand old style," it's unlikely that it cost him very much. Besides contractual pin money of $1,000 per month, the air-craft firm provided him with discretionary sums in varying amounts. Thus:

In discussions with *German consultant* last week he said that the *Jetstar* contract should be signed in September. However, he tells me that he has committed *forty-thousand Deutsch-marks* to the *political* parties and for which he will produce receipts. In addition he wants *one-hundred-thousand Deutsch-marks* for his commission and from which he will have to meet certain other *obligations* and for which there will be no receipts.[15]

It would be unfair to suggest that the propriety of all this did not bother some Lockheed officials, though their main concern seems to have been "deniability" and the "letter of the law," *vide* a telegram from Stein-rucke's Lockheed contact, N. S. Orwat:

Reference is made to . . . my recent agreement with Christian Steinrucke. It is my understanding that *an agreement of this kind may be illegal in Germany*, and I would ask that copies be limited only to those with a strict need to know. Because of security reasons, Steinrucke asked that we attempt to write an agreement that did not mention the type of air-craft involved. Attached is a draft that attempts to do just that. . . . Since Roger Smith helped to prepare it, I am sure it is legally sound [Orwat's emphasis].[16]

In rare instances, there were even more substantive doubts, worries about the unethical nature of the dealings. A 1965 memo anent Indonesia, for instance, discusses the unusual circumstance of the customer demanding that the firm *raise* its prices so that the agent (in this case the customer as well) will have a correspondingly higher "commission." "D. J. Haughton and I discussed this. I stated I felt we should hold at $1,874,000; that this hanky-panky had gone far enough. We discussed the various ethics of it, and agreed that . . . it just isn't right, and there is a limit somewhere to going along with this."[17] (As it happened, the limit was soon exceeded.)

Lockheed's problems in Indonesia, though, were in no way confined to ethical matters. Concerning the firm's original agent, "Ike" Dasaad, a Lockheed executive wrote: "There is always the possibility that the present government is merely using Dasaad and may have him on the list for liquidation somewhere down the line—but there is no reason to think so right now."[18] Indeed, the question of whether Dasaad would be liquidated or continue to function as Lockheed's agent stimulated a spate of secret inquiries: "[Ned] Ridings met with Colonel Slade, USAF air attaché, and inquired if the U.S. Embassy had any means of checking out and evaluating Dasaad's position with the new government. Slade stated that he could have the Embassy C.I.A. personnel check this out."[19] The reports of the CIA, the Embassy, various Army generals, and local businessmen, however, were completely contradictory: "well connected," said one; "in good graces," said another; "the Dasaads are completely without influence," said a third.

But the *real* problem in Indonesia was far simpler than Dasaad's complicated status: that is, the Indonesian generals simply didn't understand the etiquette of bribery. They insisted on *direct* payments from Lockheed and refused to consider the establishment of what one Lockheed official called "a nominal buffer." Instead the Indonesian Air Force (AURI) established a numbered account in Singapore. Called "the Widows and Orphans Fund," it was in the name of the omnipresent————(believed to be a different————than the————who was active in Saudi Arabia). A somewhat fearsome character given to lethal mood swings, ————declined a Lockheed request that a "third party," or cut-out, be used to launder the commissions being paid. "The advantages to be gained in mutual protection were pointed out; however,————summarily refused this suggestion on the basis that a third party would have to be paid, which would only dilute the AURI 'commission.' "[20] The same memo warns that

If Lockheed elects to do business in the prescribed AURI fashion, some of the hazards that we might be exposed to are:

1. Since we have no agency agreement in Indonesia, we have no legal means of charging off these "commissions." Thus, they may not be considered allowable deductions by the Internal Revenue Service.
2. If such payments should some day become public knowledge the repercussions could be damaging to Lockheed's name and reputation.

Despite this clairvoyant analysis, Lockheed "elected to do business the AURI way," modifying it only to the extent that "all commissions paid into Singapore must go through a 'sanitizing' process involving [Jack] Clutter's office [in Tokyo]."[21]

With the Widows and Orphans Fund established in accordance with —————'s demands, Lockheed had little trouble thereafter. A report of subsequent encounters with AURI's leaders notes, "—————was in a very jovial mood at both meetings. I learned that he had been advised of the deposit of the $100,000 'commission' in the Singapore bank just prior to our arrival. This, undoubtedly, accounted for his benign mood."[22]

Undoubtedly.

## THE JAPANESE CONNECTION

When Mitsuyasu Maeno piloted a rented Piper Cherokee into Yoshio Kodama's veranda this past spring, he wore the headband and uniform of an Imperial Army pilot and called out, as he crashed, "Long live the emperor!" It had been the battle cry of Japan's kamikaze pilots, and it had not been heard, in quite those circumstances, for precisely 30 years.

Maeno's sacrificial gesture, made in response to headlines implicating Kodama in the Lockheed scandals, appalled Japan. Not only had the country "lost face" through revelations of its government's corruption, but now the scandal was twisted in such a way that half-forgotten stereotypes were exhumed and paraded before the world's press. In need of some "fresh air," Tokyo was given a breath of the "divine wind." Even as his plane crashed, Tokyo porn palaces flickered with images of Maeno's couplings in the abysmal sex flicks of the Orient. Because it was simultaneously tragic and absurd, occurring against a background of national shame, Maeno's suicidal attack hinted at a collective Japanese pathos: the heroically suicidal youths of the Second World War, celebrated for the purity of heart perceived in the manner of their deaths, had come to this. In the new Japan of hamburgers, hard rock, Pachinko, and Quaaludes, dignity proved impossible even in the practice of ritual suicide.

And there was an even deeper irony to the affair. Maeno's intended victim, Yoshio Kodama, was himself one of the foremost celebrants of the divine wind, having only recently called for a renaissance of its fighting spirit. It was Kodama, moreover, who'd provided the kamikaze pilots of the Second World War with the planes they'd flown to such lethal effect. And it was Kodama who, in the plush Okura Hotel, had wept (discreetly) as Tokyo's assembled elite listened to the premier performance of his neo-Fascist march, "The Song of Race"; composed in 1971, it was a tune that called for a kamikaze coup d'état to restore the fading emperor to power and Japan to glory.

So when Maeno dive-bombed Kodama, it was not just masonry and metal that collided, but the depleted residue of apposite ages.

It would be surprising if Kodama did not have some sympathy for Maeno's attempt on his life, however much the man and the attempt may have shamed him. Crippled by a stroke that coincided with news of his role in the Lockheed affair, Kodama has had a year of seclusion in which to meditate upon a career of achievements and crimes in Gothic proportions.

Yoshio Kodama was an orphan raised in poverty by increasingly remote relatives. At eleven, he was duped into the service of a Korean sweatshop, an iron foundry manned by consumptive youths who were held against their will each night in barrackslike hostels owned by the company. In a practical sense, they were the unpaid property of the firm for which they worked.

Finally escaping from this servitude, Kodama made his way to Tokyo in 1929, having made the transition from childhood to adulthood without any intervening stage of adolescence. His only assets, at the time, were a few unshakable convictions derived from his experiences and the fantasies that attended them. He was convinced, for instance, that his family was a noble one, temporarily impoverished, but rooted in a tradition of samurai glory. Linking his own destiny to Japan's, he emerged from the Tokyo slums as a terrorist leader and radical patriot. An ultranationalist at fifteen, Kodama quite naturally immersed himself in the political bedlam of depression Japan, joining a score of conspiratorial "societies" with such names as the Blood Brotherhood, Holy War Execution League, Federation of Radical Patriotic Workers, and Capital Rise Asia Academy. These societies, many of them murderous and fly-by-night affairs, provided Kodama with a precarious living. Ostensibly political, they were often no more than street gangs manipulated for private ends by wealthy industrialists, the police, and the army. They fought the Communists and each other with equal frequency, and underwent a continual factionalization. Often, the societies consisted of no more than a few friends, a post-office box, and gelignite.

It was in this right-wing milieu, part underworld and part underground, that Kodama plotted in 1932 to conduct a battue of the emperor's entourage—a state massacre that would eliminate at one stroke the most powerful men in the realm. The plot went awry in a sort of "townhouse explosion," and Kodama was shot. In fact, according to former New York *Times* reporter Hugh Byas, Kodama shot himself when apprehended. "He died a few days later," Byas reported, "and was given a magnificent funeral conducted by Shinto priests and attended by nearly a thousand members of patriotic and political societies."[23]

Contrary to this mysterious report, Kodama had been sent to jail rather than the grave. Imprisoned for three years without a trial, he was held incommunicado for much of the time, finally going to court in the last days of 1935. On conviction, he spent another year in prison, devoting his time to haiku. In his spare moments, he recalls:

> My greatest pleasure was to gaze upon the sparse grass and flowers [of the exercise yard]. In season, when the cosmos were flowering, strong winds used to blow, breaking the stems of the flowers. On such occasions, I felt as badly at the sight of the windblown cosmos, as if I had my own arms broken. Often, I used to put splints on the broken stems of these flowers, but on such occasions, there were no leftist thoughts —only a deep love and a feeling of adoration of nature welled in my heart.[24]

It is a biographical curiosity that Kodama, in and out of jail throughout his youth, never returned directly to Tokyo from prison, but seemed always to have some business in Manchuria, returning home only after a journey through China. It seems worth mentioning because, at that time, Manchuria had been seized by the rebellious Japanese Expeditionary Forces. A puppet kingdom, Manchukuo, had been established by the Army and served, for a while, as its plaything. It was, in a sense, one of the most important places in the world: its temporary success encouraged the Japanese Army's dream of expansion and led directly to its imperial rampage in subsequent years.

Why Kodama should have visited Manchuria so often has never been adequately explained. U.S. Army intelligence reports suggest that he performed espionage missions and that he organized a China-wide network of Manchurian spies and collaborationists. For his part, Kodama says that he was sickened by the atrocities committed by the Japanese Army, atrocities that violated not only the rules of war, but those of nature as well, making a mockery of the samurai's chivalric code.

Despite this view, his political and military connections, coupled with his outspoken advocacy of Japan's southern expansion, combined to make him one of the Orient's most successful clandestine operators. In Shanghai, China, and Vietnam, Kodama undertook a series of secret missions, beginning in 1937, for the Army and Kempei Tai (secret police); four years later he was entrusted with the task of supplying the Japanese Naval Air Force in wartime. Establishing the Kodama Kikan, or Kodama Agency, he built a financial empire from a handful of rooms in the Shin-Asia Hotel, an empire that was to determine the political course of postwar Japan. According to a report of the U.S. Army's Counterintelligence Corps, Kodama accomplished the navy's ends at gunpoint, taking hostages and forcing Chinese villagers to sell him the goods he demanded; paying a pittance to the Chinese, he then resold the goods at fabulous profits to the Imperial Navy. Systematically looting China of its raw materials, he amassed a personal fortune of colossal dimensions. To accomplish that, he acquired heroin on the black market in Tokyo, traded it for tungsten in Shanghai, sold the tungsten for yen, used the yen to buy guns, sold the guns in Borneo for gold, exchanged the gold for industrial diamonds and, in the meanwhile, cornered the Shanghai radium market by emptying the hospitals of their supplies. In addition, he operated salt mines, iron mines, farms, fisheries, an orphanage, a molybdenum mine, and secret munitions factories throughout central China. In his heroin deals, he sometimes burned the consumer, and there were unproven allegations that the yen spent in China was counterfeit (not that it mattered, since it was useless to the Chinese in any case). He came to be regarded as "the man behind the Kempei Tai," financing its Shanghai office in return for its "physical support." Intelligence reports show that this was sometimes bloody work, revealing that Kodama was suspected of assassinating his partner.

In 1945 Kodama was 34 years old, a brigadier general, a cabinet adviser, and the possessor of a financial hoard that included half-a-roomful of platinum, sacks of industrial diamonds, an undetermined amount of foreign currency, and upward of 3.5 billion yen [about $175 million at the time]—not including illiquid assets. Just how much Kodama was worth, however, could not be exactly ascertained. All documents of the Kodama Kikan were burned at the end of the war, and Kodama himself admits that he hid most of his wealth.

Imprisoned as a war-crimes suspect in 1946, he'd been attempting to organize a new political party for Japan, a party emulating those which governed the United States. This pretense of democracy, however, failed to deceive American Occupational authorities. An intelligence assessment of Kodama concludes:

> In summary, KODAMA appears to be a man doubly dangerous. His long and fanatic involvement in ultra-nationalistic activities, violence included, and his skill in appealing to youth make him a man who, if released from internment, would surely be a grave security risk. In addition, there is the outstanding probability to be reckoned with that, as a result of his hearty cooperation with the war effort, he has a large fortune to back-up whatever activities he might see fit to undertake. His success in the difficulties of securing supplies in wartime for the Navy

mark him as one who could very easily become a big-time operator in Japan's reconstruction period. Persistent rumors as to his blackmarket profits in his Shanghai period, plus his known opportunism, are forceful arguments that he would be as unscrupulous in trade as he was in ultra-nationalism. KODAMA's past performance indicates that he is the sort of man G-2 considers more dangerous than either the superannuated ideologists or the professional men who aided Japan's wartime effort for reasons of patriotism or survival of their professional interests. . . . Dangerous potentialities for the future.[25]

Another report, prepared by Kodama's chief inquisitor, Lt. Frank O'Neill, concludes: "I am satisfied that Kodama or his associates . . . for whom he is responsible committed numerous acts of violence in China in the acquisition by foul means or fair of commodities and goods [belonging to] the Chinese."[26]

Shortly after this assessment was made, and in spite of it, Kodama was released without trial. Walking out of prison with him was Nobusuke Kishi (elected prime minister nine years later), and 17 other war-crimes suspects who would become the financial and political spine of a new, democratic Japan. Why was Kodama released? The last pages of his diary give a clue:

Who, in this age of ideological confusion, is capable of bringing the laboring masses, influenced completely by Communist ideals, and rampaging like a wounded beast, under control? . . . The bestial roar of the Communist Party [reaches] into my cell through the barred windows of Sugamo Prison . . . I can hear the dull thud of the marching feet of thousands of Communists advancing toward the bolshevization of Japan. . . . Who will fight the last fight with them? Behind the steel bars of Sugamo this young life of mine, burning with the passionate ardor of a love of my country and of justice, strains against the bars that hold it in.[27]

A few days after Kodama's release, Lt. Frank O'Neill was reported to have predicted: "Ten years from today this man Kodama is going to be a great leader of Japan."[28] He was right.

Working behind the scenes, Kodama established the Liberal Democratic Party (LDP), using funds hoarded from his Shanghai days; it soon became the most important political party in Asia, leading some to suspect that Kodama's release from Sugamo had been arranged by the fledgling CIA. Whether that is so or not, Kodama consolidated his hold over Japan's ultranationalists and reestablished contact with anti-Communist gangsters and street punks from the Tokyo Ginza. By 1958 he had again become one of the most powerful men in the Orient, almost as influential in Korea as he was in Japan. In that year, he signed the first of many contracts with the Lockheed Corporation, promising to reverse Japan's decision to outfit its born-again air force with Grumman F-11-Fs. To accomplish that reversal, he relied upon, among others, an American-born espionage agent who'd lost his citizenship by working for the Japanese in occupied Manchuria; a politician who was later jailed for embezzlement; an extreme right-wing publisher; various war-crimes suspects who'd shared the anxieties of Sugamo; and the organizer of the attack on Pearl Harbor, Gen. Minoru Genda. Appointed Commander in Chief of the Japanese Air Force (through the backing of Kodama and Kishi, then prime minister and chief of the National Defense Council), Genda was wildly enthusiastic about the Lockheed Starfighter. After testing it in California, he returned to Japan with the recommendation that only the Starfighter would do. At about the same time, Genda's recommendation was echoed by a special delegation of German Air Force officers who'd arrived in Tokyo to persuade recalcitrant Japanese of the Starfighter's dubious superiority. Supported, then, by Japan's most honored military figure, by its respected ally in the preceding war, by the prime minister, and by Kodama's political manipulations, Lockheed accomplished the impossible. Grumman's contract was canceled. A few months later, General Genda was awarded the U.S. Legion of Merit by the American Air Force—17 years after he'd annihilated its planes in Hawaii.

Indeed, 1958 was a busy year for Kodama. Besides the difficulty of arranging the Lockheed sale, he was called upon to preserve the disintegrating political position of Prime Minister Kishi. Regarded by many as an American puppet for having pushed an unpopular Japanese-American Security Treaty through the Diet, Kishi appeared to be on the way out. Kodama, however, was able to save him, rallying the right wing to his standard and provoking street demonstrations in his behalf. Those demonstrations were countered by even larger ones organized by the Left, and it appeared that President Eisenhower's impending visit to Japan would result in widespread bloodshed. With the demonstrations gathering force, U.S. and Japanese authorities called upon Kodama to take charge of "Operation Protect Ike." Moving with customary quiet, Kodama pried loose an estimated $2.3 million in "contributions" from local businessmen, ultranationalists, and racketeers. With that in hand, he hired platoons of anti-Communist street fighters, providing them with riot gear, trucks, and helicopters. At the last minute, however, Ike's visit was aborted as American authorities contemplated what appeared to be the makings of a massacre.

Sometime after Operation Protect Ike, Kodama seems to have lent his support to the Reverend Sun Myung Moon's Unification Church, gravitating toward that organization through the auspices of Ryoichi Sasagawa. An old friend of Kodama's, a veteran of Sugamo and the Shanghai-Manchuria intrigues, Sasagawa came into enormous wealth after the war, becoming, among many other things, chairman of the Japan Shipbuilding Association. An ultranationalist whose views paralleled Kodama's, Sasagawa established himself in his friend's mold, becoming one of Japan's leading *kurumaku* [literally, "black curtain": a term from the Kabuki drama which refers to someone who works "behind the scenes."] Just as Kodama financed private military exercises on the remote island of Choju, Sasagawa lavished money on Tokyo's "martial arts societies"—a euphemism that might cover everything from karate clubs to paramilitary cabals.

Sasagawa's pet project, however, was Win Over Communism (WOC), a fund-raising subsidiary of the Unification Church. Sasagawa served as WOC's chairman, and Kodama as its chief adviser. This needn't indicate any special religiosity on the part of either man; on the contrary, the Unification Church's evangelical anti-Communism is a bulwark of South Korean "stability" and, as such, protective of Kodama's investment in that country. The recipient of untold Lockheed millions, Kodama was the aircraft firm's agent in both Japan and Korea. Other corporations (notably Gulf) have been shaken down for "political contributions" by Korea's Park regime, the quid pro quo being the right to do business there. It's hard to believe that Kodama, with his influence and investments in South Korea, should not have provided Park's minions with support, financial and otherwise. If he did, then his affiliation with WOC is particularly suggestive. Specifically, it raises the possibility of the Lockheed Corporation's indirectly subsidizing the Moonies' spread from Seoul to Savannah. The money Lockheed sent to Japan was taken from Hong Kong by an apostate Spanish missionary for delivery in so-called Bekins boxes to the industry's *kurumaku* in Tokyo.

The Spanish-born priest was a naturalized Japanese citizen whose given name, Jose Gardeano, had been changed to Hoze Aramiya. Father Hoze was a courier for what Japanese police officials describe as an "underground bank." After Lockheed made an electronic transfer of funds from its Los Angeles offices to those of its Hong Kong foreign-exchange dealer, Deak & Company, Father Hoze or another secret courier then would take the money to Japan. The sums, in cash or yen bearer checks, were hand-carried aboard planes in flight bags and large attaché cases that held upward of 9,300 10,000-yen notes weighing about 27.5 pounds.

While Deak & Company served as middlemen in transfers amounting to $8.3 million between 1969 and 1975, another $4.3 million was sent by other routes, notably through Lockheed's Swiss branch. Receipts for this money came in a variety of shapes and forms. Shig Katayama, an American, says he provided the aircraft firm with blank receipts signed by himself as proprietor of the I-D Corporation's Hong Kong office. The owner of Japan's largest coffee-vending-machine company, Katayama founded I-D in the Cayman Islands three years ago. Paid $72,000 for his signatures,

Katayama is a Los Angeles resident and, apparently, I-D Corp.'s only employee.

Other Lockheed receipts were even more obvious and, occasionally, bizarre: "I received One Hundred Peanuts. s/Hiroshi Itoh."[29] Kodama's own hand written receipts looked like this:

Amount Seventy Five Million Yen Only
Have duly received the above
Showa 47th Year Nov. 6 (1972)
Kodama Yoshio

In all, Lockheed remitted about 2.33 billion yen to its Tokyo office. Receipts issued by Kodama account for about 1.72 billion yen, while the remaining $610 million appears to have gone to the Marubeni Corporation. This last amount (about $1.66 million) is thought to have been paid to high government officials. Receipts issued by the I-D Corp. are nearly identical in their yen amounts to the Marubeni Corporation's receipts for "peanuts," "units," and "pieces." Obviously, then, the money paid by Lockheed to Marubeni necessitated two sets of receipts: the "agricultural set" issued by Marubeni for the internal purpose of keeping track of the payments; and the external set "issued" by Lockheed's Hong Kong front, the I-D Corp. The former were never meant to see daylight; the latter, however, could be used for accounting purposes. According to Katayama, this was the use of the receipts he provided. By insisting, however, that he never received any cash from Lockheed, he is at odds with Lockheed executives who claim that I-D receipts reflected money actually dispersed to Katayama. (Curiously, the amount in dispute—$1.6 million—is equal to that represented by 14 bearer checks that were said to have been stolen and which, so far, have not been recovered). If Katayama is lying, it may be because he pocketed the money supposedly issued to him by Lockheed —or because he intends to protect his own financial interests in Japan by denying a direct involvement in illegal payoff. If, however, Katayama is telling the truth, and never received money Lockheed says it paid to him, then $1.6 million has disappeared entirely. Almost anyone could have it. I-D, therefore, seems never to have handled any cash: the 2.33 billion yen remitted by Lockheed is accounted for by adding Kodama's receipts to those of Marubeni. The amounts balance.

The purpose of these circumlocutions, however, is clear. Because the money was to be used in illicit lobbying operations, Lockheed did not want its remittance route traced. Neither did the firm's agents. The receipts, therefore, served three purposes: they disguised the remittance route; gave Lockheed a hold on its agents; and provided the firm with a means of justifying what it liked to call its "marketing expenses."

The ultimate goal, of course, was to sell airplanes, and in this Lockheed was successful. After years of behind-the-scenes puppeteering, involving relatively small remittances, Lockheed's patience was rewarded. On September 1, 1972, President Nixon, accompanied by Secretary of State William Rogers and National Security Adviser Henry Kissinger, met in Hawaii with Japanese Prime Minister Takuei Tanaka. As part of a U.S.-Japan trade agreement, the Japanese agreed to purchase at least $320 million in civilian aircraft from an American manufacturer within the next two years.

Within a few days, however, the Japanese Defense Council retracted its previous decision to produce anti-submarine patrol planes domestically —thereby making possible a billion-dollar sale of Lockheed P-3C Orions to Japan. A few days before that decision was formally approved, Father Hoze and his Hong Kong carriers went to work. Before a month was out, exactly 1 billion yen was delivered to Kodama in small wooden packing crates that required 15 separate deliveries.[30] The last payment took place on the day Americans went to the polls to reelect Richard Nixon.

While this financial blizzard was under way, All-Nippon Airlines canceled its option to buy ten DC-10s from McDonnell Douglas Corporation. Two weeks later, Tanaka met with ANA executives who, shortly thereafter, announced that the firm would purchase six Lockheed Tristars, later upped to 21, at a cost of $20 million apiece. The man responsible for ANA's decision is believed to have been Kenji Osano, one of the firm's directors and its largest stockholder. A confidant of Tanaka, Osano is also the owner of the hotel in which the Nixon-Tanaka talks were held.

## EPILOGUE

There is no proof that Lockheed was specifically discussed during the Nixon-Tanaka summit talks. And yet it would be careless not to speculate about the matter. Certainly the Japanese have done so. In the aftermath of the subcommittee hearings, three ANA executives have been arrested and former Prime Minister Tanaka has been jailed. No fewer than 20 Japanese industrialists and government officials have been placed under investigation.

As for Nixon, his involvement with the Lockheed Corporation is deservedly suspect. Investigators for the defunct Subcommittee on Multinational Corporations have told me, "It's absolutely incredible that Lockheed should have been the only U.S. corporation of any size *not* to have made a contribution to Nixon's 1972 reelection campaign—and yet, that's what we're told. It just doesn't make sense, not after what he did for them. I mean, he intervened *personally* to get that loan." The absence of a Lockheed contribution to the Nixon campaign is intriguing. So is Nixon's association with Khashoggi, and his appointment of senior Lockheed executives to important Air Force and ambassadorial posts. Equally suggestive is the proximity of the summit talks. So is the proximity of the summit talks to the Kodama payments, the decision against Japan's domestic production of patrol planes, and ANA's choice of the Tristar. Moreover, Nixon had himself visited Japan on a number of occasions between 1963 and 1968, conferring with business leaders and politicians there on behalf of Mudge Rose, the New York law firm in which he was then a partner. Asked if Nixon or the firm represented Lockheed during that time, Mudge Rose has so far declined to answer.

Whether or not Nixon's relationship to Lockheed becomes a subject of future investigation, the more important question of the multinationals' often subversive influence must continue to be examined. While the firms insist that their global operations make them subject to the laws of many nations (rather than to those of a single one), the truth is, as we've seen, otherwise. With the buffers provided by Swiss banks, Panamanian "research foundations," and batteries of attorneys, bagmen, cut-outs, and spies, the multinationals are often able to pick which laws they will obey, which levies shall apply. In this sense, then, the United Nations is correct in terming them *trans*nationals. While not quite sovereign states, they function as protected principalities, enjoying their status as "instruments of foreign policy." In reality, however, such policies tend increasingly to be instruments of the multinationals.

The Lockheed documents and the testimony of the firm's executives suggest an internal logic, an inevitability, to the practices which evolved. Alluding to them, Daniel Haughton told newsmen in Washington, "I haven't done anything wrong as corporate chairman. We did it playing the rules of the game. . . . I went out and increased profits and sales for shareholders and employees. If they want to change the rules of the game now, let them."

It seems a good idea, however difficult it might be to accomplish. To abide with the multinationals' immunities, out of apathy or cynicism, is a surrender to the calculus of greed. Accomplishing that surrender, we insure the subordination of democratic processes to the mechanisms of multinational profiteering. And that can only deliver us to a final bankruptcy of another kind and even greater magnitude.

## NOTES

1. Harry H. Ransom, *The Intelligence Establishment* (Cambridge, Mass.: Harvard University Press, 1970), p. 49.

2. In its Starfighter sales effort, Lockheed competed against the Grumman Corporation's F-11-F fighter. Of 900 Starfighters sold to the Germans, 174 crashed (in peacetime), killing 96 pilots. In Japan, 60 of 230 crashed.

3. Telex sent in 1972 by Lockheed officer D. O. Wood. Words in brackets have been substituted for the code words used. The hyphenated letters have also been decoded.

4. Telex dated December 11, 1972.

5. Letter from Gerald B. Juliani to Los Angeles, Georgia, and Switzerland; the letter's date is uncertain, but is believed to have been written in July 1966.

6. Undated Lockheed memo headed "Saudi Arabian Consultant: Triad Financial Establishment."

7. Cable to Robert Jackman in Paris from J. H. Wilkinson in Jidda, Saudi Arabia.

8. January 11, 1973, letter from Triad's Beirut-based Louis Lauler to Lockheed's senior vice-president of marketing, Duane Wood.

9. Antelope Cobbler is a former prime minister of Italy. The "little black book" is a reference to Lockheed codebooks, changed at regular intervals.

10. Interdepartmental communication from Allen Meyer to Walter C. Smith, head "Consultant Arrangements—Turkey," May 9, 1973.

11. IDC from Walter C. Smith to D. M. Wilder, May 7, 1973.

12. Letter from Dural to Robert F. Conley, November 30, 1973.

13. IDC from A. A. Boon Hartsinck to L. H. Arnold, March 11, 1974.

14. IDC headed "Agreement with Steinrucke/Germany on S–3A Commissions," dated March 22, 1974, prepared by A. A. Boon Hartsinck.

15. Lockheed Telex dated August 30, 1972. Italicized portions decoded, and provided by the Subcommittee on Multinational Corporations.

16. Letter to R. P. Witte from N. S. Orwat, April 1, 1974.

17. "Lockheed Private Data," memo of W. G. Myers, June 11, 1965.

18. "Lockheed Private Data," memo of D. D. Stone, November 15, 1966.

19. Letter from Ned Ridings to Dallas Cederberg, August 8, 1967, entitled "Lockheed Agent in Indonesia."

20. IDC from P. F. Dobbins to R. I. Mitchell, May 14, 1971.

21. IDC from Dallas Cederberg to B. H. Menke, May 16, 1973, "Subject: Indonesia."

22. IDC from F. S. McKinney to G. B. Methvin, May 10, 1971, "Subject: Visit to AURI Headquarters, Djakarta, Indonesia, April 28–29, 1971."

23. Hugh Byas, *Government by Assassination* (New York: Alfred A. Knopf, 1942), pp. 238–39. Mr. Byas was stationed in Tokyo by the *Times* for many years prior to World War II.

24. Yoshio Kodama, *I Was Defeated* (Japan: Radiopress, 1959), pp. 32–47. Written while imprisoned as a war-crimes suspect, Kodama's fiercely anti-Communist memoir is a self-serving document submitted to the Occupation authorities in an effort to secure his release. The non sequitur about the absence of "leftist thoughts" suggests that Kodama appropriated to himself an action he witnessed and admired in another—a "leftist."

25. G-2 Report, May 24, 1947, Far East Command, marked the attention of Col. R. E. Rudisill. The report was quietly declassified of late, and made a part of the records of the International Military Tribunal for the Far East, International Prosecution Section (IMTFE-IPS), at the National Archives.

26. "Progress Report" re Yoshio Kodama and Ryoichi Sasagawa, July 7, 1948, IMTFE-IPS.

27. Kodama, *I Was Defeated,* pp. 204–12.

28. *Ibid.,* pp. iii–iv.

29. Receipt dated August 9, 1973. Itoh was the executive director of the Marubeni Corporation, the gigantic trading company that formerly represented Lockheed in Japan. The "one hundred peanuts" referred to a transfer of 100 million yen. After the receipt became public, the Crown Record Company of Japan sought to cash in on its notoriety, cutting "Bokumo Hoshiina Peanuts," or "I Also Want Peanuts"; the rock tune, however, never really got off the ground.

30. At the official exchange rate, this would be about $2.7 million; on the black market, however, a billion yen would amount to exactly $2.5 million. Whatever the amount, the deliveries required that the courier have a strong right arm; of the *Asahi Shimbun* is correct, the money weighed 412 pounds.

# V

# *Professional Deviance*

## INTRODUCTION

The famous sociologist Everett C. Hughes is often quoted as saying that in times of social crises and rapid social change the professions are among the first institutions to be questioned and criticized. This observation seems appropriate today. And in fact most of our traditional professions, especially medicine, law, psychiatry, and education, have been under attack for several years now. And so it should be, as most of them are riddled with problems of corruption and unethical practices of various kinds. Certain routine and taken-for-granted practices of a highly dubious legal and moral nature are now found throughout the professions. More often than not, these deviant practices are not those covered by the professional "code of ethics," which is usually nothing more than a rhetorical front to persuade the naive public that the profession is taking care of its own problems. But the professions have proven even more ineffective at curtailing the abuses of their members than have official and other regulatory agencies with other forms of business deviance, as described in the chapters of the previous section. So we would be wise to view with skepticism professional claims that significant reform will come from within the professions themselves.

Part V includes five short chapters which describe certain forms of professional deviance, including those found in the practice of medicine (Chapters 11 and 12), the health care industries (Chapter 13), public school teaching (Chapter 14), and the legal profession (Chapters 11 and 15). There can be little doubt that the costs of professional deviance are very high indeed, not only the financial costs, resulting from such practices as fee-splitting or special charges in medicine and law, as noted in Chapters 11, 13, and 15, but more importantly the costs in human lives, health, and psychological well-being. Given these great costs of professional deviance, it is all the more remarkable that social scientists have done so relatively few studies in this area. And there are virtually none published on academic and university deviance, indicating that social scientists intuitively understand the strategies used by other professions of "protecting their own kind."

# 11

# Unethical Behavior: Professional Deviance

*H. Kirk Dansereau*

## PROFESSION

At this point in the development of the sociology of work, rehashing the plethora of discussions about efforts to define the term *profession* seems quite unnecessary. Although definitions and listings of criteria vary, consensus exists as to the principal characteristics that should be considered.

Following the lead of earlier writers, Krause mentions the skills and theory necessarily acquired, the nature of the relationship between the client and the practitioner, and the self-regulation within the practitioner group embodied in a code of ethics.[1] A decade earlier, Goode had written of a profession's autonomy, the existence of its own association, "prolonged specialized training in a body of abstract knowledge, and . . . a collectivity or service orientation."[2] Wilensky states:

> Any occupation wishing to exercise professional authority must find a technical base for it, assert an exclusive jurisdiction, link both skill and jurisdiction to standards of training, and convince the public that its services are uniquely trustworthy.[3]

He also points out that the differences between the professional and the lay public are: (1) The job of the professional is *technical*—based on systematic knowledge or doctrine acquired only through long prescribed training. (2) The professional man adheres to a set of *professional norms.*[4]

Using 18 occupations, he illustrates the process of professionalization in five steps, establishment of the work on a full-time basis, establishment of a training school, formation of an association, licensure, and formulation of a code of ethics. His findings indicate that the majority of the occupations studied followed the above order of development.[5]

From H. Kirk Dansereau, "Unethical Behavior: Professional Deviance." In Clifton D. Bryant, ed., *Deviant Behavior: Occupational and Organizational Bases.* Chicago: Rand-McNally, 1974, pp. 75-89. Reprinted by permission.

## ETHICS

Ethics is concerned with the determination of right and wrong in human relationships; a professional ethical code at least expresses a recognition of some of the behavioral standards endorsed by members of a profession. The fact that such codes exist is some evidence of their need; but, of course, their existence for the more recently arrived professions may well have been influenced at least minimally by an often-heard insistence that to be a profession an occupation must have its own code. MacIver speaks of professional codes as "the deliberate application of a generally accepted social standard to particular spheres of conduct."[6] He warns, however, "that group ethics will not by themselves suffice for the guidance of the group unless they are always related to the ethical standards of the community."[7]

Yet, are we professionals not honorable men? If answered affirmatively, is then such a code necessary? For reasons other than the potential unethical behavior of colleagues, two sociologists argued against a code of ethics for their own discipline. One contended that the proposed code was "equivocal or unenlighteningly vague in dealing with most of the problems distinct to social science" and encouraged his "colleagues to vote against the adoption of a code that obscures more than it illuminates, and to press instead for an officially sponsored symposium on the ethical problems of sociology." Another made the point, "A code of ethics, however, is at best an identification of issues, and it cannot fail to distort and oversimplify them."[8] He urged his *colleagues to vote against the adoption of any code of ethics by the Association.*" Herein perhaps may lie a distinction between the thinking of members of a learned society and that of members of an association more directly servicing the ills of the public.

With reference to the latter type organization, Wood quite concisely promulgates reasons for a code's existence. He claims "an ethical code is a functional necessity to the very existence of a profession in contemporary society." A second reason pertains to government-sanctioned monopoly status accorded the practitioners, preventing competition and "considerable self-regulation of recruitment and conduct standards." A third consideration is the "nonmaterial nature of professional service and often its confidential nature that lessens the effectiveness of a public or market evaluation of the 'product.'" Fourth, he posits "that so much may be at stake—is a matter that requires assurance of integrity among those who practice in these areas."[9]

Similarities in discussions of ethics are found almost without regard to the time of the writing. Different occupations may have been subject to current interest, but the basic moral themes that are stressed persist. Whether one draws upon the 1926 work of Tauesch or upon the *Annals* nearly three decades later, one sees, for example, that the professional practitioner is expected not to advertise, solicit, or accept kickbacks.[10] Influence peddling, undercover fee-splitting, and contingency fees are frowned upon; in some instances, however, the latter are permitted when limited to a percentage deemed reasonable by the profession. However, the guiding precept under which the specifics are subsumed is one of self-subordination; the interests of client, profession, and public are to supercede those of the professional himself. Infractions are expected to bring reprimand, threatened suspension, or expulsion from the association. In the most serious instances, colleagues may seek court action to have a violator's license revoked.

The blue-collar worker has considerably less opportunity than does the professional to engage in similar violations. As a hyperbolic illustration, the hod carrier does not have the lawyer's opportunity to mingle his funds with those of his employer. He can hardly split fees and is unlikely to be possessed of privileged information. Instead, the blue-collar worker can engage in some shoddy practices such as "borrowing" a few nails, boards, parts, or tools. He can occasionally get a fellow-worker to build something for him at the plant; or he may, given the capability, do it for himself. Somewhat more legally, he just goofs off, simply fails to produce.

The individual worker hardly has recourse to an action analogous to the professional's fee-raising. The counterargument that he does so in concert through his union is met with insouciance by the worker who has just won a raise. Workers, like professionals, view group solidarity and cooperation as essential to their survival even in situations in which there is an outcry that the public interest has been sabotaged. Further, workers, like professionals, often rationalize their seemingly untoward behavior in the name of their just due—apparent subordination by both of the precept of self-subordination.

## BEHAVIOR IN SELECTED OCCUPATIONS

Somewhere between the blue-collar worker and the professional lies a considerable array of occupations, many of which see themselves as professionals in their own right or well on the way to acceptance as professionals. In a single issue of a nonmetropolitan daily there were stories dealing with several such lines of work: military and diplomatic personnel, business managers, and newscasters. One had to do with the credibility of reports pertaining to the escalation of American military activity.[11] Did administration accounts, passed on to friendly governments, jibe with the report held by the Pentagon; and was the person admittedly responsible for the "leak" that precipitated the question guilty of a breach of ethics or even illegal conduct?

A second story concerned the matter of excess profits of more than $65 million during a single federal fiscal year. It is the duty of the Renegotia-tion Board to eliminate overcharges in space and defense contracts; the above amount was based on 149 determinations.[12] Are those involved in the original negotiations not somehow culpable, at least at an ethical level; or were government negotiators "taken," and are those from the private sector to be excused in the name of sharp business dealings?

Another item pointed out the lack of knowledge that employees have about their fringe benefits. The condition is blamed both on worker apa-thy and on management's lack of enthusiasm and its failure to find a way to communicate "the intricate details of its plan." The article states that some "funds are invested solely in the company's own stock. In others, fraudulent loans are made; and many plans are not insured."[13] How ethi-cal are these practices when one considers that approximately one-fourth of a pay-check is withheld for fringe benefits and an estimated $130 billion in assets is involved?

Finally, there was a wire service report about a congressional inves-tigation of a television documentary. A House subcommittee minority report arguing against subpoena of the broadcasting company and its president stated:

> The point is the subpoena is not narrowed to the specific allegations respecting "manipulative techniques," "rearrangement of the words of an individual," or making one appear to "deliver a statement which he did not in fact deliver."[14]

The minority report sought to protect against restraints on a news-man's judgment in formulating a story. Yet, is there here not some concern for ethics even in the absence of rigorous specification of complaint? Par-enthetically, about the time this last item appeared in print, a congressman appearing on non-network TV contended that four answers had been shifted in the editing of an interview conducted by a nationally known TV newscaster with a cabinet undersecretary. Whither the Television Code Seal of Good Practice?

Accountants may not accept contingency fees or split fees with a lay person. Architects may not compete with each other with regard to profes-sional fees or participate in such profits from building enterprises as "would influence his professional integrity." Engineers may not sponsor or promote "commercial or other undertakings of a speculative charac-ter," nor may they seek a position held by another engineer. Teachers may not seek employment through "indiscriminate distribution of applica-tions" or accept compensation from supply houses, having recommended purchases from them. Lawyers must set the fees they are to receive; one may not, without full knowledge of the client, accept any compensation "from other parties to the transactions in which he is employed. . . ."

Doctors may not profit from the sale of appliances or medicines or accept compensation beyond that received for professional services rendered. Rabbis are not to engage in fee-splitting; priests may not engage in specified unbecoming occupational roles; Protestant ministers may not proselytize from another church or put themselves up for consideration for another pulpit that is already occupied.[15] It seems that, although the pastor may not increase his flock by "sheep stealing" or seek greener pastures, flocks are continually having their pastors purloined by raiders who sweeten the call with a financial incentive.

The bulk of all the codes is of other than financial canons, but the smell of green is strong; and in the mind of the public, violations related to money matters probably cause more stir than all other facets of professional behavior. The business of making a living is somehow expected to be segregated from the business of being a professional at least if one is seen as "doing a little too well."

### The Pharmacist

The occupation of the independent druggist is a familiar one in which the business and professional roles are thoroughly intermingled. As noted and hypothesized by Quinney:

> Structural strain is built into retail pharmacy. The pharmacist must, therefore, make some sort of a personal adjustment to the situation.
>
> It was hypothesized that retail pharmacists resolve the dilemma of choosing between different occupational roles—professional and business—by adapting to an *occupational role organization*.[16]

Having determined the orientations as professional, business, mixed, and indifferent, he learned that there were variations in the number of prescription violators. Most violators were found in the business-oriented category, followed by the indifferent and mixed classifications; no violators were found in the professional grouping.

An AP release relates the efforts of the University of Maryland's School of Pharmacy to "remake this image of the corner druggist," that is, that he is "an impersonal dispenser of pills."[17] The fifth year in school, eliminating the older practice of apprenticeship, is designed to give the student experience in approved community and hospital pharmacies. Referring to the school's dean, the article says:

> Kinnard believes the shift in emphasis has long been needed, citing the gap between the physician's knowledge of drugs and the high number of unfavorable drug reactions suffered by patients both in and outside the hospital.

Said one Baltimore pharmacist:

I think the program is a good idea as far as theory goes, but I don't think doctors want to give up any of their powers. We're under the doctor's thumb and we're limited in what we can do.

Historically the pharmacist has been expected to recognize faulty prescriptions, in effect, to cover for a doctor's mistake. Moreover, he can beget further indebtedness by referral of patients and has a ready check on the prescription business as reciprocity.

### The Funeral Director

When it comes to being a professional, as laid out by Wilensky, the funeral director is classified as doubtful. True, he has gone through the steps; but by most people he is no doubt considered to be primarily a businessman, especially when one is reminded of the cost of the coffin. Still, during the past several years the works of Bowman and Mitford have created a somewhat sustained interest in this occupation which has undergone a metamorphosis of image from cabinet maker to undertaker to mortician to funeral director.

Throughout Bowman's book are found references to the cost of funerals. His studies reveal:

> . . . the widespread feeling that costs are much higher than they need be; that undertakers do everything in their power to raise them to the highest possible level; and that the choice by the consumer of the less costly funerals is made difficult and disagreeable.[18]

Elsewhere he notes that it is the undertaker who assumes the right to decide what shall constitute the appropriate level of expenditure "according to the client's station in life and ultimate capacity to pay."[19] High prices have led to consumer efforts to form cooperatives, but in some instances Bowman indicates that "undertakers' lobbies create difficulties for the establishment of the nonprofit groups."[20] On nonfinancial matters, he contends that the limited time involved in the relationship between the funeral director and the bereaved family and the context within which it takes place are not conducive to the operation of professionalism. Put bluntly, "Funeral directing is not a profession."[21]

Mitford's best seller in its foreword dismisses:

> . . . (misuse by undertakers of the coroner's office to secure business, bribery of hospital personnel to "steer" cases, the illegal re-use of coffins, fraudulent double charges in welfare cases) . . . [as] "not typical of the trade as a whole."[22]

Like Bowman, she presents a case for lower costs reflected in the now defunct V. A. Contract Burial Program which provided a profit for a mere $250.[23] She mentions a source of rift between mortician and florist in her chapter "The Menace of P. O." Funeral flowers account for 65 to 70 percent of the floral trade, and although they are at times a trial for the mortician, notices to Please Omit Flowers are seen as a possible move toward omitting ministers, music, and "all but the plainest caskets." Morticians are not permitted kickbacks from flower sales and in some states may not own their own flower shops. Fearful too are they that the full floral blanket will advertise for the flowers at the expense of the coffin.[24] Chapter 16, "The Nosy Clergy," presents that profession as an especial nuisance to the director. Bishop Pike feels that the funeral should be a church service rather than one conducted in a funeral home, and a California rabbi, Sidney Akselrad, feels that simplicity should prevail and that one need not "go into debt over a funeral." Mitford refers to Fulton's study which found that "Catholic priests and Protestant ministers view the purposes of the American funeral differently."[25] The priests were concerned with the honoring of "the memory and the body of the deceased." "The ministers, on the other hand, viewed the funeral in terms of the peace and understanding it brings to the survivors."[26] Although priests saw little need for change, ministers stressed the need for less pagan display, less solemnity, and less expense.[27] Such suggestions, if adopted, could greatly affect the finances of funeral directing and concomitantly increase the business emphasis at the expense of professional development.

The funeral director may not consider droll the statement: "You can always trust your undertaker; he'll be the last one to let you down." If one can believe much of what he reads, friend, rest in peace in the knowledge that there are some who, monetarily and otherwise, have let down untold numbers before your turn.

### The Lawyer[28]

The lawyer's behavior is one of perennial concern, for he is seen as one who really knows the rules and therefore stands the best chance of being able to break them with impunity. It thus behooves him to demand of himself and his colleagues special consideration of "that which is expected of a reasonable and prudent man." The profession expects admission only of the qualified, avoidance of stirring up litigation and representation even for those unable to pay.

In 1935, six lawyers were disbarred for professional misconduct. Commenting on their behavior the judges said:

> Such an agreement, to stand ready to defend future crimes, amounts to an agreement to encourage the agents to go on with conspiracy. It promises comfort to the criminal and makes his pathway as easy and safe as circumstances will permit.[29]

The practice was considered as having been "actual participation in the crime."

A particularly scathing attack on the profession was made by one lawyer who quit the profession "because he couldn't 'take' its ethics." He himself had become "adept in the juggling of facts to suit the pattern I desired." He stated:

> I found that the Canons of Ethics of the American Bar Association were glossy platitudes recited at annual conventions; to the profession at large, they were no more than fences to scale when the jumping was good.[30]

He spoke of the ambulance chaser and the bankruptcy specialist. Of accident litigation, he said, "the present slow shyster-ridden system continues solely because it is far more profitable to lawyers."[31] This criticism sounds much the same as in today's controversy over no-fault automobile insurance.

In frivolity, someone once said that abnormal psychology was a course taught by an abnormal psychologist. Wood's article on lawyers leads one to wonder whether criminal law is that practiced by criminal lawyers. Wood found little difference between criminal lawyers and civil lawyers regarding what matters constituted the basic unethical practices found in criminal law. Criminal lawyers, however, were somewhat more likely to have seen client pressure and uncertainty of fees as conditions contributing to unethical behavior. They also were more likely to have suggested that incompetent personnel and the conviction psychology of the D.A. were factors that contributed to unethical conduct in the criminal court. He also found that the better-educated lawyers were not only more indifferent to unethical practices but were no more active than others in joining professional organizations or in serving on grievance committees.[32]

A retired professor of criminal law discussed "the theory that an attorney must try to save *every* client is well established." He indicated that the crooked lawyer will frighten witnesses, bribe jurors, or resort to perjury. The goal of cross-examination was seen as that of destroying testimony, even the truth.[33] He blamed the criminal lawyer "as a protector of the guilty at the expense of truth" for a large part of the annual cost of crime.[34]

According to the work of Reichstein, ambulance chasing is rampant as a form of unethical solicitation. The chaser may be a single lawyer, a firm with an investigator-chaser, or an independent chase-entrepreneur with a network of informants.[35] One value of this practice, however, is to serve the function of ". . . equalizing the balance of power between injured parties and insurance companies by providing the former with legal representation which they might not get otherwise."[36]

Lawyers who are unfavorable toward solicitation cite unfair competition, association with fraud and client exploitation, and concern for "the public's image of the profession."[37] Some who favor solicitation rationalize the practice as a counter to the unfair practices of claim adjusters; some courts apparently concur.

Of considerable current interest is the backlog of cases jamming the courts. In many areas delays have occasioned comfortable and, in many instances, profitable waits for some lawyers. In Pittsburgh the courts have made a breakthrough in negligence cases by reducing continuances and initiating conciliation conferences before the trial date. Very few of these cases now get to the jury. Delays to build inventories of cases, to fit fees into more desirable tax years, and to impress juries have been virtually eliminated. Said Judge Ellenbogen: "Courts cannot be run just for the convenience of lawyers and judges."[38] Elsewhere the jam-up continues, sometimes for "professional reasons," meaning delay until the lawyer's fee has been guaranteed. Plea bargaining is one answer to the problem, but it may carry with it some ills, for example, giving away the defendant's rights, which may exceed the wrongs of delay.[39]

Another area of questionable legal behavior is that involving violation of customary rules of procedure. To cope with these actions it has been suggested that those who violate decorum in the courtroom be removed, that any lawyer who deliberately prevents the orderly procedure of the court be removed, that courtroom packing with adherents of defendants be controlled, that courts and bar associations act to suspend or disbar lawyers who engage in unseemly conduct, and that legislation make such conduct a felony.[40]

In this time of confrontation, demonstration, and intimidation, some young activist lawyers appear to be suffering harassment at the hands of some of their fellow professionals. A state bar association accused OEO lawyers of soliciting clients, fomenting demonstrations, and preparing leaflets on consumer boycotts. An OEO investigating team found the charges to be "without foundation."[41]

If the American Bar Association is perturbed about public attention to its members' affluence, its concern was not disclosed by its decision to have the second half of its 1971 annual convention in London. It was estimated that 15,000 American lawyers and their wives and children made the trek by plane and ship. Planned over a span of eight years, it was anticipated that the conventioneers would spend $2.5 million during their one-week stay.[42]

### The Physician

The medical doctor, ever high on the prestige list, is, ironically, traditionally more likely than any other professional to be sued for malpractice, perhaps because his is felt to be an easy mark. He must be sensitive to public criticism of rising medical costs which have been an important contribution to the Cost of Living Index, noticeably since World War II. That this condition arouses mixed feelings among practitioners is illustrated in the following excerpt from an overheard conversation.

| | |
|---|---|
| *First physician:* | Doctor why don't you get rid of that old Plymouth and get a Cadillac like mine? |
| *Second physician·* | I couldn't do that; my patients would call me an S.O.B. |
| *First physician:* | They already call you an S.O.B., so you may as well ride in comfort. |

The mass media have played a lengthy role in portraying the image of the physician. In the old cowboy movies, even Ole Drunken Doc won the battle between bottle and professional duty. Today AMA technical consultants help perpetrate an image of competence and, it may be assumed, dedication. Despite the effort at image building (or maybe because of it) Montague reports the AMA opinion survey finding that "respondents had considerably higher regard for their own family doctors than they did for doctors as a group." Further, "people liked their doctors much better than they did the medical profession." In Montague's words, "The AMA has come to be thought of as an unnecessary drag on progress."[43]

Having read the works of Bowman and Mitford, one may momentarily question the credibility of Michelfelder's book *It's Cheaper to Die*. On second thought, however, most expect to die no more than once, but in a lifetime may be subject to repeated fee-splitting, fee-raising, charges for ghost surgery (ghost surgery is nonexistent surgery, or minor surgery passed off as major surgery and billed accordingly), and the like. Michelfelder states:

What anguishes organized medicine, however, is the "sensationalism" [meaning public exposure] accompanying bona fide and legally proved revelations of such things as workmen's compensation shakedowns, rebates, deals with smaller drug firms owned by misbehaving doctors, grand jury presentments on surgery abuses and private hospitals [usually owned by doctors], and unlawful arrangements with medical supply houses, opticians, and laboratories.[44]

In 1943 Seidman wrote of "the racketeers in white who traffic in human lives." He referred to fee-splitting and fee-padding, abuses in the sale of oxygen and the rental of equipment, defective apparatus, referral fees, and fraudulent bills.[45]

*Time* subsequently reported that within the year 1,000 of New York City's 16,000 physicians had been convicted of crooked dealing in compensation cases. Steerers, usually lawyers or insurance men, receive kickbacks from the doctor's padded bill.[46]

A 1953 interview with the Director of the American College of Surgeons brought out some ideas about fee-splitting, unnecessary operations, overcharging, and ghost surgery. Fee-splitting was reported as growing, in some cases being legalized to allow appropriate compensation of the family physician. Unnecessary operations were reported to result from "plain dishonest money making," with women as the principal patients. In the case of fees, to prevent overcharges, he suggested that the patient and the doctor reach agreement before the surgery. Ghost surgery, he stated, was largely performed in unethical hospitals, but "the great majority of the hospitals are as clean as a hound's tooth."[47] (What odds would a bacteriologist give on that?)

Through the mid-1950s the theme was pretty much the same: the kickback or referral fee, fee-splitting, the use of feeders, and unnecessary surgery. An article, "Patients for Sale," was well received by the surgeons themselves, or at least by their principal spokesman. A Pennsylvania doctor commented, "We have gilding on the dome and termites in the basement."[48]

In California a committee of physicians undertook to remedy some of the most common complaints. Among other steps, they set up local schedules of fair and reasonable fees; they established a telephone-answering service and an emergency doctor-dispatching program guaranteeing medical care regardless of ability to pay. Similar concern by physicians was reported in *Newsweek*.[49]

By 1958 the doctor-merchant had come under fire. Said *Newsweek* of efforts at self-policing: "Despite this self-surveillance, physicians have sometimes been attacked by their peers as well as their patients for practices labeled 'shady,' 'selfish,' and 'money grabbing.'" The same article commented that in New York there was a tie-up between 1,500 city doctors and a dozen laboratories. The result was estimated to be an added cost of $12 million to patients.[50]

By 1962 the Senate Antitrust and Monopoly Committee had taken more than a passing interest in the doctor-merchant. Its findings revealed 3,000 doctors who owned drugstores, 2,500 ophthalmologists who sold eye glasses, and 5,000 doctors who owned stock in 150 drug-repackaging firms. At least 10,500 of the nation's 2,000,000 doctors were selling products they had prescribed.[51]

Dr. S. J. Hadfield advised:

> . . . a main object and function of a code of professional ethics is to protect the individual from the special advantages possessed by the professional as a result of his special knowledge and training.

"The Conscience of the Doctor" is tested says Dr. Hadfield in those "nontherapeutic situations where clear ethical guidance is not available." He mentions nontherapeutic abortion, contraceptive advice, and sterilization.[52] More and more new developments will repeat the test, for example, surgery before birth, germinal choice, and cloning.[53]

Dr. John Knowles intimated that within 10 more years doctors will be handed over to the government unless some of the AMA's present practices change. He said, "The price of freedom from federal control is responsibility for public interest." He continued:

> Are we asking the doctor to be beyond reproach more than the average citizen? Yes. It's my firm hope that we physicians will be in fact what society has assumed or wanted us to be since time began—above and beyond ordinary human frailties.[54]

Violations, though practiced by a minority, appear to be numerous. Young men who frown on unethical behavior have been known to have difficulty in establishing their practices; some of these same, however, have at least reduced the undesired activities in their localities. Until such time as unethical conduct is considerably reduced, the neologism, Hypocritic Oath, may in many instances supplant the venerated Oath of Hippocrates.

## CONCLUSION

This paper is oriented toward occupational deviance and its contents should in no way be construed to imply that more than a minority in any profession are crooked at either the legal or ethical level. The sense of this statement holds as well for practitioners of callings of lesser prestige. However, these minorities are supplemented by a fringe of those who engage in "marginal ethicality." It may be appropriate to paraphrase and question whether the commandment can be interpreted as: Thou shalt not steal except maybe just a little bit.

Harking back to the professions discussed herein, from the standpoint of ethics, what will be the balances sought, what designs rendered, what prescriptions proposed? What cryptic cases will plague those who would seek cures for professional ills?

Given present goals and means, current practices are likely to continue. Persistence of the competition between the business and the professional ethic will probably find mere mortals frequently succumbing to the temptation to serve Mammon. As long as professional attention is poorly balanced between cure and prevention and oriented more toward the dollar than toward service, a favorable climate for professional deviance exists. The presence of interprofessional conflicts and competitions for client loyalty are other potential contributors to that climate.

Clients seeking remedies are understandably sensitive to the treatment accorded them by the professional; had they not already felt some discomfort, they would not have sought help. To forestall any criticism, then, it is incumbent upon the professional to engage in conduct that is above reproach. More specifically, he must do what his code "guarantees": provide competent service at a fair price. Professionals must do their own internal policing or, surely, with loss of public trust, the much desired autonomy will be lost. With that will go the prestige and the professional authority that attracts much of the talent in which so many professionals take just pride.

## NOTES

1. Elliott A. Krause, *The Sociology of Occupations* (Boston: Little, Brown, 1971), pp. 75–76.
2. William Goode, " 'Professions' and 'Non-Professions,' " in *Professionalization*, ed. Howard M. Vollmer and Donald L. Mills (Englewood Cliffs, N.J.: Prentice-Hall, 1966), p. 36.
3. Harold L. Wilensky, "The Professionalization of Everyone?" *The American Journal of Sociology* 70, 2 (September 1964): 38.
4. *Ibid.*
5. *Ibid.*, pp. 142–46.
6. R. M. MacIver, "The Social Significance of Professional Ethics," *The Annals*, ed. Benson Y. Landis, 297 (January 1955): 120.
7. *Ibid.*, p. 124.
8 Howard S. Becker and Eliot Friedson, "Against the Code of Ethics," *American Sociological Review* 29 (June 1964): 409–10.
9. Arthur Lewis Wood, "Professional Ethics among Criminal Lawyers," *Social Problems* 7 (Summer 1959): 71.
10. Carl F. Taeusch, *Professional and Business Ethics* (New York: Holt and Company, 1926); and MacIver, "The Social Significance of Professional Ethics."
11. Arthur L. Gavshon, "Some U.S. Friends Are Conducting Credibility Tests," *Bowling Green–Park City Daily News*, an Associated Press release (Sunday, July 11, 1971), p. 1.
12. Jean Heller, "Report Excessive Contract Profits," *Bowling Green–Park City Daily News*, an Associated Press release (Sunday, July 11, 1971), p. 1.
13. John Cunniff, "People Know Surprisingly Little about Their Fringe Benefits," *Bowling Green–Park City Daily News*, an Associated Press release (Sunday, July 11, 1971), p. 7.
14. Peggy Simpson, "Minority Report Hits Probe of CBS," *Bowling Green–Park City Daily News*, an Associated Press release (Sunday, July 11, 1971), p. 13.
15. MacIver, "The Social Significance of Professional Ethics."
16. Earl Richard Quinney, "Occupational Structure and Criminal Behavior: Prescription Violation by Retail Pharmacists," *Social Problems* 11, 202 (Fall 1963): 181.
17. Sharon Joiner, "Hope to Remake Image of Corner Druggist," *Bowling Green–Park City Daily News*, an Associated Press release (October 6, 1971), p. 21.
18. Leroy Bowman, *The American Funeral: A Way of Death* (New York: Paperback Library, 1959), p. 51.
19. *Ibid.*, p. 60.
20. *Ibid.*, p. 131.
21. *Ibid.*, pp. 85–86.
22. Jessica Mitford, *The American Way of Death* (Greenwich, Conn.: Fawcett Publications, 1963), p. 8.
23. *Ibid.*, pp. 44–45.
24. *Ibid.*, Chap. 8, passim.

25. *Ibid.,* pp. 196–97.
26. Robert L. Fulton, "The Clergyman and the Funeral Director: A Study in Role Conflict," *Social Forces* 34 (May 1961): 318.
27. *Ibid.,* p. 319.
28. The final two professions to be discussed, law and medicine, are treated more or less historically. Such treatment permits a view of the evolution of concern for some questionable practices within these professions throughout the last few decades. However, in fullest candor, it must be admitted that, in terms of sheer simplicity, the chronologic is eminently superior to the taxonomic.
29. "Philadelphia Lawyers Disbarred," *Current Notes* (May 1935): 141–42.
30. Weyland Cross, "Ex-Lawyer," *The American Mercury* 52 (February 1941): 160.
31. *Ibid.,* p. 163.
32. Wood, "Professional Ethics among Criminal Lawyers," pp. 73, 75, 81, and 82.
33. John Barker Waite, "How Ethical Are These Lawyers?" *Reader's Digest* 71 (November 1957): 57–58.
34. *Ibid.,* p. 59.
35. Kenneth J. Reichstein, "Ambulance Chasing: A Case Study of Deviation and Control within the Legal Profession," *Social Problems* 13 (Summer 1965): 7.
36. *Ibid.,* p. 9.
37. *Ibid.,* pp. 11–12.
38. Murray Teigh Bloom, "No More Law's Delay," *National Civic Review* (March 1969): passim, 106.
39. Jack Star, "Jam-Up," *Look* 35, 6 (March 23, 1971): 34, 39.
40. Louis Nizer, "What to Do When the Judge Is Put Up against the Wall," *New York Times Magazine* (April 5, 1970), pp. 126, 128.
41. Lester Vellie, "The Angry Young Lawyers of OEO," *Reader's Digest* (May 1971): 196.
42. Anthony Collings, "15,000 Americans to Invade London for ABA Convention," *Bowling Green–Park City Daily News,* an Associated Press release (July 13, 1971), p. 3.
43. Joel B. Montague, Jr., "Medicine and the Concept of Professionalism," *Sociological Inquiry* 33 (Winter 1963): 48–50.
44. William Michelfelder, *It's Cheaper to Die* (Derby, Conn.: Monarch Books, 1961), p. 81.
45. Harold Seidman, "Racketeers in White," *Survey Graphic* 32 (August 1943).
46. "Racketeers, M.D.," *Time* 44 (July 24, 1944): 54.
47. Paul R. Hawley, "Needless Surgery—Doctors, Good and Bad," *Reader's Digest* 62 (May 1953): 53, 54, and 56.
48. Steven M. Spencer, "Patients for Sale," *Saturday Evening Post* 226 (January 16, 1954): 36.
49. Milton Silverman, "The Doctors Who Crack Down on Doctors," *Saturday Evening Post* 227 (February 12, 1955): 32–33; see also, "About Ethics," *Newsweek* 52 (June 17, 1957): 98–99.
50. "Paying the Doctors," *Newsweek* 51 (April 21, 1958): 106.
51. "The Doctors Who Profit from Prescriptions," *Consumer Reports* (May 1966): 234.
52. S. J. Hadfield, "The Conscience of the Doctor," *20th Century* 177, 1041 (1969): 14, 16.
53. David M. Rorvik, "The Unborn," *Look* 33, 22 (November 4, 1969): 75, 83.
54. John H. Knowles, "U.S. Health: Do We Face a Catastrophe?" *Look* (June 2, 1970), 74, 78.

# 12

# M.D. Degrees for Sale?

*Kit Konolige*

Nathan Lemler of Nassau County, New York, drove a Cadillac, Jaguar, or Mercedes when he wasn't riding with his chauffeur. He maintained a $1,100-a-month apartment in Miami, Fla., and another pad in Freeport, the Bahamas, but he could only visit them between his travels to Europe, Alaska, Hawaii, Puerto Rico, or Las Vegas.

Only occasionally did Lemler have to work. His lucrative business: promising to buy places in medical schools for some 50 students—at fees ranging from $5,000 to $25,000 per placement.

"If you have enough money, you can buy your way into medical school. So what else is new?" asks Dr. Albert Merlis, a New York physician and medical lawyer who was one of Lemler's clients.

Lemler's case is only the most fabulous in a series of scandals that have made it clear that admission to some medical, dental, and veterinary schools is today a high-stakes game whose players do not always observe the spirit of the Hippocratic Oath. Suspicions of unfair or illegal influence in the admissions process, once voiced only by sour losers in the game, have been confirmed by civil and criminal legal proceedings around the country:

- The speaker of the Pennsylvania House of Representatives has been indicted for allegedly extorting a total of $56,000 from parents seeking his help in gaining their children admission to medical and veterinary schools.
- In an unrelated incident, two other Pennsylvania state legislators from Philadelphia face trials on several counts of bribery and conspiracy in similar alleged schemes involving a dental school.
- Chicago Medical School in 1973 collected an average of $50,000 each in contributions—over and above tuition—from relatives and friends of 77 of its 91 entering freshmen. School officials admitted under oath that the money influenced admission chances.

• Officials of the medical college at the University of California at Davis have testified that, while no money is involved, the children of wealthy businessmen and influential politicians have been accorded special treatment when they applied.

Since influence peddling succeeds only so long as it is kept from public notice, it's impossible to say whether these are isolated examples or part of a broader but unpublicized pattern. Whatever their scope, such practices are being disclosed at a time when the Supreme Court is considering a lawsuit charging that one medical school discriminates against whites by selecting blacks ahead of them. But there has been no public outcry over "affirmative-action programs" that discriminate in favor of wealthy or politically influential applicants.

The examples just mentioned have two factors in common: medical schools that, despite high tuition and government support, need more money, and parents who are eager to spend it because an M.D. degree guarantees a lucrative career. Politicians, and private entrepreneurs such as Lemler, offer middleman services—for a price. "It's a very difficult situation, hard to deal with," notes Charles Fentress, a spokesman for the Association of American Medical Colleges.

Medical-school officials contend that even at the Chicago Medical School no potentially incompetent students were admitted, because the "contributions" were solicited and accepted only from families of applicants who had already qualified for a large "acceptable pool." But even if an American medical school would not accept a demonstrably unqualified student for any amount of money, critics say there are compelling reasons why extratuitional money should never be a factor in admissions.

First, they argue, such practices are bound sooner or later to erode the quality of the profession. Second, they discriminate against equally qualified but poorer students who have already supported their intended school by contributing through taxes to the 47 percent of all med-school funds that come from various levels of government.

## FREE REIN TO SOME

Finally, allowing a free market in professional-school admissions gives free rein to unscrupulous politicians or con men who take money on the false suggestion that they can help side-step the normal procedures. Nathan Lemler, in fact, is doing five to 14 in a federal prison not for bribery but for grand larceny—taking money on the promise that he could buy a place, which he generally could not. Two Pennsylvania legislators face trial on the same grounds.

Medical schools are more susceptible than other professional schools to monetary and political manipulation because of the legendary squeeze to enter them. Slightly more than 40,000 students apply each year, but there are only about 15,000 places available in the nation's 116 medical schools. The rarity and hence value of the M.D. degree make it in turn a prize for which, in words spoken by a parent at Lemler's trial, "I would have done anything." (Veterinary schools are even more competitive, though they have far fewer students and applicants. Entering dentistry is somewhat less competitive but still very difficult.)

## AVENUES OF INFLUENCE

The medical schools themselves, moreover, face pressures from several sources of funds, the most powerful of which are state legislators. As Joseph DiPalma, dean of Hahnemann Medical College in Philadelphia, told a drug-industry publication: "When a politician talks, a dean listens. We'd have to close our doors tomorrow if our state aid were cut off."

Control, or the suggestion of control, over those crucial funds naturally gives state legislators considerable sway over both applicants and schools. The presentment accompanying a Pennsylvania grand jury's indictment gives a fascinating glimpse of how that dual-edged power can be exercised.

Dr. Donald Goldenberg, a suburban Philadelphia dentist, became so worried about his son Andrew's application to Temple University's School of Dentistry that he contacted Samuel Biener, an old family friend with political connections. Biener, the grand jury charged, got in touch with state Sen. Francis J. Lynch, then told Goldenberg that "help" would cost $15,000.

## PRESSURES IN PENNSYLVANIA

Unfortunately for Lynch, Goldenberg was told by an alumnus at about the same time that his son had made it on his own. The dentist naturally hesitated to pay money for useless help. Apparently panicking, Lynch —according to the presentment—quickly called state Rep. Stephen R. Wojdak, chairman of the House Appropriations Committee—a major conduit for the roughly $66 million that Temple as a whole receives from the state annually. The presentment says Wojdak in turn told Thomas W. Elliott, an assistant vice-president who lobbies for Temple in Harrisburg, that he wanted young Goldenberg's letter of acceptance held up. But the admissions director, pressured by Goldenberg's alumnus friend as well as Elliott, finally sent the letter out anyway.

The grand jury made clear how the game was to be played. The presentment states:

At no time did Lynch or Wojdak make any effort to aid in the admission of Andrew Goldenberg to the Temple Dental School. Rather, they intended to collect the money after Andrew Goldenberg was successful on his own. In their capacity as public officials, they knew that they could learn, in advance of formal notification, the names of those candidates who had been accepted.

Lynch and Wojdak both have pleaded innocent.

## FAVORITISM IN CALIFORNIA

On the other hand, politicians sometimes do have actual power to influence admissions. At the University of California at Davis, according to information revealed in a civil suit, the medical-school dean, Dr. J. J. Tupper, admitted the sons of three important politicians outside normal channels.

An assistant dean testified at the time: "In a fledgling medical school like Davis [it was founded in 1968], money for capital construction and facilities is life-blood. Favorable consideration [in the Legislature] would be helpful. You can't say that because Student X was admitted, the medical school received X dollars for that consideration," the assistant dean added, but such an admission "might purchase good will."

(The allegations of political influence at the Davis medical school emerged in a landmark reverse-discrimination suit now before the U. S. Supreme Court [*The Observer,* Nov. 27, 1976]. Alan Bakke, a white applicant, sued because he says a special admissions program at Davis favors minorities and thus violates the Fourteenth Amendment's equal-protection clause. A lower court ruled for Bakke, and the University of California's regents appealed to the Supreme Court.)

## ENVIRONMENT FOR PAY-OFFS

And in Pennsylvania, according to a January indictment, House Speaker Herbert Fineman not only apparently aided the admission of students to three different professional schools in Philadelphia; he even had the power to persuade school officials to destroy potentially incriminating letters in the students' files. Fineman also has pleaded innocent.

Highlighting the pressures that create a fertile environment for pay-offs, U.S. Attorney David Marston noted: "Everybody in these transactions did something that shouldn't have been done. The schools were afraid their appropriations will be cut. . . . The parents were concerned about the prospect of their children getting into school."

If state schools such as Temple are concerned primarily about their appropriations, private schools have additional worry. They must raise enough money from private sources to supplement their smaller governmental grants. The private sector provides as much opportunity for such free traders as Nathan Lemler as the state medical schools do for politicians.

## CASH-BASED ADMISSIONS

Because Lemler was a consummate fraud—"The capacity of this defendant to manipulate appears to have no limit," his trial judge said—it is hard to determine how many medical-school places he actually bought, if any. He promised worried parents admission to a wide range of schools and contacted some of them, but in only one case is there incontrovertible evidence of cash-based admissions. That was Chicago Medical School, and testimony at Lemler's trial and in a Chicago civil suit established a clear picture of the school's procedures:

A faculty committee would cull from the several thousand applications received each year an "acceptable pool" of 300 to 350 applicants. "These applicants could be arranged in any number of arbitrary ways: the science grades, the MCAT [Medical College Admissions Test] scores, the social background of the parents, or even their heights," argued a memorandum from CMS President Dr. A. Nicholas Taylor that was offered in evidence at the Chicago trial. "If, however, a parent, friend, or foundation comes to us and says that he will give or get all or a major portion of the difference in cost of education for an applicant who has been judged acceptable by the [admissions] committee, naturally we, like any other private school, will tend to favor that applicant."

## A VICTIMLESS CRIME

The approach worked. In 1973 the school augmented its budget by nearly $4 million in extratuitional contributions from relatives and friends of incoming students. (The practice has now been stopped by the Association of American Medical Colleges.)

What can be done to stop place-buying?

One approach is to scare the participants, which is what U.S. Attorney David Marston of Philadelphia is trying to do. Before his office indicted Fineman, Marston warned that every medical-school official, politician, and parent of an applicant within his jurisdiction would be "either a Government witness or a defendant." By that he meant that those involved who didn't come forth and volunteer information would risk being indicted. His investigation is continuing.

But even when egregious influence-peddling—the kind of which Fineman stands accused—is involved, under-the-table payments represent a victimless crime that none of the parties is liable to report voluntarily. Even if every private transaction were made public, there would remain a large and troublesome gray area of post-admission gifts to a school that admitted the child of wealthy parents. As Fentress, the medical-school association's spokesman, points out, it is unlikely that medical schools would agree to controls so tight that they would restrict such sources of income and growth.

## A LOTTERY SYSTEM

The problem could be circumvented entirely, so one suggestion ran after the David miniscandal, if the hordes of similarly qualified applicants were winnowed with a straight lottery system. According to Fentress, the elements of a lottery already exist *de facto!* "I don't doubt for a minute," he remarks "that some schools just draw the names out of a hat when they're down to the last one or two places."

The experience of the University of Washington in Seattle's nursing school—apparently the only professional school in the country to have adopted a procedure for admission by lottery—shows how it could work. According to Florence Gray, associate dean for the undergraduate division, 273 students applied last year, 205 were judged "eligible" on the basis of their records, and 41 top-ranked students plus 17 members of minorities were then taken immediately. The remaining 26 places were assigned by random drawing among the remaining qualified students. "Some people are still unhappy," says Gray, "but overall there are fewer unhappy students and families. There's less uncertainty, and it's generally considered fairer."

Fairer or not, a lottery system has not been acclaimed by the nation's medical schools, and their admissions procedures seem likely to remain substantially unchanged for the immediate future. The choice among candidates whose qualifications can hardly be separated with a razor blade will continue to be the province of deans and faculty committees. And if current revelations are any guide, those persons will remain the objects of indefinite but unmistakable pressures by important and wealthy interested parties.

# 13

# A Crisis for Patients

*Howard R. and Martha E. Lewis*

If you are like most laymen, you take comfort in the belief that doctors of medicine are kept in careful rein by stringent laws, rigorous government agencies, and exacting professional groups. Unfortunately, if you think this you are mistaken.

Actually, the privately practicing physician is largely a free agent, scarcely subject to regulation. Once he secures a license he has virtually a lifetime franchise to practice at his own discretion. There are few statutory standards he must meet, for the laws are generally silent as to what constitutes acceptable performance by physicians. Even where restrictions are clear, enforcement is spotty; the state boards charged with overseeing the profession are seldom active on matters of discipline.

Within the profession itself the disciplining of colleagues has little support; physicians do not like to police their fellows, and this reluctance is reflected at every level of organized medicine. At that, the strongest penalty a medical society or hospital staff can levy is expulsion. But removal from a society or hospital has no bearing on the doctor's license; though unacceptable to his peers, the offender retains his legal privilege to treat patients. Moreover, just as the profession is slow to prosecute violators within its ranks, so also is it loath to pursue the cause of more effective laws. As a result, the inadequate statutes currently on the books are likely to remain unamended for the foreseeable future.

The Medical Disciplinary Committee, a blue-ribbon panel commissioned by the American Medical Association, has conducted the most comprehensive investigation of the medical offenders. In essence the Committee found that (a) medicine's proclaimed system of self-discipline is more illusory than real, and (b) there are no adequate laws to fill the gap. Here verbatim, as summarized by a cooperating group, are the Committee's principal conclusions:

From Howard R. and Martha E. Lewis, *The Medical Offenders* (New York: Simon and Schuster, 1970), chap. 1, pp. 21-28. Reprinted by permission.

- Discipline in the medical profession is a vague and undefined aim at both the legislative and professional levels.
- The state medical societies are generally powerless except to expel a member from the society in cases involving serious crimes or unprofessional conduct.
- State licensing boards too frequently do not have the machinery for instituting and conducting hearings on disciplinary matters.
- There is little apparent concern over such matters as narcotics addiction or fraud and deceit in practice.
- Too often a "guilty" physician is [merely] encouraged to go to another state.
- There is failure on the part of individual physicians to recognize their responsibility in reporting ethical and professional violations.
- The philosophy of present administrators of discipline . . . is very conservative and reluctant.

It merits pointing out that medicine's disciplinary vacuum creates no problem in regard to the performance of the great majority of M.D.s. The typical physician's own conscience inspires him to practice with competence and honor. Stronger regulations would probably not affect such physicians, who already represent the best that disciplinary reforms could hope to achieve.

But reform is nonetheless needed because of a minority of physicians. This fringe group benefits from the fact that few legal or professional restraints exist to curb substandard performance.

*Item:* A 77-year-old physician is home after being institutionalized for senile psychosis, an irreversible mental deterioration of the aged. He is incapable of maintaining a rational train of thought, much less a competent medical practice.

His memory fails him. His mind wanders. He dozes off in midsentence. He hears voices. He panics over imaginary threats. He explodes into incoherent rages.

Yet under the law of his state he can continue treating patients. The medical licensing statute contains no provision for suspending a physician's license on the ground that he is mentally incapacitated.

*Item:* A hospital has charged a doctor with 25 counts of unprofessional conduct. These incidents cost the lives of six patients.

In one operation he unnecessarily removed both adrenal glands from a woman, causing her death. After opening up another patient for cancer, he found none. Without the patient's permission he proceeded to remove a kidney, so negligently as to cause gangrene and kill her. During a tumor operation he ignored warnings that a sponge was missing. The patient later died of an internal abscess resulting from the sponge.

The doctor's hospital colleagues have documented his unfitness to practice and suspended him from the staff. But even with this documentation, the state medical licensing law permits him to stay in practice. Under the statute, substandard performance is not ground for discipline.

*Item:* This physician works without supervision in a hospital he owns. He is notorious for performing unnecessary surgery, often ineptly. He also overprescribes barbiturates and neglects to administer needed therapy.

One patient came to him complaining of fatigue. Without examining him, the doctor prescribed vitamin shots three times a week. The patient actually had a rapidly worsening case of tuberculosis. Its neglect, prolonged while the doctor gave useless injections, exposed five small grandchildren to mortal danger.

This error, on top of previous ones, prompted the county medical society to expel the doctor. Although his colleagues have denounced him as a "menace to the public and the profession," he will probably remain in practice indefinitely. State law would permit the suspension of his license, but the medical licensing board, which is responsible for enforcing the law, is not vigorous in its disciplinary function. Except where doctors have been found guilty of felonies, it takes no action.

## THE OFFENSES

What offenses characterize the medical offenders? In its report the AMA Medical Disciplinary Committee has sketched some types of problem doctors:

> There are the . . . narcotics addicts, the mentally incompetent, and the professionally incompetent. There are those who overcharge; there are those who charge one fee when the patient has no insurance and a much higher fee if the patient is insured. There are those who perform unnecessary surgery. There are those who consort with quacks and faddists. . . . There are the fee-splitters and the rebaters.

Some less obvious offenders fall into a gray area. While a physician may not have violated a specific provision of the law or the Principles of Medical Ethics, he may nevertheless have committed an act contrary to medicine's high ideals. "These borderline cases represent the most perplexing and disturbing problem of medical discipline," the Medical Disciplinary Committee has said.

In this limbo the Committee found the doctor "who prescribes sedatives or stimulants promiscuously to all who wish to purchase them but disguises his records so that it appears that a bona fide physician-patient relationship exists between him and his customers." Also in this gray area is the ladies' man and the heavy social drinker. "Although he seems to be professionally competent," observes the Committee, "he is not a credit to the profession."

Offenses vary in intensity from region to region. To determine the major disciplinary problems in each state, the Medical Disciplinary Committee sent questionnaires to local medical societies. The commonest complaints reported to the Committee include "unjustifiably holding oneself out as being competent; deviation from the spirit of the Hippocratic Oath; . . . substandard care."

Connecticut replied that its worst problems are with physicians who overcharge and demonstrate "lack of interest or consideration for patients." Among California's problem doctors are those who are "quacks or mentally unbalanced." Iowa cites as its chief problems drug addicts and physicians suffering from mental and nervous disorders. Georgia mentions doctors who perform unnecessary surgery. Needlessly prolonging treatment is reported a big problem in West Virginia. In Maine: cheating health insurance plans. In Massachusetts: fee-splitting. In Minnesota: incompetent surgery and the excessive ordering of laboratory tests by physicians who own their own labs. In Pennsylvania: improper attention to emergency calls. In Tennessee: incompetence.

Incompetence and negligence stand out as failings reported nationwide. By studying the grounds for professional liability claims, the AMA Law Department has found what this wrongdoing may entail. Poor surgical results, poor medical results, and errors in diagnosis account for about half of all malpractice actions. Foreign bodies left in surgical patients constitute the next largest malpractice allegation, closely followed by burns resulting from the application of heat, chemicals, and x-rays.

Other common grounds for malpractice claims include assault (performing a procedure without proper consent), abandonment (failing to complete a medical obligation), and faulty prescribing. Poor results in neuropsychiatric treatment and improper commitment of patients are occasional causes of malpractice actions. Somewhat less frequent are cases involving malfunctioning equipment and blood transfusion accidents.

Malpractice cases often reach the courts, and the physician is held financially responsible for negligence. The most severe cases of medical misconduct may also be heard by state medical licensing boards, which are empowered to revoke and suspend licenses to practice. A summary of board actions is the closest document medicine has to a police blotter. In a typical year scores of doctors have their medical licenses revoked or suspended or are put on probation. The principal offenses include narcotics addiction, illicit prescribing or sale of narcotics, alcoholism, income tax evasion, and fraud. A survey of one year's revocations shows that licenses were also lost for bribery of a public official, assault and battery, and manslaughter.

The anatomy of licensing board disciplinary proceedings is suggested by Dr. Leo T. Heywood in a study of complaints to the Nebraska Bureau of Examining Boards. Incidents of abandonment prompt a large number of complaints from patients. These cases are generally brought to the board's attention after a doctor has absented himself without notifying his patients or has refused to come to a patient's aid. Overcharging similarly spurs many protests from patients. Patients also often complain of doctors being untruthful about their qualifications to give specialized treatment.

Criminal fraud is another concern of medical licensing boards. Every board is alert to the possibility that an unqualified person may fraudulently attempt to get a license to practice medicine. Most boards have encountered a deceitful applicant who uses a real physician's name rather than his own. Or he may present a fake degree or transcript in his own name. Or he may show a concocted license, especially one from a foreign country that will be hard to check.

Dr. Heywood finds that fraud charges are registered chiefly by attorneys and by officials in insurance and government. Frauds so reported frequently involve exploitation of insurance companies, welfare agencies, and Workmen's Compensation. In recent years a number of physicians have been disciplined for entering into conspiracies with dishonest lawyers to boost personal-injury settlements. These doctors reported accident injuries that never occurred, often submitting large bills and giving false testimony as well.

In extreme cases medical societies may initiate delicensure proceedings. The grievance committee of a county medical society has referred to Dr. Heywood's board the case of a rapist who performed "immoral acts" after giving female patients "unacceptable therapeutic advice . . . concerning frustrated marital relationships." Another problem doctor was brought before the board by his medical society for mistreating psychiatric cases. He committed patients unnecessarily, then abandoned them.

## DIMENSIONS OF THE PROBLEM

How large a problem is posed by the practitioners on medicine's fringe? The best-accepted estimate has been reported by Dr. Harold E. Jervey, Jr. Dr. Jervey is a past president of the Federation of State Medical Boards, the principal association of medical licensing officials. He served as a consultant to the AMA Medical Disciplinary Committee.

Dr. Jervey and others with long experience in this field estimate that at least one physician in 20 is a severe disciplinary problem, that between 15,000 and 20,000 private practitioners (as many as one in nine) are repeatedly guilty of practices unworthy of the profession. Most of these physicians commit offenses that are unethical rather than prosecutable: substandard care, abandonment, overcharging, and the like. But, Dr. Jervey concludes, between 2,500 and 7,500 are actually breaking the law through narcotics violations, frauds, and other felonies.

"These figures I do not believe to be exaggerated," he adds. "If anything, they are too conservative."

In the purely clinical realm of diagnosis and therapy, an index of the amount of unsatisfactory service is suggested by the volume of medical malpractice claims filed in courts or with insurance companies. At least 2,000 professional-liability claims are brought against physicians each year, and the number may be as high as 5,000. The AMA Law Department has found from surveys of the profession that at least one malpractice claim has been filed against 18.6 percent of all doctors in private practice, some 32,500 practitioners.

No less than 35 percent of these charges are valid, to judge by the number of cases resulting in an award to the plaintiff. (The percentage is the same whether the case is tried in court or settled by the insurance company.) In the courts such verdicts are decided by nonphysician judges and juries, and presumably may be swayed by sympathy for the patient and other considerations aside from the medical facts. Thus are these verdicts fair? Generally, yes, says William F. Martin, legal counsel of the Medical Society of the State of New York: "Unjust recoveries in malpractice suits are remarkably rare. The laws as laid down by most of the appellate courts in this country are, on the whole, eminently fair to both the patient and the doctor."

In the observation of some doctors these malpractice figures err on the side of meagerness. While on the staff of New York's Bellevue Hospital, Dr. Vincent J. Fisher evaluated the prehospital care given by patients' private physicians. He reports that he found "poor and even harmful care" in one case out of ten. A surgeon writing under the name of Michael V. Corio has this to say: "If patients brought malpractice suits against *all* guilty doctors—and against guilty doctors only—the courts would probably be flooded with three times the number of such suits now in litigation."

Studies by health insurance plans bear out that in some quarters of medicine substandard care is commoner than generally believed. As a means of evaluating the services performed by participating physicians, health insurers often rely on "medical audits." These are detailed reviews of cases by independent specialists, who then pass judgment on the quality of diagnosis and treatment.

In New York City, one out of 16 residents is covered by a health and welfare plan negotiated by the Teamsters Union. In the course of operations, the administrators of the program asked Dr. Ray E. Trussell, director of the Columbia University School of Public Health and Administrative

Medicine, to conduct a medical audit. For 18 months, 35 faculty members and a panel of seven additional physicians probed their way through a sampling of services performed by participating doctors.

From a study of 406 cases in which the patient was hospitalized, the auditors concluded that no fewer than one out of five received "poor" care. Another one-fifth received only "fair" care. In surgical cases the quality of surgery in 20 percent of the cases was found "poor," in 26 percent merely "fair."

The auditors also found evidence of considerable milking of the program through unnecessary services. Twenty percent of the hospital admissions were found to have been needless. Of 60 hysterectomies, 20 were unnecessary and ten were of doubtful need. Of 13 cesarean sections, seven were without justification.

## APPEALS FOR REFORM

"The profession of medicine is plagued . . . by a small percentage of members who fail to recognize or refuse to abide by accepted standards of conduct," wrote Dr. J. P. Medelman, president of the Minnesota State Medical Association. Dr. Medelman's remarks appeared in an editorial in *Minnesota Medicine,* his society's journal, and they constituted the journal's first comment about medicine's disciplinary problem in at least five years.

Since the profession is generally reluctant to air its dirty linen, and since discipline is not a matter of prime interest to most practitioners, comment on the subject is infrequent. When an occasional medical leader does speak out, his words are lost in the absence of a systematic campaign of information and improvement. It is a rare physician and a rarer layman who knows how bleak a picture has been painted by knowledgeable medical leaders and how little is being done about it.

Even warnings from the profession's highest echelon have resulted in few corrective measures. In his capacity as secretary and general manager of the AMA, Dr. George F. Lull called for a prompt cleanup. "It cannot be denied that the reputation of the medical profession is being damaged seriously by the . . . malpractitioners within its ranks," he declared. "The situation must be corrected." This was in 1953.

Nor has the problem gone unnoticed by AMA presidents, and their calls for reform have similarly met with little success. When Dr. Louis Bauer was in office he sought to "drive out of the profession" all doctors guilty of unethical practices. The campaign he attempted to launch lacked general support. It lasted only as long as he held office, and so when Dr. Edward J. McCormick took up the post he started his own program to get medicine to clean house. "We cannot," he said, "protect or condone the . . . greedy and godless physicians who flagrantly violate the noble traditions of the medical profession." But Dr. McCormick's call too went unheeded.

Then, after an interval of little discussion or action, Dr. Leonard W. Larson was elected AMA president. Like Drs. Bauer and McCormick, Dr. Larson recognized that reforms were now needed, first of all in the profession's attitude toward discipline. "That small fraction of undisciplined practitioners must not be allowed to remain in the body of medicine, lest it corrupt and enervate the entire profession," he warned. "We must take a vigorous position on self-discipline, for to ignore the problem would bring on ultimate catastrophe."

But, once again, zeal for reform sparked only isolated physicians and ended in next to no improvement. As a result, the malpracticing periphery of the profession remains a major hazard. And late in this decade Dr. James Z. Appel has made yet another stab at establishing a meaningful reform program. "The emphasis must now be in the field of discipline," he declared in a statement of priorities he wished to pursue as AMA president. Once and for all, he urged his colleagues, let us police ourselves.

What is the effect of this lack of policing? The AMA Medical Disciplinary Committee found that the situation is deteriorating. In Connecticut, Delaware, Ohio, and Utah, medical societies report that the profession's discipline problem is outpacing all efforts to correct it. In Hawaii, the problem is worse than it was ten years ago.

# 14

# *Masking Official Violence: Corporal Punishment in Public Schools*

*Joseph A. Kotarba*

Government agencies of social control in our society are often caught between two morally opposing sets of expectations. On the one hand, the police, prison administrators, the military, must operate under the public mandate to insure social order. On the other hand, these agencies are prohibited, within the arena of public opinion, from utilizing unwarranted, unreasonable, or covert violence in the execution of their duties. The American ethos contains a view of government that is subservient to the will of the people and is never allowed to subjugate the citizenry, especially through the use of physical violence. Exceptions to this rule are really limited to very unusual circumstances, such as states of national emergency like war or capital punishment for certain heinous crimes.

Recent history has shown us that government leaders who publicly order their subordinates to resort to violence, even in times of great civil or organizational crisis, are likely to receive great public criticism that can be extremely damaging to their careers. The National Advisory Commission on Civil Disorders viewed the reactions of city officials during the urban riots of the early 1960s as the "indiscriminate, repressive use of force" against both innocent and culpable members of the black community. Mayor Richard J. Daley of Chicago was heavily criticized by black community leaders and the liberal press for his order to "shoot to maim" looters during the ghetto riots in 1968. Governor Nelson Rockefeller's decision to storm prisoner rebels at Attica, resulting in the death of 39 people, was often referred to as "murder" in the press.

It is clear that this kind of negative reaction to official violence results in a reluctance among governmental leaders to openly espouse or order sheer force as a necessary means of maintaining social order. Many of the same leaders have felt that, under various circumstances, physical violence is necessary to the operation of their organizations and agencies. Thus, official violence often occurs as covert operations. Since these episodes of official violence are to be kept from public observance at all costs, they are usually planned and accomplished in such a way that the executive leadership of the agencies would be held *non-accountable* in the event of public disclosure. This consideration is necessary in light of the fact that leaders are ultimately responsible for the activities of their subordinates, at least in the critics' eyes.

A good example of this type of intrigue occurred during the Kennedy administration, when the CIA plotted secret wars and assassination attempts against Cuba's Fidel Castro. President Kennedy authorized the Bay of Pigs invasion in April 1961 as a subversive operation whose goal was the overthrow of the Communist regime in Cuba. Since the operation could easily be criticized as an unreasonable, unethical, and violent interference in the internal affairs of another nation, it was necessary to protect the president from public involvement in the adventure, in case of its failure. Following the first principle of covert violence, executive non-accountability, presidential aid Arthur Schlesinger sent a then classified memorandum to Kennedy under the heading *Protection of the President:*

> The character and repute of President Kennedy constitutes one of our greatest national resources. Nothing should be done to jeopardize this invaluable asset. When lies must be told, they should be told by subordinate officials. At no point should the president be asked to lend himself to the cover operation. For this reason, there seems to be merit in Secretary Rusk's suggestion that someone other than the President make the final decision and do so in his absence—someone whose head can later be placed on the block if things go terribly wrong (quoted in Moyers, 1977).

Although the overthrow of Fidel Castro was decided upon by the president and, in Attorney General Robert Kennedy's own words, had "the top priority of the United States Government" (Moyers, 1977), it was necessary to obtain tacit yet unofficial approval from the president for the specific plans of the operation. Richard Bissell, chief of covert operations for the CIA, testified to the Senate Intelligence Committee that "a good intelligence officer conducts his conversations with the Chief of State in such a way that the Chief of State can never be proved to have explicitly authorized certain kinds of actions" (Moyers, 1977). The Senate Committee learned procedure for eliciting this tacit approval:

> The prevailing practice on all sensitive matters was to brief the President without obtaining his express approval. Maxwell Taylor testified that the President would simply listen to what the person briefing him had to say without responding affirmatively so that the record did not say that the President personally approved (Moyers, 1977).

The second principle of covert, official violence, *subordinate accountability,* is invoked when a covert operation becomes public knowledge. In this case, the executive is to place blame upon insubordinate employees for the adventure. Arthur Schlesinger offered the following advice to President Kennedy, to be used in the event of a foul-up of the Bay of Pigs invasion:

> If Castro [wins the engagement] and flies a group of captured Cubans to New York to testify that they were organized and trained by CIA, we will have to be prepared to show that the alleged CIA personnel were errant idealists or soldiers-of-fortune working on their own (Moyers, 1977).

The two principles of executive non-accountability and subordinate accountability, as they are exercised at the highest levels of government, are becoming increasingly well documented, as is apparent with the Watergate fiasco. At a lower level of government, the illicit and covert use of police violence follows the same patterns (Knapp Commission, 1971: 92; and Redlinger, 1969). At an even lower level of government, there exists a common form of official violence that, until quite recently, attracted little public concern due to the powerless nature of its victims. I am referring to the use of corporal punishment in American public education. In the remainder of this paper, I will (1) briefly sketch the history of corporal punishment in America; (2) examine the use of corporal punishment in the Chicago Public Schools, where it is "officially" banned; and (3) describe the procedures used by school officials, based on the two principles of covert, official violence, to cover up incidents of teacher violence and project the required public image of nonviolence.

There are three sources for the data used in this paper. First, I have relied on official Board of Education publications for much of the policy statements intended for the public. Second, I have utilized my five and a half years of employment with the Board of Education as a source of information on the day-to-day operations of the schools. This experience includes one-half year as a substitute teacher, four years as a classroom teacher for mildly retarded high school adolescents, and one year as team leader (i.e., assistant principal) at an elementary school I will refer to as Middle School. Third, I have interviewed various Board of Education executives, auxiliary personnel, teachers, and children concerning the problems of discipline in the schools.

## CORPORAL PUNISHMENT IN AMERICAN EDUCATION

Corporal punishment, which has been outlawed in the military and no longer officially sanctioned in prisons, has been and continues to be an accepted and desirable discipline measure for many teachers and school administrators. The idea of beating sense into children—for their own good—is deeply rooted in Judaeo-Christian folklore and the Anglo-American view of humanity (Hechinger, 1974: 84).[1] The necessity for saving children from the ravages of youth and Original Sin is proclaimed in several passages of the Bible:

> Foolishness is bound in the heart of a child; but the rod of correction shall drive it from him (Proverbs 22:15).
> Thou shalt beat him with the rod and shalt deliver his soul from hell (Proverbs 23:14).

Ever since the early eighteenth century, the authoritarian nature of education in puritan America was conducive to the use of violence for disciplining rowdies, motivating dullards, and, in general, demonstrating the all-powerful role of the teacher.[2] Besides the purging of evil, corporal punishment was seen to have the positive effect of developing a sense of "manliness." This feeling led Theodore Roosevelt, an ideal of American machismo, to write in 1899: "When it comes to discipline, I cordially agree . . . as to the need for physical punishment" (Hechinger, 1974: 84).

Corporal punishment was not, however, without its early critics in America. Henry Thoreau quit teaching after two weeks because he refused to hit children. Herman Melville left the Pittsfield Schools after less than a year of teaching in disgust over the brutality inflicted on the children in his school. Actual reforms of disciplinary policy and technique came at the end of the nineteenth century, when the enlightened educational philosophy of John Dewey and others made its mark on some school administrators.[3] The Chicago Board of Education was among the first large, urban systems to ban corporal punishment (*Rules of the Board of Education,* section 179: 1891). At the present time, only certain school districts (e.g., New York City, Boston, Baltimore, Philadelphia, San Francisco, and Washington, D.C.) and a handful of states (New Jersey, Maryland, and Massachusetts) have joined Chicago in prohibiting teacher violence. Many other school districts openly espouse corporal punishment, such as Dallas, Texas, which proudly generates and openly disseminates meticulous records on all paddlings in the city school system.[4]

The debate over corporal punishment continues and reflects many opinions on the purpose of the educational process. Opponents of corporal punishment, who are for the most part distant observers of the classroom setting and include policy-making bodies like the American Civil Liberties Union and the American Psychological Association, tend to rely on psychological and/or ethical arguments. The central arguments include the following: (1) "Corporal punishment gives the child a vision of society that relies upon force to settle conflict" (Friedenberg, 1964); (2) "[Corporal] punishment is the antithesis of democratic interpersonal exchange, and it is likely, in time, to blunt a person's feelings of indignation towards acts of injustice" (Whiteside, 1975: 161); and (3) "Corporal punishment drives aggression and antisocial tendencies underground, which leads to unpredictable eruptions of more serious violence and spiteful-ness" (Redl and Wattenberg, 1959). In other words, criticisms of cor-poral punishment are essentially concerned with the possible negative, latent functions of corporal punishment on the psyche of the child.

Proponents of corporal punishment are more likely to be active mem-bers of the teaching enterprise who look upon harsh discipline as a neces-sary and pragmatic tool for *enforcing* social control in the classroom. A 1972 survey of classroom teachers commissioned by the National Educa-tion Association "indicates that 72% of them advocate retaining corporal punishment, partly as a way of protecting themselves and others from physical injury and property damage, and also as a means of maintain-ing order in the classroom" (Whiteside, 1975: 160). It is no news that many of our urban schools—which often cater to a poor, multilingual, and multicultural student body—are nothing more than microcosms of the larger pluralistic and conflictful society:

> Each year there are some 70,000 physical assaults on teachers and hundreds of thousands of assaults on children. . . . After extensive hear-ings by his Subcommittee to Investigate Juvenile Delinquency, Senator Birch Bayh undoubtedly spoke for many teachers when he said, "The primary concern in many modern American schools is no longer educa-tion but preservation" (Moorefield, 1976: 13).[5]

## CORPORAL PUNISHMENT IN THE CHICAGO PUBLIC SCHOOLS

In spite of the October 20, 1975, U.S. Supreme Court decision allowing for a "reasonable" level of corporal punishment to be administered to a child who has been previously warned, the Chicago Board of Education has strictly adhered to its 1891 decision outlawing the practice.[6] In the words of one Board consultant on human relations, the reason is simple:

> It would be suicide for the Board to condone corporal punishment. If it did, every civil rights group in town would be down here screaming and protesting the use of violence against minority students, who comprise 76% of the student population.

The Board of Education not only prohibits corporal punishment in the schools, but insures that it does not exist "officially." The Law Depart-ment of the Board is responsible for the prosecution (legal or organiza-tional) of Board employees for flagrant violation of Board rules, including corporal punishment (see sections 2-10 and 4-30, *Rules of the Board of Education*). Yet, in the past five years, only one teacher has been tried for engaging in corporal punishment. The contradiction surfaces when one realizes that teacher violence is rampant in the schools. In my five and a half years of employment with the Board, I have never seen nor heard of any school where corporal punishment was not practiced regularly by at least some of the faculty. What really occurs is, in the day-to-day functioning of the school system, a filtering process by which knowledge of actual incidents of corporal punishment is restrained at a lower and less visible rung of the organization so that the top administration of the Board can maintain executive non-accountability. This filtering process exists because it would be impossible for the Board to eradicate corporal punishment in such a large, diffuse, and culturally conflictful system as Chicago's, even if it so desired.

The individual school principal is expected, by the Board, to regulate corporal punishment in his school and to resolve any resulting conflicts with parents or community members. Very few principals are ever able to eradicate teacher violence in their schools, for they realize that violence is sometimes necessary to maintain the public image of school-wide social order for which the principal is accountable. The office of the principal is the logical point for limiting knowledge of teacher violence, since it is the highest organizational level where disputes over corporal punishment can be handled *informally*. One Board of Education attorney explains the crucial importance of the principal's role in this matter:

> We expect the principal to take care of these matters for two reasons. First, he's the most familiar with the parties involved, the teacher, the student, and the parent. He should be able to cool everyone off. Secondly, if an incident should be brought to the attention of the next highest person in charge, you know, the district super [superintendent], then the whole thing gets put on record and all kinds of rules must be enforced. At this point, the teacher's whole career is jeopardized, simply because he lost his cool and smacked a kid. . . . The one case we did prosecute was not really over a corporal punishment issue. The principal, super, and Board simply used it to build a case against an otherwise totally incompetent teacher who they wanted to dismiss.

Within the school settings, the responses of principals to teacher violence will vary according to their moral stance on violence, the cooperation of the faculty, the types of discipline problems they encounter, etc. A few principals are strongly opposed to teacher violence and will sanction their teachers who engage in its practice. These sanctions usually involve low professional evaluations that could hurt a teacher's chance for promotion or desirable transfer and the face-to-face embarrassment of being "chewed out in the office." The pacifist approach is usually taken by principals in those few schools where order is easily maintained by non-violent measures, schools that cater to middle- and upper middle-class students from constructive home environments. Most principals, however, are less fortunate and must give their tacit approval for teachers to hit children when necessary. It is necessary for the principal to maintain his own executive non-accountability, as exemplified by one principal's annual teachers' orientation message:

> I expect classroom order and discipline to be the sole responsibility of the teacher. I also realize that different teachers utilize various discipline procedures, which I won't personally evaluate, but please don't leave any evidence that can be used against you.

It is commonly understood among the teachers that "evidence" refers to cuts, bruises, or welts inflicted on the children.

### Unstructured Teacher Violence

Corporal punishment takes the form of *unstructured teacher violence* in those schools where the decision to engage in and the responsibility of successfully accomplishing corporal punishment is left strictly in the hands of the teacher. Very few teachers enter the profession knowing that they will later resort to physical punishment as a way of maintaining order in the classroom. As Kohl (1967), Kozol (1967), and others have illustrated and the present research has verified, new teachers placed in disruptive classroom settings initially intend to react rationally and passively to problem children. When this naive idealism crumbles and a teacher first strikes a child, this act is an irrational and, above all, emotional response to an unbearable situation. In time, the teacher may rationally incorporate violence in his/her classroom style.

When I was an administrator at Middle School, one of my novice teachers was young, female, bright, and overly optimistic regarding her ability to maintain classroom order through "constructive interpersonal relationships." One afternoon early in the school year, she buzzed my office through the intercom. I immediately rushed up to her classroom, since I had been expecting trouble for several weeks. Her classes were always loud and unruly, and her attempts to reason with the children and even shout them down were to no avail. When I arrived at her class, she was standing outside the door, sobbing. After I quieted down the class, I tried to normalize the situation and console the teacher, for she was obviously more upset than the child she hit. In near hysteria, she blurted out the following:

> I hate him! Ever since school began, he's done everything he could to get on my nerves. I tried talking to him, understanding him, everything. . . . I don't care if they fire me; I don't care what the kids think. He was asking for it. I'm not gonna take that shit anymore from any kid, I don't care how underprivileged he is.

This particular teacher was soon a regular paddler. Like many other teachers, she soon realized that her peers hit children on occasion, got away with it, and had fewer problems in the classroom.

Teachers utilize various self-defense strategies in order to minimize the possibility of negative reactions from parents. One strategy is to co-opt the parents and actively seek their permission to spank the children when necessary. This permission is readily available in schools where the parents are poor, unsophisticated, and/or unable to control the children themselves. In such schools, a typical response to such a request is: "Feel free to smack him anytime he gets out of line. Maybe you can straighten him out. He won't listen to me anymore." Parental permission for corporal punishment, even when given on paper and signed, does not, of course, transcend the Board's ruling against it. Naturally, "smart" teachers won't bother to inform parents of this fact.

The most important self-protection strategy is to make sure that the parent doesn't find out about it. Many teachers will use psychological intimidation on a child, telling him/her that a spanking should be "taken like a man (or a woman)," or that "only a baby goes home crying about a spanking." This strategy relies on the child's peer pressure to act grown-up.[7]

### Structured Teacher Violence

Certain principals who favor corporal punishment will regulate its use in accord with the existing organizational structure of the school. By placing responsibility for corporal punishment on an intermediate member of the staff (e.g., the assistant principal), the principal can further remove himself from the practice and limit its use in the school. One junior high school in Chicago, with an enrollment of two thousand underprivileged black youngsters, is policed by four assistant principals. Their primary duty is to walk the corridors with a paddle, making sure that students are not roaming the school and cutting class. They are always available if a teacher has a problem with a student and are given explicit permission to use the paddle when necessary, although the teachers themselves cannot.

Middle School provides a perfect example of structured teacher violence. The school is divided into six teams, each comprised of 170 students, seven classroom teachers, two teachers' aids, a counselor, and a team leader. In theory, the team leader occupies the traditional role of assistant principal and is responsible for the instructional program and administrative requirements of the team. In practice, however, he is also responsible for maintaining social order in the team and regulating discipline practices. According to the principal's directive, a teacher who feels that a child is deserving of a whack is to petition the team leader to do it. There are two reasons why the team leader (and assistant principal in those schools using that nomenclature) is delegated this authority. First, the team leader is expected (by the principal) to rationally decide which children are deserving of physical violence and to administer it fairly and moderately. Hopefully, this will lessen the chance of a classroom teacher losing his/her temper and possibly injuring a child in a fit of rage. Second, the team leader, as a member of the administration, is held in higher esteem than a regular teacher. His status will help convince an angry parent that the child really deserved a spanking or that a teacher who might have spanked the child is really a good teacher and simply made a mistake.

Needless to say, this arrangement often puts the team leader in the middle of confrontations with angry parents. The following example demonstrates this point, and also illustrates the situation actualization of the two principles of covert, official violence. A fourteen-year-old Puerto Rican boy had been a very trying discipline problem for the teachers on one particular team at Middle School. He was constantly cutting class, fighting, stealing from other students, and was in general a totally disruptive youngster. Although he tested out as being four years behind normal progress, this factor plus his erratic behavior were insufficient evidence for the principal to place him in a special education classroom. (We later learned that the principal, being a very politically conscious person, refused to place this child in special education because he knew that the parents were very active in community politics. The principal wanted to avoid any "official"—accountable—decision that would reflect on him as racist or discriminatory.) Thus, the teachers were constantly at wits end in dealing with this child, and the team leader, not aware of the principal's political considerations, proceeded to treat the child as he would any other.

One afternoon, the team leader caught the child in an empty classroom, rifling through the other students' belongings. The team leader began scolding him and gave him a quick slap on the bottom. The child then tried to run out of the building, when the team leader grabbed for him and ripped his shirt. The child got away and, as he flew toward the exit, exclaimed: "You're gonna get it now. Wait 'til my mother sees this!" An hour later, the team leader was called to the principal's office. As he approached the office, he was intercepted by the principal and taken to a side room where a policeman was waiting. The following is a close reconstruction of the principal's statement:

> Mr. Warner, this is Officer O'Malley. He's responding to Mrs. Ortiz' call to the station. She's in my office now and is she mad! We have to cool her off. When we go back, I don't want you to say anything. The officer is going to chew both of you (i.e., the team leader and the child) out. Don't mention anything about the stealing. If she asks you if you hit George, admit it, but apologize and I'll add the fact that this rarely happens here, and in your team. Just say that you lost your temper at George for cutting class. Don't say anything else.

All three men then entered the principal's office, where the child, his mother, and a bilingual secretary who was there at the mother's request, were present. The officer proceeded to scold both the team leader and the child, the former for overreacting and the latter for not showing proper respect to the team leader. The principal, acting only as if he were a truly objective party, repeated his statement about the rarity of this type of situation in his school. After the team leader and the child were made to apologize to each other, the mother seemed satisfied and the group disbanded. The team leader later recounted to me how depressed and "ripped off" he felt at that moment.

The above is a clear demonstration of the two principles of covert, official violence. The principal disclaimed any involvement in the incident by stating that corporal punishment is truly rare in his school and, in effect, not allowed. His subordinate, the team leader, was held responsible for the incident, if not by design then by momentary loss of self-control. The precipitating factors to the event, of which the principal was clearly aware, were never mentioned. An incident of corporal punishment that was presented to a public audience as an irrational act of violence simply glossed over the rational decisions of the executive in charge that were conducive to its actualization.

### The E.R.A. Classroom

The Chicago Public Schools, being a typically modern school system, has developed numerous special programs for unusual student needs. There are classes for three levels of mental retardation, for the audibly and visually impaired, for exceptionally bright students, etc. Expectedly, the Board developed a special program for children who present unusual discipline problems in their schools. Initiated in 1968, the Early Remediation Approach to Self-Discipline Program (E.R.A.) functions to remove "severely socially maladjusted children" (i.e., "the bad boys") from the regular classroom and place them in the care of a specially trained teacher. The official goals of the program are impressive:

> The ultimate objective, which is dependent on all of the other objectives, is to motivate the child to aspire with success and to progress in behavior to that point where he can assume responsibility for his own acts. Both of these will give him the necessary social, emotional, and educational strengths to allow him to return to the regular classroom.
> . . . A key concept in changing attitudes in the child is to establish a sense of pride in self. The child's self-image should be constantly reinforced and strengthened (Board of Education, 1972).

Several of the E.R.A. classes appear to be truly effective remedial programs. District Eleven's E.R.A. classes, for example, utilize sophisticated behavioral modification techniques that apparently work. Many other schools do, however, use the E.R.A. class as a strictly supervisory dumping ground for unmanageable children. During my substitute teaching experience, 1 witnessed nine different E.R.A. classrooms where educational supplies and programs were minimal, and the usual behavior modification technique used was a large, wooden paddle. In general, the children who get beat the most in the regular classrooms receive the same treatment when placed in the E.R.A. class.

At Middle School, the E.R.A. teacher is the most valuable member of the faculty. The team leaders constantly try to "be on his good side," for he has the power to relieve them of their worst discipline problems. Placement in the E.R.A. classroom is supposed to require a lengthy battery of official acts, such as psychological examination, parent-teacher staffings, and district superintendent approval. Following these steps takes an enormous amount of time (sometimes up to a whole year). The E.R.A. teacher can, if willing, sidestep them and accept a child on a "temporary basis." Children placed in E.R.A., either formally or temporarily, are rarely able to return to the regular classroom.

The E.R.A. classroom therefore provides the most sophisticated form of structured teacher violence. Its teacher is given license to use whatever discipline measures felt necessary, as long as he doesn't return the children to the teams. By centrally locating the most disruptive children, teacher violence in the classroom is lessened. The official purpose of E.R.A., to establish positive social attitudes in the children, becomes a public front to conceal the use of regular and systemic corporal punishment.

Parents and children rarely complain about the harsh discipline meted out by the E.R.A. teacher. The parents realize that the E.R.A. class is probably the last stop for the child before placement in a correctional institution, so they are grateful for having the E.R.A. teacher forestall incarceration. The children—who often have severe emotional problems, police arrest records, and ineffective home lives—somehow feel comfortable with the military-like regimentation enforced in the E.R.A. class.

It is often written that the line separating the agent of social control and the deviant actor is symbiotic, that collaboration between the two is frequently the most expedient policy to pursue (see Manning, 1971: 178–79). The success of many E.R.A. teachers results not only from their sadistic feelings toward discipline, but from their ability to personally accept much of the deviant behavior of their children. Put differently, a successful E.R.A. teacher is one who understands and acknowledges the developing antisocial (and in some cases criminal) lifestyle of the students and tolerates its existence outside the school, as long as the student is subservient within the school. At Middle School, the majority of E.R.A. students are part of a larger, communitywide youth subculture that provides homosexual favors to adults for money. Unlike the regular classroom teachers who are shocked and offended by this behavior, the E.R.A. teacher—

himself a homosexual—acknowledges and literally enjoys this facet of his students' behavior. The students subsequently feel that their teacher's acceptance of this as well as other forms of their street behavior projects an image of a relevant teacher. One student describes his relationship with the E.R.A. teacher:

> Mr. Smith? He's an awright dude I guess. He doesn't get an attitude all the time like you teachers do. . . . Does he ever hit me? Boy, he's always whoopin' me. But that's cool. It's not like a regular teacher whoopin' me. Mr. Smith knows what's coming down in the neighborhood. Nothin' shakes him up.

## CONCLUDING REMARKS

We have seen how the Chicago Public Schools maintain the image of upholding their public mandate to produce an orderly educational environment for students. Accordingly, much of the reality of accomplishing this social order is masked from public view. I need mention that there are many teachers within the system who accomplish social order through thoughtful teaching, innovative curriculum, behavior modification, ethnic awareness, and other programs that make the educational experience meaningful and exciting for students. Creative teachers and administrators, though, are not representative of the entire school system.

One might easily say that corporal punishment really doesn't exist in the Chicago schools, for if one were to go down to the Board and ask to see records of it, they wouldn't exist. The leadership of the Board, like the leadership of any public organization, take steps to insure that knowledge of incriminating activities occurring within the organizaton is kept from public view, especially the media. Knowledge of specific acts of corporal punishment is blocked at a lower organizational level, specifically, by the principal of each school where it is practiced. The principal himself maintains executive non-accountability by either giving only his tacit approval to teachers to hit children, delegating authority to specific subordinates (i.e., the assistant principal or team leader) to regulate violence, or isolating violence in one classroom under the guise of special education. The losers in all of this organizational frontwork are the children who get a paddle instead of a worthwhile education and the teachers who must resort to violence in order to keep the peace in an otherwise chaotic school situation.

## NOTES

1. Corporal punishment has been outlawed in France since 1887. Educational philosophy on the entire continent has tended to see corporal punishment "as a relic of a more barbaric age" (Leinster-Mackay, 1977: 2).
2. Several observers have noted how corporal punishment is condoned in societies that

maintain a sense of authoritarianism. This seems to be an oversimplification of the issue (see Falk, 1941: 108).

3. In essence, Dewey (1915 and 1963) felt that education should be a continuous reconstruction of experience in which there is a development of immature experience toward experience funded with the skills and habits of intelligence. The learning experience should be attempted in a quiet atmosphere that is emotionally supportive of the immature child.

4. "Acording to Nolan Estes, a Dallas assistant school superintendent, there were 10,225 instances of corporal punishment in the city's classrooms in the 1973–74 school year . . . 'That's not 10,000 students paddled,' Estes explained; 'some of them were repeaters' " (Merlis, 1975: 425).

5. Postman and Weingartner (1969) provide a vivid account of the oft-chaotic situation teachers face when teaching in a large, urban school system.

6. In 1951, the Board of Education revised its rules, so that the current rule on teacher violence reads as follows: "Section 6-22: *Corporal Punishment Prohibited.* No employee of the Board of Education may inflict corporal punishment of any kind upon persons attending the public schools of the City of Chicago." The penalty for flagrant violation of a Board rule is dismissal.

7. I have even witnessed a teacher demand that a child not cry while being spanked!

# REFERENCES

Board of Education. "Here's the Program." E.R.A., Chicago: organizational mimeo, 1972.

Dewey, John. *The School and Society,* 2nd ed. Chicago: The University of Chicago Press, 1915.

——. *Experience and Education.* New York: Macmillan Co., 1963.

Falk, Herbert A. *Corporal Punishment.* New York: Columbia University Press, 1941.

Friedenberg, Edgar Z. *The Vanishing Adolescent.* Boston: Beacon, 1964.

Hechinger, G. and F. "Thou shalt beat him with the rod and shalt deliver his soul from hell." *New York Times Magazine,* October 6, 1974, p. 84+.

Knapp Commission. *Commission Report.* Private publication, 1971.

Kohl, Herb. *36 Children.* New York: American Library, 1967.

Kozol, Jonathon. *Death at an Early Age.* Boston: Houghton-Mifflin, 1967.

Leinster-Mackey, D. P. "Regina v. Hopley: Some Historical Notes on Corporal Punishment." *Journal of Educational Administration and History* 9, 1 (January 1977): 1–5.

Manning, Peter K. "The Police: Mandate, Strategies, and Appearances." In Jack D. Douglas, ed., *Crime and Justice in American Society.* Indianapolis: Bobbs-Merrill, 1971.

Merlis, George. "The Updated Hickory Stick." *The Nation* (November 1, 1975): 425–27.

Moorefield, Story. Untitled. *American Education* 13, 1 (1976): 12–16.

Moyers, Bill. "Open Letter to Arthur Schlesinger." *Wall Street Journal* (July 20, 1977): 15.

Postman, Neil, and C. Weingartner. *Teaching as a Subversive Activity.* New York: Delacorte Press, 1969.

Redl, Fritz, and William Wattenberg. *Mental Hygiene in Teaching,* 2nd ed. New York: Harcourt, Brace, Jovanovich, 1959.

Redlinger, L. J. "Dealing in Dope." Unpublished Ph.D. dissertation, Northwestern University, 1969.

Whiteside, Marilyn. "School Discipline: The Ongoing Crisis." *The Clearing House* 49 (December 1975): 160–62.

# 15

# *Practice of Law as a Confidence Game*

*Abraham S. Blumberg*

A recurring theme in the growing dialogue between sociology and law has been the great need for a joint effort of the two disciplines to illuminate urgent social and legal issues. Having uttered fervent public pronouncements in this vein, however, the respective practitioners often go their separate ways. Academic spokesmen for the legal profession are somewhat critical of sociologists of law because of what they perceive as the sociologist's preoccupation with the application of theory and methodology to the examination of legal phenomena, without regard to the solution of legal problems. Further, it is felt that "contemporary writing in the sociology of law . . . betrays the existence of painfully unsophisticated notions about the day-to-day operations of courts, legislatures and law offices."[1] Regardless of the merit of such criticism, scant attention—apart from explorations of the legal profession itself—has been given to the sociological examination of legal institutions or their supporting ideological assumptions. Thus, for example, very little sociological effort is expended to ascertain the validity and viability of important court decisions, which may rest on wholly erroneous assumptions about contextual realities of social structure. A particular decision may rest upon a legally impeccable rationale; at the same time it may be rendered nugatory or self-defeating by contingencies imposed by aspects of social reality of which the lawmakers are themselves unaware.

Within this context, I wish to question the impact of three recent landmark decisions of the United States Supreme Court, each hailed as destined to effect profound changes in the future of criminal law administration and enforcement in America. The first of these, *Gideon v. Wainwright*, 372 U.S. 335 (1963), required states and localities henceforth to furnish counsel in the case of indigent persons charged with a felony.[2] The

From Abraham S. Blumberg, "The Practice of Law as Confidence Game: Organizational Cooptation of a Profession," *Law and Society Review* 1 (1967): 15-39. Copyright © 1967 by Law and Society Association. Reprinted by permission.

*Gideon* ruling left several major issues unsettled, among them the vital question: What is the precise point in time at which a suspect is entitled to counsel?[3] The answer came relatively quickly in *Escobedo* v. *Illinois,* 378 U.S. 478 (1964), which has aroused a storm of controversy. Danny Escobedo confessed to the murder of his brother-in-law after the police had refused to permit retained counsel to see him, although his lawyer was present in the station house and asked to confer with his client. In a 5–4 decision, the court asserted that counsel must be permitted when the process of police investigative effort shifts from merely investigatory to that of accusatory, "when its focus is on the accused and its purpose is to elicit a confession—our adversary system begins to operate, and, under the circumstances here, the accused must be permitted to consult with his lawyer."

As a consequence, Escobedo's confession was rendered inadmissible. The decision triggered a national debate among police, district attorneys, judges, lawyers, and other law enforcement officials, which continues unabated, as to the value and propriety of confessions in criminal cases.[4] On June 13, 1966, the Supreme Court in a 5–4 decision underscored the principle enunciated in *Escobedo* in the case of *Miranda* v. *Arizona.*[5] Police interrogation of any suspect in custody, without his consent, unless a defense attorney is present, is prohibited by the self-incrimination provision of the Fifth Amendment. Regardless of the relative merit of the various shades of opinion about the role of counsel in criminal cases, the issues generated thereby will be in part resolved as additional cases move toward decision in the Supreme Court in the near future. They are of peripheral interest and not of immediate concern in this paper. However, the *Gideon, Escobedo,* and *Miranda* cases pose interesting general questions. In all three decisions, the Supreme Court reiterates the traditional legal conception of a defense lawyer based on the ideological perception of a criminal case as an *adversary, combative* proceeding, in which counsel for the defense assiduously musters all the admittedly limited resources at his command to *defend* the accused.[6] The fundamental question remains to be answered: Does the Supreme Court's conception of the role of counsel in a criminal case square with social reality?

The task of this paper is to furnish some preliminary evidence toward the illumination of that question. Little empirical understanding of the function of defense counsel exists; only some ideologically oriented generalizations and commitments. This paper is based upon observations made by the writer during many years of legal practice in the criminal courts of a large metropolitan area. No claim is made as to its methodological rigor, although it does reflect a conscious and sustained effort for participant observation.

# COURT STRUCTURE DEFINES ROLE
# OF DEFENSE LAWYER

The overwhelming majority of convictions in criminal cases (usually over 90 percent) are not the product of a combative trial-by-jury process at all, but instead merely involve the sentencing of the individual after a negotiated, bargained-for plea of guilty has been entered.[7] Although more recently the overzealous role of police and prosecutors in producing pretrial confessions and admissions has achieved a good deal of notoriety, scant attention has been paid to the organizational structure and personnel of the criminal court itself. Indeed, the extremely high conviction rate produced without the features of an adversary trial in our courts would tend to suggest that the "trial" becomes a perfunctory reiteration and validation of the pretrial interrogation and investigation.[8]

The institutional setting of the court defines a role for the defense counsel in a criminal case radically different from the one traditionally depicted.[9] Sociologists and others have focused their attention on the deprivations and social disabilities of such variables as race, ethnicity, and social class as being the source of an accused person's defeat in a criminal court. Largely overlooked is the variable of the court organization itself, which possesses a thrust, purpose, and direction of its own. It is grounded in pragmatic values, bureaucratic priorities, and administrative instruments. These exalt maximum production and the particularistic career designs of organizational incumbents, whose occupational and career commitments tend to generate a set of priorities. These priorities exert a higher claim than the stated ideological goals of "due process of law" and are often inconsistent with them.

Organizational goals and discipline impose a set of demands and conditions of practice on the respective professions in the criminal court, to which they respond by abandoning their ideological and professional commitments to the accused client in the service of these higher claims of the court organization. All court personnel, including the accused's own lawyer, tend to be coopted to become agent-mediators[10] who help the accused redefine his situation and restructure his perceptions concomitant with a plea of guilty.

Of all the occupational roles in the court the only private individual who is officially recognized as having a special status and concomitant obligations is the lawyer. His legal status is that of "an officer of the court" and he is held to a standard of ethical performance and duty to his client as well as to the court. This obligation is thought to be far higher than that expected of ordinary individuals occupying the various occupational statuses in the court community. However, lawyers, whether privately retained or of the legal-aid, public defender variety, have close and continuing relations with the prosecuting office and the court itself through discreet relations with the judges via their law secretaries or "confidential" assistants. Indeed, lines of communication, influence, and contact with those offices, as well as with the Office of the Clerk of the court, Probation Division, and with the press, are essential to present and prospective requirements of criminal law practice. Similarly, the subtle involvement of the press and other mass media in the court's organizational network is not readily discernible to the casual observer. Accused persons come and go in the court system schema, but the structure and its occupational incumbents remain to carry on their respective career, occupational, and organizational enterprises. The individual stridencies, tensions, and conflicts a given accused person's case may present to all the participants are overcome, because the formal and informal relations of all the groups in the court setting require it. The probability of continued future relations and interaction must be preserved at all costs.

This is particularly true of the "lawyer regulars," i.e., those defense lawyers who, by virtue of their continuous appearances in behalf of defendants, tend to represent the bulk of a criminal court's nonindigent case workload, and those lawyers who are not "regulars" who appear almost casually in behalf of an occasional client. Some of the "lawyer regulars" are highly visible as one moves about the major urban centers of the nation, their offices line the back streets of the courthouses, at times sharing space with bondsmen. Their political "visibility" in terms of local clubhouse ties, reaching into the judge's chambers and prosecutor's office, are also deemed essential to successful practitioners. Previous research has indicated that the "lawyer regulars" make no effort to conceal their dependence upon police, bondsmen, jail personnel. Nor do they conceal the necessity for maintaining intimate relations with all levels of personnel in the court setting as a means of obtaining, maintaining, and building their practice. These informal relations are the *sine qua non* not only of retaining a practice, but also in the negotiation of pleas and sentences.[11]

The client, then, is a secondary figure in the court system as in certain other bureaucratic settings.[12] He becomes a means to other ends of the organization's incumbents. He may present doubts, contingencies, and pressures which challenge existing informal arrangements or disrupt them; but these tend to be resolved in favor of the continuance of the organization and its relations as before. There is a greater community of interest among all the principal organizational structures and their incumbents than exists elsewhere in other settings. The accused's lawyer has far greater professional, economic, intellectual, and other ties to the various elements of the court system than he does to his own client. In short, the court is a closed community.

This is more than just the case of the usual "secrets" of bureaucracy which are fanatically defended from an outside view. Even all elements of the press are zealously determined to report on that which will not offend the board of judges, the prosecutor, probation, legal-aid, or other officials, in return for privileges and courtesies granted in the past and to be granted in the future. Rather than any view of the matter in terms of some variation of a "conspiracy" hypothesis, the simple explanation is one of an ongoing system handling delicate tensions, managing the trauma produced by law enforcement and administration, and requiring almost pathological distrust of "outsiders" bordering on group paranoia.

The hostile attitude toward "outsiders" is in large measure engendered by a defensiveness itself produced by the inherent deficiencies of assembly line justice, so characteristic of our major criminal courts. Intolerably large caseloads of defendants, which must be disposed of in an organizational context of limited resources and personnel, potentially subject the participants in the court community to harsh scrutiny from appellate courts and other public and private sources of condemnation. As a consequence, an almost irreconcilable conflict is posed in terms of intense pressures to process large numbers of cases, on the one hand, and the stringent ideological and legal requirements of "due process of law," on the other hand. A rather tenuous resolution of the dilemma has emerged in the shape of a large variety of bureaucratically ordained and controlled "work crimes," short cuts, deviations, and outright rule violations adopted as court practice in order to meet production norms. Fearfully anticipating criticism on ethical as well as legal grounds, all the significant participants in the court's social structure are bound into an organized system of complicity. This consists of a work arrangement in which the patterned, covert, informal breaches and evasions of "due process" are institutionalized but are, nevertheless, denied to exist.

These institutionalized evasions will be found to occur to some degree in all criminal courts. Their nature, scope, and complexity are largely determined by the size of the court and the character of the community in which it is located, e.g., whether it is a large, urban institution or a relatively small rural county court. In addition, idiosyncratic local conditions may contribute to a unique flavor in the character and quality of the criminal law's administration in a particular community. However, in most instances a variety of stratagems are employed—some subtle, some crude—in effectively disposing of what are often too large caseloads. A wide variety of coercive devices are employed against an accused client, couched in a depersonalized, instrumental, bureaucratic version of due process of law, and which are in reality a perfunctory obeisance to the ideology of due process. These include some very explicit pressures which are exerted in some measure by all court personnel, including judges, to plead guilty and avoid trial. In many instances the sanction of a potentially harsh sentence is utilized as the visible alternative to pleading guilty, in the case of recalcitrants. Probation and psychiatric reports are "tailored" to organizational needs, or are at least responsive to the court organization's requirements for the refurbishment of a defendant's social biography, consonant with his new status. A resourceful judge can, through his subtle domination of the proceedings, impose his will on the final outcome of a trial. Stenographers and clerks, in their function as record keepers, are on occasion pressed into service in support of a judicial need to "rewrite" the record of a courtroom event. Bail practices are usually employed for purposes other than simply assuring a defendant's presence on the date of a hearing in connection with his case. Too often, the discretionary power as to bail is part of the arsenal of weapons available to collapse the resistance of an accused person. The foregoing is a most cursory examination of some of the more prominent "short cuts" available to any court organization. There are numerous other procedural strategies constituting due process deviations, which tend to become the work style artifacts of a court's personnel. Thus, only court "regulars" who are "bound in" are really accepted; others are treated routinely and in almost a coldly correct manner.

The defense attorneys, therefore, whether of the legal-aid, public defender variety or privately retained, although operating in terms of pressures specific to their respective role and organizational obligations, ultimately are concerned with strategies which tend to lead to a plea. It is the rational, impersonal elements involving economies of time, labor, expense, and a superior commitment of the defense counsel to these rationalistic values of maximum production[13] of court organization that prevail in his relationship with a client. The lawyer "regulars" are frequently former staff members of the prosecutor's office and utilize the prestige, know-how, and contacts of their former affiliation as part of their stock in trade. Close and continuing relations between the lawyer "regular" and his former colleagues in the prosecutor's office generally overshadow the relationship between the regular and his client. The continuing colleagueship of supposedly adversary counsel rests on real professional and organizational needs of a *quid pro quo,* which goes beyond the limits of an accommodation or *modus vivendi* one might ordinarily expect under the circumstances of an otherwise seemingly adversary relationship. Indeed, the adversary features which are manifest are for the most part muted and exist even in their attenuated form largely for external consumption. The principals, lawyer and assistant district attorney, rely upon one another's cooperation for their continued professional existence, and so the bargaining between them tends usually to be "reasonable" rather than fierce.

## FEE COLLECTION AND FIXING

The real key to understanding the role of defense counsel in a criminal case is to be found in the area of the fixing of the fee to be charged and its collection. The problem of fixing and collecting the fee tends to influence to a significant degree the criminal court process itself, and not just the relationship of the lawyer and his client. In essence, a lawyer-client "confidence game" is played. A true confidence game is unlike the case of the emperor's new clothes wherein that monarch's nakedness was a result of inordinate gullibility and credulity. In a genuine confidence game, the perpetrator manipulates the basic dishonesty of his partner, the victim or mark, toward his own (the confidence operator's) ends. Thus, "the victim of a con scheme must have some larceny in his heart."[14]

Legal service lends itself particularly well to confidence games. Usually a plumber will be able to demonstrate empirically that he has performed a service by clearing up the stuffed drain, repairing the leaky faucet or pipe—and therefore merits his fee. He has rendered, when summoned, a visible, tangible boon for his client in return for the requested fee. A physician who has not performed some visible surgery or otherwise engaged in some readily discernible procedure in connection with a patient may be deemed by the patient to have "done nothing" for him. As a consequence, medical practitioners may simply prescribe or administer by injection a placebo to overcome a patient's potential reluctance or dissatisfaction in paying a requested fee "for nothing."

In the practice of law there is a special problem in this regard, no matter what the level of the practitioner or his place in the hierarchy of prestige. Much legal work is intangible either because it is simply a few words of advice, some preventive action, a telephone call, negotiation of some kind, a form filled out and filed, a hurried conference with another attorney or an official of a government agency, a letter or opinion written, or a countless variety of seemingly innocuous and even prosaic procedures and actions. These are the basic activities, apart from any possible court appearance, of almost all lawyers, at all levels of practice. Much of the activity is not in the nature of the exercise of the traditional, precise professional skills of the attorney such as library research and oral argument in connection with appellate briefs, court motions, trial work, drafting of opinions, memoranda, contracts, and other complex documents and agreements. Instead, much legal activity, whether it is at the lowest or highest "white shoe" law firm levels, is of the brokerage, agent, sales representative, lobbyist type of activity, in which the lawyer acts for someone else in pursuing the latter's interests and designs. The service is intangible.[15]

The large-scale law firm may not speak as openly of their "contacts," their "fixing" abilities, as does the lower-level lawyer. They trade instead upon a façade of thick carpeting, walnut paneling, genteel low pressure, and superficialities of traditional legal professionalism. There are occasions when even the large firm is on the defensive in connection with the fees they charge because the services rendered or results obtained do not appear to merit the fee asked.[16] Therefore, there is a recurrent problem in the legal profession in fixing the amount of fee and in justifying the basis for the requested fee.

Although the fee at times amounts to what the traffic and the conscience of the lawyer will bear, one further observation must be made with regard to the size of the fee and its collection. The defendant in a criminal case and the material gain he may have acquired during the course of his illicit activities are soon parted. Not infrequently the ill-gotten fruits of the various modes of larceny are sequestered by a defense lawyer in payment of his fee. Inexorably, the amount of the fee is a function of the dollar value of the crime committed and is frequently set with meticulous precision at a sum which bears an uncanny relationship to that of the net proceeds of the particular offense involved. On occasion, defendants have been known to commit additional offenses while at liberty on bail, in order to secure the requisite funds with which to meet their obligations for payment of legal fees. Defense lawyers condition even the most obtuse clients to recognize that there is a firm interconnection between fee payment and the zealous exercise of professional expertise, secret knowledge, and organizational "connections" in their behalf. Lawyers, therefore, seek to keep their clients in a proper state of tension and to arouse in them the precise edge of anxiety which is calculated to encourage prompt fee payment. Consequently, the client attitude in the relationship between defense counsel and an accused is in many instances a precarious admixture of hostility, mistrust, dependence, and sycophancy. By keeping his client's anxieties aroused to the proper pitch and establishing a seeming causal relationship between a requested fee and the accused's ultimate extrication from his onerous difficulties, the lawyer will have established the necessary preliminary groundwork to assure a minimum of haggling over the fee and its eventual payment.

In varying degrees, as a consequence, all law practice involves a manipulation of the client and a stage management of the lawyer-client relationship so that at least an *appearance* of help and service will be forthcoming. This is accomplished in a variety of ways, often exercised in combination with each other. At the outset, the lawyer-professional employs with suitable variation a measure of sales-puff which may range from an air of unbounding self-confidence, adequacy, and dominion over events to that of complete arrogance. This will be supplemented by the affectation of a studied, faultless mode of personal attire. In the larger firms, the furnishings and office trappings will serve as the backdrop to help in impression management and client intimidation. In all firms, solo or large-scale, an access to secret knowledge and to the seats of power and influence is inferred or presumed to a varying degree as the basic vendible commodity of the practitioners.

The lack of a visible end product offers a special complication in the course of the professional life of the criminal court lawyer with respect to his fee and in his relations with his client. The plain fact is that an accused in a criminal case always "loses" even when he has been exonerated by an acquittal, discharge, or dismissal of his case. The hostility of an accused which follows as a consequence of his arrest, incarceration, possible loss of job, expense, and other traumas connected with his case is directed, by means of displacement, toward his lawyer. It is in this sense that it may be said that a criminal lawyer never really "wins" a case. The really satisfied client is rare, since in the very nature of the situation even an accused's vindication leaves him with some degree of dissatisfaction and hostility. It is this state of affairs that makes for a lawyer-client relationship in the criminal court which tends to be a somewhat exaggerated version of the usual lawyer-client confidence game.

At the outset, because there are great risks of nonpayment of the fee, due to the impecuniousness of his clients, and the fact that a man who is sentenced to jail may be a singularly unappreciative client, the criminal lawyer collects his fee *in advance*. Often, because the lawyer and the accused both have questionable designs of their own upon each other, the confidence game can be played. The criminal lawyer must serve three major functions or, stated another way, he must solve three problems. First, he must arrange for his fee; second, he must prepare and then, if necessary, "cool out" his client in case of defeat[17] (a highly likely contingency); third, he must satisfy the court organization that he has performed adequately in the process of negotiating the plea, so as to preclude the possibility of any sort of embarrassing incident which may serve to invite "outside" scrutiny.

In assuring the attainment of one of his primary objectives, his fee, the criminal lawyer will very often enter into negotiations with the accused's kin, including collateral relatives. In many instances, the accused himself is unable to pay any sort of fee or anything more than a token fee. It then becomes important to involve as many of the accused's kin as possible in the situation. This is especially so if the attorney hopes to collect a significant part of a proposed substantial fee. It is not uncommon for several relatives to contribute toward the fee. The larger the group, the greater the possibility that the lawyer will collect a sizable fee by getting contributions from each.

A fee for a felony case which ultimately results in a plea, rather than a trial, may ordinarily range anywhere from $500 to $1,500. Should the case go to trial, the fee will be proportionately larger, depending upon the length of the trial. But the larger the fee the lawyer wishes to exact, the more impressive his performance must be, in terms of his stage-managed image as a personage of great influence and power in the court organization. Court personnel are keenly aware of the extent to which a lawyer's stock in trade involves the precarious stage management of an image which goes beyond the usual professional flamboyance, and for this reason alone the lawyer is "bound in" to the authority system of the court's organizational discipline. Therefore, to some extent, court personnel will aid the lawyer in the creation and maintenance of that impression. There is a tacit commitment to the lawyer by the court organization, apart from formal etiquette, to aid him in this. Such augmentation of the lawyer's stage-managed image as this affords is the partial basis for the *quid pro quo* which exists between the lawyer and the court organization. It tends to serve as the continuing basis for the higher loyalty of the lawyer to the organization; his relationship with his client, in contrast, is transient, ephemeral and often superficial.

## DEFENSE LAWYER AS DOUBLE AGENT

The lawyer has often been accused of stirring up unnecessary litigation, especially in the field of negligence. He is said to acquire a vested interest in a cause of action or claim which was initially his client's. The strong incentive of possible fee motivates the lawyer to promote litigation which would otherwise never have developed. However, the criminal lawyer develops a vested interest of an entirely different nature in his client's case: to limit its scope and duration rather than to do battle. Only in this way can a case be "profitable." Thus, he enlists the aid of relatives not only to assure payment of his fee, but he will also rely on these persons to help him in his agent-mediator role of convincing the accused to plead guilty and ultimately to help in "cooling out" the accused if necessary.

It is at this point that an accused-defendant may experience his first sense of "betrayal." While he had perhaps perceived the police and prosecutor to be adversaries, or possibly even the judge, the accused is wholly unprepared for his counsel's role performance as an agent-mediator. In the same vein, it is even less likely to occur to an accused that members of his own family or other kin may become agents, albeit at the behest and urging of other agents or mediators, acting on the principle that they are in reality helping an accused negotiate the best possible plea arrangement under the circumstances. Usually, it will be the lawyer who will activate next of kin in this role, his ostensible motive being to arrange for his fee. But soon latent and unstated motives will assert themselves, with entreaties by counsel to the accused's next of kin, to appeal to the accused to "help himself" by pleading. *Gemeinshaft* sentiments are to this extent exploited by a defense lawyer (or even at times by a district attorney) to achieve specific secular ends, that is, of concluding a particular matter with all possible dispatch.

The fee is often collected in stages, each installment usually payable prior to a necessary court appearance required during the course of an accused's career journey. At each stage, in his interviews and communications with the accused, or in addition, with members of his family, if they are helping with the fee payment, the lawyer employs an air of professional confidence and "inside-dopesterism" in order to assuage anxieties on all sides. He makes the necessary bland assurances, and in effect manipulates his client, who is usually willing to do and say the things, true or not, which will help his attorney extricate him. Since the dimensions of what he is essentially selling, organizational influence and expertise, are not technically and precisely measurable, the lawyer can make extravagant claims of influence and secret knowledge with impunity. Thus, lawyers frequently claim to have inside knowledge in connection with information in the hands of the D.A., police, probation officials or to have access to these functionaries. Factually, they often do, and need only to exaggerate the nature of their relationships with them to obtain the desired effective impression upon the client. But, as in the genuine confidence game, the victim who has participated is loath to do anything which will upset the lesser plea which his lawyer has "conned" him into accepting.[18]

In effect, in his role as double agent, the criminal lawyer performs an extremely vital and delicate mission for the court organization and the accused. Both principals are anxious to terminate the litigation with a minimum of expense and damage to each other. There is no other personage or role incumbent in the total court structure more strategically located, who by training and in terms of his own requirements is more ideally suited to do so than the lawyer. In recognition of this, judges will cooperate with attorneys in many important ways. For example, they will adjourn the case of an accused in jail awaiting plea or sentence if the attorney requests such action. While explicitly this may be done for some innocuous and seemingly valid reason, the tacit purpose is that pressure is being applied by the attorney for the collection of his fee, which he knows will probably not be forthcoming if the case is concluded. Judges are aware of this tactic on the part of lawyers, who, by requesting an adjournment, keep an accused incarcerated awhile longer as a not too subtle method of dunning a client for payment. However, the judges will go along with this on the ground that important ends are being served. Often, the only end served is to protect a lawyer's fee.

The judge will help an accused's lawyer in still another way. He will lend the official aura of his office and courtroom so that a lawyer can stage-manage an impression of an "all-out" performance for the accused in justification of his fee. The judge and other court personnel will serve as a backdrop for a scene charged with dramatic fire, in which the accused's lawyer makes a stirring appeal in his behalf. With a show of restrained passion, the lawyer will intone the virtues of the accused and recite the social deprivations which have reduced him to his present state. The speech varies somewhat, depending on whether the accused has been convicted after trial or has pleaded guilty. In the main, however, the incongruity, superficiality, and ritualistic character of the total performance is underscored by a visibly impassive, almost bored reaction on the part of the judge and other members of the court retinue.

Afterward, there is a hearty exchange of pleasantries between the lawyer and district attorney, wholly out of context in terms of the supposed adversary nature of the preceding events. The fiery passion in defense of his client is gone, and the lawyers for both sides resume their offstage relations, chatting amiably and perhaps including the judge in their restrained banter. No other aspect of their visible conduct so effectively serves to put even a casual observer on notice that these individuals have claims upon each other. These seemingly innocuous actions are indicative of continuing organizational and informal relations, which, in their intricacy and depth, range far beyond any priorities or claims a particular defendant may have.[19]

Criminal law practice is a unique form of private law practice since it really only appears to be private practice.[20] Actually it is bureaucratic practice, because of the legal practitioner's enmeshment in the authority, discipline, and perspectives of the court organization. Private practice, supposedly, in a professional sense, involves the maintenance of an organized, disciplined body of knowledge and learning; the individual practitioners are imbued with a spirit of autonomy and service, the earning of a livelihood being incidental. In the sense that the lawyer in the criminal court serves as a double agent, serving higher organizational rather than professional ends, he may be deemed to be engaged in bureaucratic rather than private practice. To some extent the lawyer-client "confidence game," in addition to its other functions, serves to conceal this fact.

## THE CLIENT'S PERCEPTION

The "cop-out" ceremony, in which the court process culminates, is not only invaluable for redefining the accused's perspectives of himself, but also in reiterating publicly in a formal structured ritual the accused person's guilt for the benefit of significant "others" who are observing. The accused not only is made to assert publicly his guilt of a specific crime, but also a complete recital of its details. He is further made to indicate that he is entering his plea of guilt freely, willingly, and voluntarily, and that he is not doing so because of any promises or in consideration of any commitments that may have been made to him by anyone. This last is intended as a blanket statement to shield the participants from any possible charges of "coercion" or undue influence that may have been exerted in violation of due process requirements. Its function is to preclude any later review by an appellate court on these grounds, and also to obviate any second thoughts an accused may develop in connection with his plea.

However, for the accused, the conception of self as a guilty person is in large measure a temporary role adaptation. His career socialization as an accused, if it is successful, eventuates in his acceptance and redefinition of himself as a guilty person.[21] However, the transformation is ephemeral in that he will, in private, quickly reassert his innocence. Of importance is that he accept his defeat, publicly proclaim it, and find some measure of pacification in it.[22] Almost immediately after his plea, a defendant will generally be interviewed by a representative of the probation division in connection with a presentence report which is to be prepared. The very first question to be asked of him by the probation officer is: "Are you guilty of the crime to which you pleaded?" This is by way of double affirmation of the defendant's guilt. Should the defendant now begin to make bold assertions of his innocence, despite his plea of guilty, he will be asked to withdraw his plea and stand trial on the original charges. Such a threatened possibility is, in most instances, sufficient to cause an accused to let the plea stand and to request the probation officer to overlook his exclamations of innocence. The table that follows is a breakdown of the categorized responses of a random sample of male defendants in Metropolitan Court[23] during 1962, 1963, and 1964 in connection with their statements during presentence probation interviews following their plea of guilty.

It would be well to observe at the outset that, of the 724 defendants who pleaded guilty before trial, only 43 (5.94 percent) of the total group had confessed prior to their indictment. Thus, the ultimate judicial process was predicated upon evidence independent of any confession of the accused.[24]

### TABLE 1
### Defendant Responses as to Guilt or Innocence after Pleading Guilty
### (N = 724; Years, 1962, 1963, 1964)

| Nature of Response | | N of Defendants |
|---|---|---|
| Innocent (Manipulated) | "The lawyer or judge, police or D.A. 'conned me' " | 86 |
| Innocent (Pragmatic) | "Wanted to get it over with" "You can't beat the system" "They have you over a barrel when you have a record" | 147 |
| Innocent (Advice of counsel) | "Followed my lawyer's advice" | 92 |
| Innocent (Defiant) | "Framed" "Betrayed by Complainant," "Police," "Squealers," "Lawyer," "Friends," "Wife," "Girlfriend" | 33 |
| Innocent (Adverse social data) | Blames probation officer or psychiatrist for "bad report," in cases where there was prepleading investigation | 15 |
| Guilty | "But I should have gotten a better deal" Blames lawyer, D.A., police, judge | 74 |
| Guilty | Won't say anything further | 21 |
| Fatalistic (Doesn't press his "Innocence," won't admit "Guilt") | "I did it for convenience" "My lawyer told me it was only thing I could do" "I did it because it was the best way out" | 248 |
| No Response | | 8 |
| Total | | 724 |

As the data indicate, only a relatively small number (95) out of the total number of defendants actually will even admit their guilt, following the "cop-out" ceremony. However, even though they have affirmed their guilt, many of these defendants felt that they should have been able to negotiate a more favorable plea. The largest aggregate of defendants (373) were those who reasserted their "innocence" following their public profession of guilt during the "cop-out" ceremony. These defendants employed differential degrees of fervor, solemnity, and credibility, ranging from really mild, wavering assertions of innocence which were embroidered with a variety of stock explanations and rationalizations, to those of an adamant "framed" nature. Thus, the "Innocent" group, for the most part, were largely concerned with underscoring for their probation interviewer their essential "goodness" and "worthiness," despite their formal plea of guilty. Assertion of his innocence at the post-plea stage resurrects a more respectable and acceptable self-concept for the accused defendant who has pleaded guilty. A recital of the structural exigencies which precipitated his plea of guilt serves to embellish a newly proffered claim of innocence, which many defendants mistakenly feel will stand them in good stead at the time of sentence, or ultimately with probation or parole authorities.

Relatively few (33) maintained their innocence in terms of having been "framed" by some person or agent-mediator, although a larger number (86) indicated that they had been manipulated or "conned" by an agent-mediator to plead guilty, but as indicated, their assertions of innocence were relatively mild.

A rather substantial group (147) preferred to stress the pragmatic aspects of their plea of guilty. They would only perfunctorily assert their innocence and would in general refer to some adverse aspect of their situation which they believed tended to negatively affect their bargaining leverage, including in some instances a prior criminal record.

One group of defendants (92), while maintaining their innocence, simply employed some variation of a theme of following "the advice of counsel" as a covering response to explain their guilty plea in the light of their new affirmation of innocence.

The largest single group of defendants (248) were basically fatalistic. They often verbalized weak suggestions of their innocence in rather halting terms, wholly without conviction. By the same token, they would not admit guilt readily and were generally evasive as to guilt or innocence, preferring to stress aspects of their stoic submission in their decision to plead. This sizable group of defendants appeared to perceive the total court process as being caught up in a monstrous organizational apparatus, in which the defendant role expectancies were not clearly defined. Reluctant to offend anyone in authority, fearful that clear-cut statements on their part as to their guilt or innocence would be negatively construed, they adopted a stance of passivity, resignation, and acceptance. Interestingly, they would in most instances invoke their lawyer as being the one who crystallized the available alternatives for them, and who was therefore the critical element in their decision-making process.

In order to determine which agent-mediator was most influential in altering the accused's perspectives as to his decision to plead or go to trial (regardless of the proposed basis of the plea), the same sample of defendants were asked to indicate the person who first suggested to them that they plead guilty. They were also asked to indicate which of the persons or officials who made such suggestion was most influential in affecting their final decision to plead. Table 2 indicates the breakdown of the responses to the two questions.

It is popularly assumed that the police, through forced confessions, and the district attorney, employing still other pressures, are most instrumental in the inducement of an accused to plead guilty.[25] As Table 2 indicates, it is actually the defendant's own counsel who is most effective in this role. Further, this phenomenon tends to reinforce the extremely ra-

## TABLE 2
### Role of Agent-Mediators in Defendant's Guilty Plea

| Person or Official | First Suggested Plea of Guilty | Influenced the Accused Most in His Final Decision to Plead |
|---|---|---|
| Judge | 4 | 26 |
| District attorney | 67 | 116 |
| Defense counsel | 407 | 411 |
| Probation officer | 14 | 3 |
| Psychiatrist | 8 | 1 |
| Wife | 34 | 120 |
| Friends and kin | 21 | 14 |
| Police | 14 | 4 |
| Fellow inmates | 119 | 14 |
| Others | 28 | 5 |
| No response | 8 | 10 |
| Total | 724 | 724 |

tional nature of criminal law administration, for an organization could not rely upon the sort of idiosyncratic measures employed by the police to induce confessions and maintain its efficiency, high production, and over-all rational legal character. The defense counsel becomes the ideal agent mediator since, as "officer of the court" and confidant of the accused and his kin, he lives astride both worlds and can serve the ends of the two as well as his own.[26]

While an accused's wife, for example, may be influential in making him more amenable to a plea, her agent-mediator role has, nevertheless, usually been sparked and initiated by defense counsel. Further, although a number of first suggestions of a plea came from an accused's fellow jail inmates, he intended to rely largely on his counsel as an ultimate source of influence in his final decision. The defense counsel, being a crucial figure in the total organizational scheme in constituting a new set of perspectives for the accused, the same sample of defendants were asked to indicate at which stage of their contact with counsel was the suggestion of a plea made. There are three basic kinds of defense counsel available in Metropolitan Court: legal-aid, privately retained counsel, and counsel assigned by the court (but may eventually be privately retained by the accused).

The overwhelming majority of accused persons, regardless of type of counsel, related a specific incident which indicated an urging or suggestion, during the course of either the first or second contact, that they plead guilty to a lesser charge if this could be arranged. Of all the agent-mediators, it is the lawyer who is most effective in manipulating an accused's perspectives, notwithstanding pressures that may have been previously applied by police, district attorney, judge, or any of the agent-mediators that may have been activated by them. Legal-aid and assigned counsel would apparently be more likely to suggest a possible plea at the point of initial interview as response to pressures of time. In the case of the assigned counsel, the strong possibility that there is no fee involved may be an added impetus to such a suggestion at the first contact.

In addition, there is some further evidence in Table 3 of the perfunctory, ministerial character of the system in Metropolitan Court and similar criminal courts. There is little real effort to individualize, and the lawyer's role as agent-mediator may be seen as unique in that he is in effect a double agent. Although, as "officer of the court" he mediates between the court organization and the defendant, his roles with respect to each are rent by conflicts of interest. Too often these must be resolved in favor of the organization which provides him with the means for his professional existence. Consequently, in order to reduce the strains and conflicts imposed in what is ultimately an overdemanding role obligation for him, the lawyer engages in the lawyer-client "confidence game" so as to structure more favorably an otherwise onerous role system.[27]

## CONCLUSION

Recent decisions of the Supreme Court, in the area of criminal law administration and defendant's rights, fail to take into account three crucial aspects of social structure which may tend to render the more libertarian rules as nugatory. The decisions overlook (1) the nature of courts as formal organizations; (2) the relationship that the lawyer-regular *actually* has with the court organization; and (3) the character of the lawyer-client relationship in the criminal court (the routine relationships, not those unusual ones that are described in "heroic" terms in novels, movies, and TV).

Courts, like many other modern large-scale organizations possess a

**TABLE 3**
**Stage at Which Counsel Suggested Accused Plead**
**(N = 724)**

| Contact | Counsel Type | | | | | | | |
|---|---|---|---|---|---|---|---|---|
| | Privately Retained | | Legal-aid | | Assigned | | Total | |
| | N | % | N | % | N | % | N | % |
| First | 66 | 35 | 237 | 49 | 28 | 60 | 331 | 46 |
| Second | 83 | 44 | 142 | 29 | 8 | 17 | 233 | 32 |
| Third | 29 | 15 | 63 | 13 | 4 | 9 | 96 | 13 |
| Fourth or more | 12 | 6 | 31 | 7 | 5 | 11 | 48 | 7 |
| No response | 0 | 0 | 14 | 3 | 2 | 4 | 16 | 2 |
| Total | 190 | 100 | 487 | 100* | 47 | 101* | 724 | 100 |

* Rounded percentage.

monstrous appetite for the cooptation of entire professional groups as well as individuals.[28] Almost all those who come within the ambit of organizational authority, find that their definitions, perceptions, and values have been refurbished, largely in terms favorable to the particular organization and its goals. As a result, recent Supreme Court decisions may have a long-range effect which is radically different from that intended or anticipated. The more libertarian rules will tend to produce the rather ironic end result of augmenting the *existing* organizational arrangements, enriching court organizations with more personnel and elaborate structure, which in turn will maximize organizational goals of "efficiency" and production. Thus, many defendants will find that courts will possess an even more sophisticated apparatus for processing them toward a guilty plea!

# NOTES

1. H. W. Jones, "A View from the Bridge," *Law and Society*, Supplement to summer 1965 issue of *Social Problems* 42 (1965). See G. Geis, "Sociology, Criminology, and Criminal Law," *Social Problems* 7 (1969): 40–47. N. S. Timasheff, "Growth and Scope of Sociology of Law," in *Modern Sociological Theory in Community and Change*, ed. H. Becker and A. Boskoff (New York: Holt, Rinehart, & Winston, 1957), pp. 429–49, for further evaluation of the strained relations between sociology and law.

2. This decision represented the climax of a line of cases which had begun to chip away at the notion that the Sixth Amendment of the Constitution (right to assistance of counsel) applied only to the federal government and could not be held to run against the states through the Fourteenth Amendment. An exhaustive historical analysis of the Fourteenth Amendment and the Bill of Rights will be found in C. Fairman, "Does the Fourteenth Amendment Incorporate the Bill of Rights? The Original Understanding," *Stan. L. Rev.* 2 (1949): 5–139. Since the *Gideon* decision, there is already evidence that its effect will ultimately extend to indigent persons charged with misdemeanors—and perhaps ultimately even traffic cases and other minor offenses. For a popular account of this important development in connection with the right to assistance of counsel, see A. Lewis, *Gideon's Trumpet* (New York: Random House, 1964). For a scholarly historical analysis of the right to counsel, see W. M. Beaney, *The Right to Counsel in American Courts* (Westport, Conn.: Greenwood, 1955). For a more recent comprehensive review and discussion of the right to counsel and its development, see Note, "Counsel at Interrogation," *Yale L.J.* 73 (1964): 1000–57.

With the passage of the Criminal Justice Act of 1964, indigent accused persons in the federal courts will be defended by federally paid legal counsel. For a general discussion of the nature and extent of public and private legal aid in the United States prior to the *Gideon* case, see E. A. Brownell, *Legal Aid in the United States* (Westport, Conn.: Greenwood, 1961); also R. B. von Mehren et al., *Equal Justice for the Accused* (1959).

3. In the case of federal defendants the issue is clear. In Mallory v. United States, 354 U.S. 449 (1957), the Supreme Court unequivocally indicated that a person under federal arrest must be taken "without any unnecessary delay" before a U.S. Commissioner where he will receive information as to his rights to remain silent and to assistance of counsel which will be furnished, in the event he is indigent, under the Criminal Justice Act of 1964. For a most interesting and highly documented work in connection with the general area of the Bill of Rights, see C. R. Sowle, *Police Power and Individual Freedom* (Chicago: Aldine, 1962).

4. See *N.Y. Times*, Nov. 20, 1965, p. 1, for Justice Nathan R. Sobel's statement to the

effect that based on his study of 1,000 indictments in Brooklyn, N.Y., from February–April, 1965, fewer than 10 percent involved confessions. Sobel's detailed analysis will be found in six articles which appeared in the *New York Law Journal,* beginning November 15, 1965, through November 21, 1965, titled "The Exclusionary Rules in the Law of Confessions: A Legal Perspective—A Practical Perspective." Most law enforcement officials believe that the majority of convictions in criminal cases are based upon confessions obtained by police. For example, the District Attorney of New York County (a jurisdiction which has the largest volume of cases in the United States), Frank S. Hogan, reports that confessions are crucial and indicates "if a suspect is entitled to have a lawyer during preliminary questioning . . . any lawyer worth his fee will tell him to keep his mouth shut," *N.Y. Times,* Dec. 2, 1965, p. 1. Concise discussions of the issue are to be found in D. Robinson, Jr., "Massiah, Escobedo and Rationales for the Exclusion of Confession," *J. Crim. L.C. & P.S.* 56 (1965): 412–31; D. C. Dowling, "Escobedo and Beyond: The Need for a Fourteenth Amendment Code of Criminal Procedure," *J. Crim. L.C. & P.S.* 56 (1965): 143–57.

5. Miranda v. Arizona, 384 U.S. 436 (1966).

6. Even under optimal circumstances a criminal case is a very much one-sided affair, the parties to the "contest" being decidedly unequal in strength and resources. See A. S. Goldstein, "The State and the Accused: Balance of Advantage in Criminal Procedure," *Yale L.J.* 69 (1960): 1149–99.

7. F. J. Davis et al., *Society and the Law: New Meanings for an Old Profession* (1962), p. 301; L. Orfield, *Criminal Procedure from Arrest to Appeal* (Westport, Conn.: Greenwood, 1947), p. 297.

D. J. Newman, "Pleading Guilty for Considerations: A Study of Bargain Justice," *J. Crim. L.C. & P.S.* 46 (1954): 780–90. Newman's data covered only one year, 1954, in a midwestern community, however, it is in general confirmed by my own data drawn from a far more populous area and from what is one of the major criminal courts in the country, for a period of 15 years from 1950–1964 inclusive. The English experience tends also to confirm American data, see N. Walker, *Crime and Punishment in Britain: An Analysis of the Penal System* (New York: Aldine, 1965). See also D. J. Newman, *Conviction: The Determination of Guilt or Innocence without Trial* (Boston: Little, Brown, 1966), for a comprehensive legalistic study of the guilty plea sponsored by the American Bar Foundation. The criminal court as a social system, an analysis of "bargaining," and its functions in the criminal court's organizational structure are examined in my book, *Criminal Justice* (Chicago: Quadrangle Books, 1967).

8. C. Feifer, *Justice in Moscow* (1965). The Soviet trial has been termed "an appeal from the pretrial investigation" and Feifer notes that the Soviet "trial" is simply a recapitulation of the data collected by the pretrial investigator. The notions of a trial being a "tabula rasa" and presumptions of innocence are wholly alien to Soviet notions of justice. "The closer the investigation resembles the finished script, the better" (p. 86).

9. For a concise statement of the constitutional and economic aspects of the right to legal assistance, see M. G. Paulsen, *Equal Justice for the Poor Man* (1964); for a brief traditional description of the legal profession, see P. A. Freund, "The Legal Profession," *Daedalus* (1963): 689–700.

10. I use the concept in the general sense that Erving Goffman employed it in his *Asylums: Essays on the Social Situation of Mental Patients and Other Inmates* (New York: Aldine, 1961).

11. A. L. Wood, "Informal Relations in the Practice of Criminal Law," *Am. J. Soc.* 62 (1956): 48–55; J. E. Carlin, *Lawyers on Their Own* (New Brunswick, N.J.: Rutgers Univ. Press, 1962), pp. 105–09; R. Goldfarb, *Ransom—A Critique of the American Bail System* (New York: Harper & Row, 1965), pp. 114–15. Relatively recent data as to recruitment to the legal profession and variables involved in the type of practice engaged in will be found in J. Ladinsky, "Careers of Lawyers, Law Practice, and Legal Institutions," *Am. Soc. Rev.* 28 (1963): 47–54. See also S. Warkov and J. Zelan, *Lawyers in the Making* (New York: Aldine, 1965).

12. There is a real question to be raised as to whether in certain organizational settings, a complete reversal of the bureaucratic ideal has not occurred. That is, it would seem

in some instances the organization appears to exist to serve the needs of its various occupational incumbents rather than its clients. A. Etzioni, *Modern Organizations* (Englewood Cliffs, N.J.: Prentice-Hall, 1964), pp. 94–104.

13. Three relatively recent items reported in the *N.Y. Times* tend to underscore this point as it has manifested itself in one of the major criminal courts. In one instance the Bronx County Bar Association condemned "mass assembly-line justice," which "was rushing defendants into pleas of guilty and into convictions, in violation of their legal rights." *N.Y. Times,* March 10, 1965, p. 51. Another item, appearing somewhat later that year reports a judge criticizing his own court system (the New York Criminal Court), that "pressure to set statistical records in disposing of cases had hurt the administration of justice." *N.Y. Times,* Nov. 4, 1965, p. 49. A third and most unusual recent public discussion in the press was a statement by a leading New York appellate judge decrying "instant justice" which is employed to reduce court calendar congestion "converting our courthouses into counting houses . . . as in most big cities where the volume of business tends to overpower court facilities." *N.Y. Times,* Feb. 5, 1966, p. 58.

14. R. L. Glasser, "The Confidence Game," *Fed. Prob.* 27 (1963): 47.

15. C. W. Mills, *White Collar* (New York: Oxford Univ. Press, 1951), pp. 121–29; Carlin, *Lawyers on Their Own.*

16. E. O. Smigel, *The Wall Street Lawyer* (New York: The Free Press, 1964), p. 309.

17. Talcott Parsons indicates that the social role and function of the lawyer can be therapeutic, helping his client psychologically in giving him necessary emotional support at critical times. The lawyer is also said to be acting as an agent of social control in the counseling of his client and in the influencing of his course of conduct. See T. Parsons, *Essays in Sociological Theory* (New York: The Free Press, 1954), p. 382 et seq.; E. Goffman, "On Cooling the Mark Out: Some Aspects of Adaptation to Failure," in *Human Behavior and Social Processes,* ed. A. Rose (1962), pp. 482-505. Goffman's "cooling out" analysis is especially relevant in the lawyer-accused client relationship.

18. The question has never been raised as to whether "bargain justice," "copping a plea," or justice by negotiation is a constitutional process. Although it has become the most central aspect of the process of criminal law administration, it has received virtually no close scrutiny by the appellate courts. As a consequence it is relatively free of legal control and supervision. But, apart from any questions of the legality of bargaining, in terms of the pressures and devices that are employed which tend to violate due process of law, there remain ethical and practical questions. The system of bargain-counter justice is like the proverbial iceberg, much of its danger is concealed in secret negotiations and its least alarming feature, the final pleas, being the one presented to public view. See A. S. Trebach, *The Rationing of Justice* (1964), pp. 74–94; Note, "Guilty Plea Bargaining: Compromises by Prosecutors to Secure Guilty Pleas," *U. Pa. L. Rev.* 112 (1964): 865–95.

19. For a conventional summary statement of some of the inevitable conflicting loyalties encountered in the practice of law, see E. E. Cheatham, *Cases and Materials on the Legal Profession,* 2nd ed. (1955), pp. 70–79.

20. Some lawyers at either end of the continuum of law practice appear to have grave doubts as to whether it is indeed a profession at all. Carlin, *Lawyers on Their Own,* p. 192; Smigel, *The Wall Street Lawyer,* pp. 304–05. Increasingly, it is perceived as a business with widespread evasion of the Cannons of Ethics, duplicity and chicanery being practiced in an effort to get and keep business. The poet, Carl Sandburg, epitomized this notion in the following vignette: "Have you a criminal lawyer in this burg?" "We think so but we haven't been able to prove it on him." C. Sandburg, *The People, Yes* (New York: Harcourt, Brace Jovanovich, 1936), p. 154.

Thus, while there is a considerable amount of dishonesty present in law practice involving fee-splitting, thefts from clients, influence peddling, fixing, questionable use of favors and gifts to obtain business or influence others, this sort of activity is most often attributed to the "solo" private practice lawyer. See A. L. Wood, "Professional Ethics among Criminal Lawyers," *Social Problems* (1959): 70–73. However, to some degree, large-scale "downtown" elite firms also engage in these dubious activities. The difference is that the latter firms enjoy a good deal of immunity from these harsh charges because of their institutional and organizational advantages, in terms of near monopoly over more desirable types of practice, as well as exerting great influence in the political, economic, and professional realms of power.

21. This does not mean that most of those who plead guilty are innocent of any crime. Indeed, in many instances those who have been able to negotiate a lesser plea have done so willingly and even eagerly. The system of justice-by-negotiation, without trial, probably tends to better serve the interests and requirements of guilty persons, who are thereby presented with formal alternatives of "half a loaf," in terms of, at worst, possibilities of a lesser plea and a concomitant shorter sentence as compensation for their acquiescence and participation. Having observed the prescriptive etiquette in compliance with the defendant role expectancies in this setting, he is rewarded. An innocent person, on the other hand, is confronted with the same set of rule prescriptions, structures, and legal alternatives, and in any event, for him this mode of justice is often an ineluctable bind.

22. "Any communicative network between persons whereby the public identity of an actor is transformed into something looked on as lower in the local scheme of social types will be called a 'status degradation ceremony.'" H. Garfinkel, "Conditions of Successful Degradation Ceremonies," *Am. J. Soc.* 61 (1956): 420–24. But contrary to the conception of the "cop out" as a "status degradation ceremony" is the fact that it is in reality a charade, during the course of which an accused must project an appropriate and acceptable amount of guilt, penitence, and remorse. Having adequately feigned the role of the "guilty person," his hearers will engage in the fantasy that he is contrite, and thereby merits a lesser plea. It is one of the essential functions of the criminal lawyer that he coach and direct his accused-client in that role performance. Thus, what is actually involved is not a "degradation" process at all, but is instead a highly structured system of exchange cloaked in the rituals of legalism and public professions of guilt and repentance.

23. The name is of course fictitious. However, the actual court which served as the universe from which the data were drawn is one of the largest criminal courts in the United States, dealing with felonies only. Female defendants in the years 1950 through 1964 constituted from 7–10 percent of the totals for each year.

24. My own data in this connection would appear to support Sobel's conclusion (see note 4), and appears to be at variance with the prevalent view, which stresses the importance of confessions in law enforcement and prosecution. All the persons in my sample were originally charged with felonies ranging from homicide to forgery; in most instances the original felony charges were reduced to misdemeanors by way of a negotiated lesser plea. The vast range of crime categories which are available facilitates the patterned court process of plea reduction to a lesser offense, which is also usually a socially less opprobious crime. For an illustration of this feature of the bargaining process in a court utilizing a public defender office, see D. Sudnow, "Normal Crimes: Sociological Features of the Penal Code in a Public Defender Office," *Social Problems* 12 (1964): 255–76.

25. Failures, shortcomings, and oppressive features of our system of criminal justice have been attributed to a variety of sources including "lawless" police, overzealous district attorneys, "hanging" juries, corruption and political connivance, incompetent judges, inadequacy or lack of counsel, and poverty or other social disabilities of the defendant. See A. Barth, *Law Enforcement versus the Law* (1963), for a journalist's account embodying this point of view; J. H. Skolnick, *Justice without Trial: Law Enforcement in Democratic Society* (New York: John Wiley & Sons, 1966), for a sociologist's study of the role of the police in criminal law administration. For a somewhat more detailed, albeit legalistic and somewhat technical, discussion of American police procedures, see W. R. LaFave, *Arrest: The Decision to Take a Suspect into Custody* (Boston: Little, Brown, 1965).

26. Aspects of the lawyer's ambivalences with regard to the expectancies of the various groups who have claims upon him are discussed in H. J. O'Gorman, "The Ambivalence of Lawyers," paper presented at the Eastern Sociological Association meetings, April 10, 1965.

27. W. J. Goode, "A Theory of Role Strain," *Am. Soc. Rev.* 14 (1960): 483–96; J. D. Snoek, "Role Strain in Diversified Role Sets," *Am J. Soc.* 71 (1966): 363–72.

28. Some of the resources which have become an integral part of our courts, e.g., psychiatry, social work, and probation, were originally intended as part of an ameliorative, therapeutic effort to individualize offenders. However, there is some evidence that a quite different result obtains than the one originally intended. The ameliorative instruments have been coopted by the court in order to more "efficiently" deal with a court's caseload, often to the legal disadvantage of an accused person. See F. A. Allen, *The Borderland of Criminal Justice* (Chicago: U. of Chicago Press, 1964); T. S. Szasz, *Law, Liberty and Psychiatry* (New York: Macmillan, 1963), and also Szasz's more recent, *Psychiatric Justice* (New York: Macmillan, 1965); L. Diana, "The Rights of Juvenile Delinquents: An Appraisal of Juvenile Court Procedures," *J. Crim. L.C. & P.S.* 47 (1957): 561–69.

# VI

# Solving the Problems of Business and Professional Deviance

## INTRODUCTION

There are several legitimate reasons why we are interested in the problems of business and professional deviance. Some of us may be so interested for practical reasons, such as how to avoid being victimized by such practices. Others may be interested because of what these problems tell us about the more general phenomena of deviance and social control or because of a desire to understand all facets of American society. But for virtually all of us, there is no doubt that examining the available evidence and appreciating all the complexities of business and professional deviance are *not* ends in themselves: we are also interested in *solving* these problems, if indeed they can be solved, and in learning what solutions have worked or failed in the past and those likely to work in the future. All of the chapters in Part VI address these concerns.

In "The Use of Criminal Sanctions in the Enforcement of Economic Legislation" (Chapter 16), Harry Ball and Lawrence Friedman discuss all of the complex and problematic features of trying to define what kinds of economic acts and economic sanctions are the potential candidates for official policy making in our society. While there is little evidence on this, they see as the central sociological question a concern for knowing how any given legal regulation affects the conduct of business and businessmen, how these are related to the prevailing values and moral sentiments in the community, and how this is related to the effectiveness of using sanctions to control economic activities. The little evidence bearing on this important question clearly shows there are no simple relations between individuals' attitudes or moral sentiments about laws and the extent to which they are likely to be effective (or effectively violated). Ball and Friedman seem to feel there are some grounds for thinking that using criminal sanctions for controlling economic activities might be more effective than for controlling "street crimes." But one of the major points in this debate is that we now possess very little empirical evidence to know what is likely to work or fail. Thus, for many years to come we will probably have to make these political decisions on the basis of our largely unverified commonsense knowledge about society, what might be effective, and so forth.

In Chapter 17 Gerald Seib gives us a brief account of a Dallas, Texas, ordinance aimed at curtailing automotive repair rip-offs, one which appears to have achieved some success. But Chapter 18 by Robert Wagman and Sheldon Engelmayer presents us with another account of how the official regulating processes can be corrupted by those they are mandated to audit and control, and thus emerges a "symbiotic relationship" between the controllers and the controlled. This reminds us, again, that mindless calls for uses of official state powers are most unlikely to achieve effective solutions and may even create other unintended problems. Finally, the last three chapters raise important questions about effective use of official sanctions for economic activities and analyze some possible resolutions to these dilemmas.

# 16

# *Criminal Sanctions in Enforcement of Economic Legislation*

*Harry V. Ball and Lawrence M. Friedman*

Concern over the use of criminal sanctions in the enforcement of business legislation is by no means new. As late as 1961, however, Whiting remarked that "the history of antitrust enforcement to date should not cause undue alarm to the corporate executive."[1] Two recent prosecutions have intensified the discussion and called Whiting's conclusion into question. In *United States v. McDonough Co.*[2] one president and three vice-presidents of several comparatively small garden tool manufacturing firms[3] received 90-day jail sentences and a fine of $5,000 for deliberate price fixing and market rigging. The defendants entered pleas of *nolo contendere.* The government felt that a fine would be "a sufficient deterring factor"; the defendants argued against a jail sentence, pointing out that no jail sentence had been imposed in *nolo contendere* cases during the 59-year life of the Sherman Act.[4] The judge ignored both the government and the defendants. His position was that Congress would not have provided for imprisonment in the original act and retained it thereafter unless that penalty was intended to be used whenever a sentencing court believed jail sentences proper.

In the second and more famous case, the *Electrical Equipment Antitrust Cases,*[5] the government demanded jail sentences in several instances. Moreover, the prosecutor asked the court to refuse pleas of *nolo contendere* from the individual defendants. The government argued that acceptance of such pleas "would neither foster respect for the law nor vindicate the public interest" in the light of the fact that the grand jury's indictments "charging violations of rigging and price-fixing as serious as any instances ever charged in the more than half a century life of the Sherman Act."[6] The judge agreed. The sentences imposed included, in addition to fines and probation seven straight sentences to imprisonment for 30 days and 31 suspended sentences for various periods. The court described the de-

From *Stanford Law Review*, 17 (1965): 197. Copyright 1965 by the Board of Trustees of the Leland Stanford Junior University.

fendants' conduct as a "shocking indictment of a vast section of our economy" that "flagrantly mocked the image of the economic system of free enterprise which we profess to the country and destroyed the model which we offer today as a free-world alternative to state control and eventual dictatorship."[7] Later the Attorney General of the United States classified the defendants' conduct as "a serious threat to democracy."[8]

On the other hand, many major newspapers paid little or no attention to the convictions and sentences;[9] some critics of the prosecution saw "ominous overtones" in the fact that men had been sent to jail for "something that has been going on for years as an accepted business practice"[10]; and a convicted president of one of the 29 accused corporations questioned the right of the government to enact such "regulations," much less to send a person to jail for their violation, and asserted that "price stabilization" was an essential element of "free enterprise."[11]

Perhaps these price-fixing (price-stabilizing) and market-rigging (market-stabilizing) cases are not typical of the broader class of criminal-penal laws regulating business. The defendants knew they were violating the law, they acted in secret collusion, huge sums of money were involved, and the Justice Department strove mightily to equate the conduct in the second case to a fraud against the government. Quite different are mine-run violations of regulations affecting business, especially those involving strict liability where intentional violation is not an essential element of the crime. At least these may raise more clearly the problem of what Professor Sanford Kadish has called "moral neutrality."[12] The issue is whether severe criminal sanctions ought to be imposed on those who violate the legal but not the moral code. In the view of Kadish and others, a key factor in any discussion of the propriety and effectiveness of the use of criminal sanctions in enforcing business regulations is the relationship between prevailing morality and the norms of the criminal law. Are economic crimes morally wrong? If they are, should men be sent to jail for committing them? Even the price-fixing cases raise the issue, though in a slightly different form.

This essay is an attempt to explore the relationship between popular morality and the use of criminal sanctions in regulating business practices. We shall begin by setting forth some basic distinctions necessary for a sociological analysis of the problem.

First, when we speak of using criminal sanctions, we may be referring to more than one meaning of the term *use*. One may distinguish between (a) *authorization* by the legislature of the employment of criminal sanctions, and (b) their *application* by the administrator. That is, the law may be said to "use" a sanction when a statute authorizes its use; in a second sense, the sanction is "used" only when it is actually applied. Discussing antitrust laws, for example, one might debate whether it is proper to append criminal sanctions for violations of the regulations at all; and even those who concede that it is proper may question whether it is right to unsheath the sword in particular cases. Thus, those who are distressed because even a small proportion of the implicated officials of the electrical industry were imprisoned are probably opposed to any authorization of criminal sanctions in regulating business affairs; they can hardly argue that these particular offenders merited any special leniency. On the other hand, persons who complained because criminal sanctions are rarely invoked in mine-run antitrust cases and who look upon this as an indication of favoritism to "white-collar criminals" are questioning the administration of the sanctions while conceding—or even urging—the propriety of their authorization. Problems of the legislative authorization of criminal sanctions and problems of the administrative decisions to apply the sanctions ought to be analyzed separately.

Secondly, what do we mean by the term "criminal sanctions"? Statutes aimed at economic regulation often provide multiple, alternative sanctions. Sometimes mandatory sequences of use are prescribed. The sanctions may include cease-and-desist orders (enforced through contempt proceedings), injunctive divestiture proceedings, awards of damages or treble damages, monetary fines or forfeitures (which may or may not involve imprisonment for nonpayment), seizures of goods, revocations of business or occupational licenses, prison sentences, and probation with a threat of fine or imprisonment for the violation of probation. Of these, some classes of fines, direct imprisonment, and probation with threat of fine or imprisonment for the violation of the conditions of probation are generally considered "criminal" sanctions.

However, fines or money forfeitures are widely used also as sanctions in actions formally classified as "civil proceedings." Criminologists generally approve of the use of fines as a sanction for violation of laws punishing deliberate, calculated, antisocial "profit making," because the fine divests the violator of his profits; it is a penalty which plausibly can be said to deter profit-making misconduct.[13] However, this defense of the propriety of the fine fails to distinguish a criminal fine from a civil forfeiture or from treble damages or other forms of punitive damages, which may also deter. One may, of course, ask whether money penalties are appropriate sanctions against a business organization; and there are other subsidiary questions, e.g., should the state or the victim receive the money?[14] But such questions are irrelevant to a discussion of whether the sanction of a money penalty should be "civil" or "criminal." Therefore, when one asks whether certain conduct should be subject to criminal sanctions, one is not asking whether the conduct should be subject to a money penalty. The civil law "punishes" breach of contract and torts with damage awards, but no one imagines that money damages here are criminal sanctions. For these reasons we are eliminating the fine or money penalty from our consideration of criminal sanctions.

When discussion is directed to the question of the use of "criminal" sanctions, then, the issues raised are essentially these: (a) Must the evidence establish the defendant's guilt beyond a reasonable doubt, and shall the defendant be entitled to all the procedural safeguards of criminal law? (b) Shall the defendant and his conduct be publicly labeled as criminal? (c) Shall the defendant, upon conviction, be subject to imprisonment or conditional probation with the threat of loss of liberty for violation of the conditions?

Finally, what is the meaning in this context of "economic regulation"? Professor Kadish feels there is more than one kind of economic regulation and limits his discussion of enforcement problems to regulations "which impose restrictions upon the conduct of business as part of a considered economic policy."[15] He would exclude "regulations directly affecting business conduct which are founded on interests other than economic ones; for example, laws regulating the conduct of business in the interest of public safety and general physical welfare."[16] He is concerned with those regulations intended "to protect the economic order of the community against harmful use by the individual of his property interest" and whose "central purpose . . . is to control private choice, rather than free it," in contrast to the "traditional property offenses," intended to "protect private property interests against the acquisitive behavior of others in the furtherance of free private decisions."[17] Thus, he is concerned with violations of "such laws as price controls and rationing laws, antitrust laws and other legislation designed to protect or promote competition or prevent unfair competition, export controls, small loan laws, securities regulations, and, perhaps, some tax laws."[18] For such offenses the "nature of the interest protected is by definition unique."[19]

Professor Kadish certainly has the right to specify these types of regulation, and for his purposes they may constitute a unitary category. However, his reasons for isolating them—the uniqueness of the protected interest and their origin as part of a considered economic policy—cannot be defended upon empirical grounds. Let us test some of his examples in the light of his claimed differentiae.

For Professor Kadish, the economic crime par excellence is the antitrust violation. The text of the Sherman Antitrust Act reflected legislative awareness of existing common-law doctrine concerning restraint of trade.[20] The enactment of a much-debated federal criminal statute on the subject owed more to political forces and theories operating in the late nineteenth century than it did to economic theory, policy, or ideology. The primary interest involved was and is "the emergence of the modern corporate organization as presenting a problem in the distribution of power," the continuing problem of individual freedom of choice,[21] and the functioning of democratic processes in a society where large corporations had tremendous wealth and power, including political power.[22] The basic problem has been and is "that of the control of the conduct of the business organization rather than a problem of preserving 'competition.' "[23] This was clearly recognized at the time of the enactment of the Sherman Act by proponents and opponents alike. William Graham Sumner, for example, opposed "federal interference" because he was firmly convinced that industrial "bigness" was economically desirable[24] *and* that government was too weak to resist being taken over by a business plutocracy if it sought to interfere with the trusts.[25] Arguably, considered economic policy entered the picture when the courts rejected arguments based on bigness per se and explicitly read the concepts of reasonableness[26] and control into federal antitrust law.[27] "Dissolution is not a penalty but a remedy" to be employed only "if the industry will . . . need it for its protection."[28] Economic policy in its purest form entered the arena not as the primary purpose of the legislation but as an alleviation against its strictness in the face of good faith on the part of the regulated. Much of the vagueness of antitrust regulation must be ascribed not to efforts to restrict business but to efforts to prevent the use of the "political" Sherman Act to hamstring productive efficiency.

Laws regulating maximum prices or rents represent the same basic situation. They are necessary to restrict the power of persons to use property in ways contrary to the public interest because some emergency condition has eliminated the freedom of the normal market. The crisis situation is viewed as a general threat to national health, safety, and welfare—even survival. In such a situation extraordinary powers are assumed by the agents of the politically organized community against, for example, "speculative, unwarranted and abnormal increases in rents, exactions of unjust, unreasonable, oppressive rents and rental agreements, overcrowding occupation of uninhabitable dwellings, speculative, manipulative and disruptive practices by landlords of housing accommodations, and other acts and conditions endangering the public health, safety, welfare and morals" of the community while allowing, "at the same time, to landlords, fair and equitable rents."[29] Private housing has, in the legislature's opinion, become vested with a public interest.[30] Where the distribution of power pertinent to the larger interests is not an issue—as in Honolulu during the Korean War where the rents charged workers in company housing were established as part of the collective bargaining agreement between the plantation corporations and the ILWU—the government is likely to adopt a hands-off policy.

The preceding also suggests the difficulty of maintaining Professor Kadish's claimed distinction between "economic" laws which are part of "considered economic policy" and "economic" laws relating to health and physical safety. In which category, for instance, belong the laws limiting the employment or the hours of work of women and children? These were propounded as health laws, to be sure, but another important factor was a considered economic policy giving job preference to male heads of households over the competition of women and children.[31] In general, "considered economic policy" and health and safety factors are inextricably bound together in the history of all types of regulation. For example, occupational licensing and similar laws are curious mixtures of economic policy and health and safety measures. The Wisconsin barber statute makes it unlawful "for any barber to use any instrument or article that has not been disinfected in accordance with . . . sanitary standards"; but the statute makes it equally unlawful to "advertise a definite price for any barbering service by means of displaying a sign containing such prices so that the same is visible to persons outside the barbershop."[32] The two sections of this law are, to be sure, analytically separable; but the whole statute is animated by one spirit, in which an economic aim (protecting barbers from competitors) is mixed with a public-welfare aim (improving sanitary conditions of public barbershops).

In short, Kadish's attempt to distinguish the "economic" from other forms of regulation produces numerous inconsistencies. Thus, a rent-control law directed against unjust rents is viewed by Kadish as referring to morally neutral behavior and as part of a considered economic policy; a tenement-house law that requires minimum standards of quality, regardless of the amount of rent, is presumably a health measure. In similar fashion, that part of most rent-control laws which makes it criminal for a landlord to seek to evict an existing tenant under certain circumstances would also be a regulation of morally neutral behavior. But how would Professor Kadish classify an "open occupancy" statute that makes it criminal for a landlord to discriminate on the basis of race in the initial selection of tenants?

Moreover, it is even difficult to distinguish Kadish's "pure" form of economic crimes from his "traditional property offenses." These offenses, such as robbery, blackmail, forgery, and passing worthless checks, were intended, in his words, to protect property interests "against the acquisitive behavior of others," so as to further "free private decisions."[33] To say that the traditional property offenses protect property (and thus aid private decisions) begs the question. These offenses are part of the system by which the legal order *defines* what objects and interests a particular social system chooses to protect as property.[34] All social systems protect property as they define it; in so doing they map out what types of economic exchanges are protected (these they further) and what types are not (these they discourage). In our present society you may induce a young lady to break her date and instead to go out with you on Saturday night. This is no crime (so long as she is over a certain age and you do not entice her from her family for immoral purposes); nor does it give her initial date a basis for civil action, for he had no property right in her agreement to attend the movies with him. In fact, you, the aggressor, have the benefit of the protection of the law from any physical intimidation by the first young man to keep you from "stealing his girl." But it is a crime to steal a wristwatch, a ten-dollar bill, or the sexual privileges of another man's wife. The noncriminality of inducing a girl to break a date (in legal terms, the fact that one cannot have a property interest in a rendezvous) frees private citizens to engage in vigorous courtships and vigorous competition for eventual wives and sweethearts. Laws against adultery prevent or attempt to control the exercise of "free private decisions" in competition for sexual privileges by establishing property rights.[35] Adultery is a form of trespass.

The traditional property offenses take their definition of property from the underlying assumptions of a given society and seek to use the criminal law to channel economic behavior along lines consistent with these assumptions. Therefore, they are arguably the product of considered economic policy, though so rooted in the social order that no one actually bothers much to consider them. The traditional criminal law has always aimed at regulating economic exchanges in the broadest sense. Most offenses against property (and even offenses against persons) apply social controls to limit or otherwise regulate the manner in which economic exchanges may take place, the terms of sale, and the type of commodity which may legitimately form the subject matter of a sale. Whether or not one has a marketable property interest that he may offer to another for purchase or whether he has merely a "possession" that he may not lawfully offer for sale is often a matter of the criminal law.

So, for example, you are not allowed to make a person buy his reputation ("blackmail"). The criminality of blackmail represents a social judgment that one may not manipulate as an income-producing asset knowledge about another person's past; you may not sell to that person forbearance to use your knowledge of his guilt. If, on the other hand, you acquire knowledge of a person's illustrious ancestry, or use in business the skills necessary to ascertain the ancestry of others, you may set yourself up as a genealogist and bargain with others on the basis of your skill or information. The difference between a genealogist and a blackmailer—between a genteel and a criminal profession—reflects a difference in the notions of legitimate exchange within our society. In other societies, of course, the criminal law adopts a quite different definition of what is and what is not a legitimate exchange.[36] Even within our own society, subtle distinctions are made among types of economic exchange which are criminal, those which lead to civil penalties only, and those which lead to no penalties at all but are positively encouraged by the legal order. The distinctions may at times appear anomalous. In Wisconsin if you give a worthless check to a tavern owner, you may be criminally responsible for your act, even though you are drunk on liquor he has sold you, and even though he continues to sell liquor to you on the strength of the "credit" of your check. If, however, you buy liquor on open credit from this same tavern owner, he may not even collect his debt from you through regular civil court processes. Credit sales of liquor are against public policy, and liquor debts, like gambling debts, are unenforceable. However, much of the apparent anomaly of this situation is reduced when the researcher finds that it is also criminal for a tavern owner knowingly to serve a certified alcoholic or allow him to be served.[37]

In short, Kadish's attempt to distinguish the "traditional property offenses" from his pure "economic policy" offenses turns out to be an instance of circular reasoning. The basic difference is presumably found in the fact that the traditional offenses are naturally associated with a "stigma of moral reprehensibility," while the economic offenses are "morally neutral." But he asserts that the traditional offenses possess this natural association in part precisely because they are criminal under traditional categories of crime. This seems to mean at its core that his "morally neutral" conduct is so simply because it is newly proscribed behavior.[38] Kadish adds, however, that the new crimes are morally neutral also because they "closely resemble acceptable aggressive business behavior." But the key word here is *acceptable*. Throughout one finds the hidden assumptions that business conduct not included in traditional property offenses was by definition not considered unethical or morally reprehensible, and, conversely, that all conduct proscribed by traditional property offenses is currently considered unethical or morally reprehensible. But this is precisely one of the central issues to be discussed in considering the relationship between popular morality and the criminal law relative to economic regulation.

This means that defining a pure category of economic crimes is of little value to a sociological examination of the use of criminal sanctions regulating economic transactions. It is more fruitful to begin with a broader inquiry: How does any given legal regulation affect the conduct of business and businessmen, what is its relationship in this regard to the prevailing morality, and what are the implications of this relationship to the use (in both senses) of criminal sanctions?

In pursuing this inquiry we do not assume that there are any pure "economic crimes." Some criminal statutes, like the Sherman Act, regulate the conduct of businessmen exclusively or almost so. Others, like price-control laws, regulate business transactions and control the conduct of both businessmen and nonbusinessmen, for example, consumers. Still others only rarely have special relevance to a businessman in the conduct of his business, e.g., laws against murder.[39] To deny that there is a category of pure economic crimes is not to say that laws against murder and laws against monopoly do not reflect different social forces in their inception, diffusion, moral basis, and enforceability. But it does mean that these matters should be resolved by empirical evidence and not by definition.

## LEGAL REGULATION, BUSINESS CONDUCT AND PREVAILING MORALITY

We have shown the futility of looking for pure economic crimes and have framed our inquiry in terms of the relationship between specific legal regulations, business conduct, prevailing morality, and criminal sanctions.

By "prevailing morality" we mean the current attitudes of the public (or any relevant portion of the public) toward given courses of conduct in specified circumstances. The circumstances must be given close attention. For example, a study[40] of various samples of the population of Akron, Ohio, in the mid-1930s indicated that prevailing opinion did not believe it "wrong" for West Virginia coal miners to steal coal from inoperative mines for their own use, though it was thought "wrong" if the theft were for resale for profit. It was overwhelmingly recognized that in both instances the taking was a crime. On the other hand, the populace believed it "wrong" for a corporation to close its plant and move to another community because of a strike, though it was widely recognized that such a course of action was legal. As one might expect, the opinions varied with the position of the individual in the social structure of the community.

Clearly it is important to learn which segments of the population determine the prevailing morality on any given issue. In discussions of what "ought" to be the relationship between morality and criminal law, a number of different supposedly important "publics" have been designated. Some writers have placed special emphasis upon enforcement administrators, especially judges, while others have spoken in vague terms, e.g., of the offender's "fellow men."[41] Kadish appears to be talking mostly about the public of the "regulated." Another writer has referred to "majority feelings of disgust or revulsion in the community."[42] Another has, in addition to distinguishing the administrators, sought to divide citizens into the regulated, the militant regulators, and the indifferent.[43] At least it is clear that communities, in generating standards of morality, are not to be considered as sets of isolated individuals; rather, communities are made up of persons of varying statuses and group memberships.

What is the evidence concerning the relationship between compliance with economic regulation and approval or disapproval of the regulation by the regulated? Here the general regulation of a specified area of conduct should be distinguished from particular rules or restrictions in effect at a particular point in time. We shall first consider attitudes toward general regulation. This is a relevant consideration, since the degree of approval reflects the attitude of the regulated toward the moral justification of the regulation.

The few empirical studies that have been made fail to indicate any simple relationships between the general attitudes of businessmen toward a given area of regulation and the willingness or propensity of businessmen to violate the regulations. Robert E. Lane, in his study of compliance with a wide range of governmental regulations, concluded that "there was no tendency to react against a wide range of laws, no evident general anti-regulation animus, at any one time," and that it was "the position of the firm, rather than any emotional qualities of its management, which led it to violate."[44] A study of rent-control violations in Honolulu in 1952 found no relationship between the attitude of a landlord toward the "necessity" of continued rent control and the likelihood that the landlord would violate the legal maximum rent of any particular rental unit. The study concluded that "opposition to legal rent control, as such, did not appear to play any systematic role in the act of ceiling violation."[45] Finally, in the *Electrical Equipment Cases* many company officials who actively participated in the violations believed price fixing was wrong, and there is no evidence that any substantial number of the violators believed it was right (although for a variety of reasons many thought it necessary in the circumstances).

These studies make only a negative point, that compliance and non-compliance are not wholly determined by whether persons subject to regulation approve of it—i.e., whether they deem the regulation consistent with their moral code. The extent to which compliance is related to approval, however, ought to be taken into account.[46] Regulatory laws are directed toward businessmen (just as laws against murder are directed toward members of society generally), and businessmen constitute the "public" within which compliance must be measured. To be sure, there is a wider "public" for purposes of measuring support for enforcement. Thus complete and intransigent refusal by businessmen to obey might lead to more than collapse of regulation; severe social conflict might result if the narrower "public" (businessmen) refused to obey regulatory laws widely supported by the broader "public" (the general population). Moreover, the studies indicate that "disapproval" of laws by the regulated does not necessarily result in defiance and rebellion. Grumbling acceptance of the income tax, food and drug laws, and the Clayton Act may serve the purposes of the legal order perfectly well; wild enthusiasm for regulatory measures is not necessary.

Empirical evidence tends, therefore, to show that moral approval by the regulated is not a *necessary condition* of general compliance. It is also true that general compliance—even coupled with deep public moral support—does not of itself mean that application-use of criminal sanctions (as defined above) is an appropriate technique to insure achievement of the social ends underlying given regulations with maximum efficiency. This fact is often recognized in discussion of certain sexual crimes, such as adultery, fornication, and consensual homosexuality. The general public condemns such sexual conduct and most people comply with the law. Yet arguments are continually and powerfully advanced against punishing these acts through criminal processes.[47] These arguments will be familiar to most readers. Essentially, it is argued that enforcement does more harm than good; for example, it encourages blackmail, snooping, arbitrary and unfair punishment of unlucky or unpopular offenders, and overzealous police work.

What underlies these arguments can be highlighted by considering a less flamboyant example, nonsupport of children. Here too the failure of the criminal law bears directly on the problem of economic regulation and the criminal process. Our "prevailing morality" does, of course, condemn a person's willful failure to provide support for his children; a man who neglects his children is guilty of highly immoral conduct in the eyes of the public. Most people sacrifice heavily to provide advantages for their children, and judges in good conscience vigorously denounce offenders. Yet the problem of nonsupport shows no sign of vanishing. Correctional administrators complain that child-support offenders fill too many jail cells; welfare administrators do not want to require mothers receiving Aid-to-Dependent-Children benefits to take legal action against nonsupporting fathers, feeling that such action would handicap their programs. Increasingly, law and administration seek devices to induce public condemnation of nonsupport with noncriminal sanctions (or at least without felony conviction).[48] Here again the use of criminal sanctions does not seem to provide an adequate solution to problems raised by conduct clearly condemned by prevailing morality.

It is easy to see why the "use" of criminal sanctions (in our second sense of "use") may actually impede the attainment of the ends supported by public policy and morality. The criminal law is more than a set of propositions, more than a moral code, more than a catalog of rights and wrongs. A set of precepts and definitions lies at the heart of the criminal law; but criminal law is also a technique, a mechanism; and it is administered through highly organized institutions. Criminal justice does not consist only of penal statutes; it is also judges, bailiffs, sheriffs, policemen, district attorneys, jails, work-houses, courtrooms, files, fingerprints. Violation of the criminal law may bring the violator into contact with at least a part of this complex apparatus. Any realistic discussion of the application-use of criminal sanctions must take into account the impact on the accused of one of the law's most effective sanctions: the bringing of the accused into contact with the enforcement institutions of the criminal law. The difficulty with the use of criminal sanctions in child-support cases is the impeding effect of exposing the violator to the apparatus of the criminal law; its repressive and cumbersome techniques may interfere with the goals of persuasion, negotiation, and voluntary compliance on the part of the erring father.

This does not mean that making an act formally criminal may not have, in some cases, subtle aftereffects. Labeling conduct as "criminal" may change the public attitude toward the man who breaks the law as well as the attitudes of those who are themselves tempted to break the law. We shall examine these aftereffects later. For the present, it is enough to note that there is no necessary connection between the label "crime" and public morality; nor between the forces which tend to induce compliance with statutory precepts. Criminal law, particularly as it relates to economic crime, is a set of techniques to be manipulated for social ends.

The history of criminal law is in fact a history of the reasons why techniques of criminal-law enforcement have been brought to bear in particular areas to advance social goals. One factor dictating the use of criminal sanctions has been unduly ignored in most treatments of crime. This is the fact that the cost of enforcing the criminal law is borne by the state and that the initiation of criminal process and its administration are conducted by servants of the state. This is, in fact, a major social distinction between criminal and noncriminal law. To say that breach of contract is not a crime is not a statement about the morality of breach of contract, though we may consider breach of contract highly immoral under certain circumstances. Liability for breach of contract in the twentieth century has been imposed in some situations where the prior law did not impose liability, because of popular feelings that certain kinds of breach of contract are "unfair" (that is, immoral) and should therefore give rise to liability.[49] The use of the concept of "unjust enrichment" affords a good illustration. The noncriminal nature of breach of contract means that the initial decision to "punish" a man who breaches his contract lies in the private sector and is, in fact, the exclusive decision of the man whose contract has been breached. In addition, once the aggrieved party decides to pursue his action in court, he must bear the expenses himself (though he hopes to recover some of them if he wins). He must hire his own lawyer and make arrangements to pay him. The state provides judges and courtrooms as a service; but the state has no interest in whether the plaintiff chooses to terminate his case before judgment or whether he chooses to levy execution on the goods of the defendant after judgment. The victim of theft, on the other hand, does not hire the state to punish the thief. It is generally true of theft that the state will not prosecute unless a private citizen complains. But there are many areas of criminal law where this is not so. Murder is an obvious example.[50]

We do not suggest that the only difference between criminal law and noncriminal law is that the former has socialized the process of enforcement, but this is an important distinction between the two areas, particularly with respect to economic regulation. Often the morality or immorality of proscribed conduct has little to do with whether the law labels the conduct criminal or leaves enforcement in private hands.

A striking example is usury. In Wisconsin,[51] for example, usury was considered a socially dangerous and immoral practice by most of the population, as far as we can judge, through most of the nineteenth century. It was not, however, a crime. It was discouraged by severe civil penalties under some of the statutes; under one statute, based on a New York model, the usurer was barred from recovering either principal or interest and thus might lose the entire amount of his loan.[52] Common statutory provisions called for treble damages, as in modern antitrust law. Provisions for punitive or multiple damages tend to encourage (and are meant to encourage) private enforcement. But since usury was punished only by civil sanctions, penalties inured to the private citizen who pursued his remedy. He made the choice of suing or not suing, and he saw the matter through the courts.

In 1895 usury was made a crime in Wisconsin, punishable by fine.[53] It would be a rash assumption to say that usury became a crime because in 1895 a heightened sense of the immorality of usury suddenly gripped the public. The true explanation is more subtle. In the Middle West of the nineteenth century, usury had been primarily a problem of the rate of interest on farm mortgages. By the turn of the century it became preeminently a problem of urban consumption loans. Those who suffered from usury were unable to handle enforcement themselves because of their social and economic status. Loans were small; the borrowers were in large measure landless urban workers, many of them foreign born. By contrast, the farmers in the 1850s and 1860s had had a larger voice in the affairs of the community and had been willing, to judge from court records, to enforce the usury laws. Making usury a crime was thus a legislative judgment that it was best to socialize remedial action, not because of the immorality of usury, but because under existing social conditions civil enforcement had failed.

Lending money at interest is an economic act; and usury is an economic wrong under the law of the American states. The historical development just related demonstrates that the progression from civil to criminal sanctions does not necessarily represent any change in the moral status of the act proscribed. Usury was stamped with immorality both before and after it was made criminal in Wisconsin.

It is probably more typical of economic regulatory crimes that the forbidden conduct is not considered "immoral" either before or after the imposition of criminal sanctions. Statute books are filled with economic crimes whose congruence with popular morality is either completely absent or so muted that one need not consider it. Take, for example, the Wisconsin statute which makes it a crime for any publicly supported hospital to "furnish to its inmates or patrons . . . any oleomargarine."[54] Offenders are liable to be fined "not to exceed $200 or imprisoned in the county jail not to exceed 6 months, for the first offense"; for subsequent offenses, fines may range up to $500, with imprisonment "not less than 30 days nor more than 6 months."[55] The origins and purposes of the statute are perfectly obvious; but it is dubious to assert that it arose out of popular *morality*;[56] and whether the public brands the purveyor of oleomargarine to patients in public (as opposed to private) hospitals with any special obloquy is even more dubious. Another Wisconsin statute forbids the sale of baking powder unless the label lists the ingredients, is printed "in the English language, with black ink, in type not smaller than eight point, bold-faced, Gothic capitals," and contains "the name and address of the manufacturer of such baking powder, and the words: 'This baking powder is composed of the following ingredients and none other.' "[57] This crime bears the same penalties as the crime of giving oleomargarine to hospital patients. There may be considerable popular revulsion against the selling of poisonous or harmful or deceptive foods; but surely neither before nor after the passage of the act were there any deep wellsprings of disgust against selling imported baking powder with a French label in small type-faces, or printed in green ink instead of black. The purpose of the act is regulatory; as in the case of the criminal usury law, administrative considerations probably led to the choice of criminal sanctions. Theoretically, the state could give the buyer of baking powder which did not conform to statutory standards a civil action for damages, or the right to rescind his purchase. This would certainly fail to accomplish the purpose of the statute, since the buyer of a small amount of baking powder would never bother to sue the seller. The individual transactions which form the subject of this legislation are too trivial for civil enforcement to effectuate the state's policy in regard to baking powder. The criminal law is here used as an administrative technique, as a way of socializing the costs of enforcement, which are too great for individuals profitably to bear.

Frequently, however, the general criminal processes will prove too cumbersome and inefficient to attain the state's policy goals. The next step is to vest responsibility for enforcement and administration in an administrative agency. Although mislabeling of baking powder formally remains a crime in Wisconsin, one can be fairly certain that enforcement and policing of baking-powder labels (if any) is carried out by the staff of the appropriate executive department or agency, not by the district attorneys of the various counties.

The shift to administrative enforcement takes place partly because criminal sanctions drag with them all the traditional safeguards surrounding the defendant. Proof beyond a reasonable doubt, trial by jury, and other forms of protection are required. The socialization of remedies thus has the dysfunctional result of making large-scale enforcement difficult for reasons irrelevant to the purpose of making the proscribed acts criminal.[58] Thus, transfer to an administrative agency is likely to occur as soon as such an agency is available.[59] The criminal sanctions remain as threats —they are "used" in the sense of being authorized, but no longer "used" in the sense of wholesale application to offenders.

It is not, however, only the administrators of economic regulation who sharply distinguish between their authorization to invoke criminal sanctions and the selective application of these sanctions; nor is it only the guardians of the Sherman Act who hesitate to imprison all violators. We are coming more and more to recognize how highly selective is the process by which criminal sanctions are actually invoked. All criminal sanctions are "administered" by the officials responsible for law enforcement. Even classic crimes of violence and immorality—murder, robbery, arson—are administered by public officials. Often only flagrant cases receive the full treatment. But the full treatment also serves as a threat, to induce compliance by voluntary means. The existence of criminal sanctions applicable to the proscribed conduct warns the potential offender of the availability of the full treatment, but officials are free to use lesser means or no means as the situation may demand. Thus, the administration of criminal justice is in many ways analogous not only to the criminal aspects of economic regulation, but even to noncriminal regulation by administrative agencies. In general, criminal justice involves the delegation of large areas of discretion to the administrator.[60] Almost anything that can be said about vagueness, uncertainty, and selectivity of enforcement in economic regulation by administrative agencies can also be said about the traditional areas of criminal law. Statutes creating administrative regulation often admit frankly that vast discretion is vested in the administrators —they use such terms as "public interest, convenience, and necessity."[61] Although the traditional criminal law does not specify that enforcement is selective,[62] this difference is largely a matter of form. Statutes which set up administrative agencies are almost never content to give these agencies rule-making and civil enforcement power; the statutes almost invariably add a catch-all section making violation of the statute or of the rules and regulations of the agency a crime. Like all criminal statutes, these administrative criminal laws leave the process of selection in the hands of administrators, even though no explicit mention is made of the fact.[63]

The purpose of providing for criminal sanctions is at least twofold. First, it adds dimension to the full treatment available. This strengthens the agency's position by giving it one more weapon. Flagrant, unpopular violators of the law or the rules can be told they may go to jail, or at least face the obloquy, the annoyance, the physical restraints of the criminal process. Secondly, the criminal section of the statute enables the agency to use, when necessary, the general law enforcement machinery of the state. Of course the agency will invoke criminal sanctions only in exceptional cases. A criminal trial is a slow process, heavily laden with procedural safeguards for the defendant. It is not only the business community which is chary of criminal sanctions; the administrators themselves avoid them for the same reasons that lead welfare workers to deplore excessive use of criminal law in nonsupport cases. But the fact that the agency may not wish to use the criminal process often is no reason to deny them the power to invoke it in the proper case; thus, legislatures regularly *authorize* criminal sanctions and thereby create new regulatory crimes.

## INTERACTIONS BETWEEN CRIMINAL LAW AND BUSINESS CONDUCT

Historically, growth in the number of regulatory crimes represents a broadening of the techniques for the enforcement of state policy. Nevertheless, the word "crime" has symbolic meaning for the public, and the criminal law is stained so deeply with notions of morality and immorality, public censure and punishment, that labeling an act criminal often has consequences that go far beyond mere administrative effectiveness. As noted in our discussion of criminal sanctions generally, imprisonment or threat of imprisonment and the public stigma of the criminal process are the real issues about which the discussion of criminal sanctions in regulating business revolves. It is generally accepted today that fear of criminal prosecution is an effective deterrent to businessmen, professional men, and the middle class.[64] It follows that criminal sanctions ought to be highly effective in dealing with economic crimes. Also, noncriminal sanctions are presumably made more effective if the threat of criminal prosecution lurks in the background. The study of rent control in Honolulu already alluded to provides some confirmation. The study found that some landlords wanted to violate legal ceiling rents. However, they did not do so because they were afraid of criminal prosecution. When they found out that under current policy "collusive" violations of ceilings (those agreed upon by both landlord and tenant) were not prosecuted, these landlords tended to enter into just such collusive arrangements.[65]

The very effectiveness of criminal sanctions in restraining the behavior of businessmen accounts in large part for the concern over the use of criminal-penal sanctions in regulating business. Businessmen abhor the idea of being branded criminals. Society does not particularly care whether murderers and rapists like being branded as criminals; but businessmen, after all, form a large, respectable, and influential class in our society. Therefore, effectiveness of the penal sanction in this case leads to pressure against use of the sanction. The phenomenon is a general one; middle-class persons resent being "treated like a criminal," no matter what legal rule they may violate. But rules acquire legitimacy through being adopted in the regular processes utilized in society for making rules. The legitimacy of rules derives from the use of a standardized process of adoption, as much as or more than from the subject matter with which the rules deal. Americans in general accept the proposition that it is "wrong" to violate the law, even if they feel the law acts unwisely when it prohibits certain conduct. The very fact that a criminal statute has been enacted by the legislature is a powerful factor in making the proscribed conduct illegitimate in the eyes of a potential actor, even when the actor disagrees with the purpose of the law.

Lane has suggested that there are no generic differences between the factors which produce violations of economic regulatory law and the factors which produce other criminal acts.[66] If this is true, then economic regulation through the use of criminal sanctions poses a real dilemma for society and for the businessman. The businessman may find himself impelled toward crime; he recognizes the legitimacy of the laws which define the crime he is tempted to commit; yet he cannot concede that he is a criminal. We tend to view the criminal as a person who violates laws which we cannot see ourselves violating. In the phraseology of Harry Stack Sullivan, the criminal is that person whom we perceive from the standpoint of our own self-system as "not-me."[67] In other cases, the criminal is the person who violates rules which we can imagine ourselves violating (or have violated in the past) but which we see as part of our "bad-me"; "There but for the Grace of God go I." We are willing to condemn the conduct of the "bad-me" as "wrong," but are not likely to agree to the imposition of sanctions we feel are too severe. This attitude emerges toward such crimes as drunk driving and statutory rape (where the victim is a girl who looks much older than she is).[68] Many people who condemn drunk driving and statutory rape have the uncomfortable feeling that these are crimes they have committed, are likely to commit, or could commit. The result is a tendency to distinguish between the conduct (which we condemn) and the person (with whom we readily sympathize).[69] In the case of some economic crimes, juries have found it convenient to convict the corporation (a fictional entity) rather than the human conspirators. This seems to have occurred in some price-fixing trials, to the bewilderment of legal commentators.[70] The distinction between person and conduct is particularly important in economic crimes, since these are often crimes which the businessman can see himself violating, even when he admits that violation is wrong and ought to be prevented—if for no other reason than that the law ought to be obeyed.

Obviously, distinguishing between the person and the conduct depends upon whether one identifies with the person. A stern, church-going teetotaler cannot readily sympathize with drunk drivers. He may see drunk driving not as an act committed by the "bad-me" but as one committed by the "not-me," more like murder, arson, and rape. Nonbusinessmen may similarly fail to understand business temptations. Public clamor in a form distinctly hostile to business aspirations lies at the source of some regulation of business with criminal sanctions. The outcry against the trusts which led to the Sherman Act is a good example. An official of General Electric can understand more readily how it is possible to be tempted down the primrose path of price fixing than can a factory worker. The factory worker, particularly if he has leftist leanings, may classify price fixing and restraint of trade with theft, murder, and rape. We need not confine ourselves to factory workers. Sutherland, a distinguished academic, talks about restraint of trade as a crime in the same tone one might use in speaking of murder or theft;[71] he does not seem to recognize that a roomful of Philadelphia lawyers cannot always advise a soap company whether it is criminal to buy another soap company—while any sane person would know that it is a crime to rob a stranger's house.

The difficulty of categorizing the behavior of businessmen as criminal or noncriminal does not mean that restraint of trade cannot be a "crime" in the same sense as burglary—the electrical price-fixing case, for one, proves that it can. The defendants in effect put on masks, jimmied open windows, and stole the people's money. There are crimes and there are crimes. For the mine-run economic crime, it is easy to see why the sanctions of the criminal law are not often employed. We have mentioned some reasons already; there are others. As Sutherland has pointed out, law enforcement is in the hands of members of a social class who are likely to sympathize with the businessman.[72] The nonuse of criminal sanctions to enforce antitrust laws, for example, is a consequence of the institutionalizing of a program which was originally the product of genuine popular outrage. The clamor against "the trusts" can be compared with the clamor against sex criminals, murderers, and those who plant bombs in airplanes. Ultimately, however, state and federal governments created enforcement and administrative agencies staffed with personnel who tended to treat with some understanding the problems of the businessmen whose businesses were regulated. Even when antitrust law is vigorously enforced through civil sanctions, e.g., cease-and-desist orders, the choice of such civil sanctions reflects the fact that the administrators are able to sympathize with the business position; they readily separate the "conduct" from the "person." This may well be another reason for the neglect of criminal sanctions in antitrust regulation, except for flagrant cases of willfulness and stealth. (This genuine sympathy is above and apart from another, admittedly potent, factor inducing sympathetic behavior, namely, the fact that regulators often end up in the employ of the companies they formerly regulated.)

Thus the "moral neutrality" of regulatory crimes arises out of a number of factors to which writers like Professor Kadish may give insufficient weight. The businessman can hardly be blamed for failing to sense as an abhorrent crime the commission of an act which is forbidden in or pursuant to a regulatory statute in which criminal sanctions have been authorized but which historically have not been used except in flagrant cases. Nor can he be blamed for failing to sense as "criminal" acts made criminal only in order to socialize the remedial process. But tensions and conflicts arise because of lack of understanding of these facts by the broader public and because, as noted above, the authorization of criminal sanctions may initiate a process of interaction between law and prevailing morality.

Some general features of this process of interaction are worthy of note here. The aim of regulatory law is to secure compliance by the regulated. Criminal sanctions are a technique to insure compliance. Compliance, however, can be viewed in two lights, short- and long-run compliance. When a program of economic regulation is adopted, the attention of the legislature is usually fixed on problems of short-run compliance. The symbolic value of law as law, the fact that most people want to obey the law and will do so, has important consequences for long-run compliance. American social scientists generally agree that social sanctions can be employed deliberately to modify modes of social action—not only overt behavior, but also cognitive, affective, and conative attitudes. Less technically put, social sanctions can be used to change beliefs, attitudes, and personal values and goals; they can effectuate policy considerations by influencing what a person thinks he ought to do or what he wants to do in a particular situation.

William Graham Sumner said, "Men can always perform the prescribed act, although they cannot always think or feel prescribed thoughts or emotions."[73] But he added that by changing conduct one induces new "experiences" that effect further changes in thoughts and emotions. The key technique is to maintain a sustained demand for "strict compliance with detailed and punctilious rule."[74] Legal institutions are therefore particularly appropriate vehicles for effecting changes in thoughts and emotions in the long run. The law may specify clear and unambiguous requirements, may provide a vigorous enforcement program, and can be equipped to maintain a long-continuing effort. Some authorities have suggested that administrative regulation is an especially useful tool for bringing about social change—it permits detailed specification of required conduct; it can modify the rules to plug loopholes as attempts at evasion appear; and it has great flexibility to adopt tactics and allocate resources toward enforcement of its regulations.[75]

Underlying these propositions is the assumption that people tend to think that what they do is the right thing to do, even if they began to do so because they were forced to. Eventually they begin to expect similar conduct from others and, indeed, are eager to impose it upon others. As conduct becomes formalized, it lays an ideological basis for the extension of similar social norms to situations that are perceived in "analogous" terms. Ironically, some of the participants in the electrical price-fixing case reported that they first experienced price fixing when they served as industry representatives in federal price-control programs during World War II.[76] Less dramatically, filing income tax returns and carrying drivers' licenses have become so commonplace that the public probably accepts these "customs" and, by and large, believes strongly that they are proper.

Other social scientists, however, disagree with the proposition that people learn to want to do what they have to do. Reinhard Bendix, for example, stresses how variable are the effects of coercion on personality.[77] How a person will react to a requirement that he do something he thinks wrong and does not want to do, depends on his whole arsenal of psychological resources. Certainly people are not sheep; the countless revolutions and civil wars of human history are proof enough that law does not always convert its subjects. But surely there is some tendency for persons to provide "public justifications" for what they are actually doing.[78] Thus the public morality must be under some pressure to correspond with required conduct. We should not be surprised to find an intergenerational "drift" toward increased moral justification of required conduct.

The phenomenon of intergenerational drift is probably particularly important in the case of "economic crimes." A major factor in determining whether this drift toward justification takes place is the extent to which public officials appreciate the distinction between criminal law as technique and criminal law as a reflection of popular morality. Again we may use the antitrust laws as an example of economic legislation which arose out of profound and passionate feelings of public outrage. The passion which attended the birth of the Sherman Act has certainly subsided.

At any rate, control of the trusts is no longer a major political issue. Yet antitrust laws have not become dead letters, because they have been handed over to federal agencies which have increasingly buttressed the statutes with relatively precise regulations and have built up bureaucratic structures to enforce these laws. Business, for its part, has learned to live with the antitrust laws, whatever reservations business has as to the wisdom of these laws. The businessman knows generally that these laws exist; he is accustomed to consult lawyers who advise him on the legality of proposed mergers and acquisitions; he frequently modifies his behavior in ways which take the laws into account.

Some criminal statutes, however, have become dead letters because they have not become highly institutionalized. When the moral outrage which set them in motion subsides, they lose their vitality. The classic case is that of the colonial blue laws. These laws were vigorously enforced because the society which created them believed in them passionately: men informed on their neighbors; local courts and magistrates rigorously enforced laws against Sabbath-breaking, adultery, card-playing, disobedience to parents, and fornication.[79] Formal administrative techniques were neither needed nor used; the whole society involved itself in seeking out violators and bringing them before the bar of public opinion and legal punishment. When the passion subsided, the laws ceased to be enforced, since there was no administrative structure charged with enforcement. This, then, is the point of Sumner's emphasis on the "detailed and punctilious rule"; it is only that kind of rule, when institutionalized and formalized, that can give rise to a custom capable of surmounting the loss of passion.

The electrical price-fixing cases are unusually interesting in that they seem to foreshadow a rebirth of passion in the relatively colorless field of antitrust law. The wide publicity, the newspaper harangues, the human interest stories, and the rash of lawsuits which followed in their wake certainly dramatized the antitrust laws and disturbed many businessmen. In the price-fixing case—as in "show trials" in general—the criminal law was used, whether deliberately or not, to influence behavior by the use of the mechanisms of law enforcement most open to public view—the trial, the preachments of the prosecutors, the sermons delivered by the judge. The public participated in these trials, directly (on juries, for example) and indirectly as spectators, newspaper readers, and radio and television audiences. The effect sought in such cases is twofold: first, to warn and deter those who might violate the law; second, to rekindle in the public a sense of the immorality of the defendants' acts. But it was the quality of flagrancy and stealth, combined with the magnitude of the crime, which made a "crackdown" possible. And at the same time it alerted the business community and its apologists to the dangers inherent in the mere *authorization* of criminal sanctions. This danger lies in the discretion vested in the administrators—the danger of selective use of these powerful sanctions for reasons not justified on grounds of administrative efficiency. It is precisely the same danger which some have seen in the "misuse" of tax law to put gangsters in jail, the abuse of laws against fornication, the application of trespass laws against Negro sit-in demonstrators, and the "persecution" of Communists through the use of laws which originally had nothing to do with Communism. But these are problems not peculiar to regulatory crimes; they are problems of government generally, of bureaucracy generally, the general problem of fairness in the use of administrative discretion.

It is equally clear that these are not problems peculiar to the use of *criminal* sanctions, since similar problems are raised by the variable administration of zoning laws, the "unfairness" of the licensing process, and the inequities involved in government subsidies and penalties in general. The sanctions (positive and negative) which are available to a legal system range in a continuum from cash grants on one end to death in the electric chair on the other. Historical and social realities dictate the authorization and application of sanctions (criminal and civil) in legal regulations, depending upon the ends to be achieved, the class of persons to be affected, and the behavior sought to be influenced. At every point in the process of choosing and using sanctions questions are raised—moral questions, empirical questions, questions of ends and means. Criminology in general has given up the search for general theories of "crime" and general theories of "criminal sanctions." This is all to the good; what is needed is not a theory of "crime" (let alone a theory of "economic crime") but theories of human behavior. It is not likely (at least at this stage of the development of social science) that a theory will be found to describe and predict human behavior accurately enough to fit the murderer, the corporate monopolist, the mislabeler of baking powder, and the trespasser on public grass (to mention only "criminals"). Discussions of the use of sanctions in economic regulation—whether the discussants are lawyers or social scientists—ought properly to begin by delineating exactly what sanctions and types of economic regulation are under debate.

## NOTES

1. Whiting, "Antitrust and the Corporate Executive," *Va. L. Rev.* 47 (1961): 929, 981.
2. 1959 Trade Cas. 75882 (S.D. Ohio).
3. Although the firms were "relatively small," together they controlled between 60% and 80% of the $50,000,000-per-year market. *Time*, Dec. 21, 1959, p. 76.
4. "So firmly had the custom become entrenched of imposing no heavier a penalty than a fine on a businessman entering a plea of *nolo contendere* to a charge of price-fixing or market-rigging in collusion with rivals that such a limitation of the penalty had come to be widely regarded as tantamount to a private right." Watkins, "Electrical Equipment

Antitrust Cases—Their Implications for Government and for Business," *U. Chi. L. Rev.* 29 (1961): 97, 100 n.7.

5. United States v. Westinghouse Elec. Corp., 1960 Trade Cas. 76753 (E.D. Pa.)

6. *Ibid.,* p. 76754.

7. N.Y. *Times,* Feb. 7, 1961, p. 26, col. 3.

8. TV Interview with Attorney General Robert Kennedy (quoted in J. Fuller, *The Gentlemen Conspirators* (1962), p. 176).

9. The *New Republic,* Feb. 20, 1961, p. 7.

10. This phrase is taken from a letter received by the Department of Justice after the close of the case. See J. Herling, *The Great Price Conspiracy* (Westport, Conn.: Greenwood, 1962), pp. 291-97.

11. This individual also stated: "No one attending the gatherings was so stupid he didn't know the meetings were in violation of the law. But it is the only way a business can be run. It is free enterprise." Fuller, *The Gentlemen Conspirators,* p. 14.

According to the sentencing judge, this particular executive, whom he held to be "the sole authority for price fixing" by his corporation and sentenced to pay a fine of $7,500, would have been sentenced to jail except for his and his wife's ill health and advanced age. Herling, *The Great Price Conspiracy,* p. 217.

12. Kadish, "Some Observations on the Use of Criminal Sanctions in Enforcing Economic Regulations," *U. Chicago L. Rev.* 30 (1963): 423. Kadish defines "morally neutral behavior" as conduct to which "the stigma of moral reprehensibility does not *naturally* associate itself" *because* "it is not criminal under traditional categories of crime and, apart from the regulatory prescription, closely resembles acceptable aggressive business behavior" (pp. 425–27, emphasis added).

13. *Model Penal Code* § 6.03, at 22, comment (Tent. Draft No. 2, 1953).

14. It is not inconceivable that a *civil* statute could provide for some or all of the "damages" recovered to go not to the plaintiff but to the state. Just such a provision was sometimes found in the 19th-century civil usury statutes, e.g., Minn. Gen. Stats. 1878, ch. 23, § 3, which provided that a plaintiff-borrower kept only one-half of the usurious interest he recovered in his suit against the lender; the other half went to the county treasurer for the use of schools.

15. Kadish, "Use of Criminal Sanctions in Enforcing Economic Regulations," p. 424.

16. *Ibid.* Kadish also excludes "laws indirectly affecting business conduct by their general applicability; for example, embezzlement, varieties of fraud and related white-collar offenses."

17. *Ibid.,* p. 425.

18. *Ibid.,* p. 424.

19. *Ibid.,* p. 427. Beyond this, Professor Kadish concedes that the other defining properties of the conduct proscribed by these regulations are not unique and do not necessarily distinguish it from other conduct that is "criminal." This includes his criterion of "morally neutral behavior." Other characteristics that such conduct shares or may share with other criminal conduct include: "the conduct is engaged in by persons of relatively high social and economic status; since it is motivated by economic considerations, it is calculated and deliberate rather than reactive; it is usually part of a pattern of business conduct rather than episodic in character; and it often involves group action through the corporate form (pp. 425–26).

20. "[T]he words of the Statute were chosen so as to disrupt existing patterns of conduct in the least possible degree. Words of the common law were resorted to in order to describe the conduct to be prohibited and it could be safely assumed that the courts, with the respect for precedent characteristic of the judicial process in the nineteenth century, would limit themselves to established common law doctrine in applying the Statute. The net effect would be merely to make acts involving restraint of trade monopolizing, as they were known at common law, subject to federal jurisdiction." K. Carlston, *Law and Structures of Social Action* (1956), p. 194. *Cf.* Letwin, "Congress and the Sherman Antitrust Act, *U. Chi. L. Rev.* 23 (1955): 221, 240–47.

21. "The issue of the possession of power by the corporate organization is the one central issue in the meaning of the terms 'freedom' and 'competition,' the necessity of

keeping the door open to alternatives of action by the individual, to an effective choice among the groups in which he may participate." Carlston, *Law and Structures of Social Action,* p. 210.

22. See generally Adams, *Relation of the State to Industrial Action* (1887).

23. Carlston, *Law and Structures of Social Action.*

24. Sumner, "The Concentration of Wealth: Its Economic Justification," in *Social Darwinism: Selected Essays,* ed. Persons (1963), pp. 150, 153.

25. Sumner, "Democracy and Plutocracy," in *ibid.,* pp. 136, 143–49.

26. See Standard Oil Co. v. United States, 221 U.S. 1, 60 (1911); United States v. American Tobacco Co., 221 U.S. 106, 179 (1911).

27. United States v. Corn Prods. Ref. Co., 234 Fed. 964 (S.D.N.Y. 1916).

28. United States v. Aluminum Co. of America, 148 F.2d 416, 446 (2d Cir. 1945).

29. *Honolulu, Hawaii, Ordinances* No. 941, § 11 (1951).

30. *Cf.* Block v. Hirsh, 256 U.S. 135, 155 (1920).

31. See J. Commons and J. B. Andrews, *Principles of Labor Legislation,* 4th rev. ed. (Clifton, N.J.: Kelley, 1936), p. 97: "[M]en workers undoubtedly believed that restrictions on the hours of women and children would result in decreased employment of these classes of wage earners, with consequent advantages to themselves."

32. *Wis. Stat.* §§ 148.04 (a), (14) (1961).

33. Kadish, "Use of Criminal Sanctions in Enforcing Economic Regulations," p. 424.

34. "Property is essentially the distributive system in its static aspect. It consists of the rights and duties of one person or group (the owner) as against all other persons and groups with respect to some scarce good. It is thus exclusive, for it sets off what is mine from what is thine; but it is also social, being rooted in custom and protected by law." K. Davis, *Human Society* (New York: Macmillan, 1948), p. 452.

35. See the discussion of "Sexual Property as an Institution," *ibid.,* pp. 175–94.

36. In the Soviet Union in recent years, the imposition of severe—even capital—punishment reveals how seriously the Soviets view certain types of economic exchange which in the United States are engaged in by money brokers and bankers who enjoy wealth, prestige, and high social position. Thus, speculation in foreign exchange is (since 1961) a capital offense under certain circumstances. Lipson, "Execution: Hallmark of Socialist Legality," *Problems of Communism,* No. 5 (United States Information Agency, 1962), pp. 21, 24–25.

37. *Wis. Stat.* §§ 176.26 .28, 304.22, 943.24 (1961).

38. As Morris Cohen observed in 1940 in a discussion of Garofalo's concept of natural crime, "Now if all these [e.g., prostitution, political crimes, smuggling] are not natural crimes, our prisons contain very many who have not committed any natural crime, while many who practice *gross cruelty and improbity in business* or elsewhere are not in prison at all." Cohen, *Reason and Law* (1950), p. 25. (Emphasis added.)

39. The ideal type of traditional, nonregulatory, noneconomic crime is "murder." However, the prevailing morality and the norms of the criminal law may fairly be said to condemn most severely precisely that form of murder which most closely resembles aggressive business conduct, i.e., cold, calculated murder for money, a businessman murdering his partner or competitor, a hired assassin of the "Murder, Inc." type, or a husband killing his wife to collect insurance.

40. A. W. Jones, *Life, Liberty and Property: A Study of Conflict and a Measurement of Conflicting Rights* (New York: Octagon Books, 1941).

41. H. M. Hart, "The Aims of the Criminal Law," *Law & Contemp. Prob.* 23 (1958): 401, 437.

42. Hughes, "Morals and the Criminal Law," *Yale L.J.* 71 (1962): 662, 682.

43. Llewellyn, *Jurisprudence: Realism in Theory and Practice* (Chicago: U. of Chicago Press, 1962), p. 403.

44. Lane, *The Regulation of Businessmen—Social Conditions of Government Economic Control* (1954), p. 106.

45. Ball, "Social Structure and Rent Control Violations," *Am. J. of Sociology* 65 (1960): 598, 604.

46. *Cf.* the discussion of the relationship between "personal predispositions" and "situa-

tional pressures" as these affect violations of the code of ethics of members of the New York metropolitan bar, in Carlin, "Social Control in the Legal Profession," Aug. 1963 (unpublished paper presented at the meetings of the American Sociological Association, Los Angeles, California, Aug. 28, 1963).

47. See *Model Penal Code* § 207.5, at 276–78, comment (Tent. Draft No. 4, 1955).

48. Note the interesting provisions of the *Uniform Act on Abandonment*, e.g., *Wis. Stat.* § 52.05(4) (1961): "Before the trial with the consent of the defendant, or at the trial, on entry of a plea of guilty, or after conviction, instead of imposing the penalty hereinbefore provided or in addition thereto, the court in its discretion . . . shall have the power to make an order . . . directing the defendant to pay a certain sum weekly, semimonthly, monthly, or as the circumstances may permit, for a period not exceeding 2 years, to the wife or to the guardian . . . and . . . to release the defendant from custody on probation for the period so fixed, upon . . . recognizance. . . ." There is also a tendency to treat nonsupport under misdemeanor and local ordinance provisions.

49. Conversely, the common-law courts refuse to enforce contracts which "are such as to injuriously affect, or subvert, the public interests" (without giving rise necessarily to criminal responsibility). See, e.g., Johnson v. Fargo, 184 N.Y. 379, 384, 77 N.E., 388, 390 (1906), refusing to enforce an employee's agreement in consideration of his employment by an express company, to abstain from suing his employer for personal injury damages.

50. The state may take measures to encourage the reporting of crimes committed (through payments to informers, for example); it may also take such measures by neutralizing the negative economic impact of punishment on those who are not the guilty parties. An excellent example of this is the provision found in some pre-Civil War slave codes of the South, compensating the owner of a slave executed for a capital offense, e.g., Va. Code 1849, ch. 212, § 9, at 789: "The value of a slave condemned and executed . . . shall be paid to the owner out of the treasury." No provision, of course, is made in the present law to encourage the families of persons guilty of serious crime to "inform" against the accused. This is because of the obloquy in which informers are held and the high social value placed on family cohesion, regardless of circumstance—factors which were totally lacking in the master-slave relationship.

51. See generally Friedman, "The Usury Laws of Wisconsin: A Study in Legal and Social History," *Wis. L. Rev.* (1963), 515.

52. 1851 Laws Wis., ch. 172, § 6, at 170.

53. 1895 Laws Wis., ch. 327, at 673.

54. *Wis. Stat.* § 97.47(1) (1961).

55. *Wis. Stat.* § 97.72(3) (1961).

56. See Abrahamson, "Law and the Wisconsin Dairy Industry: Quality Control of Dairy Products (1838–1929)" (S.J.D. thesis in University of Wisconsin Law School Library, June 1962), pp. 182–90.

57. *Wis. Stat.* § 97.63 (1961).

58. See Carlston, *Law and Structures of Social Action*, pp. 219–20: "[S]o long as the Sherman Act was considered as a criminal instead of a regulative statute, the trial problems of proving intent and abuse of power would tend to frustrate control and limit the sphere of application of the statute. Hence some new and simpler means must be found for obtaining jurisdiction over the defendant for purposes of regulating his business conduct. . . ."

59. See Friedman, "The Usury Laws of Wisconsin," p. 565.

60. See generally Remington and Rosenblum, "The Criminal Law and the Legislative Process," *U. Ill. L.F.* (1960): 481–99.

61. E.g., Communications Act Amendments, 1960, § 4, 74 Stat. 889, 47 U.S.C. § 309(a) (Supp. V, 1964) (radio license applications to the FCC).

62. Typically, criminal statutes are cast in the following form: "Whoever causes the death of another human being with intent to kill that person or another *shall* be sentenced to life imprisonment." *Wis. Stat.* § 940.01(1) (1961). (Emphasis added.) Nothing is said in the statute about discretion to look for, catch, and prosecute the killer. Of course this discretion exists—though in practice the police, the prosecutors, and the

judges distinguish among crimes (e.g., between murder, which tends to be vigorously investigated and prosecuted, and petty larceny, which may or may not be). In the quoted statutory provision, the word "shall" refers primarily to the absence of discretion in sentencing. The Wisconsin criminal code now usually uses the word "may" in its substantive provisions, e.g., "Whoever causes great bodily harm to another human being by conduct imminently dangerous to another and evincing a depraved mind, regardless of human life, *may* be imprisoned not more than 10 years." *Wis. Stat.* § 940.23 (1961). (Emphasis added.)

63. For example, in Wisconsin, where the licensing of real-estate brokers is within the province of the Real Estate Brokers' Board, the Board has extremely broad powers to determine the qualifications of brokers, to license them, and to revoke their licenses. Yet "any person" who "violates any provision of this chapter, shall be fined not less than $25 nor more than $5,000 or imprisoned not less than 10 days nor more than 6 months or both." *Wis. Stat.* § 136.16(1) (1961).

64. "[S]evere punishments . . . may be footless in preventing crimes of passion. But when the question is one of urging the great well-meaning public into conduct which happens to be slightly inconvenient, severe punishments in the offing—known to be in the offing—are capable of effect." Llewellyn, *Jurisprudence*, pp. 403–04.

65. Ball, "A Sociological Study of Rent Control and Rent Control Violations" (Ph.D. thesis at University of Minnesota, June 1956).

66. Lane, *The Regulation of Businessmen*, p. 107.

67. H. Sullivan, *The Interpersonal Theory of Psychiatry* (New York: W. W. Norton, 1953), pp. 162–64.

68. This distinction between the "conduct" and the "person" probably accounts for the divergent attitudes of judges and juries toward statutory rape and drunk driving recounted in Broeder, "The University of Chicago Jury Project," *Neb. L. Rev.* 38 (1959): 744, 749–50.

69. When a jury returns a verdict of "not guilty by reason of insanity," it is also distinguishing between the conduct and the person.

70. See, e.g., Comment "Increasing Community Control over Corporate Crime—A Problem in the Law of Sanctions," *Yale L.J.* 71 (1961): 280, 292–93 n. 50. In at least one instance, a judge dismissed charges against convicted individuals while allowing the verdict to stand against their corporate employer, causing the government to complain that "the court in effect is establishing the principle that there can be violation of the antitrust laws without the intervention of any human agency." Hadlick, *Criminal Prosecutions under the Sherman Anti-Trust Act* (1939), pp. 170–71.

71. See generally F. Sutherland, *White Collar Crime* (New York: Holt, Rinehart, & Winston, 1949).

72. *Ibid.*, pp. 46, 247–48; see M. Clinard, *The Black Market* (Montclair, N.J.: Patterson Smith, 1952), p. 232; Newman, "White Collar Crime," *Law & Contemp. Prob.* 23 (1958): 735, 739.

73. Sumner, *Folkways* 67 (1907).

74. Ball, Simpson, and Ikeda, "Law and Social Change: Sumner Reconsidered," *Am. J. Sociology* 68 (1962): 532, 538–39.

75. Rose, "The Use of Law to Induce Social Change," *Transactions of the Third World Congress of Sociology* 6 (1956): 52; J. Greenberg, *Race Relations and American Law* (New York: Columbia U. Press, 1959), pp. 1–30.

76. R. A. Smith, "The Incredible Electrical Conspiracy," *Fortune*, April 1961, pp. 132, 136.

77. Bendix, "Compliance Behavior and Individual Personality," *Am. J. Sociology* 58 (1952): 292, 302.

78. See generally Brehm and Cohen, *Explorations in Cognitive Dissonance* (1962).

79. See generally G. Haskins, *Law and Authority in Early Massachusetts* (Hamden, Conn.: Shoe String Press, 1960) (study of the interrelationship of law and society in the Massachusetts Bay Colony during its first decades).

# 17

# Dallas Ordinance against Car Repair Frauds

*Gerald F. Seib*

Just four days after a tuneup, including new spark plugs, and other repairs costing $173, the 1970 Pontiac Catalina stalls on the street here. Edward Meeks, called to the scene by the Pontiac's angry owner, looks over the engine, then spins out a spark plug and fingers its corroded tip.

"It's been a while since these were new," he finally says. Considering the source, that's a serious accusation. Mr. Meeks is an investigative supervisor for the Dallas Department of Consumer Affairs; he is charged with enforcing an auto-repair ordinance that local officials contend is the toughest attempt yet by a city to crack down on dishonest auto mechanics.

Since the Dallas ordinance was passed three years ago, Mr. Meeks and three assistants have handled over 10,000 complaints from people like the Pontiac's owner who suspect foul play at the repair shop. Some 191 of these complaints have been serious enough to warrant prosecution, while many more have been settled outside the courtroom; city authorities say Mr. Meeks and his staff recover almost $3,000 for consumers every month.

## PERSISTENT PROBLEM

Of course, auto repairs long have been a source of controversy throughout the country. Sen. Wendell Ford, a Kentucky Democrat who heads the Senate Consumer Subcommittee, says that letters about auto repairs make up "the single largest category of complaints" that the panel receives. In a recent Louis Harris survey, senior business managers were asked to pick the industry they thought should receive the most attention from the consumer movement: the auto-repair industry was named more often—44 percent of the time—than any other.

Federal Trade Commission officials, meanwhile, estimate that of the $40 billion spent annually on auto repairs in the U.S., $12 billion goes for unnecessary work. In addition, observers say the problem is as sensitive as it is large. "Motor-vehicle repairs are a very emotional concern because of the role of the automobile," explains Charles Vincent, director of the Dallas consumer-affairs department. In a city like Dallas, he says, "everybody has at least one car, and maybe two or three."

Dallas, along with 17 states and a handful of cities and counties, decided to combat auto-repair problems with special legislation. The Dallas auto-repair ordinance, modeled after a California statute, makes it illegal for mechanics to charge for repairs never made or to make unnecessary repairs. It also requires shops to buy a $50 license and to provide customers with written estimates, schedules of charges, and detailed invoices.

As soon as the ordinance was on the books, consumer complaints began "coming in piles," says Mr. Meeks, a 44-year-old trained mechanic who ran a garage with his father for 20 years here before taking the city job. Almost 100 complaints now stream in weekly.

## AN HONEST MISTAKE

Many reflect shoddy workmanship, honest mistakes, or simple misunderstandings—areas in which the law is of modest help. One woman, for example, recently complained that her compact car began running poorly shortly after she had paid to have it tuned up. She suspected that the tuneup hadn't been performed, but Mr. Meeks found that the shop merely had installed the wrong spark plugs.

One-fourth of the complaints, however, reflect attempts to defraud car owners, Mr. Meeks estimates. "The degree of fraud is what surprised me," he says. "When they charge you for a complete transmission rebuild and they don't do anything, that's pretty brazen."

Consider the experience of a Mexico City man who brought his expensive French Citroen to Autos Unique, located on Dallas's Ross Avenue, for a variety of repairs. He returned twice in the next two months to get the car, but each time he was told that the parts hadn't arrived. On the third trip, accompanied by his own mechanic, the man got his car and a bill for $850.

Upset, the man contacted Mr. Meeks, who along with the private mechanic dismantled the Citroen and found that four parts included on the repair bill hadn't been replaced. The proof: Citroen parts are painted in color codes, but the ones in question had been buffed down to their shiny metallic surface in an apparent attempt to make them look new. In December 1975, the shop's owner, Charles V. Plummer, pleaded no contest in a Dallas municipal court on four counts of charging for parts that weren't delivered. Mr. Plummer, who couldn't be reached for comment, was fined $400, and his auto-repair license was revoked by the city for two years. The car owner, however, didn't get his $850 back.

## GRIMY DETECTIVE WORK

Fraud isn't always so easy to detect. A Dallas resident, E. J. Howell, began to suspect that he never got the camshaft bearings and push rods he had bought from Authorized Motor Exchange when his engine's old problem, an inadequate oil supply, cropped up again after a visit to the Dallas shop. He and Mr. Meeks took the engine apart to inspect the bearings, and they discovered a small piece of felt blocking the oil's path. Had the shop disassembled the engine to install the bearings and rods, they reasoned, the obstruction would have been discovered.

In August 1976, the shop's owner, Marshall Bailey, pleaded no contest in Dallas County court to a charge of billing for parts that weren't installed and paid a $50 fine. However, Mr. Bailey says, "I was an innocent victim of circumstances because the company was in my name. I wasn't guilty of the crime I was fined for." For his part, Mr. Howell, who spent $230 on the repairs, grouses, "It didn't do me much good. I haven't seen any money yet."

Whether fraud or sloppiness, most cases are settled without litigation. Often, shops try to avoid costly, time-consuming court procedures by redoing faulty work or refunding a customer's money. Thus did Earleane Bryant receive a new engine for her Buick after Mr. Meeks had complained to the manufacturer that a local dealer wasn't honoring a new car warranty. Mr. Meeks, who worked for a short time as a Chrysler Corp. factory-service representative, found that the original engine in Mrs. Bryant's car had burned up because of mechanical failure, not because of owner abuse as the dealer had alleged.

In the case of the Pontiac Catalina stalled on a Dallas street after a tuneup and other work, Mr. Meeks concluded that the car owner hadn't received the new spark plugs and front-end alignment he had paid for. Mr. Meeks has filed a court case alleging that the shop charged for services that weren't provided.

## THE LAW'S PENALITIES

When charges are brought, the cases are usually tried in municipal court, where fines range up to $200, and two convictions mean loss of a shop's license. But in incidents involving amounts of more than $200, prosecutors can bring felony-theft charges in state district court. There, penalties are stiffer, calling for maximum fines of $5,000 and imprisonment for up to 10 years.

Recently, for instance, the former manager of an Aamco Transmission outlet here, Lawrence R. Santella, was indicted by a Dallas grand jury on a charge of felony theft for billing a customer $334 for a transmission overhaul that allegedly hadn't been done. Mr. Santella, scheduled to be tried in state court, will plead innocent, his attorney says. "My client was just an employee, and no other employee, including those who worked on the car, or the owners were charged with the crime," the attorney says.

A major purpose of the Dallas law is to get dishonest practitioners out of the auto-repair business. Yet the new law hasn't been warmly received by the industry. "The way the ordinance reads now, I think it's unconstitutional as hell," says Robert L. Stephens, owner of an independent garage and president of the local Automotive Service Council, a professional organization of auto mechanics.

Specifically, Mr. Stephens is unhappy with provisions that require mechanics to provide written estimates and forbid them to charge more than 10 percent above the estimate without first informing the customer. Such requirements, he says, prevent long-time customers from dropping off their cars with instructions to do whatever is necessary to make them run well. Other mechanics contend that the requirements force them to overestimate in order to avoid miscalculating the cost of repairs. "A person has got to protect himself," one explains.

Mr. Meeks, himself president of the Automotive Service Council before turning city sleuth, responds that mechanics are free to charge more than the original estimate as long as the customer is contacted for approval. He argues that the ordinance only requires mechanics to do what most of the 1,500 licensed shops in Dallas would do anyway.

"I'm doing everything I can to improve the image of the industry, not to destroy it," says Mr. Meeks, adding that his $18,480 annual salary is less than he earned as a garage owner. "When they complain about the regulations, I tell them, 'You've always wanted your image improved, so I'm trying to improve it. When we have a disease going around, everybody has to take the same medicine.'"

# 18

# Federal Examiners Knew Plight of U.S. National Bank Since '62

Robert Wagman and Sheldon Engelmayer

Federal regulators knew of the wrongdoings that led to the largest bank failure in U.S. history at least 10 years before it actually happened, but did nothing about them.

An investigation by North American Newspaper Alliance has uncovered evidence that the Office of the Comptroller of the Currency knew as early as September, 1962, that the U.S. National Bank, headquartered in San Diego and with branches throughout Southern California, was being improperly used by its present and chief executive officer, C. Arnholt Smith.

Smith is currently under indictment for bank fraud.

NANA's investigation has revealed that the Office of the Comptroller of the Currency through three successive administrations either ignored or sidetracked strong evidence of the bank's problems.

On October 18, 1973, James E. Smith, comptroller of the currency, declared U.S. National Bank insolvent and announced that its "good assets" and deposits had been sold to the Crocker National Bank of San Francisco. Since that time, the federal government has poured almost $200 million into the bank.

This was the first official word of what was the largest bank failure in U.S. history. The comptroller's office placed "primary responsibility" for the failure on Smith who, the government alleges, had depleted the cash reserves of the bank by almost $400 million through questionable loans to companies that he or business associates controlled.

NANA's investigation clearly shows that major responsibility must be placed with the Office of the Comptroller of the Currency.

In September 1962, Jack Coltrane was lead examiner in the annual examination of USNB. "We had finished doing the examination of a U.S. National branch and had several hours to kill before starting on the branch at Riverside," he told NANA.

From *Los Angeles Times*, Thursday, August 8, 1974, Part I, pp. 1, 20-23. Reprinted by permission.

Donald Kline, who was my assistant, and I decided to drive by what we understood to be a new building U.S. National had just completed for a new branch in Pomona.

When we got to Pomona, all we found was a vacant lot, so, we continued on to Riverside.

Early in the examination of the Riverside branch, we discovered a $710,000 loan representing the permanent financing of the branch at Pomona that had not been built.

The manager of the Riverside branch could not adequately explain what happened to the money and instead referred us to C. Arnholt Smith at the bank headquarters in San Diego.

Coltrane said he received a confusing explanation from Smith and began to trace the proceeds of the loan at the headquarters office.

We found that the money had gone from the Riverside branch to the related Westgate Realty Corp., from there to another related company, the Majestic Finance Co., where it was used as partial payment on the highspeed elevator system that was being installed in San Diego's first high-rise office building which Smith was constructing at that time.

Coltrane immediately notified his superior, Jack Baker, head examiner of the San Diego office, who in turn notified A. E. Larsen, then regional administrator of national banks in San Francisco.

Larsen flew to San Diego and numerous examiners from throughout the region were brought in to begin a major examination of the bank.

As more and more questionable activities on the part of Smith began to be uncovered, Larsen requested additional assistance from Washington. A team of top examiners from the comptroller's staff, headed by Wallace Anker, was flown out to San Diego.

As they worked 16 hours a day, seven days a week, the pattern and extent of Smith's intercompany loans became evident to the investigators.

"During this time, we reported on almost a daily basis to the comptroller of the currency, James J. Saxon, or his deputy, Justin Watson," Coltrane said.

"By the time the examination was finished, everyone on the comptroller's staff in Washington was well aware of the serious plight of the bank."

Details of the September 1962 examination have been confirmed to NANA by various examiners who took part. In addition, from a source within the comptroller's office in Washington, NANA has read memos to the file of U.S. National Bank written by Watson, in which he details the contents of various telephone conversations with the examiners in San Diego.

At the end of the examination a report was written up, signed by head examiner Baker, and forwarded to the regional office in San Francisco for retyping and transmission to Washington.

The report stated 21 percent of all loans in the bank's portfolio were to related companies.

The examiners in the field strongly urged that a copy be forwarded to the U.S. attorney in San Diego for presentation of probable federal law violations to a grand jury. It was alleged that $13 million were loans to affiliates in violation of the Federal Reserve Act.

Another examiner who took part in the examination but who asked not to be identified supports Coltrane's story completely and indicates that the evidence of federal law violations on the part of Smith appeared quite strong.

According to a spokesman for the Justice Department in Washington, however, the first it heard of alleged criminal violations on the part of Smith and the U.S. National Bank was after a June 1972 examination by William Martin. The spokesman told NANA it could find no earlier communication regarding irregularities and violations.

Through sources in the comptroller's office in Washington, NANA has been allowed to read the September 1962 report. The report is highly critical of Smith's practices but seems to fall short of the condemnation and charges of illegality that examiner Coltrane indicates were in the report when it left the San Diego office.

The report on file in Washington is signed in Jack Baker's name by the regional office in San Francisco which had power of attorney to do so. When questioned about the report, Baker declined to comment in detail about its specifics. But he generally confirmed Coltrane's recollection, including the large amount of material which was requested to be forwarded to the U.S. attorney's office. Baker told NANA that to this day he has never seen the final report that bears his signature.

Coltrane resigned from the comptroller's staff in 1967 and himself is currently under indictment in a bank manipulation case. (A federal grand jury here last May indicted Coltrane and three other persons on charges they wrongfully manipulated the funds of Southland National Bank in San Bernardino County to aid the bank's takeover in 1969 by a group of businessmen.) The record shows how thoroughly the comptroller's office understood Smith's financial empire and his intercompany dealings.

In a memo dated November 5, 1962, Deputy Comptroller Watson drew detailed diagrams of the interrelated Smith corporate setup and showed a comprehensive knowledge of how the corporate shells were being used. This diagram could just as easily fit the 1972 Martin examination.

In early December 1962, Watson met with Smith and proposed a course of action which would have had the effect of taking control of the bank out of Smith's hands. Later that month, Regional Administrator Larsen called a special meeting of the board of directors of the bank in order to present the findings of the examination and relay the government's directive.

Notes of the meeting characterized the reaction of the board as one of "complete shock." According to these notes and the board's own official minutes of the meeting, which NANA has seen, the comptroller's office listed seven courses of action for the board in order to avert any further federal action. Six of the seven items related to taking absolute control out of Smith's hands. The seventh was the hiring of an independent outside auditing firm.

It would appear that after Watson's meeting with Smith and Larsen's meeting with the board, the recommendations of the comptroller's officer were largely ignored. The bank's board of directors continued to be dominated by Smith.

In March 1963, Baker was assigned to do a special examination of the bank. Although Baker would not discuss the details of his findings, NANA, through sources within the comptroller's office, has seen a copy of Baker's report in which the condition of the bank was described as poor and it was clearly noted that the demands of the comptroller's officer were being ignored.

During this period, Smith was writing long letters to comptroller Saxon detailing how large outstanding loans to affiliated companies were being removed from the bank's books and other problems were being solved. These letters were forwarded to Baker for his comments.

In long memorandums to Saxon, Baker pointed out that Smith's actions were totally cosmetic and that, rather than eliminating affiliated loans through repayments, Smith was simply switching corporate names.

Baker was transferred to the regional office in San Francisco where he was assigned to examine banks in such places as Anchorage, Alaska. Also reassigned were Coltrane and several other junior examiners who had worked on the U.S. National Bank case. Baker, in remembering the suddenness of the transfer, told NANA that he had been deeply hurt and considered resigning.

The next examination of the U.S. National Bank was apparently done in September 1963, with Donald Butler as the examiner in charge. Butler at the time was chief examiner of the Los Angeles office.

The Butler report brought the rating of the Bank from poor to good and stated that Smith was actively solving the bank's problems. The report did not mention either of the two Baker reports directly or by implication.

When questioned, Butler was unable to recall ever having conducted an examination of U.S. National Bank in the early or mid-1960s. He did recall in great detail, however, his examination of that bank in the mid-1950s and again in 1971.

It should be noted that at the time Butler was supposedly doing this 1963 examination, he was unexpectedly transferred from Los Angeles to San Francisco. Butler does remember his shocked and indignant reaction to the transfer.

Both Baker and Butler have since retired from the comptroller's office.

Between the 1963 examination Butler does not remember making and the 1971 examination he does remember, there were 10 intervening examinations. All were favorable reports done by five different examiners. Of the five, one subsequently became a vice-president of U.S. National Bank and two others received substantial promotions within the comptroller's office. The remaining two examiners were both close to retirement when they conducted their examinations.

Some sources have suggested that the examiners during this period were given insufficient time and resources to do a complete job. Larsen vehemently denies this. Other sources also claim that the examiners were wined and dined lavishly by Smith and that he offered them jobs.

Sources say that the experiences of Butler during his 1971 examination were typical of the period. Butler, who had been transferred to the Reno office was given short notice by Larsen to fly into San Diego to examine the U.S. National Bank. As he relates it, he was unprepared and was not allowed to bring in his own people to help him, which forced him to work with junior examiners whose methods and competence were unknown to him.

"The morning I arrived at the bank to begin the examination," Butler told NANA, "Smith immediately offered me a suite and unlimited charge privileges at his ultraluxurious Westgate Hotel across the street from the bank. I declined.

"That night, Smith took all the examiners, including me, for a ride and dinner aboard his yacht."

He noted it was not customary to have lavish lunches and dinners every day during the examination period, but this was the pattern during the September 1971 examination. Butler says, however, that he refused to participate in the daily festivities but did not prohibit the junior examiners from accepting the bank's hospitality aboard Smith's yacht or at the exclusive Kona Kai Club owned by a close associate of Smith.

"About two days into the examination," Butler said, he was approached by " a former bank examiner now working for the bank. He said he understood I was about to retire and wouldn't I like to come to work for the bank. Mr. Smith had been watching me and liked my work.

"I told him that it was extremely improper to have made the offer, and even more so coming from him, a former bank examiner." Butler said he indignantly declined the offer.

"Later in the examination, Smith came to me and offered my wife and me an all-expenses-paid trip to Peru aboard one of Smith's boats." Again, Butler declined.

When asked about the examination, Butler replied that it had been rather casual and that Larsen had not given him sufficient time or personnel to examine a bank the size of U.S. National. When asked whether he was satisfied with the quality of the report and its findings, he said, "Of course not." He declined to elaborate further on his dealings with Larsen during the 1971 examination.

Larsen denies that he ever limited the amount of time an examiner could spend at a given bank.

The next examination of the bank was the one conducted in June 1972 by William Martin, which led to the bank's closing. NANA has learned that between the two examinations, it was announced to certain key officers of U.S. National Bank that Regional Administrator Larsen had agreed to become president of the bank later in the year. However, the Martin examination intervened and no official announcement was ever made about Larsen becoming affiliated with the bank.

Larsen denied to NANA that he was scheduled to become U.S. National's president or that any such offer was made. However, he did admit that "there were some offhand comments made by Smith about why didn't I come down and take over the bank, but there were no formal discussions." (Earlier this year Larsen became president of another San Diego-based bank, Southern California First National.)

In early 1969, the *Wall Street Journal* published a major investigative article on Smith and his financial empire. In the long and heavily documented story, it was clearly implied that U.S. National Bank was being used to finance many of Smith's ventures. Yet the appearance of the article did not trigger any noticeable response from the comptroller's office nor were the charges investigated in subsequent examinations.

The article did, however, prompt the Securities and Exchange Commission to launch a probe of its own. Sources close to the SEC probe allege that the office of the Comptroller of the Currency made it difficult on numerous occasions to obtain necessary data.

According to the SEC source, the refusal by the comptroller's office was based on a fear that the probe might cause a run on the bank.

Both Watson and Larsen insist that between the first Baker examination in 1962 and the Martin examination in 1972 things had improved greatly at Smith's bank and that any mistakes made in the examinations during the decade were the fault of the examiners themselves.

When the Baker examination was conducted in 1962, the amount of questioned funds totaled approximately $20 million. By 1973, that total had grown to $400 million.

# 19

# Corporations and Law: Ending the Impasse

*Christopher D. Stone*

One would not expect to find much in common in the way corporate executives and student activists look on law and authority. One group operates in the rooms and cloakrooms of power; the other cannot get any closer than the streets. When a student is busted on a marijuana charge, he is assigned a public defender; the corporation retains a battery of the highest-paid lawyers money can buy.

Yet, as one who has been dividing his time recently between businessmen and students, I can assure you that there is an unmistakable commonality: the one group is coming to feel as misunderstood, alienated, and even as "hassled" as the other.

The public is, of course, more aware of the students' worldview. We know that Watergate, marijuana laws, and pointless—to them—university regulations, have left many with a sense that the law is either irrelevant or stacked against them.

But it has yet to recognize how pervasive such attitudes are becoming in the business sector, or what the implications are. Profit and prestige are being encroached upon by the outside world's growing concern for the environment, worker health, and product safety. A jumble of federal and state agencies, many too young to know what they are supposed to be doing and not old enough to be pliable, are imposing ever-increasing demands on corporate manpower and patience. The red tape is only slightly easier to live with because the businessman knows (more than anyone) that most questions of him are the wrong ones.

The reaction can go beyond exasperation and contempt. One business acquaintance of mine, a respected mineral-company executive, refuses to believe that his endless frustrations at the hands of various governmental agencies are a traditional and inevitable (however damnable) product of bureaucracy. He has come up with his own conspiracy theory (involving the fate of various mineral-lease applications), which he defends as earnestly, and I might say as ingeniously, as the students

From the *Los Angeles Times*, Monday, October 6, 1975, Part II, p. 7. Reprinted by permission.

who land in my office with their explanations of the Kennedy assassinations. The one is as unpersuasive as the other—but as unpersuadable, too. That much foul-up, they have decided, couldn't just "happen."

The ramifications of these attitudes are serious. The law, if it is going to be truly effective, has to make sense to, and command the respect of, the community it is supposed to govern. The business community, of course, is not going to stage a sit-in at the Federal Power Commission or commit acts of civil disobedience. It has too large a stake in things to be in open contempt of society's ground rules.

What comes, instead, is an increased winking at violations of the law that are not likely to be detected and a compliance, when prudent, that is increasingly begrudging. (Resistance to law need not always take the form of foot-dragging or fudging data; one of the most effective ways for business to keep "those idiots" off its back is to answer their requests with *truckloads* of data.)

Other forms of reaction are more gross. Consider, for example, the rash of corporate bribery. It cannot be condoned, but we have to recognize that such acts are an almost inescapable product of the same trend: the more the corporation's environment is shaped by governments (through law or contract award), and the more it is all done in a way that strikes the businessman as arbitrary or uninformed, the easier it becomes for him to brush aside moral qualms.

The public, for its part, is not going to cease its demands, nor should it. Corporations *are* our society's most effective actors. It is increasingly they—and, quite likely, an ever-shrinking number of them—who are our producers, distributors, polluters, investors, farmers, and even fathers: the drug-deformed "thalidomide babies" are as corporate as they are human.

Thus, to solve society's problems means, in no small measure, to deal with corporations. Yet our present legal arrangements for doing so are doubly damned: from the businessman's point of view they are merely frustrating and costly; from society's, too often ineffectual.

To understand why we are not doing a better job of it, we must look to legal history. When the law was forming, it was individual, identifiable persons who trespassed, created nuisances, engaged in consumer frauds. The law responded with contemporary notions about individuals—what motivated them, terrified them, and constituted justice toward them. Later, as corporations became the dominant vehicle for social action, only rarely did the law meet them with specially tailored adaptations. Since a body of law addressed to "persons" already existed, it was simply transferred to corporations without distinction.

Today's giant corporations, however, are much more than persons who just happen to be especially large and powerful. They are complex sociotechnical organisms—not just men, or even men-and-machines-in-groups, but men, machines, patterns of reward, ways of doing things, all divided up into loosely coordinated clusters of cells. There is no reason to believe (as the law implicitly does) that the way "it" will respond and adapt to external threats, the way "it" will scan the environment for information, the way "it" will calculate and weigh "its" pleasures against "its" pains is like that of an actual person.

Consider, for example, the law's efforts to deter an auto company from unleashing a dangerous model on the market. If the company doesn't exercise due care, we threaten to fine it or hold it answerable in civil suits. But to the men on the assembly line, or in production design, these threats mean little. Their immediate concern is not with overall corporate profit but with the targets and objectives of their shop, their department, their plant—or with simply getting home by five.

The law's feints at the corporate bank account are hardly more intimidating to the executives at the top. Fines and judgments against the corporation are passed on to the shareholders as reduced dividends. Even in the wake of the most severe lawsuits, executive compensation and tenure seem to survive untouched.

Individual responsibility is difficult to establish in an enormously complex organization. Even where it can be proved, there is no guarantee that the individual will bear the brunt of any judgment. Typically, a corporation covers directors and officers with legal liability insurance, or indemnifies them against fines and judgments by, for example, reimbursing them with stockholders' money.

Much of the standoff and frustration is intractable. But part of it we can do something about.

First, the law is going to have to become much more sophisticated about the special institutional features of corporations that make the problems of controlling them (and of controlling the men in them) a problem distinct from controlling human beings in ordinary situations. To do so will require an "autopsy" of the actual situations in which corporate behavior got out of control. What were the organizational or managerial weaknesses? The way in which the company was defining its employees' roles? The distribution of authority? "Breaks" in the flow of information up and down the line? Pressures created by the company's special criteria for reward and advancement?

Next, as we come to understand how these critical organizational features operate, the law will have to put them to work in special situations. Where a recidivist corporate polluter is in the docket, for example, the corporation, as a condition of probation (obviously it cannot be marched to jail), could be forced to create a vice-president for environmental affairs. His powers and duties would be defined by law, not by the public relations department.

An internal information network may have to be required, too, so that if there are clues of impending environmental injury, an officer using *his* specified responsibility—not the organization's—*must* report the data to the board of directors. The minutes of their next meeting would then be required to report that the board members had seen the report (so none of them could later plead blissful ignorance).

This approach—influencing institutional direction by laying down mandatory procedural and structural requirements—is commonplace in public agencies. But we have tried it only rarely when corporations, our "private governments," are concerned. For the public, it would hold considerable advantage. Enforcement is more effective, and less costly, when you are keeping tabs on internal systems rather than on each detail of operation and production. It is, in addition, a particularly appropriate way of moving into areas where we know so little about the costs and benefits of different measures, in which hastily drafted laws, with their rigid, across-the-board application, may only make matters worse.

As for the business community, its leaders are willing to brook some changes of this sort (consumer-affairs departments, vice-presidents for social policy), but they want to do it on their own terms, under the guise of a "self-regulation" that has been altogether too cosmetic to provide the public with the assurances it needs.

Organizational requirements that have the force of law behind them will be more effective, but would they also be just one more source of counterproductive government–industry friction? Not wholly.

Viewed as an alternative to an extension of present bureaucratic control measures, there is much to recommend this approach to management. The companies would have to provide assurances that their internal regulations (for example, quality control) were being carried out effectively and in good faith—and provide the identities of those now-anonymous employees who will be on the line if they are not.

This is a lot less intrusive, and less stultifying, than having to transfer back to Washington a growing number of decisions on the most minute details of operations or having to collect and hand over ream upon ream of undigested raw data. A legal system that included such arrangements would be less a product, and less a cause, of sheer mutual frustration.

# 20

# *Is Bribery Defensible?*

*Milton S. Gwirtzman*

It has been above 110 degrees each day in the dusty Middle Eastern capital city. The American sales representative has already been through two bouts with dysentery; worse yet, the only liquor available is a foul substance called "ponzoo." After three months of presentations before lesser officials, the American is finally granted an audience with the Minister. For the nth time, he goes through his product's performance, his company's reputation, the attractive price. The Minister listens, obviously bored, then points to a round little man in the back of the room. "This is Mr. Faud," he says. "Mr. Faud will pay a visit upon you tonight."

That evening, over still more glasses of ponzoo, Faud informs the American he can have the contract if his company will pay $1 million to the Minister. A quick exchange of coded cables with the home office, and the bargain is sealed. As fast as he can clear out, the American heads for the airport and home.

This has not been an easy year for American business. Still struggling to recover from the worst sales decline in 30 years, the business community has been hit with sweeping new regulations of its products and advertising by the government, and with increasing complaints about high prices and defective merchandise by a public whose faith in the free-enterprise system, according to recent polls, has sunk to a new low.

In this already embattled atmosphere, some of the big multinational firms have been targets of a highly publicized series of revelations concerning bribery and payoffs abroad. Some of the country's flagship corporations —Exxon, Lockheed, Northrop, Gulf, United Brands—have admitted funneling massive amounts of cash to officials of foreign governments and hiding the transactions from their shareholders and directors. With their ethics as well as their profits under attack, many businessmen view themselves as Job beset by a plague of boils.

From *The New York Times,* October 5, 1975, mag., pp. 12, 24-27. © 1975 by The New York Times Company. Reprinted by permission.

Of all the tribulations, the exposure of shady foreign business practices was the most unexpected, concerning as it does a practice that has existed at least since the 1600s, when the British East India Co. won duty-free treatment for its exports by giving Mogul rulers "rare treasures," including paintings, carvings, and "costly objects made of copper, brass and stone."

Nations like Britain and Sweden, whose standards of government ethics are a good deal stricter than our own, take it for granted that their businessmen will pay bribes when operating abroad, especially in developing countries. "Without it," says *The Financial Times* of London, "business simply would not get done." The only difficulty such bribes pose for British firms, according to a recent survey by *The Financial Times,* is one of morale. Some British executives feel unfairly treated when comparing their own modest and highly taxed salaries with what *The Times* calls "the large, tax-free rewards going to an assortment of foreign middlemen."

But in the United States, this traditional way of doing business abroad has become food for scandal because of the new climate of openness and honesty that former Vice-President Agnew ruefully but accurately called, in his resignation speech, the "post-Watergate morality."

It was largely corporate funds, laundered in foreign countries and returned to the United States in black satchels, that financed the Watergate break-in and the subsequent illegal payoffs to cover it up. In the course of its investigations, the Special Prosecutor's Office found in the possession of Richard Nixon's personal secretary a list of firms that had made illegal corporate contributions to President Nixon's campaign.

The Securities and Exchange Commission, which protects shareholders by requiring companies to disclose material facts of their activities, went after the firms for failure to report these contributions to their owners. Further probing revealed that some of the devices used to hide illegal contributions had also been used to hide the bribery of foreign officials from the companies' shareholders, and even from their own auditors. The SEC then moved to require disclosure of the questionable overseas practices, arguing that, while there is no law against such payments, the amounts of the bribes and the names of the recipients were important facts that present and prospective shareholders had a right to know.

Firms caught up in these proceedings feel as if they have been hit by a ton of bricks. When the facts began to unravel about a $1.25-million bribe paid by United Brands to the former president of Honduras to reduce the tax on the production of bananas, the company's president committed suicide, its stock dropped 40 percent, its holdings in Panama were expropriated, and its tax and tariff concessions in Honduras were revoked.

The Internal Revenue Service is investigating more than 100 corporations for improperly deducting payoffs and political contributions on their tax returns. (A bribe is not a legitimate business deduction. An agent's fee is.) A series of hearings by the Senate Subcommittee on Multinational Corporations, led by Senator Frank Church of Idaho, has fueled a push for new legislation, ranging from compulsory disclosure of such payments, to their criminal prosecution, to a requirement that the State Department keep watch on American businessmen and report all suspicious activities to the appropriate U.S. authorities.

All of this presents the American businessman operating abroad with a seemingly cruel dilemma. If he keeps paying foreign officials, he runs afoul of the post-Watergate morality in all its fury. If he is prevented from making these payments, either by law or by the chilling effect of disclosure, he risks the loss of important sales and investment opportunities to foreign competitors, who can apparently continue to pass bribes without embarrassment. The Lockheed case presents the most dramatic example of this predicament; despite considerable initial pressure from Congress and the SEC, the company refused to reveal the names of the recipients of the $25 million to $30 million in bribes it admitted having paid in the last five years. The firm, represented by former Secretary of State William Rogers, argues that if the whole truth were known about what it did to secure orders for aircraft from certain foreign governments, the orders could well be canceled, the company ruined, and the $200 million in loans the government has made to keep Lockheed afloat would be lost for good. Lockheed did agree to pass no more bribes, and it subsequently lost a jumbo-jet contract in India to a French company that, Lockheed alleges, had contributed $1.5 million to the ruling Congress party.

American business activities abroad generate 15 percent of the gross national product, 30 percent of the total profits of the nation's corporations, and an estimated 10 million American jobs. In large measure, the preservation of our current fragile economic health depends upon profits from foreign investment and dollars earned through overseas sales. It is important, therefore, to consider the true extent of the problem of foreign bribery, and its underlying causes, in order to decide what might be done about it.

U.S. business abroad runs the gamut from the people who sell the American college T-shirts so popular with the young in foreign countries, to Exxon, whose revenues from foreign operations total $27 billion a year. The ordinary businessman sells to private concerns. He is not enmeshed in the kind of payoffs that have been making news. Most American exporters have dealt with upright commission merchants in Europe and elsewhere for years. They may have to cross the palm of a local customs inspector to clear a shipment, or be overly generous at holiday time, but by and large the goods they offer are purchased or rejected on the basis of price and quality. The side inducements are no different from those that are part of daily practice in almost every field of business in the United States.

In general, the larger the company, the bigger the deal. The bigger the deal, the more heavily involved the foreign government is, either as purchaser, owner of natural resources or regulator. The bigger the government's stake, the more likely it is that large amounts of money will pass under the table. From the revelations of recent months, few can contest that graft and bribery of significant proportions are widespread, particularly in the developing countries. And the system by which the U.S. government, the world's biggest arms merchant, sells its wares through private American firms is apparently shot through with corruption, not only in Asia and the Middle East, but in Europe as well.

The biggest payoffs are made by the large multinational companies, and they are part of a broader tendency to place the corporations' interests ahead of those of the countries in which they operate. Some multinationals can and have moved factories from country to country with little regard for the workers involved and shifted profits earned in one country to others where the tax systems are more indulgent.

Studies have shown that the multinational firms' ability to transfer large sums of money from one currency to another at a profit played an important role in the devaluation or revaluation of each of the world's major currencies over the past seven years and the resultant breakdown in the world monetary system that had previously been based on fixed parities between national monies. (When former President Nixon blamed the devaluation of the dollar on "international speculators," he was speaking of some of his heaviest campaign contributors.) When firms routinely engage in these kinds of maneuvers, concepts of moral ethics as well as national allegiance tend to blur. Lawyers for Investors Overseas Services, during the heyday of the Swiss-based mutual fund conglomerate once advised their chairman Bernard Cornfield, that his best option as a man with a six-figure tax bill would be to become a citizen of Iceland.

Top managers of these companies often follow a lifestyle that tends to encourage unethical practices. Some heads of multinational companies have virtually unrestricted power. Jetting around the world in their personal planes, whisked from one meeting to the next by limousine, with immediate access to millions of dollars to spend as they see fit, they are driven by one overriding goal—to improve the company's earnings.

This style of management has some advantages, but time for ethical reflection is not among them. These multinational managers are neither grafters nor thieves, but somewhere in the frenzy of travel, pressure, and ambition they may lose their ability to balance the needs of their shareholders with the accepted standards of moral behavior. It happens at home—to this day, tobacco companies refuse to concede any medical link between cancer and cigarettes. It happens far more easily abroad, where the managers feel less sense of local commitment and may not develop the ethical antennae that result from having to relate to one's neighbors.

Nor can they always look for help to their shareholders and directors. At the annual meeting of United Brands in August, the majority of shareholders were far more concerned with the company's passing its common dividend than with its massive bribes in Central America. They cheered a statement by one of their number that bribery was "essential in doing business in many parts of the world." At the annual meeting of Exxon, a resolution to require disclosure of the firm's payments abroad was defeated, 97 percent to 3 percent. Despite the devastating publicity suffered by Ashland Oil for payoffs in four countries and illegal contributions to scores of U.S. politicians, its directors recommended against firing its chief executive, Orin Atkins (who was directly responsible for most of the payments) on the ground that, since he had taken over, the corporation's net income had grown from $31 milion to $113 million.

If corporate bribery abroad has offended the post-Watergate morality, the companies implicated have nevertheless taken a greater share of the blame than they deserve. Bribery abroad is not exactly the corruption of innocents. Several of the incidents spotlighted by the Senate hearings smack more of protection and extortion than of simple bribery. In the most outrageous case, the chairman of the ruling party in South Korea threatened to close the $300-million operation of Gulf Oil in that country unless the company made a donation of $10 million to his party's presidential campaign. Gulf's chairman, Bob Dorsey, was able to shave the demand down from $10 million, which he considered "not in the interests of the company," to $3 million, which he said was.

The reasons multinationals must do business amid a profusion of outstretched hands go deep into the history and structure of the lands in which they operate. In much of Asia and Africa the market economy as we know it, in which the sale of goods and services is governed by price and quality competition, never has existed. What has developed in its stead are intricate tribal and oligarchic arrangements of social connections, family relations, and reciprocal obligations, lubricated by many forms of tribute, including currency.

In a meeting at the Department of Defense in 1973 (a report of which was subpoenaed from the files of the Northrop Corp.), Adnan Kashogghi, one of the most successful middlemen in the Middle East, justified his enormous sales commissions—$45 million on a single deal for fighter planes —by his need to cover his operating expenses and also take care of his pecuniary "loyalties" to Saudi Arabia's royal family.

Another memo explained Northrop's loss of a contract to build a communications system by noting that Saudi officials wished to help out the local agent of a Northrop competitor, one Ibriham el-Zahed. "They felt," the memo said, "that by awarding a contract to his principals, he will make enough money to pay off his debts. This may sound like an amazing reason to people sitting in Century City [Northrop's California headquarters], but can be a very valid one in Saudi Arabia."

In most developing countries, civil service salaries are deliberately low—the average Indian bureaucrat makes $1,650 a year—on the assumption that people will supplement their salaries by taking money where they can find it. Where political instability is the rule, the tenure of high officials is always uncertain and often short. Bribes provide a form of retirement fund. It is considered far more patriotic to take the money from rich foreign corporations than out of one's own country. None of this is new. Some 70 years ago, Joseph Conrad wrote, in "Nostromo," about the mythical Latin republic of Costaguana, in which a foreign-owned silver mine kept a regular payroll of government officials. The brother of the insurgent general spoke of his intention "to demand a share in every enterprise —in railways, in mines, in sugar estates, in cotton mills, in each and every undertaking—as the price of his protection." Since the voyages of discovery, foreigners have come to the Third World to extract what they could from its land and its labor. This exploitation has been countered by levies on them for the benefit of those in power at the moment. Despite their undoubted role in modernizing the economies of developing countries, foreign companies are still looked upon by the people of the Third World as latter-day conquistadors. Little wonder that when the recent revelations of bribery became sensational worldwide news, the wrath of the nations involved was directed almost solely at the companies. When Ashland admitted it had paid $150,000 to the President and Prime Minister of Gabon to protect oil concessions, the government accused the company of blackmail and racism. In fact, in much of Africa, the historic resentment of white exploitation impels black regimes to demand bribes from Western companies without moral qualms.

The responsibility for present practices must also be shared by [the U.S.] government, which not only encouraged investment in countries whose ethical standards differ from ours, but also in many respects set the pattern for the graft under censure today. American intelligence agencies have regularly dealt in bribery and payoffs wherever they seemed to be useful tools in strengthening American influence abroad and frustrating the designs of Communist nations. Bribes have been used not just to acquire useful information, but to restore the Shah to power in Iran, to purchase votes in international organizations against Cuba, and to "destabilize" the Allende government in Chile. We shall probably never know how many of the electoral campaigns of pro-West political parties were financed by secret contributions from the CIA. The important thing here is that these have been accepted tactics for more than a generation.

The rapid acceleration of American private investment in foreign lands, which began in the mid-nineteen-sixties, was seen by our foreign-policy makers as a welcome opportunity. If U.S. firms could build a nation's infrastructure, supply its consumer goods and hire a portion of its workers, the greater the likelihood the nation would be bound to ours by the safest and strongest of ties, economic self-interest. As a result, our government wrote the foreign investment laws of several developing countries and urged our multinationals to make use of them. New programs were established to insure foreign investment against the risks of war and expropriation. Embassy personnel were ordered to scout out export possibilities for American firms, which were published in *Commerce Business Daily,* the government's daily list of business opportunities.

Sometimes the government-business relationship was even closer than it seemed. After the 1967 exposé of the CIA's use of American student groups as fronts for intelligence activities, the CIA decided that new organizations were needed for the purpose of deep cover. A special office was established in Washington to place agents in overseas offices of American companies. At the same time, multinationals began recruiting former intelligence agents to run their operations abroad. Often this meant a man retired from the government, in whose service he had bribed foreign officials, to begin a new career bribing the same officials on behalf of private enterprise. When Kermit ("Kim") Roosevelt Jr., grandson of President Theodore Roosevelt, became an "international consultant" to Northrop and other clients, he was able to use the same network of spies he had run when head of operations for the CIA in the Middle East. (Roosevelt himself has not been linked to any bribe attempts. For Northrop, he concentrated on intelligence-gathering and high-level contracts. He is said to have told one old friend that he "always stayed away from the payments side.")

Armaments sales provide the most dramatic and dangerous example of corporate profit-seeking, foreign customs, and U.S. policy goals combining to create a massive networn of bribery. As cutbacks in Western defense budgets have dried up domestic markets for arms, purchases by Third World countries have increased. In addition to maintaining domestic employment and lowering the unit cost of arms produced for our own defense, such exports were considered by our government to be the most effective way of cementing diplomatic relations. Recipient countries, it was argued, would find it difficult to stay out of the U.S. orbit if they depended upon us for their military hardware, its maintenance and spare parts, and the training of personnel in its use.

When the war in Vietnam wound down, the most important market for armaments became the Middle East. For a generation, the United States and the Soviet Union, as well as Britain and France, have tried to strengthen their influence in that region by catering to the Arab rulers' fears of Israel and each other.

The sharp rise in the price of OPEC oil gave the Arabs the means to buy the most sophisticated modern weaponry. Such sales have become a vital element of the "recycling" procedure, by which Western countries try to earn back some of their petrodollars.

From less than $1 billion in 1966, the total arms imports of Middle Eastern nations, including Israel, have shot to more than $9 billion in 1974. Last year, the United States alone sold $6.5 billion worth of armaments, more than half of them going to Iran, where the Shah has expressed a keen interest in purchasing aircraft capable of delivering nuclear weapons.

Given the stiff competition from other countries and the way business is done in that region, the Middle East arms race was bound to generate millions of dollars in graft. Under recent Saudi Arabian law, no foreign company could do business without a local agent. When Northrop, with strong encouragement from the Pentagon, undertook to sell its F-5 fighter plane there, the Saudi minister of defense told [Northrop's "international consultant"] Kermit Roosevelt to advise the firm to hire Adnan Kashogghi, who had previously been the agent for Lockheed and Raytheon. To get the sale approved, the firm fattened Kashogghi's fee to include $450,000 for two Saudi air force generals who were threatening to hold up the deal.

Northrop President Thomas Jones says he knew nothing about this, but admits that on a quick trip to Jidda, the graft question was raised, and he told Kashogghi that "Northrop is a company that meets its obligations." The bribe money was deducted from Northrop's income tax and included as a reimbursable cost in its bill to the Department of Defense. Since the recent scandals, both claims have been withdrawn. Some of the fighters were transferred by the Saudis to Egypt and Syria for use against Israel. Thus the U.S. government is encouraging unethical practices in order to unload American weapons that increase the risk of war.

For all these reasons, it would be unwise, as well as unfair, simply to write off bribery abroad to corporate lust. It is a symbol of far deeper issues that really involve America's role in the world. For the past 30 years, from Dean Acheson to Henry Kissinger, the governing principle of U.S. foreign policy has been that a Communist threat to our nation's vital interests exists, sufficient to require a major American presence throughout the world and whatever means are necessary to maintain U.S. influence.

Since our multinational companies, like government agencies, are important instruments of our nation's global power, it is argued that they should not be hobbled by home-bred notions of business morality. After all, if such firms were government-owned, as many of their foreign competitors are, their managers would be servants of the state and presumably have the same license as intelligence agents to pass bribes for the good of the country. And is there really a distinction in this regard between state-owned companies and firms like Northrop and Lockheed, whose customers are governments and whose products give our policies their clout? If ending these practices means that other nations, through their instruments of power, will best us in the contest for international influence, don't we almost have to hold our noses and let the multinationals do what they say they must?

There is, of course, a growing force of opinion in this country that holds such a view of our past foreign policy to be both obsolete and dangerous, arguing that bribery abroad goes hand in hand with coziness with dictators, the excesses of the CIA, and everything else that has put us on the defensive in so many parts of the world. A foreign policy that at one stroke can justify bribes, the purchase of influence, the overthrow of governments, and assassinations of foreign leaders subverts not just the free-enterprise system, but all our national ideals. Moreover, in its own terms, it doesn't work. The brutal lesson of Vietnam and Cambodia was that a corrupt regime, no matter how great its friendship for or dependence upon the United States, does not serve our interests; no amount of armaments can save such a regime from ultimate rejection by its own people. In China, Cuba, Algeria, Vietnam and—potentially—Portugal, the issue of graft among the ruling class has been an important part of the revolutionary appeal of Communist movements. The people who have taken over in these countries whatever their other failings, usually are fanatically puritanical when it comes to rejecting bribes. If American policy results in more revolutions, not only will U.S. influence be destroyed, but trade will cease and the assets of American firms will be expropriated. Thus even by the test of the most single-minded corporate manager, bribery is ultimately bad for business.

These opposite views of American foreign policy cannot be resolved by argument. With the right pair of candidates, they may be a central issue in next year's presidential election. One thing is certain, however: to implement this last view will require far greater changes in how our country acts abroad than the mere cessation of graft. If that is all that changes, business will be handicapped in many foreign countries and our economy may suffer as a result.

Yet this may be exactly what occurs. The investigations by Congress and the SEC have enjoyed a remarkable staying power on the front pages of the nation's press. The revelations undoubtedly have struck a sensitive national nerve. A sufficient head of steam exists in Congress to push through new laws outlawing both bribery and political contributions abroad. Whether such a law is sensible or even enforceable is another question. It has always been difficult to give extraterritorial effect to American criminal law, in countries where local law is different. Robert Vesco in Costa Rica and the Vietnam draft resisters in Canada and Scandinavia are testimony to that. To prove a case of bribery abroad might well require evidence and witnesses American courts cannot command, any more than Bolivia has been able to force Mr. Dorsey of Gulf to come to that country and testify about his company's activities there. The task of keeping watch on what businessmen and foreign officials do would radically change the atmosphere of our embassies and cause widespread resentment abroad. If businessmen avoid our embassies, the important work they are doing to identify trade opportunities could well be wasted.

There is more to be said for a new law making it easier for the SEC to require disclosure of foreign bribes. Forty years of experience with securities legislation has shown that if gamey activities must be exposed in public, they will usually—but not always—die a natural death. If disclosure is to be mandated, however, it should be limited to payments made in the future. Some exposure of past activities has been necessary to focus public concern on the issue. But aside from providing an unending spectacle, there is little reason to continue to call business executives on the carpet to account for activities that were not only legal, but practiced by their competitors, accepted and expected by the host countries, condoned and in some cases encouraged by our own government.

It would be far better if reform could be coordinated with other countries and with international organizations. Since the United States puts up such a large share of the capital of the World Bank and the Inter-American Development Bank and other international lending organizations we could ask that these agencies strengthen their procedures against payoffs on projects financed with their loans.

In a recent interview on West German television, an official of that country's Finance Ministry admitted it was "morally indefensible" to allow German companies to deduct foreign bribes on their tax returns, but, he said, he feared that if West Germany changed its laws, its firms would be "out of business . . . the others would get the business in our stead."

The best place to initiate common reform may be in the Organization for Economic Cooperation and Development, whose membership comprises all the Western industrialized nations, and which is now working on guidelines for the conduct of both multinational companies and the countries in which they operate. If the United States were to insist on strong prohibitions against bribery in this document, member nations might, in concert, adopt such strictures for themselves.

In addition, former Under Secretary of State George Ball has proposed an international companies law, similar to the one being written for the European Common Market. Under Ball's proposal, multinationals would derive their right to do business not from the state of Delaware, or even from one country, but from an international authority. Companies would have to meet world standards in all their activities, from capital transfers to tax procedures, or lose the right to do business in the countries that adhere to the law.

All these proposals are fraught with the delay and frustration that come with any attempt to break new ground in international law. But if they could be implemented, it would not be the first time that nations found themselves able to do together what none dared do alone.

Yet even if we have to act alone, it will not be the first time. Last year, we were ready to impeach a president for actions that are accepted practices abroad. Watergate showed not that America was the most corrupt of nations, but that it was the most sensitive.

The truth is that we have stood for worthy ideals even while playing international hardball. The export of Marshall Plan aid, Food for Peace, and the Peace Corps volunteers were actions others admired and then followed. One of our ideals is that we are an open society that lets its conduct hang out for ethical inspection. Perhaps the export of the new morality born of the Watergate tragedy would not hurt us in this wearied world.

# 21

# *White-Collar Crime and the Criminal Process*

President's Commission on Law Enforcement
and Administration of Justice

## EFFECTIVENESS OF CRIMINAL SANCTIONS

. . . Most persons convicted of common-law crimes are likely to be young and to have serious educational and vocational lacks which rehabilitation programs can help meet. Presumably such programs are far less significant and will often be irrelevant for the white-collar offender.

Furthermore, with respect to many kinds of white-collar offenders long periods of incarceration or supervision are not needed to protect society from further criminality. For example, there appears to be only a negligible amount of recidivism among those convicted of certain white-collar crimes. Thus of the 1,186 persons convicted of criminal tax fraud in 1963 and 1964, only two persons were repeat offenders.[1] On the other hand, among some classes of white-collar offenders, such as those guilty of cheating consumers, recidivism may be a serious problem.

There is, unfortunately, no hard evidence available regarding the deterrent effect of criminal sanctions. This was vividly illustrated when in a 1964 tax case the Justice Department was asked to submit a memorandum to the court justifying imposition of a four-month jail term and a $10,000 fine as a deterrent. The only significant data produced were figures indicating that recidivism among tax violators was minimal and a case study from Israel which indicated that since 1956, when the government had adopted a program of criminal prosecutions for tax evasion, there had been a graphic increase in the amount of income declared for taxation.[2] There is a clear need for further research into the effectiveness

From "White Collar Crime," *Task Force Report: Crime and Its Impact—An Assessment,* Task Force on Assessment—The President's Commission on Law Enforcement and Administration of Justice. Washington, D.C.: U.S. Government Printing Office, 1967, pp. 104-08.

of criminal sanctions in this area. We need to know, for example, more about the comparative deterrent effects of prosecution, publicity, a jail sentence, a criminal fine, and civil damages. To this end, the IRS and the Justice Department recently engaged the National Opinion Research Center of the University of Chicago to conduct a survey of public attitudes toward the administration, enforcement, and infringement of the tax laws.

Despite the lack of hard evidence, common sense notions about how people behave support the thesis that the condemnatory and deterrent aspects of criminal sanctions are likely to be peculiarly effective in the white-collar area. Persons who have standing and roots in a community, and are prepared for and engaged in legitimate occupations, can be expected to be particularly susceptible to the threat of criminal prosecution. Criminal proceedings and the imposition of sanctions have a much sharper impact upon those who have not been hardened by previous contact with the criminal justice system. Moreover, white-collar crimes as a class are more likely than common law crimes to be preceded by some deliberation; there is therefore more often an opportunity to calculate the risk objectively.

It appears further that jail sentences, however short, would constitute particularly significant deterrents for white-collar crime. The imposition of jail sentences may be the only way adequately to symbolize society's condemnation of the behavior in question, particularly where it is not on its face brutal or repulsive. And jail may be the only sanction available which will serve as an adequate deterrent.

These impressions are supported by the opinions of those who have had experience with the enforcement of the tax and antitrust laws.

No one in direct contact with the living reality of business conduct in the United States is unaware of the effect the imprisonment of seven high officials in the Electrical Machinery Industry in 1960 had on the conspiratorial price fixing in many areas of our economy; similar sentences in a few cases each decade would almost completely cleanse our economy of the cancer of collusive price fixing and the mere prospect of such sentences is itself the strongest available deterrent to such activities.[3]

The Department of Justice believes that imprisonment may often be the appropriate penalty for a clear-cut antitrust violation, such as price fixing. The attached paper [refers to Attachment A, pp. 109–112, not included in this selection] points out that criminal fines or civil damages may be inadequate for a number of reasons: present statutory maximums often make criminal fines trivial for corporations[4] in proportion both to their ability to pay and to the profits resulting from the criminal violations; in a number of states corporate executives may be lawfully reimbursed by the corporation for fines imposed on them; and since discovery of criminal violations of the antitrust laws is very difficult, even substantial civil penalties may not constitute adequate deterrents.[5]

Significantly, the Antitrust Division does not feel that lengthy prison sentences are ordinarily called for. It "rarely recommends jail sentences greater than 6 months—recommendations of 30-day imprisonment are most frequent."

In tax cases, the Justice Department also considers criminal sanctions, and jail sentences in particular, of significant value as deterrents. It is the Tax Division's policy to recommend jail sentences for all defendants convicted of tax fraud whenever the court requests a recommendation. James V. Bennett, former director of the Federal Bureau of Prisons, has taken the position that the effort to deter misconduct by imposing relatively harsh penalties, while often a feeble thing in regard to traditional crime, "has had a most benign effect on those who do not like to pay taxes."[6]

But it is clear that the criminal law is not an appropriate means of dealing with all kinds of white-collar misconduct. Since white-collar misconduct usually does not involve an act which, like robbery, burglary, or rape, is of a simple and dramatic predatory nature, it is inevitable that one of the critical and difficult issues is determining when the violation is clear-cut enough to warrant use of society's ultimate method of control. A great deal of business is now subject to regulations whose interpretation is not at all clear. The language of the Sherman Act, for example, is extremely broad and abstract and has been subject to varying administrative and judicial interpretations. As pointed out in the attached paper, the Antitrust Division's solution has been to seek criminal sanctions only where there has been an intentional violation of clear and established rules of law. Where misconduct does not constitute such a violation, the Antitrust Division pursues civil remedies in place of criminal sanctions.

But the law is often adequately unambiguous. The offenders in the *Electrical Equipment* cases were, for example, quite aware that their activities were in violation of the law. As one of the violators testified:

> [I]t was considered discreet to not be too obvious and to minimize telephone calls, to use plain envelopes if mailing material to each other, not to be seen together traveling, and so forth . . . not leave wastepaper, of which there was a lot, strewn around a room when leaving.[7]

The list of executives in attendance at meetings was referred to as the "Christmas card list" and the meetings as "choir practice."[8] The executives filed false travel vouchers in order to conceal their visits to the cities in which meetings were held.[9]

Aside from the question of ambiguity of the violation, it is important to recognize that a decision to use criminal sanctions involves costs and disadvantages which must be analyzed against the gains to be achieved and the alternative methods available to seek compliance. As discussed above, against many types of white-collar offenders application of criminal sanctions is likely to be highly effective in terms of deterrence. But this "economy" of sanction does not argue for an indiscriminate increase in the use of criminal sanctions. Among the economic and social costs involved in using criminal sanctions are the loss of services or serious curtailment of the usefullness of highly productive members of society and the danger that greatly increased use of the criminal law would dilute its condemnatory effect. And there are many situations in which use of criminal sanctions may not be the most effective means of obtaining compliance with the law. Thus it is apparent that use of the withholding tax scheme has proved an extraordinarily efficient and effective method of preventing tax fraud. This is of course true in other areas of the law as well. Increased use of locks may be far more effective in reducing burglary and auto theft than an increase in police patrol. But the threat of criminal sanctions will often be an economical way to obtain compliance. In the tax area, for example, 80 million income tax returns are filed annually. It would be impractical to audit all of these and investigate all cases in which there was some reason for suspicion. The Tax Division audits only 4 percent of all returns filed. And the withholding tax scheme, while highly effective, can only insure that income earned in the course of some regular employment is reported. The government must therefore depend to a great extent on the deterrent effect of the threat of criminal sanctions.

Careful thought must be given to determining those areas in which use of criminal sanctions is appropriate and in which other means of enforcement will suffice. And sound prosecutorial discretion must be exercised in deciding which cases, among those that might technically involve criminal violations, should be selected for prosecution.

## PRACTICAL PROBLEMS WITH THE USE OF CRIMINAL SANCTIONS

There are practical obstacles to enforcement of the laws relating to white-collar crime because of factors peculiar to this kind of criminality.

As noted previously, it is often extremely difficult even to discover the existence of white-collar crimes; it is similarly difficult to secure evidence of criminal guilt. White-collar crime may not stand out as unusual conduct when committed as would, for example, theft, burglary, or assault. It may involve acts of omission rather than commission, which are less likely to be observed or noticed. It is often committed in the privacy of a business office or home. In addition, there may be no single victim or group of victims to complain to law enforcement authorities. Or victims may be unaware at the time of the offense that they have been victimized. Victims of consumer fraud are but one example. Moreover, the crime itself may be difficult to identify. It is often committed in the course of ordinary business activity and may not be significantly distinguishable from non-criminal business conduct. Especially where financial offenses are involved, the crime may be so technical that discovery is possible only after detailed and lengthy audit or economic analysis by specially trained law enforcement personnel with expertise in fields such as accounting and economics. Careful scrutiny of a huge mass of data for weeks or months may be necessary to produce the required evidence of criminality. A complicated security fraud investigation, for example, may involve several years of investigation by a team of law enforcement personnel.

A pervasive problem affecting enforcement is the fact that white-collar crime is often business crime and business crime is often corporate crime. Where corporate defendants are involved, the only criminal sanction available is the fine. As noted previously, fines may be inadequate as deterrents for a variety of reasons. There are also serious practical problems in imposing sanctions upon corporate employees. It is very difficult to obtain the conviction of the true policy formulators in large, complex corporations. The top executives do not ordinarily carry out the overt criminal acts—it is the lower or middle management officials who, for example, attend price-fixing meetings. Under traditional doctrines of complicity, to hold a superior responsible he must be shown actually to have participated in his subordinate's criminal activities, as by ordering the conduct or encouraging or aiding in its performance. It is very difficult to obtain evidence of such participation. Difficulties of proof have prevented the prosecution of top management in many Sherman Act cases.[10]

## RESISTANCE TO THE USE OF CRIMINAL SANCTIONS

As important as the practical obstacles to effective law enforcement is society's reluctance to impose criminal sanctions upon the white-collar offender. Thus despite the apparent effect of the *Electrical Equipment* cases, in which seven individual executives received and served jail sentences, since that case no antitrust defendant has been imprisoned. In seven cases since then, involving 45 individual defendants, prison sentences were imposed, but in each case the sentence was suspended. During this time the government has recommended that, out of 58 cases in which individual defendants were charged with criminal violations, prison sentences be imposed but suspended in seven cases, and imposed and served in 27 cases. The recommendations covered 105 individual defendants. Similarly, Marshall Clinard's study of a variety of rationing and other controls during the Second World War revealed that the sentences imposed on OPA violators after conviction were relatively mild.[11]

While little is known of the public attitude toward white-collar crime, it is apparent that the present concern with crime is not directed at white-collar crime but at "crime on the streets." As one executive convicted and sentenced to jail in the *Electrical Equipment* conspiracy said:

> [O]n the bright side for me personally have been the letters and calls from people all over the country, the community, the shops and offices here, expressing confidence in me and support. This demonstration has been a warm and humbling experience for me.[12]

But one attempt to measure public reactions to a form of white-collar crime—violations of the Federal Food, Drug and Cosmetic Act—indicated that the public would treat offenders more severely than the courts, although not as severely as persons guilty of such crimes as larceny and burglary. Consumers were asked to judge cases of food law violation in terms of how they would punish the offender. Six actual cases were selected, representing three types of violation—misbranding, distasteful but not physically harmful adulteration, and physically harmful adulteration. Fifty-eight percent of the consumers felt that penalties should have been more severe than the actual court decisions, and yet within the maximum penalty provided by the federal law, a one-year prison sentence on first conviction. Twenty-two percent of the sample chose penalties equal to or less harsh than the one actually imposed, while almost 20 percent felt that the violators should receive a prison term longer than a year.[13]

The very characteristics which make white-collar criminals particularly deterrable may make it difficult to obtain the sanctions necessary to deter. They generally have families, an established place in the community, and a spotless record. They often occupy managerial or executive roles in their business and a leadership position in their community.

In the *Electrical Equipment* cases the defendants included several vice-presidents of the General Electric Corporation and the Westinghouse Electric Corporation. They were described by a newspaper reporter as "typical business men in appearance, men who would never be taken for lawbreakers."[14] Several were deacons or vestrymen of their churches. One was president of his local chamber of commerce, another a hospital board member, another chief fund raiser for the Community Chest, another a bank director, another director of the taxpayer's association, another organizer of the local little league.

The highest paid executive to be given a jail sentence was a General Electric vice-president, earning $135,000 a year. He was married and the father of three children. He had served in the Navy during the Second

World War, rising to the rank of lieutenant commander, was director of the Schenectady Boy's Club, on the board of trustees of a girl's finishing school, and was a member of the Governor's Temporary State Committee on Economic Expansion in New York.

Obviously there is resistance to subjecting defendants who are performing useful functions in society to criminal sanctions and especially to prison sentences. Clinard's study of OPA violators found that one reason for the light sentences imposed was "the fact that the offenders seldom had a criminal past or other circumstances which would warrant a severe sentence. As the judges on occasion stated from the bench, they 'would not make criminals of reputable businessmen.' "[15] On the other hand Judge Skelly Wright, in considering the question of whether an income tax violator ought to be sentenced to jail, took the position that "the only real purpose of an income tax sentence is its deterrent value. Unless we use the income tax sentence as a deterrent, we are overlooking one of our responsibilities as judges."[16]

In addition to the standing of the offenders, there are a number of aspects of white-collar offenses that may encourage public and official reluctance to use criminal sanctions, as well as provide rationalizations for the violators themselves. Thus Cressey's study of embezzlement found rationalization to be an important factor in offenders' patterns of misconduct. They distinguished embezzlement sharply from robbery or theft. He found, for example, that independent businessmen who converted "deposits" which had been entrusted to them because of their business positions, convinced themselves "either (a) that they were merely borrowing the money which they converted, or (b) that the funds entrusted to them were really theirs."[17] It has been argued that use of criminal sanctions to enforce much of the law in this area is inappropriate because the conduct proscribed is "morally neutral."[18] The soundness of some of the regulatory laws that have grown up in recent decades is a subject of continuing debate. And the very fact that they are so recent in comparison with the laws prohibiting such conduct as larceny and assault makes it unlikely that they will enjoy similar acceptance for some time. Many of the defendants in the *Electrical Equipment* cases argued that their behavior, while technically criminal, had really served a worthwhile purpose by "stabilizing prices." They frequently combined this altruistic interpretation with an attempted distinction among illegal, criminal, and immoral acts, expressing the view that what they had done might have been designated by the statutes as criminal, but either they were unaware of such a designation or they thought it unreasonable that acts with admirable consequences should be considered criminal. The fact that the line between legitimate and illegitimate behavior is sometimes fuzzy and seems occasionally arbitrary does not help in obtaining popular support for the law.

Thus the fine line between legal tax avoidance and illegal evasion may make it hard for the violator himself or others to accept the appropriateness of criminal sanctions even where the violation is not close to the line.

But most white-collar crime is not at all morally neutral. Most fraud involves preying upon the weak and ignorant; violation of food and drug laws may cause death or serious injury; embezzlement is, very simply, a form of theft; tax fraud involves cheating the government and, indirectly, other taxpayers.

Reluctance to see criminal sanctions used in the white-collar area derives also from the fact that there is often no particular victim or group of victims. The harm is not as apparent, and certainly not as dramatic. Where loss is spread throughout society, the harm to any particular individual is minimal. As Sanford H. Kadish has pointed out:

> . . . it is possible to reason convincingly that the harm done to the economic order by violations of many of these regulatory laws are of a magnitude that dwarf in significance the lower class property offenses. But the point is that these perceptions require distinguishing and reasoning processes that are not the normal governors of the passion of moral disapproval, and are not dramatically obvious to a public long conditioned to responding approvingly to the production of profit through business shrewdness, especially in the absence of live and visible victims.[19]

Moreover, where corporate misconduct is involved, the offenders—and particularly the offenders against whom evidence of guilt can be obtained—act as part of a corporate hierarchy and, ordinarily, follow a pattern of corporate behavior. Individual responsibility is therefore reduced—the offenders are often following orders from above, either explicit or implicit. Moreover, the fact that acts are performed to further the interests of the corporation, and not merely the offenders' personal interests, helps to rationalize misconduct. Thus in the *Electrical Equipment* cases, personal explanations for the acts were, for the most part, sought in the structure of corporate pressures. The defendants almost invariably testified that they came new to a job, found price fixing an established way of life, and simply entered into it as they did into other aspects of their job. This is illustrative of a pattern that Senator Everett Dirksen of Illinois, during the subcommittee hearings, labeled "imbued fraud."[20] There was testimony that, if one employee refused to engage in price fixing, the responsibility would simply be delegated to another. Prior to imposing sentence in the *Electrical Equipment* cases, Judge T. Cullen Ganey criticized the corporations as the major culprits, but he did not excuse the offenders:

> . . . they were torn between conscience and an approved corporate policy, with the rewarding objectives of promotion, comfortable secur-

ity, and large salaries. They were the organization or company men, the conformist who goes along with his superiors and finds balm for his conscience in additional comforts and security of his place in the corporate setup.[21]

And in his study of embezzlement Cressey found that offenders rationalized on the basis "that 'everyone' in business in some way or other converts or misapplies deposits so that it is not entirely wrong."[22] Criminal conduct that accords with such an accepted "system" and is in response to such pressures is not unique to white-collar offenders, as the Commission's work on juvenile delinquency, organized crime, and professional crime indicates.

There is strong evidence that many white-collar offenders do not think of themselves as criminals. Cameron's study of middle-class shoplifters who had stolen from a large department store in Chicago gave some indication of the potential educative effect of the use of criminal sanctions. Shoplifters generally do not think of themselves as thieves, Cameron points out, and "even when arrested, they resist strongly being pushed to admit their behavior is theft. Again and again store people explain to pilferers, that they are under arrest as thieves, that they will, in the normal course of events, be taken in a police van to jail, held in jail until bond is raised, and tried in a court before a judge and sentenced." Interrogation procedures at the store are directed specifically and consciously toward breaking down any illusion that the shoplifter may possess that his behavior is merely regarded as "naughty" or "bad."

> In the course of this investigation, it becomes increasingly clear to the pilferer that he is considered a thief and is in imminent danger of being hauled into court and publicly exhibited as such. This realization is often accompanied by a dramatic change in attitude and by severe emotional disturbance.[23]
>
> • • •
>
> Because the adult pilferer does not think of himself, prior to his arrest, as a thief and can conceive of no in-group support for himself in that role, his arrest forces him to reject the role . . . [and] is in itself sufficient to cause him to redefine his situation.[24]

And Cressey found that "among the violators interviewed, the accountants, bankers, business executives and independent businessmen all reported that the possibility of stealing or robbing to obtain the needed funds never occurred to them, although many objective opportunities for such crimes were present."[25]

Application of criminal sanctions in this area raises some of the most delicate and perplexing problems confronting the criminal justice system. The sensitivity of successful members of society to the threat of criminal prosecution is indicative not only of the potential success of criminal sanctions in deterring misconduct, but of their potentially destructive effect upon the offenders. Criminal sanctions may help to educate the public to realize the seriousness of misconduct which is not on its face abhorrent, yet their indiscriminate use in areas where public opinion has not crystallized may seriously weaken the condemnatory effect of the criminal law. Imprisonment may be unnecessary for purposes of rehabilitation and incapacitation, although very effective as a deterrent.

## NOTES

1. See Robert E. Lane, "Why Businessmen Violate the Law," *J. Crim. L., C. & P.S.* 44 (1953): 151.

2. Government brief, United States v. Dugan (Dist. Ct. Mass., 1964), U.S. Department of Justice files 5-36-2843.

3. Spivack (Director of Operations, Antitrust Division, U.S. Department of Justice), "Antitrust Enforcement, a Primer," *Conn. B. J.* 37 (1963): 375, 382.

4. Between 1890 and 1955 the Sherman Act provided for a fine not to exceed $5,000. This amount was raised to $50,000 in 1955.

5. See Alan M. Dershowitz, "Increasing Community Control over Corporate Crime: A Problem in the Law of Sanctions," *Yale L.J.* 71 (1961): 280.

6. James V. Bennett, "After Sentence—What?" *J. Crim. L., C. & P.S.* 45 (1955): 537.

7. U.S. Senate, Subcommittee on Antitrust and Monopoly, Committee on the Judiciary, 87th Cong., 1st Sess., 1961, "Administered Price Hearings," pt. 28, p. 17395 (hereinafter cited as *Hearings*).

8. *Ibid.*, pt. 27, p. 17100.

9. *Ibid.*, pt. 27, p. 16760.

10. Dershowitz has recommended imposing upon corporate executives a duty, enforceable by criminal sanctions, to exercise reasonable care in preventing acquisitive crime within the area of corporate business under their control. Dershowitz, "Increasing Community Control over Corporate Crime."

11. Marshall Clinard, "Criminological Theories of Violations of Wartime Regulations," *Amer. Soc. Rev.* 11 (1946): 258, 261.

12. *Schenectady & Union-Star,* February 10, 1961.

13. Donald J. Newman, "Public Attitudes toward a Form of White Collar Crime," *Social Problems* 4 (Jan. 1957): 228, 230, 231.

14. *New York Times,* February 7, 1961, pp. 1, 26 col. 3.

15. Clinard, "Criminological Theories of Violations of Wartime Regulations," pp. 258, 263.

16. Skelly Wright, "Sentencing the Income Tax Violator, Statement of the Basic Problem," delivered before the Sentencing Institute for the Fifth Circuit, *F.R.D.* 30 (1962): 185, 302, 304–305.

17. Donald Cressey, *Other People's Money* (Glencoe, Ill.: The Free Press, 1953), p. 102.

18. Sanford H. Kadish, "Some Observations on the Use of Criminal Sanctions in Enforcing Economic Regulations," *U. Chicago L. Rev.* 30 (1963): 423, 435.

19. *Ibid.*, p. 436.

20. *Hearings,* pt. 27, p. 16773.

21. *New York Times,* February 7, 1961, p. 26.

22. Cressey, *Other People's Money,* p. 102.

23. Mary Cameron, *The Booster and the Snitch* (New York: The Free Press, 1965), p. 162.

24. *Ibid.*, p. 165.

25. Cressey, *Other People's Money,* p. 140.